HAPPY MEAT

CULTURE AND ECONOMIC LIFE

HAPPY MEAT

The Sadness and Joy of a Paradoxical Idea

JOSÉE JOHNSTON, SHYON BAUMANN,
EMILY HUDDART, AND MERIN OLESCHUK

STANFORD UNIVERSITY PRESS
Stanford, California

Stanford University Press
Stanford, California

Library of Congress Cataloging-in-Publication Data
Names: Johnston, Josée, author. | Baumann, Shyon, author. |
   Huddart, Emily, author. | Oleschuk, Merin, author.
Title: Happy meat : the sadness and joy of a paradoxical idea / Josée
   Johnston, Shyon Baumann, Emily Huddart, and Merin Oleschuk.
Other titles: Culture and economic life.
Description: Stanford, California : Stanford University Press, 2025. |
   Series: Culture and economic life | Includes bibliographical references
   and index.
Identifiers: LCCN 2024043898 (print) | LCCN 2024043899 (ebook) | ISBN
   9781503638334 (cloth) | ISBN 9781503642836 (paperback) | ISBN
   9781503642843 (ebook)
Subjects: LCSH: Meat—Moral and ethical aspects. | Meat industry and
   trade—Moral and ethical aspects. | Animal welfare.
Classification: LCC GT2868.55 .J65 2025 (print) | LCC GT2868.55 (ebook) |
   DDC 179/.3—dc23/eng/20241208
LC record available at https://lccn.loc.gov/2024043898
LC ebook record available at https://lccn.loc.gov/2024043899

Cover design: Katrina Noble
Cover illustration: Jenny Nystrøm, Æggene Hönsenes Fagforening, ca. 1909–1911,
   Nasjonalbiblioteket / National Library of Norway
Typeset by Newgen in 10/14 Minion Pro

The authorized representative in the EU for product safety and compliance is: Mare
Nostrum Group B.V. | Mauritskade 21D | 1091 GC Amsterdam | The Netherlands | Email
address: gpsr@mare-nostrum.co.uk | KVK chamber of commerce number: 96249943

Contents

Acknowledgments

Eating meat is a banal occurrence, but it can carry profound personal significance and sometimes evokes strong emotions. We are grateful to everyone who welcomed us into their kitchens, farms, restaurants, and lives to us during this research. Their honest, on-the-ground perspectives form the heart of this book and encourage us to work toward a more thoughtful approach to eating animals.

To the consumers who participated in our research: thank you for your candor about the joys and challenges of eating meat. The thousands of survey respondents were anonymous to us, and we don't know if any of them will even know about this book. But still, we are grateful for the time they took to allow us to learn about their thoughts, practices, feelings, values, and opinions about meat. We are particularly indebted to the sixty-seven participants in our focus groups. We gained incredible insights from these focus groups, whose diverse experiences produced such lively conversations and incredible stories. We learned so much about the complexities of the "happy meat" narrative from these candid discussions, and we are deeply appreciative of the honesty with which participants revealed their struggles —the emotional tensions, incomplete information, and economic constraints that challenge their ethical ideals and taste preferences. Their willingness to share their personal experiences has significantly enriched our understanding how people struggle to make "good" food choices on a daily basis.

We spoke with seventy-five people who work on the production side of happy meat—all of them admirable, inspiring, interesting, thoughtful, and determined. Many of them generously opened their homes and workplaces to us so that we could see firsthand the work they do, including their successes but also their challenges. We were deeply impressed by the skills and effort required to run operations that entail significant risk, demand countless hours of labor, offer uncertain financial rewards, and also help make the meat industry more sustainable and humane. They are idealists who put their ideas into practice. Their willingness to talk to researchers doing academic work revealed not only their generosity but also their curiosity and desire to think hard about important questions related to their work.

Writing a book is a big job. As academics, we devote a large part of our work time to research. That work does not always fit into a standard workday, like when we were traveling to rural areas to speak with farmers and ranchers. Book writing sometimes requires working late to meet a deadline—for passing a chapter over to a coauthor or for sending material to the publisher. Because books are big projects, they require a consistent focus and long hours to maintain (or regain) the flow. For all these reasons, work sometimes got in the way of family time, and so we would like to acknowledge our families for their help and forbearance as we got this work done.

We also want to acknowledge the input of our many great colleagues at our respective institutions as well as colleagues who provided insightful and helpful feedback at conferences. Many graduate students at the University of Toronto helped us make this research happen and inspired us with their own work on the food industry. A big thanks to Anelyse Weiler, Michael Lawler, Michael Chrobok, Tyler Bateman, Brody Trottier, Rebecca Lennox, and Jordan Foster. We'd like to give a special shout out to our colleagues at the Culinaria Research Centre at the University of Toronto. This interdisciplinary group of food scholars has been an invaluable resource, offering a welcoming space for feedback and a seemingly infinite knowledge about food. The collaborative spirit and intellectual rigor of all these individuals have not only enhanced the quality of our research but also deepened our understanding of the complex issues surrounding meat. While we are grateful for all the contributions and support we've received, all errors, omissions, or oversights are entirely our own.

HAPPY MEAT

INTRODUCTION   How Did Meat Become "Happy"?

HAVE YOU EVER HEARD of Colin the chicken? Colin is the bird featured in a now-classic piece of sketch comedy from *Portlandia*.[1] The scene unfolds at a trendy restaurant where a couple, Peter and Nance, grill the waitress, Dana, about their lunch choice: chicken. Forget cooking methods or seasoning—they crave details about the chicken's life. Was it raised humanely? Locally? Dana launches into a detailed bio: Colin is a heritage chicken, woodland raised and fed a diet of sheep's milk, soy, and hazelnuts; he lived just outside of Portland. Peter fixates on locality, while Nance frets about organic certification and the chicken's roaming privileges.

The absurdity escalates. Dana returns with a folder—Colin's "papers." Peter enthusiastically looks at Colin's photo, saying, "He looks like a happy little guy who runs around." He asks if Colin had friends to pal around with and "put his little wing around." Dana reassures them that the "chickens are very happy." Nance remains unconvinced, questioning the authenticity of this "organic" operation. Peter follows up, "Yeah, it's not some guy on a yacht who lives in Miami who just says he is 'organic'?" The couple tells Dana that they are going to go check out the farm and asks her to "hold their seats." Peter and Nance venture thirty minutes outside Portland to verify Colin's idyllic existence for themselves.

Portlandia's "Colin the chicken" sketch exemplifies the show's humor, poking fun at hipsters, left-leaning Portland, and ethical consumers. It also satirizes consumer anxieties around meat: the animal's life, its diet, ethical certifications (genuine or misleading?), and even farmers' morals. Are they passionate animal stewards or profit-driven yacht owners? Beneath the humor of Peter and Nance's interrogation of the restaurant server, their fixation on Colin's happiness taps into genuine concerns held by many meat eaters. Are the animals we eat raised by somebody who prioritizes their well-being, or are they simply driven by profit? Was the animal "happy"?

While Nance and Peter are ridiculous figures that we are invited to mock, their quest for transparency reflects a growing desire for a more ethical food system. Their journey to discover the backstory of their meaty meal is based on a powerful cultural narrative of the empowered ethical consumer. Good consumers aren't just looking for a tasty lunch; they seek answers. Is the meat local? Ethically raised? Humane? Good consumers strive to see beyond misleading labels. They may even visit farms, seeking firsthand knowledge of how their food is produced. Ultimately, they are expected to "vote with their forks," supporting responsible producers and avoiding corporations that exploit animals and farmers.

The narrative of Colin the chicken emerges at a time when consumers have myriad concerns about meat-eating. Investigative reports and activist exposés have shed light on the often-grim realities of industrialized meat production, where most North American meat originates. Concentrated animal feeding operations (CAFOs), commonly known as factory farms, raise animals in relatively crowded conditions that make a "happy" life difficult to envision. Meat production is linked to global and local environmental problems including deforestation, antibiotic resistance, water contamination, and climate change.[2] Simultaneously, consumers wonder if eating meat is healthy. Certain kinds of meat (e.g., processed meat) have been linked to cancer and heart disease, and meat products are also a common source of microbial contamination (e.g., E. coli, listeria) that causes widespread illness and even death.[3]

Beyond health and environmental issues, the COVID-19 pandemic exposed the precarious working conditions in meatpacking plants, which are disproportionately staffed by racially minoritized workers. The high rates of illness among slaughterhouse workers underscored the strenuous nature of their labor, the vulnerability of this workforce, and the prevailing perception of the meat industry as a vital, non-negotiable institution.[4] Even beyond these systemic concerns, some people feel visceral disgust toward meat and dislike handling raw meat, especially when parts of an animal's body, like the head, skin, or feet are left intact.[5] Others simply feel a moral aversion to eating animals, especially ones that are cute, smart, or charismatic.

Despite the myriad factors that might discourage meat consumption—from ethical concerns to environmental impacts, health risks, and labor abuses—meat remains a dietary staple for the vast majority of North Americans. This apparent contradiction fueled our curiosity and ultimately led to the writing of this book. Although meat's reputation may be tarnished, rates of vegetarianism remain relatively low in places like Europe, Canada, and the United States, hovering between 5 and 8 percent. Canadians eat a little less meat than Americans, but comparatively speaking, both countries consume a lot of animal flesh, especially when compared to most people on the planet.[6] In our own survey research (see Appendix), over 96 percent of respondents reported eating meat at least once a week, with more than half consuming it five times or more each week. This aligns with trends observed by social psychologist Hank Rothgerber, who notes that meat consumption in the United States increased from 176 to 240 pounds annually between 1970 and 2015, with "the fastest rate in four decades" occurring "during 2015." Rothgerber translates these numbers into animals: "the number of creatures killed to satisfy a family of four ballooned from 56 animals a year to 1,332 animals" during that period.[7] To put this in perspective, Canadians and Americans consume far more meat than the global average. In 2023, Canadians ate 56.5 kg of beef, pork, and poultry per capita, while Americans consumed a staggering 82.6 kg/capita.[8] This starkly contrasts with the global average of 28.1 kg/capita for all types of meat.[9]

North America might love its meat, but there has been a changing of the guard on dinner plates. Beef is slowly getting pushed aside, while poultry—the vast majority of which is chicken—has taken center stage. Colin the chicken, it turns out, is exceedingly popular. Both the United States and Canada have seen a significant decline in beef consumption over the past decades; in the U.S., it dropped from 30.7 kg (1990) to 25.2 kg (2023), while in Canada it went from 25 kg to 17 kg. This trend coincides with a rise in poultry consumption, jumping from 24.1 kg to 35.7 kg in the United States and 16.4 kg to 24.3 kg in Canada over the same period.[10] To put this in more relatable terms, in 2023 the average American ate the equivalent of about sixty-six more boneless, skinless chicken breasts than they did in 1990.

This shift reveals a key point: by and large, most Americans and Canadians continue to eat a lot of meat. Even though consumers express negative perceptions of meat production, they simultaneously associate meat, especially lean meats, with health, muscles, and vitality.[11] This aligns with deeply rooted cultural beliefs about meat as a natural, essential part of the human diet,[12] a notion reflected in the popularity of meat-centric diets like Paleo and the even more extreme "carnivore" diet.[13]

While certainly not disappearing from the menu, meat inhabits a complicated cultural terrain fraught with ethical (animal welfare, health, and sustainability) concerns. This complexity constitutes the core of the *meat paradox*.[14] A paradox describes a situation where two contradictory ideas are simultaneously true. As Carl Jung noted, paradoxes are a rich analytic tool, offering a nuanced understanding of reality that provides a "faithful picture of the real state of affairs."[15] The meat paradox encapsulates the simultaneous existence of deep concern for animal welfare and the environmental harms of industrial meat production, alongside the persistent consumption of animals—what sociologist Paula Arcari describes as the ongoing edibility of "food" animals.[16] We take the meat paradox as a starting point for our exploration, enabling us to examine it through a sociological lens and investigate individual and collective efforts to resolve this paradox through the phenomenon of *happy meat.*

Happy meat is a colloquial term used to describe meat that originates from animals raised under humane and ethical conditions, often in contrast to conventional factory farming. We heard the term frequently in our conversations with consumers, and it was often used with a hint of playful skepticism or irony. While the term *happy meat* was not our initial focus in this research project, it inductively took center stage. It captured the positive attributes that meat consumers and producers associated with ethical, healthy, and sustainable meat—qualities that consumers valued, even if they didn't feel like they could always afford them.

As we explore throughout this book, happy meat embodies the consumer desire to have a more ethically and emotionally satisfying meat-eating experience, one that transcends the guilt and unease associated with industrial production. It signifies meat raised with higher welfare standards, often invoking images of small, humane farms with ethical producers who prioritize sustainability and view animals as individuals, not faceless commodities. The producers didn't typically use the term *happy meat,* though many did embody the sustainable, small-farmer ideals that consumers associated with happy meat. As researchers, we often drove away from farm visits with a happy feeling, inspired by spending time with hard-working, committed producers who clearly care deeply about the land and the animals in their charge. At the same time, this positive feeling was tempered by the knowledge that only a small percentage of the population can access or afford meat raised this way.

Drawing on interviews with producers, focus groups with consumers, survey research, and illustrative discourse analysis, we intend in this book to reveal the sadnesses as well as the pleasures of happy meat. Although people use the term *happy* in relation to meat, many meat eaters and producers acknowledge the darker realities: the inescapable connection to animal death as well as broader environmental concerns, like the climate crisis. While the somewhat cheeky term *happy meat* was not part of our original research plan, we came to see it as aptly capturing the emotional tenor of the contemporary meat paradox. Meat remains a source of enjoyment, pleasure, and cultural identity, yet a layer of irony, even agony, lurks beneath it.

Our study of the cultural politics of happy meat is indebted to Sara Ahmed's influential work *The Promise of Happiness*.[17] Ahmed challenges a conventional view of happiness as a purely individual experience, emphasizing its social and political dimensions. From this perspective, the salient issue is not whether you and I feel good—or whether Colin the chicken is *truly* happy—but rather how the collective pursuit of happiness reveals what we value and prioritize. Crucially, Ahmed focuses on the act of attributing happiness—studying how and why we label certain things or experiences as "happy." This perspective is particularly relevant to our study of happy meat. By examining why consumers and producers attribute happiness to meat, we can gain valuable insights into the underlying values shaping our food choices. The concept of happy meat itself becomes a site of inquiry. While we use the term *happy meat* throughout this book without quotation marks for readability, we encourage readers to mentally enclose it within them. This serves as a way of maintaining some skepticism that a farm animal could lead a life described as straightforwardly happy; it can also encourage the reader to think, as we have, about happiness as an object of inquiry rather than a straightforward emotion.

Ahmed's work and our own research for this book suggest that assigning happiness to meat may function as a way of managing discomfort with the act of consuming animals today. This is the heart of the meat paradox. By labeling meat as "happy," we socially construct a positive valuation of products that we may find deeply troubling (a topic we explore in Chapters 3 and 4). Additionally, attributing happiness to meat can be a way to socially manage the negative elements of this niche market; happy meat is an expensive product that is linked to pleasure, indulgence, and social status (a topic we explore in Chapter 7). Through an Ahmed-inspired research lens, happy meat is more than a simple marketing term; it is a powerful cultural tool that shapes how we navigate the challenges of eating a highly contested food that many people remain deeply attached to. By investigating the work that happy meat does, as Ahmed encourages us to do, we gain a deeper understanding of the values, anxieties, and social forces that influence our relationship with meat and animals.

Having emphasized our focus on happy meat as a site of cultural inquiry, it's useful to take a moment to say what this book does *not* attempt to do. We draw from and are sympathetic to an animal rights perspective on meat-eating and find great value in posthumanist approaches that identify the speciesism, anthropocentrism, and often overlooked vitality of animals in agriculture.[18] However, this book does not assume that all animal husbandry is ethically or ecologically indefensible.[19] We recognize that North American rates of meat consumption are ecologically unsustainable, but our aim is not to take a normative stance on the morality or environmental defensibility of meat-eating itself.[20] We have a specific sociological goal: to keep the meat paradox in full view, dissecting its alluring and disquieting elements. We explore how happy meat narratives can simultaneously ease consumers' anxieties about animal welfare and obscure harsh realities of industrial production.[21] Moreover, we do not attempt to map all the labor issues at play in the meat commodity chain. Other scholars have addressed this critical topic,[22] and we aim to stay focused on our primary goal, which is to understand how "happy meat" narratives function within the broader context of the meat paradox, enabling continued consumption and potentially deflecting systemic critiques.

We take a narrative approach to unravel the tensions of happy meat. This approach draws attention to familiar storylines and characters that both producers and consumers bring up when describing their meat-eating ideals and practices. Stories related to happy meat helped people reconcile meat's contradictory status, offering them the possibility of more comfortably experiencing the pleasure of eating a food overlaid with animal death and environmental degradation. Ultimately, a narrative approach is ideal for revealing the complex, contradictory position happy meat occupies in the contemporary foodscape.

In the remainder of this chapter, we further examine the idea of the meat paradox—what it is, how scholars have studied it, and how it operates. We explain how it has been explored in numerous academic traditions and tell the reader what we think we can bring to the table as sociologists who study culture, gender, health, and the environment. Finally, we introduce the data we collected to examine this topic and outline our plan for the chapters that follow.

The Meat Paradox: Loving Animals While Also Eating Them

In basic terms, the meat paradox puts a name to what is likely a common experience: we eat animals, but we don't always feel straightforwardly good about doing so.[23] The meat paradox is not simply an individual struggle—it's also a collective phenomenon. On an individual level, we grapple with the guilt of enjoying a fast-food hamburger—the pleasure of the taste colliding with concerns about calories, climate impact, and eating an animal. Collectively, the paradox is evident in high meat consumption, despite growing cultural discomfort with industrialized meat production and slaughter. Critical films like the Korean feature *Okja* and the documentary *Cowspiracy* exemplify this unease.[24] While critiques of the meat industry gain traction, consumption remains high, and the concept of the meat paradox is particularly useful for capturing this contradiction.[25]

To better understand the multifaceted concept of the meat paradox, we outline how it has been studied by various academic fields, starting with psychology, a foundational disciplinary perspective. While this review can only offer a brief sketch of this multidisciplinary field, it lays the groundwork for our own sociological perspective on the meat paradox.

Psychological Studies of the Meat Paradox

Psychological studies of the meat paradox call attention to the cognitive dissonance involved in caring about animals while also eating them. As Hank Rothgerber notes, "while individuals want farmed animals to be humanely treated, they simultaneously eat meat derived almost entirely from factory farms documented for their abysmal treatment of animals."[26] How do consumers sustain this meat-related cognitive dissonance?

Psychologists have identified various strategies people use to justify eating animals.[27] Rothgerber helpfully groups these strategies into two categories: *apologetic* and *unapologetic*.[28] Apologetic strategies aim to downplay meat's origin in an animal. Eaters may use euphemistic labels (e.g., *steak* versus *cow*) or deny animals emotions, cognition, and moral status.[29] These apologetic strategies make it easier to avoid thinking about the fact that meat was once alive.[30] In a study of Danish consumers, Holm and Møhl found that consumers prefer ground meat because it is "not associated with any living animal."[31] Another apologetic strategy involves emphasizing one's efforts to reduce meat consumption—a move that Rothgerber calls "perceived behavioral change."[32]

Unapologetic strategies for dealing with the meat paradox involve explicit rationales that justify meat-eating.[33] These justifications can include taste, health, and religion (e.g., "God gave us animals to eat") or invoking a species hierarchy that separates acceptable from unacceptable animals to eat.[34] Psychologists have identified four key unapologetic rationales known as "the 4 Ns": meat is nice, normal, necessary, and natural.[35] These rationales enable consumers to manage the cognitive dissonance between their animal ideals and meat-eating behaviors. Some research suggests that challenging people's meat consumption can backfire, strengthening these justifications and even increasing meat intake. As Rothgerber writes, "By reassuring themselves that eating meat is morally justifiable, the behavior becomes more attractive."[36]

The meat paradox also has a gendered dimension, with femininity having strong associations with vegetarianism and caring for animals.[37] Drawing on numerous studies, Rothgerber writes that "gender is the single biggest predictor of attitudes towards animals and consumption of animals."[38] Women are more upset by animal harm, more likely to underreport their meat consumption, more likely to express greater disgust for meat (especially red meat), and more likely to embrace vegetarianism.[39] Men are more comfortable with an unapologetic approach to meat-eating, while women favor apologetic, avoidant strategies.[40] These psychological findings highlight the importance of gender in understanding the meat paradox, a topic we explore in Chapter 7.

Economists and Historians Take on the Meat Paradox

Economists think about the meat paradox through the lens of "utility," a concept measuring satisfaction gained from consuming something. For example, Hestermann and colleagues explain that animal welfare concerns create a tradeoff for consumers. On the one hand, there's the positive utility gained from meat consumption—like pleasure and satiety. On the other hand, there's the negative "disutility"—the guilt or discomfort stemming from awareness of animal suffering.[41]

Hestermann and colleagues have challenged the simple idea that informing people about the meat industry will automatically reduce consumption. Their model suggests the opposite: heavy meat eaters might engage in self-deception to justify their choices. In other words, providing more information about industrialized meat operations might not change habits. Instead, devoted meat eaters might downplay the information to maintain high consumption while minimizing guilt. Providing more information about meat could backfire for eaters who are information-averse and whose enjoyment of meat is unrelated to external factors like price. For these consumers, exposure to the negative externalities of meat production might paradoxically strengthen strategies of denial and lead to more unapologetic meat-eating.[42]

Beyond individual consumer strategies, we can gain further insight into the meat paradox by examining the broader shifts in our relationship with animals and food production. Historian Richard Bulliet, in his seminal work *Hunters, Herders, and Hamburgers*, identifies a cultural transition from a "domestic" to a "post-domestic" era.[43] In the domestic past, people lived in close proximity to farm animals and regularly witnessed the realities of slaughter. This exposure to death, while not always pleasant, normalized animal death. However, modern post-domestic consumers, who largely live in urban areas, primarily encounter animals as pets or neatly packaged cuts of meat. This social and geographical distance from industrialized slaughterhouses has created a disconnect where the realities of meat production are obscured from everyday life. This disconnect, Bulliet argues, has profound implications for our emotional responses to meat. With minimal exposure to farm animals or slaughter, yet unprecedented access to abundant meat, post-domestic consumers experience a paradox: they consume more meat than ever but often harbor guilt, shame, and disgust toward the industrial processes that make it possible. Bulliet eloquently captures this paradox when he describes how contemporary eaters "consume animal products in abundance, but psychologically, [they] experience feelings of guilt, shame, and disgust when they think (as seldom as possible) about the industrial processes by which domestic animals are rendered into products."[44] The very systems that make meat affordable and plentiful generate a sense of horror when eaters confront the reality of how they operate. Bulliet's identification of the profoundly emotional dimension of mass meat production systems remains prescient and will be explored further in later chapters.

Social and Cultural Contours of the Meat Paradox

Sociological research can add insight into the social underpinnings of the meat paradox, including how it manifests in diverse cultural and relational contexts. For example, a Danish study used focus groups to identify context-specific moral logics people employ to make sense of meat-eating.[45] When thinking about the context of meat *consumption*, consumers draw on moral logics that emphasize the flavor and value of meat. However, when consumers are asked to think about meat *production,* they acknowledge the negative environmental and animal welfare impacts of factory farming. This highlights the cultural fluidity of the meat paradox. Moral justifications for meat consumption differ depending on whether we are contemplating what to eat for dinner or imagining factory farms. These moral considerations are meaningful, but they do not significantly overlap, and this helps us understand how consumers can enjoy meat while temporarily pushing ethical concerns aside.

Sociologists also show how public discourse shapes consumer understandings of meat. For example, Robert Chiles argues that the physical distancing of production facilities in rural areas, combined with the mass media's minimal coverage and consumers' avoidance tendencies, creates a suppressive feedback loop that normalizes meat consumption.[46] To better understand how meat is discussed in the public sphere, we (Johnston and Baumann) worked with Tyler Bateman to use computational text analysis to investigate how meat is covered in a large sample of 2,461 news articles and news blog posts.[47] Similar to Chiles's findings, our study shows that public discourse tends to downplay the problematic aspects of meat production and overwhelmingly frames meat as a "non-problem." Dominant media tend to depict meat as benign, focusing on economic factors like production costs or consumer issues relating to taste and health. When risks are mentioned, they are usually framed as economic threats to the industry or individualized health concerns (e.g., avoiding salmonella from raw chicken). Meat is only rarely framed as an environmental problem or a source of labor injustices. Overall, we draw the conclusion that readers of popular media could easily be left without a clear imperative to change their meat habits, since the presentation of meat as normal and unproblematic weakens any sense of urgency to address meat's collective risks.

While the dominant media portrays meat as normal and unproblematic, that's not the whole story. Meat is a polysemic topic, meaning that there is no singular, simple message in meat discourse. While meat is often framed as good in the dominant public sphere (e.g., it is delicious, healthy, a source of strength), it is sometimes depicted as harmful (e.g., it hurts animals, causes climate change, poses health risks). Scholars have not fully grasped how meat eaters navigate these conflicting messages, especially given the increasing public attention given to factory farming, animal welfare, and climate change. The matter of shifting consumer understandings of meat is where we focus our attention next.

Meat's Myriad Meanings: Our Past Research on Meat Eaters

For some time now we have been interested in understanding what meat means to people. How does the polysemic nature of meat filter into everyday consumer practices and taste preferences, which we know are not purely driven by ethical principles but are strongly shaped by habit and routines?[48] How do people grapple with anxieties surrounding meat production while maintaining their established, habitual food practices and their emotional connection to a meat-centric diet?

In our past research, we (Johnston, Baumann, and Oleschuk) carried out interviews with a diverse sample of meat eaters and vegetarians in the Toronto area, speaking with people from multiple religions, ethnicities, and class backgrounds.[49] We were not seeking consumers with any particular interest in ethical or happy meat; we simply wanted to understand why this diverse group of people eats (or avoids) meat and the meanings they associate with it. To analyze how people talked about meat in their daily lives, we turned to the concept of *cultural repertoires*. This concept highlights the taken-for-granted scripts people employ to make sense of their daily lives, particularly when it comes to managing contradictions.[50]

Here we draw inspiration from Ann Swidler's influential work on cultural repertoires, notably in her book *Talk of Love*, which examined how individuals employ different cultural tools to manage the contradictions inherent in love.[51] This concept allows us to see culture as a flexible tool kit, rather than a fixed set of values, and allows us to better understand how people navigate the complexities of meat-eating.[52] By moving beyond a singular, monolithic view of "meat culture," we open the door to understanding how people make sense of meat-eating in the face of deep-seated contradictions.

Our prior work revealed how people manage the contradictions they experience when eating meat—like continuing to eat meat while acknowledging ethical and environmental concerns.[53] Another important contradiction we observed relates to meat's contested status as a healthy food. Meat was simultaneously seen as health-promoting (e.g., providing protein as well as vitamins and minerals like iron) and unhealthy (e.g., making people fat, causing cancer). This contradiction frequently manifested in the same interviewee.[54] While meat-eating was associated with healthy protein and muscle building, as we explore below, it was *simultaneously* and consistently linked to a negative meat-eating figure: an unthinking, unhealthy, overweight, male meat eater.[55] Given these negative associations, how do people make sense of their continued meat consumption? Put differently, how do cultural repertoires equip people to navigate the complex and often contradictory messages surrounding meat?

Meat-Eating Cultural Repertoires

Our prior research identified four key cultural repertoires that people use to make sense of their meat-eating: 1) meat and muscles, 2) cultural preservation, 3) consumer apathy, and 4) consumer sovereignty. The *meat and muscles* cultural repertoire connects meat-eating to an embodied form of masculinity emphasizing strength, athleticism, and a muscular physique. In essence, it suggests that meat builds muscle, which reinforces hegemonic ideas about masculinity. Men from various backgrounds (different ages, ethnicities, religions) frequently drew from this repertoire to connect meat-eating to their embodied sense of masculinity. Interestingly, women also occasionally referenced this repertoire, particularly when explaining why men eat more meat than women did.

A second key repertoire is *cultural preservation*. A diverse set of eaters in our study used this repertoire to link meat consumption with maintaining and protecting culture, revealing a strongly felt connection between meat-eating and ethnocultural identity.[56] For many interviewees, except those with religious vegetarian backgrounds, meat was a staple in a variety of dishes that connected them to their cultural heritage. These dishes weren't just meals; they embodied social connections, rituals, and traditions that bound individuals, families, and communities together. Interviewees felt strongly that these dishes were essential for expressing their cultural heritage, especially in a larger context of white privilege and negative judgments about their cultural practices. This repertoire highlights how meat consumption can be a way to resist cultural homogenization and xenophobia.

The third cultural repertoire that consumers employed to make sense of meat-eating is *consumer apathy*. This repertoire helped people manage the emotional distance between their meat-eating and the realities of factory farming. It frames meat consumption as unpolitical, even mindless, especially when meat-eating is seen as unavoidable. This cultural repertoire downplays ethical conflicts and allows people to focus on their individual desires rather than grapple with complex food system issues. Common phrases used within this repertoire include "I try not to think about it," "I block it out," or "I put it in the back of my mind." By compartmentalizing disturbing information, consumers distance themselves from the emotional weight of meat production. The consumer apathy repertoire frames consumers as powerless in the face of an inevitable meat industry ("I can't change it"). This repertoire was articulated without a sense of shame or stigma, suggesting a widespread acceptance in the broader culture. The consumer apathy script goes beyond individual disinterest and illuminates a collective cultural narrative that prioritizes self-gratification, downplays animal welfare issues, normalizes feelings of powerlessness against corporate giants, and enables the cognitive delinking of meat from its animal origins.

In contrast to the "consumer apathy" repertoire's emphasis on the right to not care, the *consumer sovereignty* repertoire emphasizes consumers' right to make autonomous choices in the marketplace. Common sentiments signaling this repertoire include "it's my right to eat meat" or "eating meat is a personal choice." This repertoire presents consumer choice as a foundational expression of individual autonomy.[57] By exercising their autonomy to pursue self-interest, people affirm their identity as independent, self-determining individuals. Choice is a powerful idea in consumer society, linked to both pleasure and a sense of control in an uncertain, risk-filled environment.[58] A key tenet of the consumer sovereignty repertoire is the consumer's right to choose, regardless of the chosen option. Of course, this cultural repertoire's emphasis on individual choice can operate ideologically to obfuscate the collective consequences of widespread meat-eating.

To sum up these multidisciplinary insights, the concept of the meat paradox offers a powerful lens for understanding the complexities and contradictions of meat-eating. It helps us move beyond simply urging people to care about injustices in the meat industry. The paradox highlights that eaters can reconcile negative ideas about meat production with entrenched consumption habits fueled by positive associations like cultural identity, physical strength, and consumer choice. Our sociological approach excavates the cultural and political contradictions surrounding meat, examining how various cultural repertoires help consumers navigate these complexities in everyday life. This book builds on our own research and other sociological studies, alongside insights from diverse disciplinary perspectives, to analyze the phenomenon of happy meat—a concept that integrates emotional experiences of contemporary meat consumption with production practices aimed at ameliorating the harmful impacts of eating animals.

Enter Happy Meat: How We Study the Meat Paradox

The idea of "happy meat" embodies the very contradictions at the heart of contemporary meat consumption. As we've discussed, it captures a fundamental paradox—that meat can be a source of pleasure, happiness, and a rewarding part of a good life, yet is inseparable from sadness, suffering, and death. Even without using this term explicitly, the consumers we interviewed valued and sought a form of meat-eating that resolves this difficult paradox.

The goal of this book is to probe the emotional and cultural contours of the meat paradox and examine the strategies consumers use to address it through the lens of happy meat. As we explore how happy meat works to resolve the meat paradox for consumers, we also consider the complications that arise in that resolution. We do this by highlighting the often-neglected perspective of producers, examining the emotional and logistical challenges they face raising animals for food that complicate the reality of consumers' happy meat stories. We believe that our data on producers represent an important dimension of food scholarship, particularly in a field that often silos consumer issues from rural concerns. Importantly, this book also focuses on the implications of turning to happy meat to resolve the meat paradox. We connect happy meat to critical issues of intersectional inequality (gender, race, class), health, and sustainability. Although happy meat offers a sense of comfort about consuming animals, we argue that its discursive emphasis can silence critical voices and obscure the painful realities of mass-scaled meat production and consumption.

An Overview of Our Methods

This book weaves together empirical details and observations with narratives about the people involved in happy meat—both those who raise it and those who consume it. While facts and figures are important for grounding us in the material realities of the meat industry, stories offer an additional dimension that allows us to appreciate meat's paradoxical status. The stories of farmers, ranchers, and eaters can illuminate the fraught, contradictory world of contemporary meat consumption, while also helping to advance a core value of the sociological enterprise: to render the social world comprehensible and relatable. Here, we share the stories entrusted to us during our research, offering readers a sense of connection to those who may display similar values or practices, while fostering empathy and curiosity toward people with different dietary choices.

Our exploration of happy meat utilized a multi-method approach, gathering various types of data between 2017 and 2022.[59] We aimed to collect a rich trove of data offering insight into both producer and consumer perspectives on the meat paradox and happy meat. This included analyzing popular culture representations of happy meat, interviewing producers, visiting farms, conducting consumer focus groups, and administering a survey. We started the project thinking about alternative food systems and used the term *alternative meat*. As our research progressed, the term *alternative meat* shifted to signify plant-based substitutes like Beyond Meat. To reflect this evolving foodscape, we adopted the terms *ethical meat* and *happy meat* to ground our analysis specifically in animal protein.

To understand the existing foodscape and evolving conversations about meat ethics, we examined American and Canadian popular culture and meat marketing. We assessed how meat is framed as positive, ethical, sustainable, and humane, despite ongoing critiques of its social, environmental, and animal welfare impacts. We started with a broad-brushed approach: we read books on meat-focused cookery and whole animal butchery, reviewed marketing material and news coverage of meat products, and paid attention to how meat was represented in food discourse. This initial exploration led to a more specific study of how fast-food companies portray hamburgers as a positive dietary choice.[60] We also analyzed thousands of North American news articles (1980–2017) on the meat industry using the computational text analysis method of topic-modeling, which provides a broad characterization of the changing topical foci of the news over decades.

Our fieldwork began with fifty site visits and seventy-six in-depth interviews with ethical meat producers across Western (British Columbia, Alberta, and Saskatchewan) and Central Canada (Ontario) (see Appendix). These producers spanned diverse roles in ethical meat production, from farmers raising

free-range animals and small-scale abattoir operators to butchers and restau-
rateurs focused on whole animal butchery. To gain a visceral understanding
of the process, we immersed ourselves in production events, especially those
associated with our interviewees. We spent an afternoon touring a small slaughterhouse, observing the process from live cattle, to the kill floor, to making final
finished products like sausage. We attended a course on whole animal butchery,
breaking down a whole pig and turning it into finished cuts of meat. We visited
numerous butcher shops, taking field notes, snapping photos, observing how
meat was marketed, and listening to the questions customers asked employees.

Complementing our work with producers, we explored consumer perspectives through focus groups with concerned meat eaters. We used focus groups
to capture the kinds of dialogue that surrounds meat as a controversial product. We had previously interviewed vegetarians and meat consumers where
concerns about meat emerged naturally, but now we were specifically looking
for people who seek out happy meat.[61] This is a group of consumers that goes
by various labels: flexitarians, conscientious omnivores, or simply ethical meat
consumers. When we imagined our ideal focus group participant, we pictured
somebody who purchases meat from a butcher or a small farmer or who looks
for meat labeled as "ethical" in some way. We weren't sure if people would use
labels like "flexitarian" or "conscientious omnivore" to describe themselves, but
we knew that we wanted to talk to people who had a desire to circumscribe their
meat-eating in some significant way. We ended up finding an extensive range
of perspectives in these focus groups: some people ate almost no meat, others
restricted themselves to carefully sourced meat, while still others thought about
buying happy meat in aspirational (rather than practical) terms. To encompass
these diverse perspectives in our focus groups, we identified "concerned omnivore" as the most fitting term for our participants.[62] In total, we spoke with
sixty-seven concerned omnivores in Toronto and Vancouver. The sample was
purposive, meaning we specifically recruited individuals interested in happy
meat. We aimed for maximum variation in our sample, which means we aimed
to get as much diversity, or variation, on key measures as possible, especially
income, gender, family status, race, and ethnicity.

To capture broader public perspectives on meat consumption, we conducted a large-scale survey in 2019. A survey research firm recruited a diverse
sample of 2,328 Canadians, ensuring representation according to national
quotas across income, education, gender, race, age (18+), and province of residence. The survey explored general food attitudes alongside specific questions

on meat. Questions investigated what people knew, liked, and disliked about meat production conditions and their views on different kinds of meat. We also asked consumers about their views on politics, economics, and culture to better understand how these factors related to their choices and beliefs about meat. This comprehensive survey (over 80 questions, 15-minute completion time) provides an excellent "big picture" view of public perceptions of meat and decision-making around consumption and is notably distinct from prior research often focused on small samples or atypical populations such as vegetarians or students.

The Chapters Ahead

Through a carefully structured journey, the book explores different ways that happy meat is a paradoxical idea. Part I charts the key cultural and discursive landscape of happy meat, what we call the *ethical meatscape*, and highlights the disconnect between widespread meat enjoyment and widespread discomfort about industrialized meat. This sets the stage for Part II, which explores the emotional dimensions of happy meat consumption. We argue that happy meat is not just something that people buy or think about; it's also a way for people to search for a positive *feeling* to envelop meat-eating. Part III centers the experiences of livestock farmers to deepen our understanding of the phenomenon of happy meat. By examining the work involved with raising pigs, chickens, and cows, we can see through the good/evil binary often assumed to characterize meat production. Finally, while the idea of happy meat might reflect a collective desire for a shift to a better way for society to eat meat, Part IV examines how happy meat can paradoxically function at an individual level to serve individuals' self-oriented purposes. We reveal how happy meat—and cheap meat—are used to draw social boundaries, reinforce inequalities, and contour debates about meat's impact on health and the environment. Next, we outline the book's chapters in greater detail.

Part I—Situating Happy Meat

Chapter 1: Exploring the Ethical Meatscape

The *ethical meatscape* captures the cultural (discursive) and the material (ecological) dimensions of meat. We trace the emergence of this concept and explore how it is understood in contemporary discourse. We also introduce narrative analysis, the analytic orientation employed throughout the book, arguing that stories play a crucial role in shaping how people understand and talk about happy meat. Happy meat is not an abstract concept; it is grounded in narratives featuring happy animals, lush pastures, and caring farmers.

Chapter 2: No Reservations? The Complicated Case of Regular (but Conflicted) Meat-Eating

The meat paradox holds space for the widespread consumption of meat and the discomfort many people feel about it. While our focus in this book is on happy meat, we also need to understand the more fundamental relationships that people have to meat of all kinds in order to understand the context in which happy meat-eating occurs. We leverage data from our survey and focus groups to examine the prevalence and relational context of meat eating. While survey data confirm that most people eat meat and believe doing so is necessary, their beliefs and emotions convey significant reservations about how much meat people eat and how animals are treated.

Part II—The Emotions of Eating Meat

Chapter 3: Meat is Disgusting . . . and Delicious!

The meat paradox involves powerful yet contradictory emotions. Our focus group conversations revealed that while consumers sometimes found meat off-putting or even disgusting, almost everyone emphasized its pleasures, reflecting a kind of emotional tug-of-war. *Factory farm disgust* is a specific aversion triggered by the realities of industrial meat production.

Chapter 4: Happy Meat Makes Me Feel Good

Happy meat is a potential solution to manage uncomfortable feelings about meat. Positive narratives around happy meat, like imagining free-roaming animals, help consumers mitigate negative emotions. However, consumers also express skepticism about happy meat stories and worry that happy meat imagery might be used to obfuscate ongoing factory farm practices. Despite this skepticism, such narratives remain influential and elicit positive emotions, which helps to explain why concerned consumers continue to eat meat.

Part III—Raising Happy Animals

Chapter 5: The Reality Behind Raising Happy Meat: Beyond a Good/Evil Binary

Chapter 5 shifts the focus to producers, exploring the complexities of ethically raising—and confining—animals for food. Here we juxtapose consumers' ideals of a happy animal with producers' realities on the farm. This chapter highlights the limitations of the simple "sad/caged" versus "happy/free" binary that dominates the ethical meatscape, as producers' stories reveal the immense gray area between these two extremes. This exploration raises questions about the degree of confinement that remains ethical and how well consumers understand the challenges of producing happy meat. With a focus on raising pigs, we introduce and explore the concept of animal "vitality" and the caring work of farmers who are committed to nurturing and supporting animals that they will eventually have to send to slaughter.

Chapter 6: Producing Happy Meat at Scale: Managing Vital Animals and Thinking Sustainably

We elaborate and extend the argument on animal vitality in the previous chapter, exploring the lived experiences of farmers raising happy chickens and cattle. By juxtaposing these two species, we explore the unique challenges and complexities inherent in meeting ethical standards for animals with vastly different needs, resource constraints, and shifting consumer preferences. Through the voices of the farmers themselves, we gain insights into the delicate balancing act they perform, striving to reconcile consumer desires for idyllic pasture settings with the practical constraints of time, resources, and emotional labor. These producer perspectives reveal the often-overlooked emotional dimensions of animal agriculture and add depth to the happy meat narrative, showcasing the interplay of values, animal vitality, and pragmatic compromises that shapes the work of raising animals for food.

Part IV—The Boundary Work of Happy Meat

Chapter 7: Other People's Meat

It is a truism in sociology that cultural practices both bring people together and keep them apart. In spite of its progressive potential, happy meat is no exception. Paradoxically, consumers may use their consumption of "happy meat" to create social boundaries, positioning themselves against those who consume "cheap meat." This "boundary work" can reinforce existing social inequalities, as cheap meat becomes associated with disgust, poor hygiene, health hazards, and the lower social classes, particularly when linked to discount supermarkets or ethnic grocery stores. By the same token, many consumers hesitate to unequivocally declare happy meat a more ethical option due to its connection with affluence and privilege. They drew clearer boundaries along gender lines, imagining the typical happy meat consumer as feminine and overly concerned with appearances. Yet, despite this negative stereotype, happy meat also evoked positive connotations: conscientious consumption, an appreciation for high-quality foods, and a desire to provide children with a healthy diet. Overall, we see how happy meat functions not as a simple taste preference but as a significant boundary object revealing the interplay of ethics, class, gender, and consumption choices.

Chapter 8: Meat Makes Us Healthy and Whole—and Can Even Heal the Planet

Here we examine the health and sustainability claims surrounding happy meat, focusing on the blurry boundary between "healthy" and "unhealthy" meat, both for humans and the planet. The inconsistent portrayal of meat's health benefits in public discourse leaves consumers feeling confused and overwhelmed, caught between scientific information and personal intuition. Despite uncertainty about meat's health status, we observed a relatively consistent belief that meat is unsustainable and contributes to the climate crisis. Consumers often turn to happy meat as a solution for a healthy body and a healthy planet, a response to the increasing moral scrutiny of meat. However, this strategy is not without its challenges: affordability and trust in production practices remain significant hurdles. Moreover, the idea that happy meat can be a solution to the ethical and environmental dilemmas of conventional meat, allowing for guilt-free consumption, creates its own set of tensions and paradoxical outcomes.

Conclusion: How Can We Eat Ethically When Meat Is Murder?

The conclusion grapples with the ethical challenge of being a meat eater in today's world. The story of happy meat is ethically complex and deeply paradoxical. While the story of happy meat reflects a genuine desire to improve the food system, an inherent paradox remains: happy animals are ultimately raised for slaughter. Drawing on extensive research, we argue for navigating this ethical meatscape with extreme caution. Ambiguity surrounds ethical meat production, corporate transparency is usually lacking, and the climate crisis adds urgency, particularly given that the most recent data on emissions of methane and nitrous oxide (emissions associated with agriculture) show that 2023 saw the highest levels of emissions in recorded history.[63] The conclusion highlights a key tension inherent to many ethical consumption projects: the onus is on consumers to make ethical choices, but most consumers face financial, logistical, and emotional obstacles to sourcing happy meat. Furthermore, cultural norms, food habits, and emotional attachments make it difficult to give up meat entirely. Consumers believe that people should eat less meat, but they also want market reform and stronger government regulations to promote sustainable production. The book concludes by situating these observations within the growing public debate about meat-eating and emphasizes the need for structural solutions to address pressing issues like public health, farmer livelihood, animal welfare, and the climate crisis.

PART I   **Situating Happy Meat**

ONE

Exploring the Ethical Meatscape

THE SUPERMARKET AISLE CAN be a bewildering place for a conscientious consumer, especially one who eats animal products. Take eggs, for example. Staring down a confusing array of labels—"cage-free," "free-run," "free-range"—the shopper must balance ethical and budgetary concerns. It is cheaper to buy "cage eggs," but who wants to admit that they deliberately choose eggs from an animal living in a cage? The consumer may also wonder if free-range chickens *actually* live an idyllic life outdoors—is the higher price justified? And what about heritage chickens that lay beautiful eggs in various shades of brown and even light blue? Are these eggs healthier, more delicious, or more ethical than their generic white counterparts? Buying eggs from a "happy" hen might seem relatively simple, especially if you have enough money, but trying to understand the underlying reality behind supermarket eggs can be a time-consuming and frustrating process.[1]

The complexities of happy animal products extend beyond the supermarket, permeating the daily lives of farmers who grapple with ethical considerations and practical challenges. As we'll explore in Chapters 5 and 6, the process of raising a happy, free-ranging farm animal is far more complicated than most consumers, ourselves included, might imagine. One Alberta farmer, Sheila, recounted her shock and disbelief as she witnessed how her cute yellow chicks transformed into aggressive birds prone to pecking, fighting, and even cannibalism in an outdoor pasture environment.[2] Similarly, another farmer, Matthew, highlighted the complex issue of animal welfare in the context of caged versus free-range laying hens. While acknowledging that a barn of caged layers is "not a very pleasant sight," he also argued that farmers have an economic motivation to keep caged animals happy, healthy, and productive. Stressed birds, he explained, lay fewer eggs, and caged birds can produce eggs "at the highest level possible." Although Matthew was not raising caged laying hens, he insisted that "every farmer has to keep their animals as comfortable and as happy as possible. . . . There's a built-in incentive for the farmer to treat their animals really well." Other farmers articulated the same sentiment about a "built-in" incentive to consider animal welfare and emphasized how confinement can even offer benefits, like protection against threats like aggressive behavior, inclement weather, and predators like hawks and coyotes.[3]

Thinking about Sheila and Matthew's perspectives on chickens, as well as the bewildering array of supermarket eggs, we can start to appreciate the complexity of happy meat. This complexity presents a rich field of inquiry for food scholars. The example of happy chickens not only highlights the often-opaque material realities of animal agriculture (e.g., how was this animal treated? Is this a sustainable practice?) but also invites investigation into the evolving cultural politics of meat.[4] It prompts us to examine the motivations behind consumers' preference for happy meat as well as the reasons why industrialized meat is perceived as undesirable or even gross.

Let's consider another example from Matthew's chicken farm that speaks to the material ambiguity and shifting cultural politics of meat-eating. Matthew started his business raising chickens in barns but added pasture-raised chickens in response to consumer demand. Canadian consumers, like consumers elsewhere, increasingly consider the emotional lives and well-being of farm animals in their consumer decisions. In doing so, they frequently connect outdoor living with happier animals and more delicious meat.[5] Matthew radiated a calm, even-keeled demeanor but nonetheless betrayed a hint of frustration with consumers' preferences. He explained that he charges significantly more for pasture-raised poultry, in part because of outdoor birds' higher mortality rate compared to barn-raised birds. Matthew says, "When you make this choice [to raise chickens outside] . . . we're condemning 10 percent of those birds to die before they would normally die." In contrast to Matthew's uncertainty—which was echoed by many producers—about whether outdoor animals have a better life, the consumers we spoke with were unanimous in their belief that a chicken living outside is a happy chicken.[6]

How do consumers come to develop such strong, consistent ideas about what constitutes a happy chicken? Who or what shapes the collective understanding of what constitutes "good" meat? This book explores these questions by examining the *narratives* that weave together the idea of happy meat through stories of contented animals, verdant pastures, and caring farmers. We ground happy meat in the concept of the *ethical meatscape*, a tool for grappling with the complex terrain of human-animal interactions as they relate to food.[7] Briefly, the ethical meatscape refers to the broad cultural and material context of production and consumption surrounding ethical meat choices.

The heart of our exploration lies in the stories people tell about happy meat. In the next section, we introduce the concept of narrative analysis, which is a tool for decoding these narratives and uncovering their underlying significance. We then unpack the concept of the ethical meatscape, exploring how it emerged and who it involves. Throughout the chapter, we aim to provide concrete examples from our research, giving a voice to the human and animal characters that populate the stories of happy meat.

Narrative Analysis: The Story of Happy Meat

Happy meat is more than a consumer aspiration or a marketing ploy—it is also a story. Scholars from various disciplines recognize the power of stories in shaping human experience, cognition, and even political conflicts.[8] We directly saw the importance of stories when we held our focus groups. Participants frequently expressed themselves by telling a story to explain their relationship to food and meat-eating more specifically. Participants not only shared stories about their own meat experiences; they also revealed how they were influenced by external narratives. Jun, a forty-four-year-old Chinese Canadian father, told us that his food heroes were an elderly Italian couple who lived next door. He was drawn to their cooking not just for the flavors but also for the stories woven into their food: "One thing I like about their cooking is they have a lot of stories to tell." Jun makes clear that these stories are "not just about the food" but include their family histories and life struggles. His neighbors' food stories not only taught Jun to understand their Italian culture and cooking but also imparted broader life lessons.

At its core, a story is a way of giving meaning to a sequence of events, a cast of characters, and our experiences. Stories also reflect who we are and how we want to be seen; as Raul Lejano, Mrill Ingram, and Helen Ingram argue, stories help the storyteller convey their identity and their place in a broader group.[9] Lois Presser further explains that stories can offer broader cultural insights by making points "that are generalizable, and usually have to do with right living—that is, with morality."[10] While stories are studied in different ways in different disciplines, there are some key building blocks that scholars agree on: conflict, central characters (villains and protagonists), context and setting, themes and meaning, as well as a broader logic or point.[11] These elements form the framework of a story, although not all elements are present in every narrative analysis.[12] In Figure 1.1, we visually demonstrate how these key elements function in the context of happy meat narratives, the focus of this book.

There are several important reasons to examine stories, particularly those surrounding meat. First, studying narratives unveils power dynamics and the formation of hegemonic common sense.[13] As the cultural politics of meat-eating shift, understanding the stories we tell about meat can help us understand this shift. Indigenous Canadian writer Harold Johnson writes, "To change our

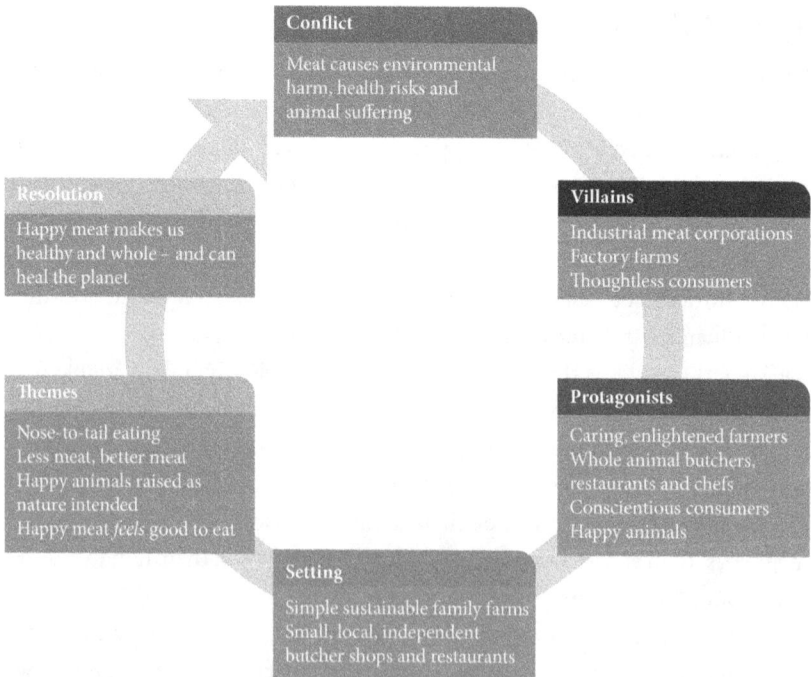

FIGURE 1.1: Key elements in the happy meat story.

Conflict
Meat causes environmental harm, health risks and animal suffering

Villains
Industrial meat corporations
Factory farms
Thoughtless consumers

Protagonists
Caring, enlightened farmers
Whole animal butchers, restaurants and chefs
Conscientious consumers
Happy animals

Setting
Simple sustainable family farms
Small, local, independent butcher shops and restaurants

Themes
Nose-to-tail eating
Less meat, better meat
Happy animals raised as nature intended
Happy meat *feels* good to eat

Resolution
Happy meat makes us healthy and whole – and can heal the planet

Source: Author.

circumstances, we need to change our story: edit it, modify it, or completely re-write it."[14] Narrative scholars emphasize that stories are neither static nor neutral. They reflect, reproduce, and potentially challenge power structures.[15] Sociologist Christopher George Takacs highlights this, noting that stories "are not benign vessels—they are laden with status-signals conveying important information about the storyteller."[16] Embedded in power relationships, stories reflect the storytellers' power and status. However, this influence is not absolute, as stories gain and lose power over time. The storytelling process is also dynamic and involves active participation through the telling and retelling of a story. For that reason, stories are best seen as plurivocal and dialogical, involving a dynamic process of claims-making rather than a static, monolithic form of power.[17]

Narrative ambiguity, as sociologist Francesca Polletta argues, represents an important part of a story's power.[18] Indeed, Wendy Griswold's research on novels suggests that ambiguity and plurivocality can be a strength—up to a point.[19] Successful literary works often strike a successful balance between generating a shared sense of common understanding while permitting a variety of interpretations. In the case of the happy meat narrative, we will see how ambiguity allows diverse actors to find common ground in a single storyline, despite holding together diverse viewpoints and interpretations.

Another reason we focus on the stories surrounding happy meat is because of their unique suitability for sociological analysis. The meat paradox, as explored in psychological literature, is relatively individualistic. Psychological studies provide valuable insights into the cognitive strategies consumers employ to reconcile their love for animals with meat consumption. However, a narrative approach to the meat paradox offers a more sociologically grounded, collectively oriented perspective. This allows us to take into consideration all the elements of the story (see Figure 1.1): the material settings of production and consumption, the real and imagined relationships between different characters (e.g., farmers and animals, consumers and producers, chefs and butchers), and the cultural themes embedded within the happy meat narrative.

Narrative analysis also serves to redirect our focus beyond facts and logic, as stories possess a unique power to evoke emotions and deeper understanding. This is particularly relevant to understanding meat-eating, which like many other consumer decisions is not exclusively a logical, considered decision but rather involves ingrained habits and emotional attachments. Meat-eating invokes positive emotions, like pleasure and familiarity, but people can also be profoundly disgusted by meat. Given the increasingly charged cultural politics of meat, we argue that studying the stories we tell about meat can provide tremendous insight into our complex, often contradictory feelings about meat.

Emotions are woven into the very fabric of narratives. Stories trigger feelings and provide an avenue for exploring and experiencing them.[20] Storytelling can compensate for the limitations of logical deliberation, bringing in personal experiences that imbue daily life with meaning.[21] Emotion is also a key part of how we evaluate stories. A stirring narrative stimulates an emotional reaction in the listener. Put simply, good stories make us feel things. Lois Presser argues that narrative analysis can be a useful tool to understand "emotional arousal," allowing us to better understand how narratives "get to us."[22] Studying the emotional tenor of stories allows scholars to understand which issues become politicized and which remain uncontroversial, unveiling possibilities for resistance and collective action.[23] In this way, "narrative analysis can provide a close-up view of how individuals create the motivation to act" or provide the rationalization for maintaining the status quo.[24] In this book, studying stories allows us to understand how meat has become a salient political issue that many people have strong feelings about.

Sociologist Arlie Russell Hochschild's concept of a "deep story" is particularly helpful when examining the happy meat narrative.[25] A deep story "*feels* as if it were true"; it has a narrative that resonates emotionally and can prioritize feelings over objective facts and reality.[26] The happy meat story exhibits the qualities of a deep story. While the science and facts of animal production play a role, the emotional core lies with an emotional impression of animals raised humanely in open spaces, surrounded by grass and sunshine, and cared for by conscientious farmers. As a deep story, happy meat stories don't always have a clear relationship to material realities. Recall Matthew's observation that pasture-raised chickens die at a significantly higher rate than chickens raised in a barn.[27] While happy meat stories can have a tenuous relationship to material realities, they conjure associations of sustainability, pleasure, and ethical consumption that take on a life of their own.

Examples of Happy Meat Stories

Chipotle's award-winning commercial, "The Scarecrow," serves as a powerful illustration of the happy meat narrative.[28] Fiona Apple's melancholic voice narrates over animations that expose the viewer, along with an innocent scarecrow protagonist, to the horrors of factory farming. The scarecrow encounters menacing red-eyed mechanical crows, frightened chickens being injected with steroids that induce plumper specimens, cows confined in metal boxes with only their heads sticking out, and assembly-line boxes plastered with stickers reading "100% beef-ish!" The viewer is invited to identify with the scarecrow, experiencing his disillusionment as he commutes to work through a dystopian landscape of corporate greenwashing and environmental exploitation.

This is a dark story, but it takes a hopeful turn. The scarecrow resists the industrial factory farm system, returning to his brightly colored, cheerful home, where he grows vegetables and prepares delicious burritos in his old-fashioned family kitchen. He then sells this wholesome food to customers under an inspirational banner: "Cultivate a better world." Chipotle's advertisement leverages viewers' worst fears of factory farming (confinement, chemical injections, animal cruelty, corporate misdirection) but offers redemption through a burrito made with care. The story invites identification with the disillusioned scarecrow and his fight against environmental degradation, animal cruelty, and corporate deception, while providing a feeling that change is possible.

"The Scarecrow" is illustrative of the general happy meat narrative, in that it pulls together various threads to provide a coherent, morally charged message: industrialized meat production is wrong. Further, the commercial utilizes a clear narrative structure, following the scarecrow's journey through a dystopian, factory-farm landscape, which encourages viewers' sense of unease. This emotional tension is crucial. The advertisement doesn't rely on facts about industrialized agriculture; it evokes empathy for the plight of the animals and the scarecrow. This emotional resonance strengthens the moral message and leaves viewers relieved as the film's denouement introduces a wholesome Chipotle burrito.

Just as every good story needs a hero, compelling stories also require a formidable villain to oppose them.[29] In the happy meat narrative, that villain is the industrial meat system. In "The Scarecrow," the factory-farm antagonist provides a force for the scarecrow protagonist to oppose, adding dramatic tension and strengthening the story's emotional resonance and moral messaging. Factory farms are a recurring villain across popular media. We see this in the film *Chicken Run*, where the chicken coop is portrayed as a kind of concentration camp, positioning meat eaters as outsiders to the animal experience and highlighting the industry's cruelty.[30] Chipotle utilizes a similar strategy, contrasting a heartless system of industrialized meat-eating with the scarecrows' idyllic home and handmade burritos, reinforcing an association of happy meat with ethical consumption. While factory farms are a commonplace, generic villain, the "happy meat" narrative also contains a more specific antagonistic force: corporations. Chipotle's scarecrow commercial, ironically itself sponsored by a large company, unintentionally highlights a vulnerability within the happy meat narrative: large corporations have the power to manipulate not just consumers but also the very storyline promoted by small, sustainable meat producers.

How Scholars Understand Meat through Narrative Analysis

Our analysis of happy meat narratives can benefit from a broader understanding of how scholars have used stories to think about the place of meat in contemporary life. Lois Presser, a narrative criminologist, offers a unique perspective by examining agriculture, meat, and animals within the framework of *zemiology*, the study of mass harm. Her research identifies the stories people tell to rationalize causing harm to one another, including the harm inflicted on farm animals through meat consumption.[31] Presser identifies a curious narrative silence surrounding meat itself.[32] Presser found that meat eaters, when interviewed about harm, rarely felt compelled to tell a story to justify this practice.[33] Presser attributes this silence to the deeply ingrained, habitual, mundane nature of eating meat.[34] The "story of meat," she argues, is so entrenched in our customs and our ideas of the natural order that it often goes untold.[35]

Presser's observation about the "taken-for-granted"-ness of meat finds support in the work of other scholars. Feminist scholar Carol Adams introduced a powerful concept, the "absent referent," to highlight how meat's origins in living, breathing animals are typically obscured and made invisible in everyday life.[36] For example, we don't talk about eating "pigs" or "cows" but instead talk about "bacon" or "pork," "beef" or "a steak." The absent referent extends beyond language, reflecting the broader cultural disconnect between meat production practices and daily meat consumption. Because of this distancing from "absent" animals, people may not feel compelled to tell a story justifying why they eat meat or ethically wrestle with the implications of their food choices.

Presser argues that when stories about meat *do* emerge, they often frame meat consumption as inevitable, normal, or invisible. Chipotle's commercial exemplifies this. Here, farm animals disappear from the narrative once the scarecrow opens his "better world" burrito business. This invisibility, a portrayal of animals as lacking agency or subjectivity, is a common theme in meat-eating narratives. Animals are cast as objects destined to be eaten, which reinforces the normalization of killing animals for food.[37] Presser describes this dynamic as a "power paradox," a concept applicable to meat-eating and other situations of mass harm.[38] The power paradox describes a contradiction where a person or group feels empowered and justified in inflicting harm, yet simultaneously feels powerless to resist acting as they do.

The *power paradox* is a useful tool for understanding dominant meat narratives. On one hand, the meat eater perceives meat-eating as a right, and they can experience a powerful form of entitlement to this food. This stems from multiple factors, like culture, the perceived healthfulness of meat, and cultural norms (like the idea that humans have dominion over animals and that eating them is our biological destiny).[39] However, the power paradox has a flip side: a sense of powerlessness. Here, the narrative portrays meat-eating as an inevitable part of humans' struggle to survive. The meat eater is a victim of a broader system, lacking the power to avoid meat, change the system, or resist the allure of tempting foods like burgers, bacon, and barbecue.[40] The theme of powerlessness can obscure eaters' sense of responsibility for their choices, allowing them to avoid thinking about the harm inflicted on animals through their diet.[41] While mainstream discourse typically frames meat as inevitable and unremarkable, a key premise of this book is that the cultural politics of meat is in flux. Critical perspectives on industrial meat have gained traction in the dominant public sphere, and some eaters are questioning their complicity in a system of animal exploitation and environmental harm. This questioning opens the door for alternative stories, most notably the happy meat narrative.[42]

Presser implicitly acknowledges the happy meat story when she cites a "deviant" case in her study involving Tina, a former vegetarian. While disgusted by the "factory environment" of conventional meat, Tina feels comfortable eating meat from free-range buffalo purchased by her in-laws.[43] Tina's story contains the kernel of the "deep story" of happy meat: factory farming feels cruel, but when exposed to a mode of eating meat that feels better, a consumer *can* eat meat (in this case, free-range buffalo) with a clear conscience. Presser notes that this story contains a basic narrative structure: a problem is identified (factory farming), a solution is found (ethical meat), and a "moral conclusion is drawn—that eating meat from an animal not made to suffer is okay."[44]

While Tina was an exception in Presser's study, her story reflects a core dimension of the happy meat phenomenon. Today's consumers, increasingly aware of the ethical costs of industrial meat, feel compelled to tell stories that make sense of and justify meat-eating. This reflects a growing discomfort with industrialized meat production, a sentiment shared by former vegetarians like Tina but also lifelong meat eaters.[45] This shared unease fuels the search for alternative narratives that center happy meat—and helps explain why Chipotle felt motivated to produce their own version of the happy meat story. The happy meat narrative provides a framework for various actors—consumers, producers, even large corporations—to grapple with their roles in the meat industry and moralize their meat consumption.

Despite its singular label, the happy meat story encompasses multiple related storylines. This narrative flexibility can unite diverse voices, bridge divides, and serve as a political resource.[46] Narratives, as Polletta suggests, allow "diverse groups to see their interests as alike enough to act collectively."[47] Presser reinforces this point, stating, "The more ambiguous a story, the more people can make that story their own."[48] We have frequently observed how an ambiguous, flexible happy meat narrative allows diverse actors—producers, consumers, corporate advertisers—to coalesce under a shared banner of alternatives to mainstream industrial meat. However, this united narrative front does not erase underlying diversity. Different actors within the happy meat narrative have disparate interests, expectations, and ideas about what counts as "good" meat. In the following chapters, we explore this complexity, mapping out the unified strands of the happy meat narrative, while acknowledging the differences and inequalities that undergird them.

The Ethical Meatscape: Where the Happy Meat Story Takes Place

Having emphasized the importance of narratives for understanding happy meat, we now unpack a key tool for understanding this storyline: the ethical meatscape. The concept of the ethical meatscape stems from the broader idea of a foodscape.[49] A foodscape involves a world of food that is culturally mediated and socially constructed but simultaneously rooted in material production, markets, and everyday practices.[50] Unlike a "food environment," a concept that primarily refers to the physical availability of food, a foodscape aims to capture how our social and cultural interpretations shape our interactions with the material world of food.[51] Imagine a foodscape like a landscape painting of a farm, portraying buildings, farm equipment, farmers, and animals, but the artist's choices—and our culture and social constructions—inevitably shape how we perceive the landscape.

An ethical meatscape is a specific kind of foodscape focused on meat—and, more specifically, meat that is understood as sustainable, humane, and healthy.[52] Like others, we use the term *ethical* to indicate an alternative to the conventional food system, not to claim inherent moral superiority for these products. The ethical foodscape is not a unitary, monolithic space. It offers a diversity of products that make a wide array of promises, from improving human health to protecting the environment, fairly treating producers, and promoting animal welfare.[53] Ethical meat is part of a larger movement toward alternative food systems, sometimes referred to as alternative food networks (AFNs).[54] The "alternative-ness" of AFNs is a topic of frequent debate—what truly separates them from mainstream food? This question is not easily resolved and makes up an essential part of ethical foodscapes. Are genetically modified foods always a bad idea? Is local food superior to long-distance organics? Should producers prioritize sustainability as well as fair labor practices? These ongoing conversations reflect the dynamic political and cultural context surrounding ethical food and ethical meat more specifically.

Meat occupies a particularly prominent space in the ethical foodscape. This is due, in no small part, to growing consumer awareness of the ethical and environmental limitations of factory-farming.[55] Mirroring the broader ethical foodscape, the ethical meatscape brings together a variety of actors—small farmers, hipster butchers, concerned consumers, and food corporations—ultimately connecting caring producers with conscientious consumers. The ethical meatscape is bound together by a deep story: thoughtfully raised animal products contribute to a collective good, offering improved animal welfare, revitalized rural economies, healthy food, and environmental protection. In this narrative, meat producers lovingly provide products that are naturally raised, sustainable, and free of antibiotics and hormones. As we'll explore in Chapter 4, consumers are drawn to these products based on a feeling that happy meat is not only delicious to eat but is also ethically sound and good for the planet.

FIGURE 1.2: A "happy chicken" offered for sale in a
boutique butcher shop in Vancouver.

Source: Author photo.

In addition to its cultural richness, the ethical meatscape is also connected
to the *material* world—a world of blood and flesh, feathers and bone, money
and markets. Consumers navigate this space making consumption choices
that may or may not meaningfully translate into real-world gains for animals
or sustainability. Put differently, the happy meat narrative, with its characters,
themes, and ideals, is not a perfect photorealistic representation of the messy
material realities of meat production. As the geographer Mara Miele observes,
the "invention" of the happy chicken is "ambivalent but also precarious," since
"many important areas of animals' lives remain opaque."[56]

A potent example of this slippery material-culture relationship is nose-
to-tail eating, which involves eating and valuing every part of an animal. We
encountered this idea regularly in our research on happy meat and in popular
reference guides on the subject. For example, the *Home Butchering Handbook*
suggests that breaking down your own animals "allows more of the animal
to be used," implying that buying parts of animals at the grocery store will

generate food waste.[57] During interviews, producers routinely valorized the idea of a home cook transforming a whole, free-range bird into several family meals. In this storyline, the wasteful, bland, and disconnected industrialized meat system is symbolized by a boneless, skinless chicken breast packaged on a Styrofoam tray—everything the whole-chicken approach opposes.

As an example of this esteem for whole chickens, consider Hayun, a young Korean-Canadian woman we met in a Toronto focus group. Hayun talked about the importance of introducing people to whole chickens in her community cooking classes, saying, "Especially with people who are younger, they're really uncomfortable with bones, and if it's not already cut for you and de-boned, no skin, whatever, they're not really comfortable with it." For Hayun and other concerned meat consumers we spoke with, embracing whole-animal eating is central to ethical consumption as it minimizes food waste and reconnects consumers with the reality of meat as part of a whole creature, with bones, skin, and fat. For Hayun, working with a whole chicken also holds cultural significance, as it enables her to make bone broth, which she sees as a valuable element of Korean culture. Bone broth is a bridge for Hayun, connecting chicken bones to a much broader physical and cultural context. This connection challenges the prevailing tendency to fetishize meat, seeing a piece of animal flesh in isolation from the rest of its body and the larger production context. Hayun strongly resists this, saying, "even just a chicken thigh is part of something bigger."

The story of nose-to-tail eating, where every part of an animal is carefully utilized, holds a significant place in the ethical meatscape. However, like all narratives, it has an imperfect relationship to the complex realities of meat production. Conscientious meat eaters may be unaware that industrialized agriculture is organized around a principle of eliminating waste and extracting value. Every last part of an animal is meticulously transformed into a multitude of products, from familiar items like leather and pet food to lesser-known applications like ramen flavoring, biofuel, and glues. Alex Blanchette's insightful book *Porkopolis* sheds light on the ruthless but rational efficiencies of industrial pig production.[58]

The efficiency of industrialized meat stands in stark contrast to the experiences of some small meat producers we interviewed. These producers sometimes struggled to use the entire animal in a cost-effective way, since their small-scale operations lacked access to global commodity networks that efficiently monetize every element of a carcass. Sheila and Derek, ranchers in

Alberta, recounted their initial excitement at selling large volumes of prime cuts of beef to an upscale restaurant. They felt honored and validated to have their beef featured on this high-end menu. However, this deal left them with a freezer full of tougher, less valued cuts, ultimately forcing them to consume this lower-value meat themselves for years, even as the quality deteriorated due to prolonged storage in their freezer. Jeremy, a rancher and slaughter-house owner, shared a similar dilemma. While consumers prize well-marbled beef, his small operation couldn't utilize the vast quantities of fat produced. "It's limitless," he lamented, "and it crushes me to throw it away." His kids learned to make soap using the excess fat, but it barely made a dent in the surplus: "You couldn't in a million years use all the beef fat from a plant that kills 10 beef a week."

These stories highlight a stark contrast between the efficiency of indus-trial meat production, which maximizes profit by utilizing every part of the animal, and the challenges faced by small-scale producers, who often lack the infrastructure and market access to do the same. This is not to suggest that industrial slaughterhouses are ethically superior due to their efficiencies—an argument that Blanchette explicitly rejects.[59] Instead, the case of nose-to-tail eating highlights how the happy meat narrative, while emotionally resonant, doesn't perfectly capture the material realities of either factory farming or ethical meat production. Still, it is a deep story—it is a story that feels true—and for that reason it remains powerful. For many consumers in our focus groups, cooking a whole chicken simply *feels* more responsible than buying a package of pre-cut breasts. In part, this is because the happy meat narrative paints a picture of humanely raised animals who enjoy their lives and then are killed in a respectful slaughter process that minimizes waste. Every morsel of meat is savored, all fat is rendered, and bones are transformed into flavorful broths. While this ideal may not always be achievable, it serves as an aspira-tional framework for a more ethical relationship with meat that filters into the everyday consciousness of concerned consumers.

The Ethical Meatscape: Unraveling its Origins, Key Players, and Major Concerns

While minimizing food waste is an important issue for concerned eaters, it represents just one facet of a broader ethical meatscape. Within this food-scape, a multitude of concerns about industrial meat converge, centering on three primary areas: 1) environmental impacts, 2) human health risks, and 3) moral considerations, especially relating to animal suffering.[60] In the following chapters, we draw from diverse data sources to unpack these consumer worries, exploring the motivations and practices of a growing group of consumers who are questioning the meat status quo.[61] Food writers and academics have suggested various terms to describe these concerned meat eaters: flexitarians, conscientious omnivores, semi-vegetarians, VB6 (vegan before 6 p.m. dinnertime), critical consumers, or mindful meat eaters. These consumers have varying levels of concern and commitment to change but share an intention to eat "quality" meat that feels sustainable and humane and also tastes good.[62] This demand has fueled a proliferation of labels and marketing terms like *pasture-raised, free-run, free-range, humanely raised, happy, natural, organic,* and *antibiotic-* and *hormone-free.* Discussion about the meaningfulness of these labels is itself a key element of the ethical meatscape. They reflect how we are collectively struggling to understand the potential and limitations of a strategy that maintains meat-eating while objecting to many aspects of factory farming.

Environmental sociologists highlight a key obstacle for conscientious consumers, including ethical meat eaters: our daily habits don't always reflect our values. Practical considerations like habit, convenience, and cost often trump good intentions when it comes to food choices.[63] The disconnect can be especially profound for ethical meat eaters, who face uncertainty about which meat products represent meaningful alternatives to the industrial mainstream. To investigate this point, psychologist Hank Rothgerber uses survey data to compare conscientious omnivores to vegetarians.[64] He finds that conscientious omnivores have relatively vague commitments compared to vegetarians and are more likely to "cheat" on their diets. Rothgerber partially attributes this lapse in ethics to the difficulty of discerning the ethical backstory of a meat product. Unlike vegetarians who might simply check for the presence of meat, ethical meat eaters face a more complex task—deciphering the ethical treatment of the animal behind the meal.

Seeing the gap between ethical meat eater ideals and their real-life practices might tempt some readers to dismiss them as uncommitted or hypocritical. We resist that temptation and instead work to better understand the myriad concerns meat eaters express about industrial meat. While searching for ethical meat options might seem like a relatively minor, impotent response to a massive, industrialized meat system, it signals a growing desire for a more mindful, responsible approach to meat consumption. As Miele writes, "Even if the 'happy chicken' might be seen as a weak invention, fraught with ambivalence and ambiguities, it has achieved important effects; it has suggested a more complex moral relationship between human and nonhuman animals . . . we might say that the happy chicken has shown that chickens' lives should be better."[65] In this spirit, we aim to engage with concerned meat eaters on their terms. This includes recognizing how everyday practices are shaped by a mixture of ethical ideals, social relationships, and habits as well as practical considerations of cost, availability, and convenience.

Origins of the Ethical Meatscape

Imagine a world where meat consumption, sustainability, and animal welfare are not at odds. This is the world imagined within the ethical meatscape, which began to emerge in the early 2000s. While critical voices against industrial meat production existed earlier, Michael Pollan's influential writings in that period crystallized and amplified these concerns for a broader audience, particularly in North America.[66] His 2002 essay "An Animal's Place" outlined the ethical arguments against factory farming: "The American industrial animal farm offers a nightmarish glimpse of what capitalism can look like in the absence of moral or regulatory constraint."[67] This critique was not new for Pollan. His earlier article "Power Steer" used a personal narrative to critique factory farming; he bought a cow and followed it from a grassy field to a grim feedlot, where it was fed antibiotic-laced feed and given a steroid injection and ultimately became a box of steaks.[68]

Significantly, Pollan does not end either article with an argument for vegetarianism. Instead, he proposes a path for more ethical meat-eating and suggests the importance of sourcing from smaller, sustainable operations: "the ranches where cattle still spend their lives on grass, the poultry farms where chickens still go outside and the hog farms where pigs live as they did 50 years ago—in contact with the sun, the earth, and the gaze of a farmer."[69] On these farms, Pollan argues, animals contribute ecological value by adding to the nutrient-rich soil of the farm and can have a good life before they are slaughtered and eaten. Pollan followed up these essays with his best-selling book *The Omnivore's Dilemma*, which concludes with an idyllic meal featuring a wild boar that he personally shoots, breaks down, and serves to friends.[70] Overall, Pollan's influential writings offered meat-loving consumers an ethical alternative to vegetarianism and conventional meat, as long the consumer was willing to step beyond the faceless industrial food system and search out natural, wild, or pasture-raised animals.[71]

While we intuitively sensed that Pollan's writings were influential in the emergence of the ethical meatscape, we wanted to get a more systematic read on the shifting public discourse around meat. We collected articles from six leading North American newspapers (1980–2017) and generated a sample of over fifteen thousand news articles. Using topic modeling, a technique that identifies recurring themes in big datasets, we analyzed the articles by decade.[72] This analysis revealed a significant shift: major themes of ethical meat discourse were relatively absent in the 1980s and 1990s but became prominent in the 2000s and continued throughout the 2010s. This pattern suggests that Pollan's writing was perfectly timed to usher in and articulate key themes and concerns within the ethical meatscape.

While Pollan is an important figure in the emergence of the ethical meatscape, our investigation into broad discursive trends revealed a cultural shift toward ethical meat consumption in the 2000s. Besides our topic-modeling data, there were other emergent signs of a collective yearning for a different, more transparent way of eating meat: the rise of small butcher shops, the surge of butchery tattoos on hipster's biceps, the trend of charcuterie plates on restaurant menus, and the critical acclaim given to nose-to-tail restaurant chefs like Fergus Henderson (of St. John in London) with his signature bone marrow dish. Popular books also emerged to articulate options for eating meat ethically. For example, Catherine Friend's *The Compassionate Carnivore* balanced her experience raising sheep with advice for promoting more careful, compassionate meat consumption.[73]

The ethical butcher emerged as a particularly charismatic figure who could offer advice to concerned consumers. Christine Jeske explores the trend of these "rock-star" butchers who are no longer seen as simple meat processors but as knowledgeable agents whose ties to farmers allows meat to act as a mode of "re-enchantment" with the natural world.[74] Berlin Reed's *The Ethical Butcher: How Thoughtful Eating Can Change Your World* details his transformation from a rebellious Seattle upstart with the word "vegan" tattooed on his neck to a passionate advocate for whole-animal butchery.[75] Reed's journey embodies the ethical meatscape ideal of taking personal responsibility for meat consumption. Like Pollan, Reed rejects the idea that vegetarianism is the only ethical option: "Not until I slaughtered my first animal would I feel so tangibly and personally accountable for the life lost in order to feed us."[76] Reed is sympathetic to his former militant-vegan self but describes "coming out of [a] haze," "shedding the dogma that demonized meat and animal farming," and "escaping from Herbivore Island."[77]

The ethical meatscape positions the conscientious meat eater as a central figure, which aligns with the broader cultural ethos of consumer-citizenship.[78] These meat eaters take responsibility for their meat purchases, beyond simply grabbing a package of chicken breast at the grocery store. They might choose to hunt their own food or learn home butchery, crafting sausages from ethically sourced animals. The *Home Butchering Handbook,* for instance, not only offers practical advice to the reader interested in breaking down whole animals at home, it also explores the motivations behind this trend.[79] It aims to reach eaters "seeking to take greater responsibility" for food ethics or those yearning for "a more balanced and self-sufficient way of life"; these eaters know that "the best quality meat is the result of personalized attention."[80] This valuation of home butchery reflects a desire to reclaim agency within the food system; it offers eaters a chance to secede from a system of depersonalized, fast-moving animal carcasses in factory farms that promote dangerous work and create food safety issues through fecal contamination and unsanitary tools.[81] The conscientious eater aims to build a relationship with a local farmer that will allow them to purchase and potentially butcher a whole animal. The goal is to fully acknowledge, and perhaps even partake in, the transformation of farm animal into meat. This represents a significant departure from the sanitized, often obscured system of industrial meat production, where the animal's life and death are largely hidden from view.

As is made clear in the ideal of home butchery, the culinary vision in the ethical meatscape is personal, sustainable, and small in scale. The small-scale descriptor applies not only to farm size but also to portion control. The happy ending in an ethical meat story often involves eating a delicious, carefully prepared, *limited* serving of meat. Chef Dan Barber, a champion of sustainable food, envisions a similar future in his book *The Third Plate*. He proposes a shift away from the traditional "hulking piece of protein," toward higher-quality, smaller cuts of sustainable meat accompanied by beautifully prepared vegetables.[82] Imagine braised beef with a "*carrot steak* dominating the plate," instead of a giant ribeye.[83] Barber's "third plate" perfectly captures the "less meat, better meat" ideal prevalent in the ethical meatscape.

Barber's vision showcases another morality tale embedded in the happy meat story: ethical meat *tastes* and nourishes your body better than conventional meat. These themes of ethics, health, and taste resonate deeply with food scholars who emphasize two important cues for regulating food intake: what we feel we *should* eat (normative cues) and what we *want* to eat (sensory cues).[84] Happy meat fits the bill for both dimensions, as it is assumed to taste more delicious than factory farm meat (sensory cue), while simultaneously being a healthier and more ethical choice (normative cues). One doesn't necessarily mourn the loss of a giant, industrial steak if a small piece of braised meat, perhaps accompanied by a "carrot steak," is more sustainable *and* delicious.

Mark Schatzker's book *Steak: One Man's Search for the World's Tastiest Piece of Beef* captures the connection between normative sensory cues in the ethical meatscape.[85] He embarks on a sixty-thousand-mile culinary adventure to find the steak that delivers the purest flavor. His quest leads him to conclude that a top-shelf, USDA Prime, feedlot-fattened steak is less delicious than a "Choice"-graded steak with a "gorgeous Maillard crust" from a cow finished on a stretch of grass.[86] This conclusion might surprise those who assume Prime-graded meat must be the best there is. Schatzker argues that the key to this steak's deliciousness is its fat. Grass-finished cattle develop fat rich in omega-3 fatty acids, offering a healthier and more nuanced flavor. He emphasizes the importance of savoring this difference in its rawest form: "When a feedlot steak is raw, it is almost totally without flavor. A raw grass-fed steak, on the other hand, has depth—not the depth of a cooked grass-fed steak, but enough flavor to enable you to taste and enjoy the meat you're eating."[87] Schatzker's journey ends with an emotional account of eating steak sourced from a grass-fed and -finished cow raised on the Alderspring Ranch in Idaho. His words capture the strong aesthetic and emotional dimensions of his story of happy meat:

> I would like to tell you how that steak tasted, but the truth is, we lack an adequate meat vocabulary. . . . What I can tell you about that steak is how it made me feel. The flavor reached deep into my subcortex and uncorked a sensation that bubbled up and drowned out every other thought, concern, and anxiety drifting through the chaos and endless dialogue that rage in the mind. I chewed, swallowed, cut more steak, and chewed, sustaining my state of mind with each bite. It is the feeling that no human, or animal, for that matter, ever tires of experiencing. It is a feeling that makes life, for all of its pain, frustration, and sadness, worth living. The feeling is joy.[88]

The ethical meatscape offers "joy" for the eater—and even a reason for living. But what about the animal that loses its life? How prominent are happy animals as characters—minor or major—in these happy meat stories? While authors in the ethical meatscape honor the animals we eat, they rarely feature them as central characters in the narrative.[89] The idea of a happy animal (like a "happy chicken") is an important social construct, but it often remains an abstract, spectral character. Miele, whom we earlier identified as portraying the life of a happy chicken as "opaque," also describes the happy chicken as an ambivalent character, since the happiness of the chicken is often viewed instrumentally as a means of maximizing eating pleasure.[90] At the heart of the happy meat narrative lies a vexing ethical dilemma: does it genuinely prioritize the well-being of animals, or is it primarily a tool for alleviating the guilt of concerned consumers? This tension, far from being a minor detail, is a defining feature of the ethical meatscape.

While animals aren't always the protagonists of happy meat narratives, their well-being is often a prominent moral theme. Consider Schatzker's experience sharing a grass-finished steak with Temple Grandin, the renowned animal behaviorist who designs humane slaughterhouses. In keeping with the ethical meatscape's interest in happy meat, Schatzker asks Grandin specifically about a cow's happiness.[91] Grandin suggests that well-managed feedlots can provide some happiness, but then Schatzker asks Grandin where she would like to live if she was reincarnated as a cow; she answers quickly, "I think I would choose being in the field. . . . This right here is cattle heaven."[92] This exchange highlights a key aspiration of the "happy meat" narrative: to reconcile ethical eating with both animal welfare and culinary pleasure. It offers a seductive vision where sustainable practices, happy animals, and delicious meals coexist, temporarily resolving the inherent tension of consuming animal life.

How does the happy meat story sustain a sense of dramatic tension? This tension is often created by placing a delicious, ethically sourced product against a hegemonic background of industrial farming. Recall that the common villain in the happy meat story is the factory farm, depicted as "environmentally and economically corrupt and unsustainable at the level of both the individual farmer and society as a whole."[93] In contrast, alternative agriculture emerges as a "salvation story" where people must find their way through the morass of conventional farming and come to achieve personal, environmental, and/or economic redemption.[94] Nature becomes a teacher and partner, fostering an "ethical, mutually beneficial relationship."[95] A key figure in this redemption narrative is the awakened farmer, who rejects the reductionist, domineering approach of industrial agriculture, instead learning from and working alongside the animals and plants they share the land with.[96] This salvation story offers hope, a vision of enlightened animal husbandry and a less guilt-inducing way of eating animals.

Going Forward: Unity and Division within the Happy Meat Story

This chapter explored the happy meat narrative, a story that allows concerned consumers a way to eat meat and, at least temporarily, to feel good about their choices. We introduced the diverse set of actors who occupy the ethical meatscape, united by a common desire for meat that aligns with values of animal welfare, sustainability, and small-scale agriculture. Drawing on Hochschild's concept of a "deep story," we see the happy meat narrative as more than just a marketing ploy.[97] It resonates emotionally, feeling true even when it doesn't perfectly align with reality. This approach allows us to appreciate the often-overlooked emotional dimensions of meat consumption. This is a finding that struck us deeply and consistently: people's decisions to eat (or not eat) meat are connected to the habits and emotions of daily foodwork. People often want to eat meat because it feels good, and eating ethical meat can feel particularly good for consumers, as we will explore more in Chapter 3.

In the ethical meatscape, there is a significant, but imperfect, relationship between cultural ideals and material realities. The narrative ideals of small-scale, sustainable, free-ranging animals do not always align with the complex reality of raising animals for food, as we explore in Part III of this book. To be clear, our goal is not to study the objective happiness of farm animals.[98] Instead, we investigate what work is accomplished through the cultural politics of "happy meat." Here we draw inspiration from Sara Ahmed, who rejects the idea of happiness as a universal or neutral concept and investigates how the notion of happiness can be harnessed to unveil power relations and cultural values.[99] Animal happiness, like human happiness, is not a simple or singular pursuit but a powerful tool for discerning how a society shapes, interprets, and values the connection between living animals and the practice of consuming their bodies.

In the pages that follow, we will see how the distinction between "happy/ethical" and "unhappy/industrial" meat can be surprisingly blurry, as is the

FIGURE 1.3: These chickens spent a lot of time pecking out in the field, and their lives, at least in this moment, represent many consumers' ideal of happy meat.

Source: Author photo.

case in alternative food networks more generally.[100] To return to the example of eggs introduced at the beginning of this chapter, the wide range of options can overwhelm the consumer, and the value proposition of "premium" eggs is not always clear. During our research in British Columbia, we visited a particularly idyllic egg farm run by a farmer called Mitchell (to whom we will return in Chapter 6). These chickens lived in a spacious, clean environment surrounded by a bountiful orchard of fruit and nut trees. Unlike conventional practices, Mitchell's laying hens lived out their natural lives, even after their egg production declined. Seeing this operation firsthand helped us understand why these eggs were so expensive. Yet we *still* have moments of confusion encountering egg options back home in our local grocery store. The actual conditions of production are not readily transparent, and we are left wondering, does spending $10 or $12 on a carton of eggs mean that the chickens lived a decent life, or are we simply paying a premium to feel better? The answer remains frustratingly elusive. However, what persists is a unifying ideal of happy animals that produce happy meat.

In presenting happy meat stories throughout this book, we squarely acknowledge our role as researchers and writers shaping these stories. We take that responsibility seriously, aiming not to present the definitive happy meat story but rather to interrogate the complexities, contradictions, and implications inherent in contemporary meat narratives. When introducing our participants, we have made deliberate choices about which demographic characteristics to include, prioritizing those that are directly relevant to their story. This may involve highlighting the parental status of a father negotiating meaty meals with his family or identifying a participant's ethnic background as they grapple with balancing their desire to minimize meat against cultural norms in their ethnic community. We have endeavored to strike a balance between consistency and representing our participants in their full complexity within the constraints of space. This reflects the interpretive nature of sociological inquiry—work that we undertake with care, mindful of how our power and positionality shapes the storytelling process.[101] Ultimately, our goal is to paint a nuanced portrait of the "happy meat" phenomenon, one that invites critical reflection and dialogue about the ethical, social, and environmental implications of our meaty food choices.

TWO   No Reservations? The Complicated Case
of Regular (but Conflicted) Meat-Eating

ANTHONY BOURDAIN WAS A foodie's foodie. A longtime chef, Bourdain became famous for his food-focused television shows *No Reservations* and *Parts Unknown*.[1] In *No Reservations*, Bourdain traveled the world, sampling food and narrating his gustatorial experiences. Bourdain famously had "no reservations" when it came to eating foods—often unusual meat dishes—that many North American eaters fear. Bourdain's willingness to sample such diverse foods raises important questions: How do we come to fear some kinds of meat and crave others? And how common is it to really have no reservations about meat?

Our food preferences feel innate and personal, yet they are deeply rooted in our cultural backgrounds and social contexts. For example, a North American consumer in the 1970s likely felt deep reservations about eating horsemeat, but this was not the case for many French eaters at the time. But today, French consumers eat a fraction of the horsemeat they ate mere decades ago, a shift attributed to younger consumers' squeamishness about eating horses.[2] Perhaps motivated by a similar moral sensibility, many North American eaters feel an aversion to eating fluffy, cute animals like bunnies, even though there is a strong environmental argument to incorporate more rabbit meat in our diet.[3] Religious beliefs can also powerfully influence dietary choices. Hinduism, for instance, prohibits beef consumption, contributing to a strong taboo against eating beef among Hindus.[4] These examples illustrate that there are few meats that are universally embraced and that our cultural context plays a critical role in shaping how we feel about meat as well as our eating practices.[5]

Of course, while many people eat meat regularly, especially mainstream meats like chicken, beef, and pork, not everybody does so with Bourdain's no-holds-barred enthusiasm. In this chapter, we draw primarily from our survey data—and secondarily from our focus groups—to share what we saw and learned about people's complex orientations toward meat. Our questions explore people's attitudes about meat broadly, rather than focusing on happy meat alone. These findings provide crucial context about people's thoughts, feelings, and practices relating to meat, helping us interpret our more targeted findings on happy meat.

Our findings reveal a spectrum of meat-eating practices. Some eaters share Bourdain's openness to new culinary experiences and diverse meat palates. Others feel disgusted by meat and horrified by animal cruelty. Still others experience eating meat as either a necessary evil (e.g., I need the protein, I live with people who love eating meat) or a practice they engage in but feel guilty about. This range of orientations toward meat powerfully illuminates one key finding in particular: *few* people have no reservations when it comes to eating meat. Even among enthusiastic meat eaters, we observed complex emotions and ethical concerns.

The Complicated Terrain of Meat-Eating

One of the most iconic advertisements of the 1980s was a campaign for the fast-food chain Wendy's. It featured three elderly white women investigating a seemingly oversized hamburger bun, remarking on its size and airiness. Lifting the top of the bun, we are shown a very small hamburger patty and we hear one of the women repeatedly exclaim, "Where's the beef?" This viral catchphrase appeared on T-shirts and frisbees, inspiring songs and even a board game. The slogan "where's the beef?" captures a simple and straightforward desire for meat in all its deliciousness and stands in contrast to contemporary concerns about health and ethics associated with meat production and consumption. It elides the themes we described in the previous chapter as motivating the rise of the ethical meatscape, from cancer and E. coli to animal welfare and climate change. Indeed, if one were to speculate on the attitudes that the "where's the beef?" women have toward meat, it would be reasonable to guess they would emphasize a preference for larger portions and a focus on taste and satisfaction. This perspective exemplifies the traditional, uncritical approach to meat consumption that has been challenged by the rise of happy meat.

This chapter illuminates a disconnect between the popular image of the enthusiastic, "where's the beef?" meat eater and the realities of contemporary meat consumption. We begin by examining contemporary research on meat-eating and meat eaters to determine how common it is for meat eaters to have no reservations and to better understand the concerns that meat-eating and meat-abstaining consumers have about animal protein. To do so, we rely on the work of scholars who have studied the motivations of those who adopt vegetarian and vegan diets.[6] Compared to careful social scientific analyses of meat-abstaining subcultures, there is less research exploring meat eaters' discomfort and skepticism about industrially produced meat—as well as their desire for ethical meat alternatives.[7] As social psychologist Hank Rothgerber writes, "Researchers have largely lagged behind the public's interest in and consumption of ethical meat products."[8] Nonetheless, we can learn a great deal from existing research about the prevalence of vegetarian (versus meat-eating) diets and people's reasons for becoming vegetarian and vegan.[9]

As we review research on meat-eating and vegetarianism throughout this chapter and book, there is one point we want to emphasize at the outset: existing data suggest that the vast majority of people (i.e., over 95% of the population) in countries like the United States and Canada include meat in their diets. Also, as noted in the introduction, they eat meat in relatively large amounts compared to global averages. Based on these numbers alone, we might think that most North American consumers are living some version of the enthusiastic, "where's the beef?" meat eater in everyday life, floating from fast-food hamburgers to steak dinners to buckets of fried chicken.

As food and culture scholars, we realize that the situation of meat-eating is far from simple. Yes, people in North America continue to eat meat at relatively high rates. However, that does not mean people necessarily eat meat without reservations or without experiencing tensions, discomfort, and negative feelings about meat consumption. Our goal here is to move beyond overarching trends to unpack the complexity of people's ideas about meat. We aim to make sense of the reluctance and reservations consumers have about meat, especially as people learn more about industrialized meat production. In this chapter, we draw primarily from our survey data to get a big-picture sense of people's complex orientations toward meat—a picture that considers the contradictions between how people think and feel about meat and what ends up on their plate. In addition to people's general orientation toward meat, we think there is an additional piece of the puzzle: the social relationships and intimacies that shape orientations toward meat. We see these relationships and intimacies as crucial elements of the social context in which people's meat behaviors, emotions, beliefs, and identities exist. To capture this relational, contextual data, in the final section of this chapter we turn to our focus group conversations, which shed light on how meat makes up a key part of the social fabric of everyday life.

Breaking Down the Dimensions of a Meat Orientation

Before exploring our data, we want to introduce the theoretical framework we employ to understand orientations toward meat-eating. A cornerstone of this framework is the psychological tripartite model of attitudes.[10] Meat attitudes, like other attitudes, comprise three key dimensions—behaviors and practices, beliefs and cognition, and affect and emotions. When confronted with an object or issue, people's responses can range from highly positive to highly negative; if we want to comprehensively understand the basis of these responses, all three elements of the model must be considered.[11]

While the psychological tripartite model effectively captures individual responses to meat, as sociologists we argue that two additional dimensions are important for a comprehensive understanding of individuals' orientations to meat: identity and social context. Identity refers to how people see themselves and how they wish to be seen by others, including how they construct identities around food choices (e.g., as a "committed vegan" or an "enthusiastic foodie").[12] Social context also shapes orientations to meat and meat-eating. Recognizing that there is no singular "meat eater" or "vegetarian," we acknowledge that the expression of these labels varies according to the social contexts we inhabit.[13] Social context matters at different levels—the family relationships of the household and broader social ties among friends, colleagues, and wider society all influence our dietary choices. By incorporating identity and social context into our analysis, we move beyond an individualistic understanding of meat attitudes. This expanded framework allows us to examine how social forces intersect with personal experiences to shape the landscape of meat-eating.

Next, we describe how each dimension—behaviors, thoughts, emotions, identity, and social context—is necessary to gain a holistic picture of meat consumption. Prior research on meat-eating and vegetarianism underscores this point. Focusing solely on a single dimension, such as frequency of meat consumption, provides an incomplete understanding. For example, a behavioral question like "how often do you eat meat?" doesn't reveal an individual's underlying thoughts or emotions about meat. Yet relying on self-reported diet labels (e.g., "vegan") without asking people how frequently they eat meat or other animal products also misses a crucial dimension and risks overestimating meat abstinence. As our data will demonstrate, dietary practices can sometimes contradict identity (e.g., a vegetarian who occasionally eats meat).[14] Furthermore, neglecting the social context turns our attention away from the meanings people attach to meat consumption, which can elucidate meat's enduring popularity despite high levels of concern about its effects on human health, the environment, and animal welfare. By examining all dimensions— feelings about meat production, beliefs and ideas surrounding meat, actual meat-eating practices, and identity within social contexts—we gain a richer understanding of society's complex relationship with animal protein.

Behaviors and Practices: Frequency Does Not Equal Affinity

Research about the behavioral dimension of meat consumption suggests that a clear majority of consumers love meat, since most studies find high levels of routine meat consumption and low levels of meat avoidance. For example, a study of meat consumers in the United Kingdom used a series of government surveys of households spanning several decades. The surveys asked respondents about the purchase of categories of foods within the household. The author calculated rates of vegetarianism based on the nonpurchase of any kind of meat and calculated rates of veganism by also factoring in the nonpurchase of eggs or dairy. Ultimately, the study reported that vegetarianism in the U.K. fluctuated minimally around a yearly proportion of 2.8 percent of households from 1992 to 2014 and a yearly proportion of 0.5 percent for vegans.[15] This means that around 97 percent of U.K. households consumed meat during that period. The U.K. is not particularly exceptional when it comes to Western countries. Survey-based studies from the United States and Canada have similarly found that less than 5 percent of households adhere to vegetarian or vegan diets.[16] If we are using these behavioral figures to describe people's meat attitudes, we would likely conclude that most people have a positive orientation toward meat. Surely, how people behave is a central component to their orientation and cannot be ignored. But eating behavior should not be taken as the only—or the ultimate—signal of people's orientation toward meat.

Cognition: Conflicted and Contradictory Beliefs about Meat Consumption

Examining the cognitive dimensions of this orientation complicates the picture of meat-eating. Research on veganism and vegetarianism has explored the specific ideas and values held by those who abstain from eating meat.[17] There is a small but growing body of research on cognition about meat among consumers indicating that people can hold negative ideas about meat and its production even as they continue to consume animal protein.[18]

What sorts of beliefs about meat and animal agriculture do consumers hold? Research suggests that consumer beliefs about meat and animal agriculture are complex, often marked by a degree of cognitive skepticism. Research by food scientist Genero Miranda-de la Lama and his coauthors revealed that while Mexican survey respondents often lacked detailed knowledge of animal living conditions, many were aware of potential problems in meat production.[19] This finding aligns with a comprehensive review of thirty-four studies, suggesting that 23 to 35 percent of meat eaters recognize the negative environmental impact of meat.[20] While this awareness is not universal, it highlights that a significant proportion of consumers view meat as environmentally problematic—a highly significant finding at a moment when environmental issues hold a prominent place in public consciousness.[21]

Beyond environmental concerns, a 2019 Gallup survey of American adults revealed a range of motivations behind efforts to reduce meat consumption. While health concerns were indeed a salient issue, mentioned by 90 percent of respondents, a significant proportion also expressed concerns about environmental impact (70%), food safety (65%), and animal welfare (65%).[22] These findings suggest that while health plays a major role in dietary choices, it is not the sole factor shaping individuals' attitudes toward meat. The interconnectedness of these cognitive concerns highlights the multifaceted nature of consumer attitudes, with ethical, environmental, and health-related considerations all contributing to a complex decision-making landscape. Even if beliefs don't straightforwardly predict eating practices, they nonetheless reveal a wariness toward meat that many consumers might not hold for other foods they regularly eat.

Emotions: How Do We Feel about Meat?

The third key dimension of our orientation toward meat involves the realm of affect and emotion.[23] Most people intuitively recognize that eating is an emotional act—something captured in the commonplace quip about "eating your feelings" when you overindulge at a time of emotional strife. Considering how people subjectively experience meat is an important factor that adds color to our overall picture of a meat orientation.[24]

A focus on deliciousness is a particularly important affective response associated with a positive attitude toward meat.[25] On the flip side, disgust and sadness for animals are prevalent feelings evoked by meat that are related to a negative attitude toward meat-eating. A team of Norwegian psychologists found that perceptions of animal cuteness can increase empathy toward animals, which in turn makes people less oriented toward eating or enjoying meat.[26] Some members of this research team found, in another study, that the presentation or representation of meat and its relationship to a living animal—for instance, meat served with the head attached or meat advertisements featuring live animals—affected the extent to which consumers could dissociate meat from its animal origins.[27] This dissociation, in turn, was related to greater or lesser feelings of empathy or disgust.[28] Studies beyond a focus on meat also demonstrate the importance of emotion for understanding food choices, consumption decisions, and behavior in general.[29] In sum, how we feel about meat is a vital part of understanding our overall orientation toward meat.

Identity: Constructing the Self Through an Orientation to Meat

Identity, the fourth dimension of our framework, explores how individuals construct their self-image in relation to meat consumption. This is often reflected through dietary labels. These labels include long-established terms like *vegetarian* and *vegan,* which have been used widely in public discourse for many years.[30] Other labels used to describe meat-eating and meat-restricting habits, like *flexitarian* or *pescatarian,* are more recent and niche.[31] Interestingly, the dominant cultural identity of "meat eater" often remains unlabeled, considered the norm and thus not warranting a specific designation. In our research, we use the term *omnivore* to categorize people who report that they regularly include meat in their diet.[32] While analytically useful, the *omnivore* term cannot capture the emotional and cognitive reservations held by meat eaters (as we explore below), as it is not a label many people would use to describe their default way of eating.

In contrast, the identity labels of vegetarian and vegan are much more symbolically rich and have been shown to have positive schematic associations with health, wealth, thinness, and attractiveness.[33] Studies relying on self-reported dietary labels often report higher rates of vegetarianism and veganism compared to those based on actual consumption data.[34] In other words, more people *identify* themselves as vegetarian than *practice* a strict vegetarian diet. This suggests we should be wary when reading a headline claiming that plant-based diets are on the rise, since these studies are often based on survey respondents' self-reported labels. Even so, we feel that it is significant that a substantial proportion of people want to describe their diet as something other than the mainstream, "normal" meat-eating identity.[35] The contrast between self-reported diet labels and self-reported meat intake adds nuance to our big-picture project of mapping people's orientations toward meat. It highlights the importance of considering both the aspirational aspect of identity (how individuals want to be seen) and the behavioral reality (what they actually eat).

Social Context: How Is Meat-Eating Connected to Our Relationships?

The final dimension of meat-related orientations is social context, encompassing the social relationships and environments within which individuals form and express their attitudes toward meat. While psychological research prioritizes individual thoughts, feelings, and behaviors, as sociologists we also emphasize the importance of understanding meat-eating within its broader social context. Despite its significance, research on the social dimensions of meat-eating remains rather limited. This is likely because most of the research on meat orientations has been done by psychologists rather than sociologists, and psychologists tend to prioritize individuals' thoughts, feelings, and behaviors.

Our own sociological research has shed light on the importance of social context for understanding how people approach meat-eating. Interviews we conducted with people in the Toronto area revealed that individuals often justify their meat-eating habits by referencing their position in social space.[36] For example, people would justify meat-eating as something that was "normal" for men or as an important way to maintain ethno-cultural belonging. In another study, we found that the social context of gender shapes how mothers communicate with their children about where meat comes from.[37] We observed a paradox whereby mothers feel it is important to educate children about ethical food choices—including following the locavore advice of knowing where your food comes from. At the same time, some mothers wanted to protect children's innocence about meat and deliberately worked to shield their kids from knowledge of how meat gets on the plate. More generally, our findings have consistently shown the vital role that social identities—as a man, or a good mother, or a member of an ethnocultural community—and social relationships play in shaping individuals' complex, often ambivalent relationships with meat. In this book, we aim to further illuminate the ways social context shapes meat consumption, allowing us to better understand why discomfort and concern do not necessarily inspire significant meat reduction.

Before proceeding with the findings from our survey and focus groups, it is worth repeating an essential paradox in meat consumption: while most people eat meat, a significant proportion experience cognitive and emotional tensions surrounding their dietary choices. To unravel this complexity, we must consider not only individuals' thoughts, feelings, and behaviors but also their self-identified dietary labels and the social contexts that influence their decision to eat (or not eat) meat. In the following sections, we explore data from our survey and focus groups, aiming to shed light on the nuanced and often contradictory nature of this everyday practice.

Exploring Orientations toward Meat

Meat-Eating Behaviors and Diet Labels:
Measuring Meat-Eating and Avoidance

The first dimension of orientations toward meat that we examine in our data is behaviors. Within our focus group participants, we specifically sought out people who had concerns about the meat they consumed. It was therefore not surprising that we found a lot of them were frequent meat eaters—even though we noticed that it was common for people to minimize the amount of meat they ate.[38] While we gained valuable insights from in-depth conversations, we look to our survey to gain a more accurate sense of meat-eating behaviors at the population level. Our survey was designed to represent the average consumer.[39] We asked respondents how many days per week they usually eat meat, with answer options that ranged from "never" to "every day." We found that it is extremely uncommon for people to avoid meat in a typical week. Fewer than 4 percent of our survey respondents (only 91 people out of 2,328) told us that they eat no meat in a typical week. Over half of our survey respondents eat meat five times per week or more. As with prior research, we found that behaviors, on their own, indicate a pervasively enthusiastic orientation toward meat in society.

Alongside these questions about frequency of meat consumption, we also asked survey respondents about their personal diet labels or identities. In our survey, we asked people to choose from five diet labels, which correspond to a range of orientations toward meat. The most meat-centered label available in the survey—and the label selected by 79% of respondents—was "omnivore," defined as a diet that includes meat.[40] The remaining labels conveyed varying degrees of reservations toward meat. The "Flexitarian: I try to limit my meat consumption" option was selected by 14.2% of respondents. Few existing surveys include this option, which is a shortcoming of prior research. The next label was "Pescatarian: I don't eat meat, but I do eat fish," and we found that only 2.2% of survey respondents selected this label. The more common meat-avoiding diet labels were "Vegetarian: I don't eat meat or fish, but I do eat eggs and/or dairy," and "Vegan: I don't eat meat, fish, eggs, or dairy." In our survey, 3.0% of respondents chose the label of vegetarian and 1.6% chose the label of vegan.

Our survey data suggest that both dietary behavior and self-identification reflect a generally meat-positive orientation for the majority of the population. But a key question remains: how closely do meat-eating behaviors and identities align? For instance, how common is it to be a vegetarian who occasionally eats a piece of bacon or a chicken sandwich?

Survey respondents identifying as vegetarian or vegan generally reported the lowest (or no) meat consumption. However, we also found that dietary labels overestimate the extent to which our pescatarian, vegetarian, and vegan respondents exclude meat (and dairy and eggs for vegans) from their diets. For example, although 2.2% (51 respondents) of our sample identifies as pescatarian, almost a third of these self-identified pescatarians reported eating meat occasionally. Likewise, among the 3.0% (70 respondents) who identify as vegetarian, our follow-up questions about eating practices reveal that 14.3% of self-identified vegetarians reported that they eat fish at least occasionally, and an additional 25.7% of vegetarians said that they eat meat or fish occasionally. As such, the label "vegetarian" applies to only 60% of vegetarians in the way that many people think of it, as completely abstaining from meat and fish consumption. We found similar patterns among vegans as well. While 1.6% (37 respondents) of the sample identifies as vegan, follow-up questions about practices indicate that 13.5% of self-labeled vegans described their diet as one that avoids all meat but not necessarily other animal products and would thus be better described as vegetarian. Moreover, 18.9% of self-identified vegans indicated that they eat meat at least occasionally. Accordingly, only 67.6% of people in our sample who identify as vegan abstained from consuming all animal products.

If we were to offer a general assessment of meat orientations based on behavior and self-concepts, we would have to say that people in general are strongly and positively oriented toward eating meat. The proportion of meat avoiders, whether by practice or by self-reported labels, is quite small. At the same time, the presence of discrepancies between labels and practices high-lights the need to think about meat orientations as multidimensional. We also need to be aware that these dimensions can sometimes be in tension, pro-ducing complicated orientations. So far, we've only examined meat behavior and identity labels, and our picture of overall meat orientations will get more complicated as we consider how people think about meat.

Cognition and Diet Labels: Unpacking Reservations about Meat

How and what do people think about meat? Do their thoughts and beliefs indicate as strong an orientation toward meat as their behaviors and identi-ties? In our survey, we asked key questions that aimed to measure opinions on some of the most talked-about issues with meat. Specifically, we asked people how much they agree with the following four statements:

1. "Eating meat is necessary for a healthy diet."
2. "It is normal to eat meat."
3. "People should eat less meat."
4. "The way that meat is produced in this country is a big problem."

For each question, survey respondents could strongly agree, agree, neither agree nor disagree, disagree, or strongly disagree. We found some fascinating results that significantly complicate our earlier picture based on behavior and dietary labels. Public discourse often portrays meat as an essential part of a healthy diet, rich in protein and iron. Yet, only 48.5% of respondents agreed or strongly agreed that eating meat is necessary for a healthy diet, suggesting that a significant portion of people do not view meat as a dietary requirement. Interestingly, while 73.9% agreed or strongly agreed that eating meat is normal, highlighting its cultural prominence, a sizable minority (26.1%) questions this norm. A significant portion of respondents (36.9%) agreed or strongly agreed that we should eat less meat, and 34.6% expressed concern about current production methods. These findings indicate that for many, beliefs about meat are less positive than their behavior and identity suggest. These findings raise compelling questions: How do these ambivalent beliefs align with self-identifications as vegetarian or omnivore? And more broadly, how can we reconcile these seemingly contradictory views to better understand the diverse spectrum of meat-related orientations? How well are these beliefs about meat aligned with people's self-identifications as vegetarian or omnivorous? How do they help us to characterize people's meat orientations?

Examining respondents' level of agreement with our statements according to the diet labels they chose (Table 2.1), two patterns stand out. First, as expected, vegetarians and vegans generally express more negative views on meat

TABLE 2.1: Thoughts about Meat by Diet Label: Percent Agreeing or Strongly Agreeing

	Positive orientations			Negative orientations
	Eating meat is necessary for a healthy diet.	It is normal to eat meat.	People should eat less meat.	The way that meat is produced in this country is a big problem.
Full Sample (2,328)	48.5%	73.9%	36.9%	34.6%
Omnivore (1,839)	55.4%	82.5%	27.5%	32.9%
Flexitarian (331)	29.3%	49.5%	68.4%	55.9%
Pescatarian (51)	9.8%	31.4%	58.4%	60.8%
Vegetarian (70)	8.6%	22.9%	78.0%	83.6%
Vegan (37)	5.4%	18.9%	82.8%	83.8%

Source: Author created.

compared to omnivores. For instance, while 55.4% of omnivores consider meat necessary for a healthy diet, only 8.6% of vegetarians share this view. While 83.6% of vegetarians thought that meat production is problematic, only 32.9% of omnivores felt the same way.

The second trend is more revealing: even among those who identify as omnivores, a significant portion harbors reservations about meat. While some meat eaters express no such qualms, a considerable number question the normalcy of meat consumption, its necessity, the ethics of its production, and whether it should be eaten in large quantities. For instance, over a quarter (27.5%) of omnivores believe people should eat less meat, a sentiment shared by 68.4% of flexitarians. Moreover, 32.9% of omnivores and 55.9% of flexitarians express concerns about meat production methods. On the flip side, 22.0% of vegetarians did *not* agree that people should eat less meat! These findings underscore the fact that while dietary labels offer some predictive power regarding attitudes toward meat, they do not fully capture the nuanced and sometimes contradictory beliefs held by individuals across different dietary groups.

Affect and Diet Labels: Studying People's Ideas of Deliciousness and Disgust

Turning next to the emotional dimensions of meat consumption, our survey explored how people felt about several aspects of meat consumption and production. Perhaps not surprisingly, 90.9% of respondents agreed or strongly agreed that "meat can be delicious." This positive affective association undoubtedly plays a significant role in the widespread consumption and enjoyment of meat, a theme we explore further with our qualitative data in Chapter 3. However, the emotional landscape is not solely positive. A notable 32.0% of survey respondents agreed or strongly agreed with the statement, "I feel bad for animals when I eat meat" and 36.8% agreed or strongly agreed with the sentiment, "Sometimes I'm grossed out by meat."

While many people undeniably enjoy meat without experiencing negative affect—finding it delicious, not gross, and expressing no qualms about consuming animals—our findings highlight a significant counternarrative that is worth emphasizing. A substantial portion of the population grapples with a mix of positive and negative feelings about meat, experiencing discomfort, guilt, or disgust alongside the pleasure of consumption.[41] This raises further questions: how do these emotional responses vary by people's dietary labels? Do they reveal further inconsistencies between different dimensions of meat orientation?

Our data reveal stark differences in emotional responses to meat across dietary identities (See Table 2.2). As expected, omnivores in our sample had the most positive feelings about meat; 94.7% of them found it delicious, and only 5.9% reported feeling bad for animals when they eat meat. However, a notable 29.4% of omnivores agreed that they are sometimes grossed out by meat, highlighting a potential conflict even within this group. Flexitarians broadly report finding meat delicious (91.8%), but more than half (58.3%) admit that they are sometimes grossed out by meat, suggesting that emotional ambivalence toward meat consumption is quite common.

At the other end of the spectrum, vegetarians and vegans are unsurprisingly most likely to feel bad for animals and to be grossed out by meat. Yet a significant proportion of them acknowledge meat's potential for deliciousness: 34.3% of vegetarians and 45.9% of vegans. This reveals a nuanced understanding that extends beyond simple aversion. These findings underscore a key point: emotional responses to meat are complex and can vary even within seemingly cohesive dietary groups. While dietary labels offer some insight, they don't fully capture the diverse range of emotions individuals may experience.

TABLE 2.2: Feelings about Meat by Diet Label: Percent Agreeing or Strongly Agreeing

	Positive orientation	Negative orientation	
	Meat can be delicious.	I feel bad for animals when I eat meat.	Sometimes I'm grossed out by meat.
Full Sample (2,328)	90.9%	32.0%	36.8%
Omnivore (1,839)	94.7%	5.9%	29.4%
Flexitarian (331)	91.8%	16.7%	58.3%
Pescatarian (51)	62.7%	13.9%	64.7%
Vegetarian (70)	34.3%	30.0%	82.9%
Vegan (37)	45.9%	37.8%	91.9%

Source: Author created.

Social Context: How Social Relationships Shape Meat-Eating

To examine the final dimension of meat orientation, social context, we draw from focus group data. These rich narratives reveal how meat intertwines with individual's daily lives, relationships, and personal histories, highlighting the critical influence of social setting on shaping thoughts, feelings and behaviors. While individual factors like beliefs and emotions are undoubtedly important, they cannot fully account for the complex, often contradictory nature of meat consumption. To have a thorough account of meat orientation, we must recognize the dynamic interplay between personal factors and social context. While understanding the social context of meat-eating is an important task for the remaining chapters of this book, here we lay the foundation for subsequent discussions by examining how social relationships intersect with and shape people's identities, feelings, and practices surrounding meat.

Hailey's story vividly illustrates how the complex interplay between emotions, ideas, identity and social relationships can shape someone's orientation to meat. Introducing herself in our Vancouver focus group, Hailey, a forty-two-year-old U.K. transplant, immediately signaled a complicated relationship with meat: "I do eat meat. But I don't eat a lot of meat." She explained that she grew up in an English family that ate a *lot* of meat, particularly ham and bacon. When she moved out, she found herself eating meat less and less frequently.

Hailey's ambivalence toward meat was evident throughout the focus group. For example, she said, "I really like English bacon. And I love ham too, but I do have very mixed feelings about eating pigs because they're so intelligent and sweet." She admitted to being "very selective about what I eat based on the cuteness of the animal," sheepishly describing this cute-centric approach as "really bad." This internal conflict led her to consume less "cute" animals, like chicken and fish, while maintaining a mostly vegetarian diet at home.

However, Hailey's aversion to eating meat was not unwavering. Her yearning for the familiar tastes of home combined with the cultural significance of meat within her family often overrode her personal reservations. While she admitted feeling "more guilt about eating certain things," on a recent trip back to the U.K. Hailey found herself enjoying traditional foods: "I was eating meat pies, and I was eating everything with meat and going for the Sunday lunches with roast pork and applesauce and all those lovely things." Hailey's narrative highlights how social ties and cultural norms can override personal reservations, highlighting the powerful influence of social context on our dietary choices.

Grant's story offers another compelling example of how social relationships shape meat consumption. Grant, a fifty-year-old who works at a nonprofit organization, told us that he eats meat almost every day of the week. From that fact alone, Grant might seem like a "where's the beef?" kind of meat eater. But Grant's story of meat-eating is peppered with anecdotes of self-doubt and uncertainty when it comes to eating meat. Grant tells the focus group that he ate a pescatarian diet for nearly twenty years "and really liked it." However, he also reports that he has eaten meat regularly since he got married and had a child, since his wife and child are both extremely fond of meat. For Grant, eating meat is often uncomfortable. Despite enjoying the taste and convenience of meat, Grant frequently feels conflicted, as if his actions betray his underlying values.

For both Hailey and Grant, meat-eating was not simply an individual preference but a social practice deeply embedded in his relationship, family dynamics, and busy work schedule. It is impossible to understand how and why Hailey and Grant eat meat without factoring in the relational elements shaping their meat consumption, especially since both have significant reservations about eating animals. The influence of family relationships on meat orientation was variable, impacted by the social setting and context (e.g., Hailey eating meat with her English family versus cooking vegetarian meals for herself). Both of their stories underscore the importance of analyzing meat consumption not solely as an individual choice but as a dynamic process influenced by interpersonal connections and social contexts.

The significance of social cues shaping self-understanding and identity around meat was readily apparent in a Vancouver focus group, where we were shocked to hear two ostensibly omnivorous participants, Mahir, a thirty-one-year-old man, and Aanchal, a fifty-two-year-old woman, articulate *vegetarian* eating principles. This directly contradicted what we had seen on their participant recruitment screening forms, where they had identified as meat eaters. Part of this contradictory revelation appeared to be social and relational. In the focus group conversation, Mahir and Aanchal established an immediate friendliness with each other. Early on in the discussion, they bonded over a shared perspective that "meat is murder," to use Mahir's terms (and the title of the well-known song and album by the Smiths). Heartened by their shared conviction, Aanchal spoke at length about her favorite vegetarian recipes, while Mahir nodded approvingly.

After recovering from our surprise at these participants' vegetarian convictions, we worked to move the group toward a nonjudgmental discussion of meat consumption, encouraging participants to air their concerns about meat while also working to create an open atmosphere where participants could discuss what they liked and disliked about eating meat. As the discussion unfolded, Mahir revealed that he likes to eat lamb that comes from his family's farm. Aanchal spoke proudly of the deliciousness of her chicken curries. She reported that while the rest of her family practices a vegetarian diet, she would made these dishes for herself to enjoy. Mahir appeared more oriented toward meat *because of* his family relationships, while Aanchal's positive orientation toward meat existed *despite* her family relationships. Within the focus group setting, their instant conversational rapport allowed Aanchal and Mahir to share their sincere reservations about eating meat ("meat is murder"), but the friendly, open-minded group atmosphere also allowed them to share that they actually quite enjoyed eating lamb (Mahir) and chicken curry (Aanchal). We interpret these inconsistencies not as hypocrisy but as evidence of the complex relationship between social context and food-related behaviors, identities, and values. This highlights how social cues and group dynamics can either amplify or suppress certain aspects of one's meat orientation, underscoring the importance of considering these complex relational interactions when analyzing food choices.

Conclusion: Understanding the Meat-Eater Who *Has* Reservations

In this chapter, we have drawn on our survey research to provide a broad-brush picture of the consumers who populate the ethical meatscape. Here are some important findings to emphasize. The proportion of respondents who eat no meat or fish is extremely small (1.76%); the proportion of people who eat no animal-derived food at all is smaller still (1.08%). In contrast, over 96% of our survey respondents reported eating meat at least once a week, with over 50% of respondents eating meat five or more times per week. If we only looked at the behavioral dimension of people's orientations toward meat, it would appear as though there are (virtually) no reservations when it comes to putting meat on the table. Looking at our survey data on meat-eating practices, it's clear that a lot of people eat meat, they eat it frequently, and they mostly consume meat that comes from mainstream sources.

While our findings confirm the prevalence of meat consumption, a simple pro-meat versus anti-meat framework does not come close to describing the situation, a finding that our focus group data helps to flesh out. Beneath the surface of routine behavior lies a complex landscape of cognitive and affective responses. Many consumers, even those who regularly eat meat, harbor negative beliefs and emotions about it. They sometimes find it gross, express skepticism about industrial methods of raising animals, and believe that society overconsumes animal products. Whether eaters' concerns are centered on health or altruistic concerns about animal welfare and climate change, we observed deep reservations about the way we produce and consume meat. Yet, despite these reservations, meat remains a staple for many. Consumers keep eating meat because it helps them consolidate their relationships, it conveys a sense of home, it feels normal, and it tastes good, delivering a jolt of positive emotion and sensory pleasure.

These conflicting attitudes raise important questions about the role of happy meat when navigating this ethical and emotional minefield. How do consumers grapple with the tension between their enjoyment of meat and their concerns about its production and consumption? Can the promises of happy meat—raised with higher welfare standards and promising reduced environmental impact—offer a solution, however partial, that aligns with consumers' palates and principles? These questions lie at the heart of our investigation, as we explore the motivations and rationalizations shaping consumer choice in the evolving meatscape. In the next chapter, we turn to our focus group data to further explore these tensions, listening to people's narratives to see how straightforward it can be to simultaneously experience meat as delicious and delightful to eat but also devastating for the environment and disgusting to encounter.

PART II   **The Emotions of Eating Meat**

THREE   Meat Is Disgusting . . . and Delicious!

IN A VANCOUVER APARTMENT filled with the laughter of good friends sharing after-work beers, Cameron, a self-described "foodie" and enthusiastic meat eater, grapples with the ethical implications of his dietary choices. Amidst assertions of his fondness for eating good meat, Cameron also remarked, "Humanity as a whole overconsumes meat in a tragic way." His words betray both enjoyment and concern.

Cameron isn't alone in his ambivalence. The focus group, composed of five friends in their twenties—Cameron, Oliver, Palmer, Max, and Elaine—embodies the emotional complexities of meat-eating. While all are passionate about food and enjoy eating meat, they are also concerned about industrialized meat production and try to eat meat responsibly. Oliver, for instance, buys deli meat for quick lunches but tries to limit dinners to plant-based fare that he cooks with his vegetarian girlfriend. Similarly, Cameron is working to be more "vegetable forward" in his cooking style, even as he can't imagine fully giving up meat. Cameron finds the versatility of cooking meat "amazing" and "alluring" and justifies his meat consumption by sourcing through high-end butcher shops and occasionally going on hunting trips, which he sees as the pinnacle of ethical consumption. Everyone agrees that current levels of meat consumption are not sustainable, and the group discusses the negative impact of overconsumption on both the environment and our bodies. Oliver mentions a documentary, *Cowspiracy*, as a turning point in his awareness of the environmental impact of the beef industry. Cameron enthusiastically chimes in, "That [documentary] changed me for a week, hard!"[1]

Stories about the lives and deaths of meat animals, and the environmental impact of meat production, are often emotionally charged. These stories regularly provoke sadness, discomfort, guilt, and even disgust, conjuring up a host of reasons not to eat meat. As we saw with Cameron's response, industrial meat narratives can trigger a desire for change. Yet, as Cameron joked, this impulse lasted about a week. Why do stories about meat prompt powerful emotional responses but often fail to translate into lasting changes to meat-eating behaviors? This is the crux of the meat paradox raised in the introduction.

This chapter travels into the emotional heart of the meat paradox as it unfolds in our daily encounters with meat and the stories that surround it. Building on themes from Chapters 1 and 2, we explore how meat-eating has become wrapped up in social debates about what is good and bad to eat. We draw on the psychological concept of *moralization*, which describes how certain issues or entities take on a moral significance.[2] As we will see, meat moralization is not a dry, abstract conversation about ethics. Instead, our focus group data suggest that meat moralization is a deeply emotional process, one that can sensorially influence how and when meat is perceived as delicious or disgusting.

Our exploration of the emotional spectrum of meat-eating begins with pleasure. The sensory experience of meat, which involves its delicious taste and positive emotional associations, emerges as a critical factor for understanding its persistence. For eaters like Cameron, the taste of meat is a pleasure they are reluctant to give up. However, this is only one side of the story. In the second part of the chapter, we examine the negative emotional pole, examining how meat becomes entangled in moralization processes, triggering feelings of discomfort, guilt, and disgust. Finally, we explore the dynamic interplay between delight and disgust. We argue that this intertwining of positive and negative emotions around meat reflects a complex, nonlinear process of meat moralization. Even eaters with strong concerns about meat production find ways to navigate their conflicting feelings, allowing them to continue to consume meat.[3]

The Pleasures of Meat and the Four Ns

It may be self-evident, but our focus groups repeatedly affirmed a key aspect of meat's appeal: its deliciousness. How does the pleasurable taste of meat fit into existing scholarship? Melanie Joy, in her seminal writing, explored the rationalizations people use to justify meat consumption and identified three core justifications: meat-eating is normal, natural, and necessary.[4] Social psychologist Jared Piazza and colleagues, building on Joy's framework, identified a fourth "N": meat is "nice," meaning delicious.[5] Piazza argued that taste had been overlooked because it doesn't provide a particularly compelling moral justification for eating animals; it might feel ethically flimsy to say that we kill animals because we like the taste of them. However, research by Piazza and others suggests that meat's deliciousness plays a significant role in dietary choices.[6] A study of Australian women found that "meat appreciation and enjoyment" provided a major obstacle to adopting a vegetarian diet.[7] Complementary research suggests that the perceived tastiness of vegetarian diets is a strong predictor of openness to vegetarianism.[8]

Our survey research offers further empirical confirmation that meat is widely seen as "nice." As detailed in Chapter 2, our meat consumption survey included questions about meat's deliciousness. Recall that 90.9% of our respondents thought that meat can be delicious—including a significant portion of vegetarians (34.3%) and vegans (45.9%). These figures highlight the enduring salience of deliciousness in peoples' understandings of meat, even among those who consciously limit or eliminate meat from their diet. Reinforcing this idea, over half of the surveyed participants explicitly mentioned the difficulty of giving up meat due to its taste, underlying the critical role of pleasure in maintaining meat consumption.

The "niceness" of meat goes beyond individual taste preference and can play a crucial role in fostering a sense of collective belonging. Meat consumption sits at the center of many ethnonational and religious traditions and taboos, serving as markers of group boundaries and identity.[9] As anthropologist Mary Douglas famously argued, food taboos and meat-eating practices play a critical role defining the boundaries of "in-groups," with shared enjoyment of specific dishes reinforcing a sense of community and belonging.[10] The pleasure derived from meat-eating is thus a socially situated phenomenon, deeply embedded within ethnocultural, religious, and familial contexts. The "niceness" of meat is reinforced through positive associations with shared family meals, community events, and collective identities.[11] Furthermore, our social lives often revolve around meat-based meals. Indeed, 25 percent of our survey participants said their family would complain if they cooked vegetarian meals. These findings underscore the extent to which meat is woven into the fabric of our social interactions.

Our previous qualitative research with meat eaters in a diverse urban setting provided clear evidence of the collective nature of meat tastes. We witnessed firsthand how the pleasures of culturally specific meat-based dishes are
linked to a desire to preserve ethnocultural culinary traditions—particularly
in a larger context marked by racism and cultural xenophobia.[12] Interviews
with culturally diverse participants revealed that meat is far from a neutral
food, serving instead as a symbolically loaded ingredient that positively connects eaters to shared histories, rituals, and communities. Participating in rituals around eating or preparing meat dishes gave people a feeling of pleasure,
belonging, and shared identity. For example, Hannah, an Eritrean-Canadian
woman in her twenties, expressed concerns about the environmental impact
of meat-eating but also enthusiastically described eating meat-based Eritrean
dishes, especially those prepared by her father. Hannah said that meat is "incorporated into every aspect of our culture, whether it be weddings, baby
showers. Even when someone passes away, they cook meat for the family. . . .
If you were to take [meat] away from the Eritrean culture, you wouldn't have
what makes the Eritrean culture the Eritrean culture. It's a part of what it
means to be Eritrean."[13] Critiques of meat-eating in contexts such as Hannah's
can consequently be perceived as an attack on the pleasurable, symbolically
rich domains of one's culture.

In sum, prior research on meat-eating—including our own interview and
survey research—suggests that it is important to take the pleasures of meat
seriously, both as an individual taste preference and as part of one's ethnocultural identity. For many eaters, meat is necessary precisely because meat
is nice. The pleasures of meat-eating are an important piece in understanding
why people maintain their meat-eating practices, even in the face of compelling reasons to change those practices.[14] In the next section, we draw from our
focus group discussions with concerned meat eaters to explore meat's delicious qualities.

Meat Is Incomparably Delicious: "For Taste, It's Meat for Me!"

Our focus group conversations revealed the depths of participants' attachment to meat, as people shared stories about meaty foods they loved, craved,
and couldn't live without. Even though many participants had dabbled in
meat reduction, and most expressed concerns about its negative environmental associations, eliminating meat remained a challenge. When asked why

they remained committed meat eaters, all referenced the incomparable taste or satiation meat provided. Max grew up in a vegetarian household. However, as he explained, it was the taste of meat that motivated him to incorporate meat into his adult diet: "I got my first taste of meat as a young kid, and it's not comparable. I mean, you can argue health, you can argue other things, but for taste, it's meat for me!" Oliver also spent time as a vegetarian in the past, and at the time of the interview, seemed committed to preparing vegetarian dinners with his girlfriend. He nonetheless found it impossible to give up meat completely. Oliver liked to occasionally indulge in his favorite food, fried chicken, saying, "When I started eating meat again, when I had fried chicken again, I was like, fuck . . . [sighing]." When asked to articulate what it was about meat that appealed to them, the group had a dynamic discussion. Oliver named texture: "Texture is a big one." Palmer chimed in, "Flavor." Max interrupted, "Yeah, I guess flavor would be—" and Palmer picked up the thread, "You can't replicate that flavor from other things, you know, that are not meat." The group then debated the relative merits of meat's flavor and texture, framed by Cameron's comments: "Yeah, flavor. Or—you know, it's different. I guess meat does have a flavor, but it's like, I guess it's almost more texture-based, isn't it?" Palmer explained, "It is, but also—I was making, I've been making a Bolognese with veggie ground round. I get it quite close. And then recently, just this week, I actually did it with the actual ground beef." He went on, "For a while I couldn't tell the difference; it was quite good with the veggie ground round, and then the other day I had a proper ground beef, and I was like, 'Oh, man!'" Cameron affirmed this: "There is a difference!" Max summed up the group's discussion: "I know! That's the brutal truth of it."

Focus group discussions revealed a bittersweet attachment to meat. The undeniable pleasures of meat were a recurring theme, but they were discussed with a mixture of resignation and humor, especially when conversations turned to meat's negative health and environmental impacts. A common sentiment emerged: "I know it's bad, but I just can't quit!" This is what Dahlia, a self-described foodie, stated. She acknowledged the difficulty of sourcing ethical meat, but ultimately confessed, "At the end of the day, what trumps it all, as a meat eater, is I love my meat, I love a good-tasting steak!" Tom, a Toronto-based man in his thirties, echoed this sentiment: "I love meat. [Laughs.] I have had reservations recently about meat based on the overall [environmental] impact that it has. . . . But I love hamburgers, and I don't think I could live without a hamburger." Heather also described an internal struggle, feeling obligated to eat less meat while craving its taste: "People who do not eat meat talk about how healthy they feel," she admitted, "and I'd like to try it [vegetarianism]. But, like I say, I enjoy it [meat]! And I need to eat protein, so it's not going to happen." Dahlia, Tom, and Heather's ambivalence underscores how meat's pleasures uneasily intermingle with a sense that one should eat less meat and be a responsible consumer.

For people who valued the pleasures of meat, the prospect of moving toward a vegetarian diet felt daunting, even though many recognized vegetarianism as an ethical, healthy choice. Minel, a woman in her twenties, exemplified this sentiment. She expressed admiration for her vegetarian and vegan friends, describing them as people who had "made great choices . . . that have really good benefits to the world and the earth." However, she found vegetarianism personally unappealing: "meat enhances dishes that I already like." Minel gave a specific example: "I have a butternut squash soup recipe that I love, but if you sprinkle a little bacon on top, or if you cook the bacon first and then cook the onions in the bacon fat, and then you sprinkle that bacon on top, it just takes it to the next level." Minel's candid admission, "sometimes nothing does it like meat," underscored the powerful role of pleasure in her dietary choices, despite her extensive knowledge of the ethical and environmental implications of meat.

Focus group discussions underscored how the pleasures of meat extend beyond individual tastes and are deeply rooted in collective stories, dishes, and culinary pleasures. Hayun, a Korean-Canadian participant in her twenties, described feeling social pressure to adopt a vegetarian diet in her left-leaning social circles. However, this pressure conflicted with her Korean cultural identity, which included culturally significant meat dishes. As Hayun explained, "In terms of eating meat, I think a lot about how a lot of my cultural foods, they can be, it's not so meat-heavy, but there are integral dishes that are very important to my health and my fulfillment of life as well as my ability to connect, and remember, and just be myself." For Hayun, the very "fulfillment of life" is tied to the pleasures she derives from Korean dishes including meat. These pleasures are culturally rooted and familial. Hayun emphasized the particular importance of bone broth in her family food traditions and described her father warmly as "a very big broth man." Hayun perceives that the taste of meat provides her with essential familial and cultural connections that she would find difficult to access as a vegetarian.

Similarly, Elaine, a French expatriate in her thirties who has lived in Vancouver for ten years, highlighted the role of meat in maintaining her cultural identity. She spoke nostalgically about France's renowned charcuterie and high-quality meats and how giving them up would feel like denying her culture. Elaine declared, "I will never give up my *saucisson* [French sausage]! [Laughing.]" For Elaine, giving up meat felt like a betrayal of her cultural heritage, as it was deeply connected to her sense of identity as well as cherished memories of home. These connections made a vegetarian lifestyle seem both impossible and unappealing.

These narratives, however, are not simply pro-meat. Both Hayun and Elaine observed growing social acceptance of vegetarian and vegan diets and expressed positive views about these choices. While attached to her French culinary heritage, Elaine expressed her admiration for a vegan family she followed on social media, particularly the children's enthusiastic embrace of veganism. She says, "I like how the kids are actually loving it [being vegan]. The kids are big animal lovers so they just don't want to [eat meat]. I think the kids actually made it happen for the family because they just thought that it [eating meat] was so cruel." This admiration reflects Elaine's awareness that vegetarianism aligns with a broader social shift legitimizing the virtue and values of responsible eating.[15] However, despite their appreciation for plant-based lifestyles, neither Hayun nor Elaine expressed a desire to abandon the pleasures of their own culturally significant meat-based meals.

Hayun's and Elaine's stories, alongside our previous research with ethnoculturally diverse communities, suggests that even as consumers become more aware of the ethical and environmental implications of meat-eating, cultural and personal attachments to meat can remain remarkably robust.[16] Part of the pleasure of meat-eating stems from the shared social ties and sense of belonging it reinforces. These sensory orientations play an important role in boundary work (a key topic in Chapter 7).[17] Put simply, enjoying meat can be a way to demarcate who fits in and who doesn't. In this way, those who abstain from meat risk being implicitly or explicitly criticized for deviating from shared taste pleasures.

Felipe, a Latinx participant in his twenties, echoed Hayun and Elaine's sentiments, emphasizing the connection between meat, pleasure, and cultural identity. Describing his Colombian background, he explained how meat is deeply engrained in his culture, stating, "Meat is in everything we do." When the group discussed what meat dish they would miss if they gave up eating

meat, Felipe described his affection for ajiaco and cuchuco, traditional Colombian soups made with various meats, and emphasized their central role in
family gatherings and celebrations. For Felipe, these meat dishes are a conduit
for culinary pleasure and also for cultural belonging.

However, Felipe reveals how these culinary associations can act as a dou-
ble-edged sword. He recounted his vegetarian aunt's experiences of being
teased at family gatherings, illustrating how meat-eating can function as a
form of boundary work: "I feel like I had such a negative stigma of anyone
that avoided meat because it was kind of something that was ridiculed in my
family." Felipe's story underscores the potential for exclusion and ridicule
faced by those who deviate from cultural norms around meat consumption.
Felipe's personal connection to meat, rooted in "fond cultural and social
memories," emphasizes how for many of our participants, the pleasures of
eating meat were not easily separated from cultural boundaries and belonging
across generations and geographic space.

While the pleasure of eating meat was a resounding theme in our focus
groups, these pleasures were not without complications. Even if eaters can
justify eating meat by telling themselves it is *normal*, *necessary* for a healthy
diet, *natural* for humans, and *nice* to eat, they do not completely detach from
the ethical implications of eating animals. The awareness of meat's origins,
as psychologists have noted, can create a tension that eaters try to manage by
disassociating from meat's origins, specifically the realities of animal suffering. However, we were struck by how frequently our participants acknowledged that the meat on their plate originated in a living, breathing animal.
This awareness, in turn, paves the way for the exploration of difficult emotions
of meat-eating, such as disgust, to which we turn next.

Meat Is Disgusting: Confronting the Blood on Your Plates, or "Maybe It Should Hurt a Little"

At the core of the meat paradox lies the uneasy coexistence of pleasure and discomfort. Even among enthusiastic meat eaters, conversations revealed flickers
of unease when confronted with the loss of life that meat-eating inevitably
entails. This disquiet stemmed in part from an awareness of meat's inherent
animality and the acknowledgment of animal slaughter that underpins every
meat-based meal. However, discomfort extended beyond the recognition of
eating a once-living creature. Knowledge of industrialized meat's negative

health impacts and environmental burden also cast a shadow, prompting questions about the appropriate frequency and quantity of meat consumption.

Our focus group discussions provided rich insights into consumers' emotional reservations about meat. These conversations revealed how the ethical tensions inherent in meat-eating manifest not only through conscious thought processes but also through embodied experiences. Before exploring the "meat is disgusting" theme in our data, we will offer a brief review of the literature—psychological and sociological—that examines how emotions, particularly disgust, influence meat eating. Our hope is that by understanding how emotions shape meat-eating (and abstention), we can illuminate possibilities for shifting meat-eating in a more sustainable direction.

Understanding Meat: Emotions, Disgust, and Moralization

Eating meat is an emotional business. Psychological research often focuses on one particular emotion, disgust, exploring how people experience and manage disgust and how it shapes meat eaters' and vegetarians' attitudes toward meat.[18] Scholars suggest that a key trigger for disgust is the connection to our own animality—the recognition that we, like farm animals, are living, breathing, bleeding, mortal creatures.[19] This concept, referred to as *animal reminder disgust*, is particularly relevant to meat consumption.[20] Of all the foods humans consume, meat is the most significant reminder of our animal nature as it is composed of flesh itself—unlike, say, a bowl of coleslaw.

Numerous studies have confirmed that animal reminder disgust can affect people's enjoyment of meat. To manage this disgust, consumers may disassociate meat from living animals, death, or slaughter.[21] Research demonstrates that less recognizable meat products, like sausages, trigger less disgust and emotional response compared to whole animals such as a roast pig.[22] Cultural conditioning plays an important role in shaping this kind of disgust, as familiarity with different animals will vary in different cultural settings.[23] For instance, Western eaters accustomed to seeing whole roasted chickens or turkeys experience less disgust compared to unfamiliar options like a whole roast pig.[24] Besides cross-cultural variation, research also suggests a significant gender difference, with women typically exhibiting greater sensitivity to disgust and a more apologetic approach to meat-eating. Paul Rozin and colleagues write that "the strongest correlate of sensitivity to disgust is gender."[25]

Disgust toward meat, therefore, is not a simple individual response; it is culturally constructed and interwoven with moral values.[26] As with all emotions, the feelings surrounding meat are not merely individual reactions but carry social and cultural significance, impacting both personal agency and broader social practices.[27] As Arlie Russell Hochschild, a seminal figure in the sociology of emotions, advises, we should consider "the simple assumption that what we feel is fully as important to the outcome of social affairs as what we think or do."[28] Translated into the realm of meat consumption, our meat *emotions* are a critical element for understanding our meat-eating *practices* and the persistent meat paradox.

With growing concerns about the ethical, health, and environmental consequences of meat consumption, understanding the socio-emotional apparatus influencing our ability to limit meat consumption becomes crucial. In a significant 1997 article, Rozin and colleagues pinpoint the significance of disgust in meat abstinence.[29] Their research reveals that ethically oriented vegetarians, compared to those focused on health benefits, experience stronger negative emotions toward meat, view it as morally compromising, and are less tempted to succumb to meat consumption under pressure (e.g., when they are hungry, have a strong craving). Rozin suggests that moral vegetarians may be more likely to abstain from eating meat because they "have the strong force of morality behind them."[30]

Extending from their sample of vegetarians, Rozin and colleagues propose that emotions like disgust play a key role "moralizing" consumption. This process imbues previously neutral objectives or activities with moral significance, potentially diminishing the pleasure and thrill of consumption.[31] Importantly, moralization not only manifests in an individual's psyche but also operates on a collective, cultural level. While rooted in psychology, the concept of moralization has significant sociological and cultural implications. Moralization transforms individual preferences into shared collective values that are internalized and durable, invoke an emotional response, and influence consumption patterns, ultimately shaping culturally supported and institutionalized practices.

The concept of moralization offers a powerful lens for understanding how we might shift our meat consumption patterns. While Rozin's work predates ours by nearly three decades, it remains highly relevant for navigating the evolving moral controversies surrounding meat.[32] We argue that moralization extends beyond vegetarians; it also impacts meat eaters, particularly those expressing concerns about meat-eating. Recent research by Buttlar and Walther supports this idea; they found that among ethically motivated meat reducers, disgust plays a key role.[33] Individuals who found meat disgusting were more likely to experience ambivalence about eating it, while those who did not experience disgust continued eating meat irrespective of their ethical concerns. As Buttlar and Walther summarize, disgust seems to be "a central process variable that may help people to eschew meat."[34] This suggests that emotions, particularly disgust, can drive a search for cognitive consistency: if meat is morally problematic *and* disgusting, then why eat it? Negative emotions like disgust can trigger a hedonic shift, where once pleasurable experiences like the taste of meat become less appealing or even unpleasant. In essence, a key aspect of meat moralization involves meat becoming gross, at least in certain forms and circumstances.[35] These changes can potentially undergird a process of meat reduction or even elimination, addressing the meat paradox at its core.

Sociologists can build on and enrich scholarship on meat moralization. We can interrogate the range of emotional reactions to meat, examining how emotions intersect with daily food practices and ethical motivations for maintaining or minimizing meat-eating. We can shed light on the specific contexts where meat is perceived as gross, disgusting, and unappealing—and when it retains its hedonic thrill. In broad terms, sociologists bring a valuable structural perspective to the emotional landscape of meat-eating, while still taking everyday experience seriously. By adopting a structural perspective that respects individual experiences, sociologists can address what Thomas Scheff calls the "inside-outside" problem in emotion research: "If one ignores the context in which emotions arise, it will inevitably be difficult to understand their place in human behavior."[36]

Our chapter, and indeed this entire book, aims to bridge this gap by connecting the structural factors shaping meat-related emotions and moralization with the stories eaters tell about meat and their everyday lives. We explore how consumers react—emotionally, cognitively, and practically—to greater awareness of factory farming, animal welfare, environmental degradation, and other harrowing issues related to meat. Appreciating structural factors in the industrial meatscape is essential for understanding contemporary emotional reactions to meat and developing a better understanding of the ongoing moralization of meat. This holistic perspective allows us to better appreciate the conditions under which meat becomes "gross" or ethically problematic, as well as the strategies individuals employ to navigate these complex emotions.

Our Data on Disgust: Meat Can Be Gross

To begin exploring the emotional landscape of meat consumption, we briefly revisit our survey data. This research snapshot reveals the prevalence of disgust toward meat, as well as significant signs of meat moralization. As shown in Chapter 2, over one-third of survey respondents (36.8%) reported being sometimes disgusted by meat. Notably, disgust was not limited to vegans or vegetarians (although the vast majority of them were sometimes disgusted by meat). Nearly a third of omnivores and over half of self-described flexitarians reported the same. It turns out that a significant part of the population, even those who consume meat regularly, find meat a bit gross—at least on occasion. However, our survey doesn't fully illuminate the underlying reasons for this disgust, nor does it identify the specific narratives and images that evoke it. Understanding these factors is crucial for comprehending the rise of concerned omnivores and their role in the evolving ethical meatscape. In the next chapter, we will explore how negative emotional associations toward meat are resolved through stories of happy meat. But first, let's explore what aspects of meat people find disgusting, uncomfortable, and "bad." Only by understanding these aversions can we fully grasp why certain qualities of meat come to be perceived as ethical, appealing, and "good."

Meat Is Disgusting: Classic Examples of Animal Reminder Disgust

Everyday encounters at the supermarket or restaurant or in the kitchen can remind consumers of the animal origins of meat and lead to feelings of discomfort or even disgust. Consider this exchange between Hailey (42) and Sandra (34), participants in one of our Vancouver focus groups, where they share the disgust they feel managing the "fleshiness" of raw meat:

> Hailey: I don't—I've never been keen on . . . like, when you have to be in cooking classes and have to slice up the flesh. It [meat] feels very much like flesh when slicing it.
> Sandra: Yeah. I agree with that, actually. I don't like cooking [meat].
> Hailey: I don't really like that part. So, at home [I don't cook much meat]. But when I go out, it's a different story.
> Mindy: Oh, when it's prepared for you, then it's a pass?
> Sandra: You just don't like touching the raw stuff?
> Hailey: I don't.
> Sandra: That's like me. I kind of just dump it in the pan without touching it.

This avoidance aligns with existing research, revealing that consumers often employ strategies to distance themselves from the realities of animal slaughter.[37] For some, like Hailey, this means eating meat only when prepared by others, while others prefer ground meat that obscures its connection to the whole animal. Many participants openly acknowledged their discomfort with meat's origins in a living animal, expressing unease at the appearance of blood in red meat, animal carcasses being butchered, or roasted whole animals. Sandra, for instance, described her disgust at the pig roasts common in her Italian-Canadian cultural community: "They've got the head and everything!" She found the sight of "the full animal, from the butcher, with the blood and everything" repulsive, yet admitted that she found roast pork "delicious." Sandra described how she would strategically avoid looking at the whole animal at a pig roast, joking, "You bring me a plate. I'll eat it over here," that is, away from the animal. She resolved her inner conflict by avoiding the pig carcass, highlighting the tension between enjoyment and aversion that characterizes the experience of many meat eaters.

In focus group discussions, women were more vocal than men about their discomfort and disgust regarding harming animals or handling meat, especially raw meat. This gendered trend is exemplified by Roberta, a Vancouver mother of four. Like others, she expressed a strong aversion to raw meat: "I don't really even touch the meat that I make. I don't really like cutting any type of meat, and I usually buy things pre-cut." To underscore her point about not touching raw meat, she contrasted her revulsion with her husband's enthusiastic embrace of steak:

> He'll kiss his steak because he loves it! If it's a beautiful piece of steak. He loves it so much! Then if it's, what is it called? The ground meat, he will break it up with his hand! I can't do that. I got to use a fork or spoon or whatever. I can't. I don't want the . . . I don't want to have the blood on my hands.

Roberta's story demonstrates clear gendered patterns in our data: women were more likely to express disgust toward raw meat, whereas men often reveled in their carnivorous enjoyment. This aligns with existing research showing that women generally eat less meat, are more likely to be vegetarian, and express more discomfort about meat.[38] Our survey data support this trend, with women (46%) being significantly more likely than men (26%) to agree or strongly agree with the statement "Sometimes I'm grossed out by meat." Of course, this doesn't mean that all women are averse to meat, and a notable minority of men do experience disgust, but the gender difference is substantial.

As we'll explore further, many women develop specific food practices to navigate discomfort and reconcile the reality of meat's animal origins with their dietary choices.

Meat Is Emotionally Complicated

So far, our findings reveal a complex emotional landscape surrounding meat, encompassing not only straightforward delight and disgust but also ambivalent feelings that blend positive and negative reactions. These discussions of meat's emotional and moral complexity suggest that the social process of meat moralization is far from straightforward or linear and frequently involves a delicate balancing act of conflicting emotions and values.

"The Bloodier the Better": The Value in Confronting the Whole Animal

While many consumers expressed discomfort with the inherent loss of life that underlies meat-eating, not all sought to repress this reality. Unlike Sandra, many participants did not want to eat their plate of roast pork away from the body of the pig. Some embraced this connection as a mark of ethical superiority and a higher standard of meat consumption. This sentiment was particularly prevalent among men, like Jason, a man in his sixties who only bought meat from high-end butchers or Whole Foods Market and expressed disdain for those who "don't want to deal with the realities of where meat comes from." He views squeamishness toward raw meat as a kind of moral failing, believing it is cowardly to not fully embrace raw meat and its animal origins. He says, "I know a lot of people who are very squeamish about raw meat. My youngest sister can't touch chicken in any form without wearing fucking rubber gloves, you know. It's like, what the hell is that about?"

In a focus group comprised of dedicated meat eaters, the discussion celebrated people who enthusiastically ate meat, acknowledged its animal origins and displayed no signs of animal reminder disgust. When asked if they had ever felt disgust when dealing with raw meat, we received a crystal-clear response from Aaron, a man in his thirties who followed an all-meat "carnivore" diet: "No, not at all. . . . The bloodier the better. Yeah, it makes me hungry. Just like [how] people get aroused when they smell baked bread, that's what my body craves." His younger friend Markus, a former vegetarian turned butcher, admitted experiencing an initial discomfort he proudly overcame. In Markus's story, he had once been a vegetarian who put his "head in the sand"

and accepted the "easy" path of thinking that vegetarianism was the "most ethical option": "I mean it sounds great, right? You're not killing anything? Well, not directly, at least!" Markus described himself transitioning from a closed-minded vegetarian who didn't "want to think about the whole life and death question" to a clear-eyed ethical meat eater who accepted the whole "life and death question" of meat as an essential part of "being human." For Markus, a return to meat-eating reflected an evolution toward greater wisdom: "Everyone has to, at one point, come to terms with death, and whether you do it in your lifetime or at the end, sooner or later you have to." His narrative positions the open embrace of meat and its origins as a marker of maturity and even enlightenment.

Just as Markus viewed facing death and consuming meat as a kind of positive character development, other participants expressed pride in confronting animal death and actively engaging with whole animal bodies. In the same focus group, Bonnie, a butcher shop manager in her thirties, intentionally visits ranches with slaughterhouses to honor the reality of the animals' death: "I do make a point of walking through [the slaughterhouse] and just, like, honoring the fact that this is a part of the process, and I can't just hide from it." For Namita, a sixty-year-old married woman, connecting meat to the whole animal was a source of pride and celebration. Inspired by the aroma of roasting Easter lamb in her Greek neighborhood, she and her husband Carl rented a roaster to cook a whole lamb and, later, a pig. Namita conveyed a sense of pride as she described these events, emphasizing the visceral connection of "roast[ing] the entire animal, which is just looking you in the face!" They shared these feasts with friends, turning whole animal roasts into a meaningful family tradition. This practice demonstrated a conscious embrace of meat's origins, transforming the act of meat consumption into a communal celebration oriented around a whole animal.

In telling her story, Namita contrasted her perspective with her friend, Heather, who was also in the focus group. Heather had declined Namita's dinner invitations due to her discomfort with the sight of a whole roasted animal. Put simply, she found it gross. In recounting their conversation, Namita expressed a belief that confronting the reality of an animal's death, even if it evokes disgust, is a morally sound position. She said, "It's good once in a while to be faced with the fact that we actually took out an entire animal. . . . It's good for us to know that! Because when you go buy a piece of meat, you're not thinking about the original form [of the animal's body].

Not usually." While Heather prioritizes avoiding discomfort and disassociation, Namita and Carl advocate for an active experience that embraces meat's origin in a whole animal.

Another focus group discussion evoked the idea that confronting discomfort and resisting disgust toward meat is ethically meaningful. Minel, a well-traveled woman in her late twenties, recounted witnessing a pig being slaughtered during an educational exchange in Southeast Asia. While acknowledging the sadness of the animal's death, she differentiated herself from her companions who refused to eat the meat, advocating for embracing the "guilt and sadness" of meat. Minel suggests that "maybe it [eating meat] should hurt a little," explaining that part of ethical meat consumption is "recognizing that a thing was alive and now it is dead, and you are enjoying it." Minel's perspective resonated with others in the group. Felipe and Ellen, while admitting occasional disgust with meat, also valued pushing through the disgust, embracing the pain and discomfort as a moral imperative. Felipe said, "If it hurt a little, then people would probably eat less meat. Or they'd be more thoughtful when they would eat meat." Felipe's words highlight a central tenet of meat moralization: confronting the uncomfortable emotions related to meat might encourage moderation and greater ethical consideration.

In sum, these stories of meat-eating among concerned omnivores reveal an important dimension of meat moralization—and an alternative ethical food pathway to vegetarianism. Rather than succumbing to denial or disgust, these participants suggest that a principled omnivore response can involve acknowledging and processing the negative emotions associated with eating meat and harming animals. By embracing discomfort, sadness, or even pain, the concerned meat eater reports that they experience a deeper connection to their food choices and the animals that sustain them. Their approach challenges the vegetarian idea of complete abstention from meat and instead puts forward a morally engaged, "eyes wide open" form of ethical meat-eating.

I Know Too Much about Meat—and I Feel
Conflicted, Guilty, and Uncomfortable

The narratives explored in this chapter reveal a significant tension in the ethical meatscape: the discomfort and disgust associated with animal death that is inherent to any meat consumption, and the positive valorization of confronting this reality and embracing the associated negative emotions. While the previous section highlighted the ethical significance of acknowledging animal death, this section explores critiques of industrialized factory farming, which is the predominant mode of meat production. This shift in focus expands the scope of meat moralization beyond the acceptance of animal death to encompass a broader critique of the modern meat production system and its ethical implications.

Concerned omnivores are not simply upset about eating *any* animal; their emotional response is amplified when the animal has been raised in industrialized agriculture. Rather than simple animal reminder disgust, we offer a more precise term to capture this complex emotional response: *factory farm disgust*. This emotional and cognitive category encompasses feelings of not only disgust but also sadness, guilt, and anger, intertwined with the sensory pleasures derived from eating meat.[39] Factory farm disgust is a dynamic process that involves balancing the enjoyment of meat with knowledge of its origins. Notably, this disgust doesn't necessitate firsthand experience with factory farming. As psychologist Johannes Simons and his colleagues suggest, the lack of personal experience can paradoxically fuel "nightmarish fantasies" about industrial farming, constructed from media images and their own imagination.[40]

A vividly negative emotional reaction to factory farming was widespread in our focus groups, although the specific ethical concerns varied. Heather, a married woman in her sixties, emphasized a concern with animal welfare, questioning the conditions under which her food was raised: "When I eat [meat], there is often this little thing in the back of my mind asking about the way that that animal was raised. I do have those moments of conscience." Yasir, a former vegetarian in his thirties, expressed lingering guilt over meat's environmental impact: "I love eating meat . . . but I also aspire to be an environmentalist, and I know that meat production is one of the largest producers of greenhouse gases, so I'm just constantly trying to balance that." For both Yasir and Heather, the pleasures of meat comingle with emotional reminders of its connections to ethical issues and environmental harms, demonstrating the conflicting feelings that can accompany conscious omnivorism.

Like Yasir, Ellen, a woman in her twenties, grappled with balancing her love of meat against an awareness of its negative health and environmental implications. While she enjoyed meat when offered, she actively limits her personal purchases: "If someone puts meat on a plate in front of me, I will eat it, but I don't tend to buy meat myself." Ellen's university nutrition classes had instilled in her a sense of guilt around meat, especially red meat, and she discussed its saturated fat content and link to health problems. This guilt manifested both physically, as a "heavy" feeling in her stomach, and emotion-ally: "if I have red meat. . . . I definitely feel a little bit—guilty. . . . I know that it is the worst meat for the environment in a lot of ways." Ellen's experience demonstrates a hedonic shift associated with the moralization of meat, espe-cially beef, where increased knowledge of negative consequences diminishes enjoyment and introduces guilt. This shift illustrates how moralization can alter the sensory experience of meat and decreases pleasure, even for eaters who still want to include meat in their diet.

Ellen's story exemplifies how knowledge of the industrialized meat system can evoke negative emotional reactions to meat-eating. This phenomenon surfaced repeatedly in focus group discussions, particularly when partici-pants reflected on the environmental consequences of meat-eating. Consider Mindy, a Vancouver resident in her thirties who was originally from the Phil-ippines. Mindy was trying to cut back on meat for health reasons, despite her fondness for pork dishes central to Filipino cuisine. While health issues were a primary motivator for Mindy's dietary choices, she also expressed deep dis-tress over the environmental impact of meat. Recent news stories about the Amazon rainforest's destruction left her feeling troubled, angry, and guilty. Mindy became visibly upset as she described how our dietary behaviors were "choking the planet." Her reaction underscored the complex emotions inter-twined with her food choices; despite continuing to eat meat regularly, Min-dy's enthusiasm for meaty foods was tinged with conflicting feelings.

A similar conflict emerged for Heather, quoted earlier, who has cultural roots in the West Indies. Like Mindy, Heather also loved eating meat, reflect-ing how certain West Indian dishes (e.g., pelau) would be incomplete without meat. However, unlike Mindy, Heather viewed meat as essential for her health and well-being. She believed that daily meat consumption was necessary to feel healthy, energetic, and full. Despite her strong personal convictions about daily meat eating, Heather was not a straightforward meat enthusiast. During the focus group discussion, she became emotional when the topic of disgust or discomfort around meat arose. She explained that while she felt completely comfortable handling raw meat, her unease stemmed from meat's environ-mental impact:

> For me, it goes back to the environment. I'm not sure that's part of the ques-tion you are asking [about discomfort]? But that's how I feel. Too much of the environment has been destroyed to satisfy the desire of primarily North

and South Americans . . . but primarily North Americans, to provide us with
meat. And it continues to grow . . . the increasing destruction of rainforests
and the planet, to provide more and more meat.

Although Heather could not imagine eliminating meat from her diet, she
grappled with strong negative emotions regarding the environmental consequences of industrialized animal agriculture, especially in relation to
overconsumption, deforestation, and climate change. While she did not experience the visceral animal reminder disgust, the broader issues of mass-scale
production evoked strong negative feelings.

Heather's dismay about factory farming exemplifies how meat can be negatively associated with systemic issues of industrialized animal agriculture
and environmental destruction, a perspective common in our focus group
conversations. This observation supports our argument that the moralization
of meat is an evolving process. While it encompasses a general aversion to
killing and consuming animals (animal reminder disgust), the moralization
of meat can also invoke the more specific and distinct factory farm disgust.
Individuals like Heather demonstrate that factory farm disgust can coexist
with continued meat-eating, as it did not alter her dietary habits. However,
our data also reveal instances where this variety of disgust can lead to significant shifts in dietary choices.

This shift was most clearly demonstrated by Hope, a woman in her
twenties in a focus group consisting of friends in a cookbook club. Hope, a
semi-regular meat eater, expressed strong criticism of factory farming. She
was not disgusted by the sight or smell of raw meat, even saying, "I like cutting it and breaking it down. I'm really into that!" However, she found meat
from a grocery store deeply repulsive due to her awareness of industrialized
meat production. This awareness led to a hedonic shift where she could no
longer enjoy conventionally sourced meat. Hope's embodied and visceral
reaction to grocery store meat is evident in her statement: "I won't eat it,
honestly, from any grocery store. I would rather just not eat meat. I can't,
mentally. I don't want to do it." This disgust caused awkward social interactions with friends in her cookbook club, as she knew some members purchased meat from discount grocery stores, which she found "gross." Even
when she knows the person who bought it and is consuming a homemade
meat-based dish in that person's home, she expresses the following feelings
about it:

I'm kind of like, "I don't want to eat it." And I hate it, because you feel like if you go to someone's house, you can't be like, "I eat meat, but not *this* meat." [Laughter.] But I find it really hard to swallow. . . . I don't feel comfortable with it, I find it really hard to even digest it. I'm just so turned off.

Hope's experience highlights the potential of factory farm disgust to influence the broader process of meat moralization, suggesting that some consumers can become so repulsed by the idea of eating industrialized-raised meat that their consumption patterns shift away from conventional products.

Delight in the Abject: The Thrill of Being Bad

We now return to the first theme of this chapter, "meat is delicious," and connect it to the second theme, "meat is disgusting." While these themes may seem diametrically opposed, our focus group interviews with concerned omnivores revealed a specific narrative that stitches these seemingly incongruous storylines together. This narrative aligns with what psychoanalytic thinker Julia Kristeva calls *the abject*—a concept describing something fear-inducing and repellent but also fascinating.[41] In the context of meat consumption, this translates to a paradoxical delight in disgust. Activities deemed contaminating or dirty can evoke fear and revulsion, but they can also be attractive, fun, or seductive.[42] Transgression, in this sense, can be powerfully enticing. We observed this dynamic among participants who expressed a certain pleasure or thrill in abject meat experiences.

Even people with a strong critique of industrialized meat expressed a thrill in consuming forbidden, "dirty" meat items. This delight in the abject was evident when participants described enjoying parts of an animal that their peers considered gross or inedible. For example, Diane, a woman in her forties, enthusiastically shared her fondness for her favorite meat dish, steak tartare, a raw beef preparation. Diane's answer stood out, since most people described more commonplace dishes like steak when asked about their favorites. She also talked about her adventurous experiences at an edgy, meat-focused restaurant in Toronto, saying with pride, "I definitely have had horse and brain and tongue and things of that nature." While open to experimentation in a dining setting, Diane admitted she wouldn't try cooking these dishes at home and still found certain items like blood sausage intolerable "because it just tastes too much like blood. [Laughing.]" This suggests that even for adventurous eaters like Diane, there is a boundary of disgust that they are hesitant to cross. Nevertheless, Diane's pride in overcoming her fears and embracing "gross" foods highlights the allure of the abject, living on the knife's edge of disgust and deliciousness.

A different manifestation of delight in the abject arose in discussions about fast food, a category commonly associated with ill health, indulgence, and obesity. While many participants denied eating or enjoying fast food, describing it as gross, low-quality, and unhealthy, some conversations revealed a contrasting sentiment—delight in the very "junkiness" of fast food. In a focus group with Torontonians in their twenties, a discussion about the popular Canadian fast-food chain A&W's marketing claims of producing a more ethical fast-food burger led to a surprising exchange.[43] Danielle expressed a preference for A&W, saying, "At least I know that it's Canadian beef, or raised without antibiotics." However, Amber challenged this perspective, stating that she views fast food as inherently low in quality and does not prioritize sourcing when indulging in it. In her words, "I feel fast food is delicious, but it's also garbage. It sort of feels like where I eat my garbage, you know? [Laughter.]" This sentiment resonated with the group, eliciting laughter and nods of agreement. This exchange highlights the acceptance of indulgence in guilt-producing "garbage" foods, where concerns about sourcing and production are temporarily suspended for the sake of pleasure.

A similar theme of fast-food abjection emerged in another Toronto focus group. In this discussion, Karsten, who described his partner as extremely health-oriented, revealed that he had a secret habit of eating McDonald's burgers. Despite his commitment to ethical eating, he confessed: "I don't tell anyone. I don't tell [my partner]. I just don't tell people. I just go do it. . . . It just feels like a weird escape. I associate it with my teenage years, I think. I just go and eat—usually too much, too. Excessive." Karsten's description combined delight with confession, fostering a sense of camaraderie and shared transgression within the group. After Karsten's confession, another participant, Ellen, quipped, "If you're going to do it wrong, do it right," which produced gales of laughter. The shared experience of transgression highlights the importance of acknowledging and investigating spaces for indulgence within the broader context of meat moralization. While factory farms were viewed as producing disgusting or even inedible foods, a countercurrent of abject eating experiences was also present, where people describe the delight and deliciousness of "bad" meat.

Conclusion: Complex Feelings in the Industrial Meatscape

Meat presents a paradox: it is both easy and difficult to love. It connects us to important traditions, affirms cultural identity, and offers gustatory pleasure. In our focus group conversations with concerned meat eaters, meat was generally seen as "nice," aligning with the 4-N framework of meat-eating.[44] Participants emphasized its irresistible deliciousness and the challenge of giving it up, even when confronted with the harsh realities of the industrialized meat system.

However, the enjoyment of meat often comes with emotional conflict and cognitive dissonance. Our participants grappled with conflicting emotions, including pleasure intertwined with guilt, disgust, and sadness. We observed both the classic animal reminder disgust associated with consuming animal flesh and a distinct feeling of factory farm disgust stemming from the environmental and ethical concerns of industrialized meat production. The latter form of disgust, often accompanied by feelings of anger, guilt, and despair, highlights the moral complexities surrounding meat for a significant portion of meat eaters. This is likely why more than one-third of our survey participants agreed that the way meat is produced today is a problem. These negative feelings raise questions about the morality and deliciousness of industrialized meat for a significant percentage of meat eaters.

Drawing on the work of psychologist Paul Rozin and his colleagues, we can contextualize the negative emotions surrounding meat as part of a larger process of meat moralization.[45] This process involves a shift in perception, where meat moves from a taken-for-granted food to one laced with guilt, sadness, disgust, and ethical quandaries. It is important to note that meat moralization is not a categorical switch from amoral to moral but rather involves a gradual shift along a continuum.[46] Psychological research on animal reminder disgust reveals that meat has long been a contentious food item, given its origins in a living animal. However, the emergence of factory farm disgust signifies a new phase of meat moralization. Consumers are now not only aware of the individual animal sacrificed for their meal but also increasingly conscious of the problematic system of industrialized meat production on a mass scale.

Meat moralization is not a linear path that inevitably leads to vegetarianism or veganism. Instead, it can prompt concerned consumers to adopt a more conscientious approach to meat consumption. This can involve acknowledging the animal origins of meat, working to stay connected to the animal's body (e.g., breaking down a whole chicken), and actively resisting the dissociation from meat's animality. For some, this heightened awareness may result in a loss of taste for conventional meat, as they become "too informed" to enjoy products they associate with factory farming. This can manifest in avoiding fast food, rejecting supermarket meat, or seeking out niche, artis-anal experiences (e.g., chef-made charcuterie plates) that feel distanced from industrialized practices.

We also emphasize that the meat moralization process is not absolute. The allure of the abject—the simultaneous repulsion and attraction to that which is taboo or transgressive—plays a role in continued meat consumption. Even people who saw meat through a highly moralized lens employ various strate-gies to distance themselves from disturbing aspects of meat production. These strategies include surrendering to the abject pleasures of fast-food burgers, eating a piece of roast pork only at a safe physical distance from the rest of the animal's carcass, or unironically observing that the documentary *Cowspiracy* led to (only) one week's worth of strict meat avoidance. These strategies reveal the complex interplay between pleasure, disgust, and morality in the realm of meat consumption.

The moralization of meat creates a space for the emergence of happy meat, a concept that promises to reconcile the pleasures of meat consumption with ethical and environmental concerns. As we will see in the next chapter, this al-ternative narrative centers on ethically, sustainably raised animals and offers a potential solution for consumers grappling with the negative emotions associ-ated with factory farming. We explore our data to examine how "happy meat" can resolve the meat paradox for concerned eaters.

FOUR Happy Meat Makes Me Feel Good

IN AN INTERVIEW ROOM on the University of British Columbia's Vancouver campus, Jun, Ivan, Madia, and Peter sit together, their shared experiences as parents weaving a common thread through their diverse backgrounds. As the discussion unfolds, a significant point of connection emerges: an emotionally charged relationship to meat. All participants consider themselves conscientious meat eaters, but they approach meat-eating from different perspectives and with different priorities. Jun, a Chinese-born filmmaker, has done extensive research on the health issues associated with meat, even going to a research library to read academic articles on the topic. Jun is deeply concerned about his kids' health and the quality of the food his family eats, regretfully saying, "Children, all they know about is hamburgers and stuff." Lamenting the lack of tofu in his family's diet and disturbed by "shocking" documentaries exposing animal cruelty, Jun has become increasingly selective about his meat and egg purchases.

Ivan, a British-born father, introduces himself with a grin as "a big meat eater." He loves the taste of meat and prioritizes protein to fuel his gym workouts. While open about his carnivorous tendencies, Ivan is mindful to "eat meat that is as cruelty-free as it possibly can be." Madia, a Honduran immigrant and mother of two, chimes in with a contrasting perspective. She identifies as "environmentally conscious" and is well versed in meat's ecological impacts. Still, she harbors a certain pessimism about her family's ability to reduce its meat consumption. In an effort to mitigate its impact, Madia tries to purchase meat directly from farmers, striving to minimize food miles, packaging, and her overall carbon footprint.

Peter, who makes many funny observations that produce gales of laughter in the group, is an articulate computer science graduate student and a father of one child. His relationship with meat is deeply rooted in his upbringing in a rural agricultural community. Childhood friendships with children of farmers instilled in him a powerful narrative of ranching centered on compassion and love between humans and animals. As Peter says, "I always felt like the people who were farmers or are farmers, I saw that they had a very compassionate view of the livestock and animals that they took care of. I didn't think there was any cruelty or malice in how they were treated." Peter concludes, "Actually, they [the animals] were loved, to tell the truth."

Peter's fellow focus group members do not share his firsthand experience with ranching, yet they all readily evoke elements of a strikingly similar narrative when envisioning happy meat. This shared storyline features animals grazing in open, grassy pastures, free to roam, and uncontaminated by toxic chemicals or antibiotics. They envision humane, swift deaths and dedicated farmers who lovingly care for their animals while nurturing sustainable ecosystems and operating with full transparency. Ivan, for example, emphasizes the importance of freely roaming animals: "Ethical would be if the animal was brought up as close to nature as possible—like, with natural grown feed, space to run around in, et cetera." Madia agrees, adding, "It's also not using any antibiotics or hormones, anything that can be detrimental to the animals. Grass-fed as well." Talking about a friend who is a hunter, Jun introduces the idea of "being conscientious of the animal's well-being" so it "doesn't suffer very much" when it dies. He also likes the idea of making "use of the whole animal so it's not wasteful." In addition to telling stories about the happy meat they try to eat, Jun, Ivan, Madia, and Peter also rely on stories about happy meat told by producers. For instance, Madia recommends a website where farmers narrate their own stories, fostering a sense of trust that allows her to feel good about purchasing meat from the site.

This focus group discussion reveals the pivotal role that narratives of ethical farming play in shaping perceptions of acceptable meat choices and mitigating discomfort with industrialized meat production. The participants all experience meat moralization and grapple with the ethical complexities inherent in the consumption of animal products. None of them have adopted a vegetarian diet, but they all draw upon various elements of a culturally shared narrative about happy meat. This narrative, encompassing themes of humane treatment, environmental sustainability, and transparency, serves as a guide for their food choices and helps them reconcile their ethical concerns with their continued consumption of meat.

To understand the affective foundations of the happy meat storyline, we draw from the emotionally laden conversations about meat we had with focus group participants like Jun, Ivan, Madia, and Peter. These conversations illuminate two crucial points for our analysis. First, consumers draw from various elements of the happy meat storyline to manage the meat paradox, the inherent conflict between loving animals and eating them. By consuming happy meat, individuals attempt to alleviate the complex emotional tension of meat-eating. As Peter says, "When I go to the grocery store, if there is a choice between something like free-range or I know that there is an ethical way that the animals were raised or treated, I feel compelled to take that as a consumer." While Peter feels "compelled" to buy the more ethical meat option, this isn't a particularly pious moment. Peter doesn't take himself, or this choice, too seriously; he later jokes to the group about how buying into the transparently self-serving ethical meat marketing of large corporations makes him feel like a good person. Peter's self-deprecating quip underscores a second key finding: consumers engage with happy meat stories in ways that are emotionally complex, contradictory, and reflexive. These narratives are not simple one-time solutions to resolve ethical dilemmas but rather ongoing tools for navigating the complexities of meat consumption. They provide a framework for continuously managing the guilt and discomfort associated with eating animals, offering a sense of moral agency and a way to reconcile conflicting values.

In the first part of this chapter, we unpack the multifaceted nature of the happy meat narrative, exploring how consumers selectively engage with its diverse elements to justify and find comfort in their meat consumption. We shift our focus in the second part to the emotional ambiguities inherent in this narrative. Consumers, we reveal, are far from naïve. They regularly acknowledge the ethical inconsistencies and potential for corporate manipulation within happy meat claims, even while acknowledging their persuasive power. This complex interplay of belief, skepticism, and emotional engagement underscores the vital role that narratives play in shaping the specific meat choices of concerned meat eaters as well as ethical consumption in a general sense.

Happy Stories about Happy Meat

In our focus groups, stories about happy meat often emerged as a direct response to discussions about the negative emotions associated with industrialized meat production. A bleak tableau of factory farming commonly served as a foil for consumers and inspired an alternate vision of verdant pastures where contented animals roamed freely—a stark contrast that allowed them to feel better about their meat consumption. For instance, Sandra, a thirty-four-year-old research analyst, explained that when she thought about happy meat, "I think of some guy with a farmer's hat, out in the field where the animals are just frolicking about [laughter]," a vision that countered the constant new stories about "animal abuse at factory farms." Kaitlynn, a thirty-eight-year-old marketing professional, echoed Sandra's sentiment, emphasizing the importance of "free range" animals "being out, and not just being [in] this sort of factory farm." She succinctly captured this idyllic image, stating, "Free range [chickens], running around a farm. [Laughter.] Happy animals!" Sandra affirmed this image, remarking, "Chickens at the farm, yeah. They look happy." For meat eaters like Kaitlynn and Sandra, imagining happy animals living outdoors provided a comforting antidote to the unsettling images of animals confined to harsh, crowded conditions in factory farms.

The tendency to contrast a negative meat scene with a positive happy scene was also evident in a focus group involving Priya, a research scientist who was raised as a vegetarian. Priya described how her guilt about eating meat was eased by avoiding products from crowded factory farm conditions. She recalled the upsetting images she has seen in animal welfare documentaries, saying, "I don't know the truth in it, complete truth in it." She continued, "I have never visited these places myself, so there might be some ignorance to what I'm saying, but I don't want to buy my meat from a place where hundreds of animals were kept in a place where there should be just ten or twenty [animals]." Priya's opinion highlights how, even in the absence of direct experience, the visceral nature of these negative representations fuels a desire for an alternative, small-scale narrative of animal husbandry.

At this point in the conversation, Ella—a woman in her thirties who lives alone and loves to cook—joined in. Ella emphasized her preference for meat sourced from animals raised in "good conditions," stating, "I would want to know that an animal lives in good conditions and is happy and is eating well." To illustrate this point, Ella told a story:

I've never actually been happier eating meat than last year in California. I went by a ranch, and then I went across the street from the ranch to this very casual burger joint, but they were serving the meat from that ranch. And I just saw those guys [cows] roaming around and I was like, "This is gonna be good meat!" And some people would be saddened by that, but I was just like, "Those are some happy cows." And that makes me happy that I ate [them]. I know that there's a flip argument to that, but to me, it's like, they got to their final point while being very happy cows and eating good grass. That's a good cycle of life to me.

By citing the "flip argument," Ella implicitly acknowledged the moralization of meat, including the hurt involved in killing an animal and the ethical considerations of vegetarianism. But rather than abstain from eating meat, she seeks to reconcile her consumption with her values by focusing on the perceived quality of life of the animal she consumes. Ella feels positively about eating "good meat" from "very happy" animals that lived a life outside "eating good grass." Her experience demonstrates a strategy for temporarily resolving the meat paradox. By associating meat with positive emotions like happiness and satisfaction derived from the belief that the animals lived a "good cycle of life," Ella emotionally justifies her dietary choice.

This emotional justification aligns with feminist theorist Sara Ahmed's insights in *The Promise of Happiness*, which explores the cultural expectation that doing the "right" thing should lead to happiness.[1] When participants like Ella described being positively affected by the experience of buying and eating ethical meat, they echo this logic: they feel they are allowed to experience happiness because they made an extra effort to prioritize the life of the animal they are eating. Purchasing the "right" meat product becomes a pathway to a sense of happiness and ethical consistency—even if this happy feeling is fleeting and the ethical dilemmas of meat re-emerge at the next meal.

The desire for emotional reassurance found in "happy meat" narratives extended beyond individual experiences. Participants in focus group conversations drew on idyllic images of farms they had visited—or ones they imagined—to resolve the meat paradox. For instance, Ellen, a young Torontonian working as a nutritionist, described a storybook image of a serene farm oasis operated by her uncle, which she described as an "ecosystem" of healthy soil and mutually nourishing crops and livestock. Ellen's story about her uncle's farm served as a happy meat reference point for the remainder of this focus group discussion, offering a comforting contrast to the perceived ethical shortcomings of industrial meat production. Later in the conversation, Karsten criticized a corporate meat product for its lack of transparency and referenced this idyllic farm:

> It [corporate meat] kind of feels like the antithesis of what you [Ellen] described on your uncle's farm. Just as you start to figure out what the supply chain of that [corporate meat] would have to be, at some point it just feels like it's too far from someone who can say, "The barley comes from here, the beef is from here in my backyard." . . . It's just too far removed from that model [of Ellen's uncle's farm].

The corporate meat industry, with its opaque supply chains and industrialized practices, serves as a foil to the idealized happy meat narrative. In contrast, Ellen's uncle's farm represents transparency, traceability, and a direct connection to the land, offering a moral reference point and emotional good feelings that the industrial system lacks.

The stark contrast between bad meat and happy meat narratives was also evident in a Toronto focus group involving Rochelle and Mary, two women in their sixties with shared experiences working in the film industry. They recounted a work trip to Denmark, where they encountered two very different kinds of pig farms: a negative scene of factory farming and a positive scene of happy meat run by a caring farmer. Rochelle explained how "Denmark is a massive pork-producing nation, right, and it's all commercially raised. You would go, like, a few miles outside of [a] farm and it would stink, it was so gross. . . . You never once saw a pig. They were all in great giant, you know, silos or whatever they are." Mary agreed with Rochelle's negative assessment of large-scale pork production, saying that the word "slaughter" applies to the death that happens in these kinds of facilities where animals are killed "en masse"—a scene which she thought "would be horrific."

In stark contrast, Mary introduced a second experience: an idyllic Danish pig farm where the "end of life" for animals was handled with remarkable care and respect:

> The killing or end of life of pigs was just done so beautifully. I worried about it all night the night before. I thought, "I don't think I can go and watch an animal be killed." [But] it really was quite lovely. If they had to die, they did it very nicely. Then we experienced the pig being taken back and completely butchered from start to finish, and it was quite fascinating. It didn't bother me at all—I mean, from the skinning, to taking all the

organs out, and what they keep and what they don't, and why they weigh this, and the inspector coming in and inspecting the meat and making sure that everything was properly done. So I found that quite fascinating, and it didn't bother me at all.

Mary was explicit that the emotional dimension of meat varies tremendously depending on the context of production. She remembered the industrial facility as "horrific," but the Danish farm death scene was "done so beautifully," "quite lovely," and not at all upsetting.

Mary's depiction of porcine death was so positive that it sparked questions from her fellow focus group participants. What made an animal's death "lovely"? Mary explained that the pig's idyllic life, grazing freely in fields while eating a wholesome diet, was key to her perception of their death as peaceful:

> These pigs, first of all, they lived a beautiful life in great big fields. They just grazed on the land, and the feed that was given to them was made by hand. I can't remember exactly what the recipe was, but they had lovely grain that was given to them. Plus, they ate vegetables and Jerusalem artichokes that just grew wild, and they moved from pasture to pasture. So, once they finished in one, then they were moved to another. They had little huts outside, so they always lived outside, and they were never put in pens or in barns en masse.

This connection between a happy life and a dignified death became a recurring theme in our focus groups, with participants often referencing similar experiences to emotionally resolve the meat paradox. Mary's detailed account of the slaughter process is worth examining closely, as the death experience itself is an important part of the story of how these happy meat animals are moralized:

> So, the end of the life. Basically, the pigs are in a field, and a man, the owner who ran the farm, calls them up, and he's got some feed, so they will come because pigs want to eat all the time. So, they all came up, and he throws some grain around and then they all start snuffling and eating on the ground and so then he walks around. So, let's say there's half a dozen great big hogs standing there eating, and he checks each one out and he looks at their haunches and the whole size of the hog and decides which one he's going to slaughter. Then what he does is, he takes—it's like if you were charging your battery. He comes up beside them, and they're still eating, and puts an

electric thing on each side of their neck, and it immediately kills them. Then he puts a chain around the back legs. . . . And then they take the pig out on a chain and hang it up on a hook and let it bleed out so he's hanging from his feet. They let it bleed out, and the other pigs, they don't blink an eye. There's no fear, they just continue to eat, and then they take them to the butchering place where they take the skin off. But back to your question. It [death] was done so quickly and so quietly so there was no squealing; there was nothing.

Rochelle, who witnessed this event alongside Mary, summarized the moral resolution of the story: "The real main point was that everybody, I think, collectively felt it [death] . . . was so peaceful, and they [the pigs] were nonplussed." She noted that the reality of slaughter can mean "for some people, 'Now I'm a vegetarian.' But it didn't work that way for me." Rochelle contrasted this experience with other instances of inhuman animal slaughter she had witnessed. These experiences aligned with Rozin's theory of moralization (explored in Chapter 3), by prompting deeper reflection on meat consumption. However, rather than leading to vegetarianism, these experiences caused Rochelle and Mary to closely examine the ethics of eating meat. For both women, meat became deeply moralized through both positive and negative experiences with animal slaughter. Instead of viewing meat casually or inconsequentially, Rochelle reported that these experiences increased her respect for the "creature" that becomes meat. Meat moralization did not lead to abstention but rather a commitment to mindful consumption and, whenever possible, to seek out meat sources where animals graze freely in the outdoors—like the happy outdoor Danish pigs.

The storylines across our participants' accounts of happy and unhappy animals resonate with another concept from Ahmed's *The Promise of Happiness*: the idea that when happiness is ascribed to an object (be it a nation, a family, or an animal), it enhances its social value and positive evaluation of that object.[2] Challenging this positive assessment can be socially disruptive and can even be perceived as a violation of social norms. Ahmed's concept of the "affect alien" captures this phenomenon: a being who deviates from socially acceptable emotional responses, becoming "alien" or estranged from normative affective expectations. This concept highlights how certain feelings are sanctioned while others are marginalized. As an example, imagine the "melancholic migrant" who refuses to happily assimilate into their new environment, instead calling attention to the systems of global inequality and oppression shaping migration pathways. In the context of meat, the "affect alien" could be the individual who questions the narrative of "happy meat," disrupting the comfortable narrative of a happy animal death.

The concept of the affect alien might apply to animals that are raised for human consumption, regardless of the farming method. When we prioritize a socially constructed narrative of "happy" animals, obfuscating their needs and preferences, we essentially render them affect aliens. This was highlighted by Matthew, the chicken farmer we introduced in Chapter 1, who described his own struggle with the happy animal narrative. Matthew explained to us that he is "condemning" a significant portion of his birds to die when he raises them in a pasture, a practice driven, in part, by consumers' perceptions of what animals want. Similarly, Rochelle and Mary's accounts of the seemingly peaceful slaughter of pigs are valid within their experience but raise questions about the broader implications of the happy animal narrative. Does this emphasis on a "lovely" death primarily serve to alleviate our own discomfort, obscuring the inherent ethical dilemmas of animal agriculture?

By applying the affect alien concept to animals, we are prompted to examine how our desire for emotionally pleasurable meat consumption can inadvertently lead to the erasure of animals' experiences and agency. This obfuscation, which we explore further in Chapters 5 and 6, raises concerns about the potential of the happy meat narrative to mask the inherent complexities and ethical challenges of animal agriculture. Indeed, Ahmed's work encourages us to critically examine the happy meat narrative. While well intentioned, this narrative often relies on an imaginary of happy animals that frolic outdoors and are cared for by conscientious farmers to create positive emotions around meat eating. Despite this potential for oversimplification, elements of the happy meat storyline resonated deeply with our participants and appeared across various focus group conversations. These stories evoke positive emotions and project an image of ethical acceptability, reinforcing consumers' belief that meat production can be both compassionate and sustainable.

The power of storytelling shaping consumer trust was evident in a Toronto focus group discussion. Participants Priya and Selena both emphasized the importance of narratives that connect them to the origins of meat, particularly when it comes to inspiring trust in a store or restaurant. Selena explained that she looks at "what people are saying about [the restaurant], or what their catchline seems to be as a restaurant. Some menus will say, 'All of our animals are'—whatever—'happy animals.'" Priya concurred, adding, "I like the story aspect. I like to know what they're doing, where it came from, why it is special. Especially if I'm eating steak, for instance. I want to know which farm it came from."

Anton, another Toronto participant, spoke eloquently about how the story of local meat is different from the "fake" stories presented in corporate meat marketing. He criticized corporate campaigns on the specific grounds that they did *not* have a convincing story: "You can't really tell what the story is! You know, that's something that connects us as humans to each other and to the environment around us. It's all kind of designed in such a way to, you know, come across as appealing, but I'm not seeing the accountability there. I'm not following the storyline."

These accounts underscore how storytelling can be a powerful tool building trust and shaping purchasing decisions. Consumers increasingly seek out narratives that not only provide information about a product but also foster an emotional connection to its origins and production. The absence of a convincing story results in more than just a lack of information; it can contribute to a deep emotional disconnect between eaters, the animals they consume, and the environment. The work of the happy meat story is to bridge these gaps, offering a seemingly transparent commodity chain from pasture to plate. Significantly, this story functions as an emotional salve, assuaging the uncomfortable feelings that arise in the context of meat moralization. It reinforces the belief that if consumers and producers are doing the "right" thing when it comes to raising and eating animals, then they deserve to feel happy about these choices.[3]

This emotional connection is further strengthened when consumers have direct experiences with "happy animals," as seen in the stories of Rochelle and Mary, who witnessed firsthand the humane treatment of pigs on a Danish farm. However, our findings reveal that even imagined encounters with idyllic farms can carry significant weight. Participants easily envisioned themselves visiting farms, interacting with the farmer, and feeling affirmed by the quality of the lives that the animals enjoy. For example, Ivan described his ideal meat sourcing as follows: "If you go to the farm, you can experience how the animals are. You can say, 'Oh, look at that one. Kill it.' [Laughter.] It's not going to be frozen, it's not going to be transported a load of miles, so it's from pasture to your plate as close as possible." Even though very few participants described directly purchasing meat from farmers, this idealized vision echoed the sentiment and scene that many valorized. These farm experiences, whether rooted in reality or not, highlight the value placed on personal, experiential connections for building trust and positive emotions around meat consumption.

The visit-the-farm storyline came out clearly in a focus group with participants who were devoted to a meat-intensive diet. Aaron, a thirty-four-year-old who followed an all-meat diet, put it this way: "The closer to the farm, the better." Aaron described the advice he regularly dispenses to others as, "Ask around. Visit a farm. Try and buy local as much as possible." Aaron told us that there is one farm that he particularly likes because they offer farm tours. He said, "I don't know if it [farm visits] was so much intended as a marketing tool, but just offering to visit the farm, they seemed very open. . . . I think that's very disarming, in a good way, and encouraging." Markus, a twenty-year-old man who works as a meat-cutter, agreed, saying, "Like Aaron said, the closer to the farm, the better, honestly. If you can get a chance to visit the farm, it's great, right? Get to see what it's like." During our discussion, an interesting revelation surfaced: neither Aaron nor Markus had ever visited a farm. Despite this lack of direct experience, they expressed an emotional and ethical connection to the idea of touring these farms. They could imagine themselves—and other consumers—driving out of the city to witness the sustainable and humane practices involved in raising the animals that constitute their all-meat diets.

Participants envisioning their visits to happy meat farms drew on the power of imagery, and we were surprised to realize that visual representations of happy meat often held as much sway as textual descriptions or information. The importance of imagery was revealed in a Vancouver group that included Dan, a middle-aged British-Canadian man. Dan expressed significant ethical concerns about industrially produced meat, concerns that were shared by his wife, a life-long vegetarian. Dan said, "I love eating meat for sure . . . [but] I do have concerns these days when I see images of these factory farms. I don't like that. So, I am more conscious of my meat purchases these days. So I try to buy from smaller butchers that source their meat locally." The peace of mind that Dan experienced shopping at his local butcher was linked with a happy scene he encountered at the shop. Dan explained: "The butcher where I get most of my meat, they actually have a little iPad set up there with little videos of the animals frolicking at the farm. . . . You can see how well they're being treated." For Dan, seeing negative images of factory farms on social media had worked to moralize meat, making it a contentious food that he felt increasingly conflicted about enjoying. However, the happy meat images featured on the iPad at the butcher shop served as a counterbalance, helping Dan feel better about eating a food that he loved.

The trust Dan placed in his local butcher played a crucial role in shaping his positive assessment of eating meat. This sentiment resonated throughout our focus groups, with participants consistently highlighting the importance of a personal connection to the source of their meat, whether through farmers markets, local butchers, or even the simple fact of knowing the farmer's name. Max, in a Vancouver focus group, idealized local farmers who have a "little setup outside of their driveway," explaining that this is "really trustworthy." Hope, a Toronto woman in her twenties, explained that when it comes to sourcing ethical meat, "farmers markets, for me, would be the number-one closest source, and then butchers a second." Hope connected her preferences for direct purchasing to her childhood, recounting that, growing up, "we always bought a cow and had it in the freezer all winter, and we only bought meat from people that we knew." Tom, a thirty-three-year-old Torontonian who works in marketing, also fondly recounted his childhood experiences eating meat. To convey just how idyllic these experiences were, Tom told the group, "We practically knew the farmer's name."

This emphasis on personal connection reveals a deeper skepticism toward large-scale, industrial meat production. Participants assumed that small-scale farmers possessed greater knowledge and care for their animals and viewed corporate grocers and other intermediaries with suspicion, perceiving them as either ignorant of or dishonest about the origins of their meat. Although direct sourcing emerged as the highest status of happy meat consumption, it seemed like a rare occurrence in people's routine purchasing practices. As a result, local butchers emerged as a trusted alternative, fulfilling the desire for transparency and ethical sourcing.

This trust in butchers was evident in several focus group discussions. Rochelle, when asked about her confidence in her neighborhood butcher, simply laughed and said, "Because they tell me that they do [buy from reputable farmers] . . .and they have their farmers listed. You can ask them." In an animated Vancouver discussion where participants shared their mistrust of food labels, Max said that while "it's tough to use labels," he explained that he ideally purchases meat at a butcher—a figure he placed at the top of the "kind of hierarchy of where you try to go first" to buy ethical meat. According to Max, a butcher is "maybe sourcing his meat from farms that are ethical, and he'll usually say where he gets them from." Max's fellow participants agreed that they are more inclined to trust meat from a butcher, even in the absence of specific labels.

In a Toronto focus group, Ellen and Felipe concluded that rather than look for labels, it would be far more useful to "talk to the butcher and actually ask them questions." Meat from a butcher shop, participants explained, is more likely to have been lovingly cared for, living a "natural" life and sold by people with a discerning eye for quality and animal contentment. Even Mindy, who is happy to trust the labels at restaurants and grocery stores, said that she would ideally buy meat at "the small shop, the butcher shop." These accounts demonstrating the enduring appeal of a local butcher as a trusted source of ethical meat, especially if purchasing directly from a farmer feels impractical for routine food shopping.

The Emotional Ambiguities of Happy Meat

Happy meat scenes and images of happy animals being raised by caring farmers make people feel better about eating meat, but this doesn't mean that their concerns about industrially raised animals evaporate. Meat moralization is a process, not an end-state. Consumers are not dupes, mindlessly embracing every product that includes an image of an animal frolicking outside in a field. Happy meat storylines made people feel good about eating meat, but participants articulated a lingering uncertainty about whether those images truly reflected reality. Sometimes, consumers openly acknowledged that they didn't know much about the farm their meat came from.

Reacting to Dan's description of the iPad on the counter at the butcher, his friend Grant chimed in saying, "We love small butchers!" But then he added, "I probably take a shortcut" by relying on butchers and happy pastoral images for reassurance. Grant recalled one of those times at a butcher shop when he realized he was relying on images to feel good about his meat purchasing:

> I think about one of the places I buy meat. . . . So, I remember looking around to try to figure out where are you getting all this stuff. Eventually I saw . . . a big poster naming some local farm. I realize that I'm basically going off that one poster! That it is what it is. And [I'm assuming that] that nice-looking, whatever picture on it is accurate and reflects everything that's happening at that farm.

Grant's reflexivity about his meat sourcing makes clear that people don't necessarily take happy meat stories at face value. Many conscientious consumers we spoke with expressed awareness that stories about happy meat are often romanticized and entail a certain level of manipulation by producers, especially larger corporations (a topic we discuss further in Chapter 8). Yet at the same time that participants expressed skepticism, they also admitted that happy meat imagery was highly effective in making them feel good about their meat consumption, regardless of the underlying truth.

Let's return to the focus group introduced at the outset of this chapter involving Jun, Ivan, Media, and Peter. As the group critiqued the manipulation of supermarket and fast-food marketing campaigns that employ happy meat stories, Peter admitted that these kinds of corporate meat campaigns are "very effective with me." In a discussion of a conventional grocery store chain's "Free From" meat brand that has a farmer (Matt Fischer) on the package, Peter said:

> That farmer kind of looks like my friend I graduated with in 2003 from high school. . . . They make me feel good. Seeing Mr. Matt Fischer on this product, it makes me feel good, too. I'm like, "Oh, I'm helping a real person, not just a faceless conglomerate." Even though I know [the brand] . . . it is a large conglomerate. For me, they make me feel good about myself and my choices.

Ivan immediately agreed with Peter, saying: "I would say exactly the same. They use very good marketing. It makes it a more human focus. You're looking at a real person. You just envision him at his happy little farm running around." Madia, who earlier in the focus group highlighted the trust she gained from happy meat stories on a website for ordering meat directly from producers, felt similarly and foregrounded the redemptive role that happy meat stories play at her favorite fast-food chain: "For fast food, we have this conception that it's not the best food to have. But if I choose something like A&W, where they have better meat [meaning, more ethically treated], like you said, pay the extra two dollars, *I feel better about myself*" (emphasis ours).

Other focus group participants described a process of skeptically accepting the terms of happy meat stories so they can feel good about their meat choices, at least temporarily. Ella reflected openly about how she "probably relies on some blissful ignorance," even as she said she is "trying to make really informed choices." Ella stated a preference for buying meat from two small European neighborhood butchers, as she perceived that the meat from these butchers is more ethically sourced than that from a grocery store. Ella admitted, however, that this assumption is not based on concrete evidence:

I probably could admit that I'm maybe not thinking as much as I need to, in the sense that I think it's definitely more complicated than saying, "Butcher shop meat is good; grocery store meat is bad." I'm working along those lines, but I don't think that's actually probably true. I think there's probably lots of decent meat at some grocery stores. And probably not all butchers are pure, either. I think I just feel better going to a butcher and being quite confident that it's one link to a farmer . . . whereas the grocery store is just so much more complex.

Ella acknowledged that her operating assumption—that a butcher buys directly from a responsible farmer—is based more on feeling rather than established facts.[4] This mirrors a common thread in the happy meat narrative that we've observed: a reliance on a trust intermediary, in this case a butcher, to act as a mediator between consumers and producers. For Ella, the butcher provided reassurance, bolstering her decision to frequent her neighborhood butcher shop. In this narrative, the butcher becomes a symbol of transparency and ethical sourcing, even if the reality may be more complex. This reliance on trust and intuition highlights the emotional dimension of meat consumption, where consumers seek reassurance and a sense of moral rightness through the happy meat narrative, even if it involves spending more on meat than they might at the grocery store.

To close this chapter, we want to acknowledge the significant privilege embedded in the happy meat storyline. Not everybody can afford to pay a price premium based on a feeling that meat is ethically sourced—an issue that we explore more in Chapter 7 when we discuss the intersectional boundary work that occurs around the categories of cheap meat and happy meat. Ethical meat is generally regarded as more expensive, and cheap meat is viewed with suspicion. As Ivan succinctly noted, "If it's less expensive, you know it's not—the animal hasn't been as well maintained." Setting aside these class and boundary issues for now, we want to emphasize that participating in the happy meat storyline requires economic capital as well as cultural capital, promising social status and distinction to those who can fully and comprehensively engage with its ideals and practices. The ideal-typical happy meat purchase might involve buying a grass-finished cow directly from a farmer that you had a personal relationship with, one who is practicing sustainable pasture management and giving farm tours. It might then entail storing the meat in your chest freezer to be eaten at responsible intervals and in modest quantities.

While engaging with the happy meat storyline requires economic and cultural capital, the exercise and manifestation of privilege in our diverse focus group population was far from straightforward. The complex relationship between privilege and ethical meat stories is especially tangled now that the ideals and images of happy meat have become mass-market buzzwords. Elements of the happy meat storyline are visible in boutique butchers and upscale farmers markets—but these elements are also present in corporate supermarket meat aisles where "natural," "antibiotic-free," and "happy" meat products are commonplace. Indeed, some consumers we spoke with believed that corporate chains are the best places to acquire ethical meat. They found the happy meat narratives presented by large retailers more reliable and reassuring than those offered by smaller establishments. Peter said, "Before I was married, I always bought my meat from Costco, just because I trust Costco. I feel like they would do their due diligence on any product they have. But my wife, she goes to a butcher and talks to people over the counter." Living with his wife, who preferred to buy meat and ask questions at a local butcher, led Peter to withdraw some of the trust he was giving Costco, but it did not disappear entirely.

Peter's admission about the confidence he places in trusted corporate brands like Costco was a sentiment echoed in other focus groups. Multiple participants expressed faith in premium brands to sell an ethical form of meat. This makes some sense, especially given the common equation between higher prices, superior quality, and ethical practices. Ivan said he likes to shop at the British Columbia supermarket chain Save-On-Foods because, "I just thought they have better quality. A lot of their stuff, it's more expensive, but you can see it's better quality. You know that it's coming from a better environment." Although participants in this focus group recognized the value in getting meat directly from an independent butcher, especially a butcher who has a close relationship with a responsible farmer, there was also some fear and skepticism associated with this approach. Madia said, "For me, it's how much do I know about this place [the butcher]? You talked about Costco. We know the brand. We know what it's about [implying quality]." In contrast, Madia says, "a small butchery—how much do I know about how they process the meat? Where do they get it from? How is it handled?"

These elements of risk and uncertainty can also overlap with feelings of guilt and sadness that come with facing a whole animal, which is more likely to happen in a butcher shop than a supermarket grocery aisle. Peter tried to explain why it's hard for him to be completely on board with his wife's commitment to shopping at an independent butcher shop: "I feel like going to the butcher. . . . I feel like I'm getting anxiety from it." When asked to explain his anxiety, this conversation followed:

> Peter: It's weird. Like, I've been to farms, I've worked on farms. I've seen cows, I've petted cows, I've hugged cows. I've eaten meat my whole life. Maybe because I don't have much experience or confidence in doing that. Maybe I have anxiety or maybe even guilt, too.
> Ivan: Is it because it's a little bit too real with you seeing the dead animal hanging there?
> Peter: Yes, too real. Yes, you took the words out of my mouth. Too real.
> Ivan: It's not nicely packaged. It's just a corpse almost.
> Peter: Exactly. Yes. He picked the words out of my mouth there. Too real.

The interaction between Peter and Ivan shows themes of animal reminder disgust and guilt that can make people feel uncomfortable about eating meat and raise the meat paradox to the fore of their consciousness (see Chapter 3).[5]

Although it was a minority perspective, some participants in our focus groups shared Peter and Madia's wariness about small butcher shops and believed that shopping at a big corporate store is a safer and more reliable channel to purchase ethical meat. Aanchal, a middle-aged South Asian mother with a high income, was wary of the meat available at small shops: "I wouldn't go to the butcher at all because I don't trust them. All of the meat is sitting over there. . . . I don't want to go to the unbranded shops [because] whatever product they have, they actually have a long time. It's not that fresh." Aanchal did not purchase meat frequently, but when she did, she purchased meat at "brand-name stores" like major Canadian grocery chains and Costco: "We know that always everything is fresh, and it's branded." As documented in other research, some food shoppers, especially those with less economic or cultural capital, may find security in corporate branding, as large corporate brands connote reliability and consistency.[6] In addition, participants from specific ethnocultural backgrounds may have negative connotations of small meat shops, which contrast with the positive image of "hipster" butchers with iPads frequented by consumers like Dan and Grant.[7]

For consumers like Aanchal, corporate brands represent predictability and safety, alleviating concerns about meat quality and freshness they associate with smaller shops. The corporate "happy meat" narrative, with its promises of ethical sourcing and stringent quality control, resonated with several participants in her focus group. When Aanchal mentioned the large grocery chains where she likes to buy meat, Amanda, a low-income Filipino mother with a young child, agreed that high-end supermarkets were an appealing option. Amanda responded, "The quality is mostly the most important thing when you're buying food." When we asked the group where they would shop for meat if money were no object, Aanchal laughed and immediately said, "I would still go to Superstore," referencing a large Canadian grocery chain. This led to the following exchange with Mahir, a thirty-one-year-old Arab-Canadian father who worked in construction:

> Mahir: I wouldn't go to Superstore. Because Superstore, I don't know where the meat came from. I don't know anything about the meat. But I would probably go to a nice farm that I trust and see how the animals are raised.
>
> Aanchal: But it's hard to find a good farm market here in BC [British Colombia] area! You never know how they are treating the animals until you are going to stay there.

This exchange revealed both the cultural expansiveness of the happy meat storyline as well as the complex intersectional relationship between economic capital, cultural capital, and ethnocultural background. The happy meat story was pervasively articulated in our focus groups, but it was not universally endorsed. Although Mahir lived on a very low income, the happy meat story is evident in his desire to go directly to a farm so he can see how the animals are raised and trust that the meat is of high quality and from well-cared-for animals. He couldn't access this kind of meat in his daily life, but he still held it up as how he would ideally obtain meat—directly from a farmer. Aanchal had more financial flexibility than Mahir, but she was skeptical about getting happy meat directly from a farmer and did not automatically trust a small butcher; instead, she preferred a corporate brand (Superstore) that she would deputize to make good decisions for her about ethical meat.[8]

The happy meat storyline, with its direct access to a farmer, also held no appeal for Amanda, the low-income Filipino mom. Her focus was on purchasing high-quality, healthy meat to protect the health of her young daughter. This was clear when she told us that she had signed up to participate in the focus group in order to learn more about healthy foods for family meals. When we asked Amanda where she would buy meat if money was no object, she struggled with the question. After initially responding, "If I had a car, I would really like to go to Costco," Amanda gave another answer: "Walmart." At the mention of Walmart, Mahir reacted with shock and dismay, saying, "Wow." Amanda tried to explain herself: "I just say Walmart because, like to be honest, like it's hard to budget now because with the prices going up, I would probably just go Walmart." After the group encouraged her to think more expansively, Amanda responded by naming Save-On-Foods, the mainstream supermarket chain mentioned positively by Ivan: "Well, I guess Save-On-Foods. . . . Save-On-Foods has the highest quality. . . . It probably would be the best of the best."

Amanda displayed a limited range of cultural capital and economic capital when it came to the ethical meatscape. Her story suggests that the full expression of the happy meat storyline may have limited purchase with some low-income shoppers who are struggling to make ends meet. For Amanda, it would feel good to shop for meat products at mainstream supermarkets, and she trusts them to sell high-quality meats that are naturally raised, healthy, and perhaps organic. However, Mahir's response also speaks to the importance of not essentializing the experience of low-income consumers. Even with a limited income, Mahir articulated tremendous skepticism of corporate meat marketing, and he fully endorsed the happy meat narrative of shortening the commodity chain and having direct contact with animals on a "nice farm." This highlights the diversity of perspectives and priorities within the ethical meatscape, even among those facing similar financial constraints.

Conclusion

We end this chapter on happy meat where we began, with our focus group involving Jun, Ivan, Madia, and Peter. Each of these participants came to Canada from a different part of the world: China, Britain, Honduras, and Korea, respectively. The meanings they attributed to meat reflect their diverse histories, experiences, and ethno-cultural identities. However, despite these differences, they shared common concerns about the safety, sustainability, and ethics of industrialized meat. They all worried about the healthfulness of cheap meat, and they all expressed concerns about how the animals were being raised. Their overlapping concerns showcase common threads of a happier meat narrative—lush green fields, caring farmers, sustainable agricultural practices, happy animals, and quick, painless deaths.

These focus group participants hoped that by eating better-quality, happier meat, they could address concerns about industrialized meat and safeguard their families' health. Put simply, happy meat helped them address the moralization of meat that they were all grappling with. The happy meat narrative reinforced the belief that "good" meat, happy meat, can be a source of physical health and emotional well-being. Importantly, eating happier meat not only provided positive feelings but also offered an alternative to vegetarianism or veganism that allowed them to continue enjoying animal protein while assuaging their anxieties about its production and impact. Happy meat thus serves a dual purpose: it provides positive feelings associated with ethical consumption and justifies the continued inclusion of meat in our diets.

Indeed, vegetarians reading this chapter might wonder: if consumers are concerned about the ill effects of industrial agriculture, why not just give up eating meat? It is worth briefly reflecting on that question, drawing insight from Madia's perspective. As noted in the introduction, Madia was highly aware of the environmental impact of meat but admitted that she found it hard to cut down on her meat consumption:

> For me, it's a habit. It's the way I was raised. It's the way we have dinners. It's not a dinner if there's not some sort of meat that comes with it. If it's just carbs, or veggies, then we're missing something. I don't have anything against people who are vegetarian, it's just I don't think I would be full. How can you survive on tofu and things like that?

Madia told us that in her weekly meal planning, she always includes meat. She asked, "What does a day without meat look like?" and answered her own question by saying that "it feels very foreign" and "it will take me like twice the time to try to figure out what that might look like." The other focus group participants were highly sympathetic to Madia's concerns about meatless meals. They discussed what would happen if they tried to eliminate meat or even cut down on meat. Madia said that not only does this idea seem logistically difficult, but it would cause familial conflict: "Oh, they would not like it. The kids would not like it. They would be, 'Where's the chicken? Where's my chicken nuggets?' Plus, if it's just vegetarian, can I really do a whole week? Because wouldn't the veggies go bad? Or the salad? . . . I think it's more preparation. No, they would not like it."

Madia's experience was far from unique. Among our survey respondents, 51 percent agreed with the statement, "It would be difficult to eat less meat because I share meals with other people." One quarter of all survey respondents, and one-third of women, reported that if they were asked to reduce their meat consumption, they would be held back from doing so because their family would complain.

Even though the other focus group members came from very different cultural backgrounds and had kids of different ages, they all agreed with Madia that giving up meat would create difficulties—logistical and emotional—for family foodwork. Jun described a meatless meal as follows: "Oh, complaining. Last week, my twelve-year-old boy, he complained [about a meatless meal]. Two days he didn't eat meat, but we know that he ate fish, seafood, and tofu." Even with fish or seafood, Jun faced complaints from his twelve-year-old son. This experience not only caused him stress but also triggered a sense of loss over traditional Chinese plant-based dishes fading away in his children's palate: "I noticed gradually tofu disappear in my life now. I notice that. Very sad."

Peter described an imagined scenario that would follow a switch to meatless cooking in his household: "A lot of tears from my daughter. My wife would not be very happy with me. She'd probably say, 'Have you lost your mind?' Yes, it'd be very hard. I don't know what I would replace it with. I can't eat Beyond Meat every day." These accounts reveal the emotional and logistical hurdles of transitioning away from meat-centric meals, particularly in family contexts where dietary habits and preferences are deeply ingrained. Reducing or eliminating meat can be difficult because doing so disrupts daily routines and creates tension around family and cultural traditions.

These challenges highlight the tough emotional work that would be required to reduce meat intake and switch to more plant-based diets. This finding resonates with other research on family foodwork, which shows that attempting change—like asking male family members or children to help more with foodwork—can feel like more trouble than it's worth. In the memorable words of one participant in a study on family foodwork administered by Brenda Beagan and colleagues who was asked why she didn't ask her family to help out: "It's just easier for me to do it. . . . I would love to be able to change it, but is it worth the hassle for me?"[9] The analogue for participants in our study might be: *it's just easier for me to cook happy meat than no meat.* Reducing conflict and cooking meals that family members enjoy eating are key sources of emotional gratification—and cause significant stress when meals aren't perceived as delicious or satisfying.[10]

Cooking meat, especially within the happy meat narrative, offers more than just an enjoyable meal. By embracing this narrative, consumers can enjoy the familiar comforts of meat-based meals while simultaneously addressing moral concerns. This approach brings emotional gratification through the idea of supporting ethical farming, ensuring animal welfare, and promoting sustainability. It also mitigates potential familial conflict, alleviates guilt associated with meat consumption, and fosters a sense of contributing to the greater good.

In contrast, switching to plant-based meals can involve considerable emotional costs: soothing disappointed children and spouses, navigating potential cultural disconnects, and managing the stress and potential waste of uneaten food.[11] The happy meat story not only allows a reprieve from these challenges, allowing families to keep meat on the dinner table, but it promises the emotional payoff of providing a food that is liked and has positive emotions baked into it. Ultimately, for those able to participate in the happy meat narrative, cooking and consuming meat becomes more than a matter of taste or nutrition. It is part of a coping mechanism for navigating the increasingly fraught ethical landscape of food decision-making. This narrative deftly combines gustatory pleasure with a sense of ethical worthiness, providing a palatable compromise between longstanding dietary habits and contemporary moral concerns.

PART III   **Raising Happy Animals**

FIVE

The Reality Behind Raising Happy Meat: Beyond a Good/Evil Binary

IN THIS CHAPTER, WE explore the complexities of raising "happy meat," drawing on our interviews and observations with producers who grapple with balancing animal welfare and the practicalities of farming. We begin by examining the pervasive "happy meat" binary, which contrasts idyllic images of free-roaming animals with the grim realities of factory farming. This binary, while appealing in its simplicity, tends to obfuscate the nuanced realities of ethical animal husbandry. In this section of the book, we use examples from pig, chicken, and beef farming to explore the challenges producers face meeting consumer expectations while respecting the vitality and unique needs of these animals.

Ultimately, we advocate for a deeper understanding of the ethical meat landscape, one that moves beyond simplistic binaries of good and evil and embraces the complexities inherent in raising animals for food. Our point is not simply that most consumers do not appreciate the challenges of raising animals for food—although that is certainly true. Indeed, we reveal some of our own naiveté and embarrassing misconceptions about pigs, chickens, and cattle in the pages that follow. Rather than centering meat eaters' ignorance, we aim to explore what gets lost in the middle of a consumer imaginary based on a binary of good and evil.

To carry out this exploration, we target the tension between a happy meat imaginary and the lived realities facing producers who must keep animals alive and safe while ensuring their farms' financial viability. We suggest that what gets missed in the dualistic good/evil framing of meat are the complexities of animals' needs and desires as well as the creative and resourceful way farmers respond to these challenges. In the middle ground, we will see that animals have a vital presence on farms, acting in ways that complicate farmers' best-laid plans and challenge consumers' idealized notions of farm animal happiness and freedom.

Questioning the Commonplace Happy Meat Binary

We begin our discussion of meat production by briefly exploring consumer alienation from meat sources. While consumers might try to ignore the origins of meat, this ignorance is rarely complete. Instead, our data reveal an ever-evolving meat imaginary, a dynamic and often dualistic understanding of how meat is produced. The meat imaginary is not a static story of ignorance but a kind of two-sided coin with contrasting narratives. On the dark side of the coin, consumers imagine industrial animal agriculture as a grim landscape involving crowded, cramped conditions and suffering animals. In a German study, psychologist Johannes Simon and colleagues described how consumers connected factory farms with concentration camps and described common associations such as "large numbers of animals, extremely long barns, heaps of meat, and everything hidden away behind closed doors."[1] if you saw the celebrated Korean film *Okja*, you can likely recall the dystopian images of slaughterhouse confinement and the plight of the titular character, *Okja*, a beloved super-pig set to be slaughtered by an evil meat corporation.[2]

Simultaneously, consumers conjure an idealized counternarrative: happy meat produced from animals that roam free in lush, green pastures. The consumers in Simon's study described "small family farms with a limited number of animals, operating as in the 'good old days,'" where animals lead a happy life. This duality—the juxtaposition of industrial horror and pastoral bliss—illustrates that the contemporary food disconnection stems not from complete repression or ignorance but from a dichotomous perception of animal agriculture as either wholly good or entirely bad.

This happy meat binary can be conceptualized as a narrative with two contrasting scenes. The first, "sad meat" scenes feature pigs or other livestock that are confined, tortured, and treated with unimaginable cruelty.[3] These images of animal confinement and cruelty are featured in viral videos, films, and documentaries, and they fuel the imaginations of meat eaters and vegetarians alike.[4] These scenes often involve a struggle to help an animal achieve freedom and avoid death. The second, "happy meat" scenes portray animals living comfortably in bucolic settings or otherwise enjoying the freedoms that humans prize so much for themselves. To illustrate the contrast, think of the film franchise *Babe*, where a lovable pig escapes confinement—as well as certain death—and goes on wild adventures.[5] We also see this plotline in E. B. White's beloved children's novel *Charlotte's Web*, in which the pig Wilbur, aided by a savvy spider named Charlotte, avoids slaughter and is free to live out his life with his friends in the barn.[6]

This stark dichotomy between happy/free and sad/confined animals, often portrayed in popular culture, was not merely a theoretical construct; it also surfaced vividly in our focus group discussions. In one group, Mahir, an Arab-Canadian father living in Vancouver, gave a lengthy stream-of-consciousness commentary on factory farming that temporarily silenced everyone in the group. He spoke in conspiratorial tones: "There's a lot of things that we don't know, behind the scenes, what they do and how these animals grow." He then painted a picture of "thousands and thousands of chickens" that are "sleeping on each other," saying, "I think that makes it very unethical and dangerous for us to consume that kind of meat, right?" Mahir then shifted to speak about animal slaughter: "They have to get the animals to go through the death process. . . . It's just, like, painful. It's uncalled for. And it's just because some greedy people . . . just to feed ourselves, basically! I think this is a major point that makes our meat unethical." Mahir's negative meat scene featured oppressed animals, manipulative capitalists, and selfish eaters.

On the flip side, focus group participants conveyed clear and consistent ideas of what a happy farm animal looked like. For example, in one group, Malwina, a Polish-Canadian woman in her sixties, described a scene of idyllic, happy chickens raised by her grandmother: "When my grandparents, who were farmers, grow animals like chickens, they just walk out in the front of the house, free on the grass. They eat worms, grass, and other things." She continued, emphasizing the care provided: "They also eat feed, which they get from my grandmother. All other animals, like pigs, also have enough space and also get care from [my grandparents]." Malwina concluded by affirming the ethical treatment of the animals: "They were treated the . . . correct way."

Malwina and Mahir's emotionally laden comments speak to the affective highs and lows that accompany contrasting scenes of happy/free and sad/confined animals. Conventional meat production invokes upsetting feelings and images of unnecessary animal suffering, as vividly described by Mahir. In contrast, the concept of "happy meat" can be a source of positive emotions, such as pride and a sense of moral correctness. This is evident in Malwina's account of farm animals that were treated "correctly" and allowed to roam "free on the grass."

Ethically oriented producers and corporations are aware of consumer preferences for meat that comes from free-ranging, happy animals. The happy animal prototype is evident in marketing materials like a paper insert we found in a carton of "Vital Farms" eggs featuring "Eager Emmy," the "Bird of the Month." She is a handsome red hen posing in front of a fallen tree, and the accompanying text emphasizes her daily adventures in the fresh air and sunshine, suggesting a joyful and fulfilling life. Not only does Emmy get to live "simply, and beautifully," but she also offers inspiration to the consumers who eat her eggs, delivering messages like the following: *Get outside more. Socialize with friends. Engage in self-care. Be yourself. Make sure eating is always pleasurable.* The positive depiction of Emmy the chicken speaks to the strong cultural value placed on happiness and freedom for farm animals, echoing Miele's observations about the marketing of free-range birds in the U.K. as inherently more "friendly" due to their perceived greater freedom.[7]

The positive imagery surrounding Eager Emmy serves a dual purpose: it not only assuages consumer concerns about animal welfare by depicting a seemingly idyllic life, but it also leverages a deeper cultural yearning for happiness, capitalizing on what Sara Ahmed calls "happy objects."[8] As Ahmed notes, the promise of "happy objects" (like Emmy the chicken) extends beyond present-day satisfaction—they are aspirational symbols imbued with positive affect and social value. As such, happy objects can be deployed to justify and legitimize practices or products, promising a brighter future and a sense of moral righteousness. By associating "happy chickens" with feelings of future contentment, this marketing strategy effectively imbues both the animals themselves *and the act of consuming animal products* with the promise of happiness. This emotional appeal, rooted in the aspiration for a better future, is a potent tool for shaping consumer choices and cultivating a more positive perception of the ethical meatscape. In this way, the image of a happy chicken stands in stark contrast to the misery imbued in popular depictions of factory farming and offers a hopeful alternative.

However, this emotionally charged binary raises questions about what gets overlooked in this simplistic framing. What purpose does this binary serve, and what is the allure of eating a "happy" animal? Psychological research on meat consumption, as discussed in Chapters 3 and 4, suggests that eating happy meat can alleviate negative feelings and cognitive dissonance associated with the meat paradox—the tension between loving animals and participating in animal suffering and death. However, a sociological perspective reveals that the appeal of happy animals extends beyond any individual psyche and is deeply embedded in social dynamics. As Ahmed's concept of "happy objects" suggests, these idealized representations of animals can gain social value and be used to justify and legitimize meat consumption, potentially masking the ethical complexities inherent in animal agriculture. In other words, the "happy animal" narrative can function as a powerful social tool, enabling consumers to reconcile their enjoyment of meat with their ethical concerns while potentially masking the ethical complexities and externalities of animal agriculture.

Indeed, we suggest that a bifurcated framing of meat as either "happy" or "unhappy" works to obscure the nuanced realities of farming. Binaries offer clarity in an ambiguous world but also tend to obscure the middle ground occupied by farmers who must balance animal welfare and financial viability. While no one desires animals suffering in cramped cages, the reality for most farmers lies in the muddy middle ground between free-living farm "pets" and factory farm dystopia. For example, farmers routinely use various confinement techniques—fences, crates, pens, barns—not out of cruelty but as essential tools for animal management. In our research, the consistent disconnect between consumer expectations and the realities of farming raised questions about the degree of confinement that is ethically acceptable and whether consumers could ever fully grasp the complexities of raising animals for food.

As food scholars have long emphasized, most eaters are profoundly alienated from food production.[9] Farmer and author Wendell Berry made the famous pronouncement that "eating is an agricultural act," but he also realized that "most eaters are no longer aware that this is true."[10] Food alienation is perhaps most profound when it comes to meat-eating.[11] This is not an accident. As food scholar Warren Belasco writes, the "main thrust" of the meat industry "over 150 years has been to insulate consumers from any contact with the disassembly of warm-blooded mammals into refrigerated, plastic-wrapped chops and patties."[12] Consumers' alienation from meat production has many consequences, including collective ignorance about what is involved in raising animals and producing meat.[13] While some consumers may have experience growing fruits or vegetables, very few have firsthand knowledge of raising or slaughtering farm animals.

Animal confinement—keeping animals indoors, often in cramped quarters with limited space to move—is a key issue that highlights consumer alienation from the food system. A concern about confinement frequently arose in our focus group discussions and is a central issue for many consumers wary of industrial agriculture. Our survey results further underscore these concerns: 57% of respondents believe it's wrong for animals to spend their lives indoors, and 70% find it unethical for animals to live in crowded conditions. Notably, over 95% of these respondents consume meat, revealing a stark example of the meat paradox. Although most meat eaters express discomfort with confinement in conventional industrial agriculture, it is not clear that they are able to easily align these ethical concerns with their dietary choices.

The producers we interviewed are certainly aware of consumers' concerns about animal confinement, especially in industrialized animal agriculture. Their own practices for raising animals were often shaped by an aversion to industrialized methods of raising large numbers of animals in confined spaces. In their farming practices, they sought to do things differently—to give animals freedom, space, and time outdoors to express their natural behaviors. However, caring for animals does not translate into a simple or straightforward prescription for *how* farm animals should live happy lives with as much free movement as possible. Moreover, pigs, chickens, and cattle are distinctly different species, and while they have some common ways of living happily, they also have some important physiological and behavioral differences.

It's an especially difficult matter given that most farm animals can't survive independently and have been bred to live alongside humans. It is an obvious point but one worth emphasizing: the pigs, chickens, and cows we eat have been domesticated through human intervention over centuries. For that reason, it is perhaps not surprising that many farmers we spoke with emphasized how animals benefit from confinement, which is part of the care they give to animals. When it came to confinement, farmers had to balance competing objectives: a generally felt desire to let animals express their natural instincts (rooting in the mud, grazing in grassy fields, pecking for bugs and grubs outdoors) while also keeping animals safe, comfortable, and healthy. Overlaid against these challenges, farmers must consider how to keep their operations profitable and their prices accessible to consumers. Allowing animals freedom of movement is important, but this emphasis can occlude attention to other important factors like the absence of stress, extreme weather, hunger, thirst, or injury—factors that might paradoxically be heightened in free-range, outdoor animal husbandry.[14]

The consumer aversion to animal confinement, however, doesn't translate into a clear vision of what constitutes a "happy" life for farm animals. This returns us to the broader question raised above: what gets missed in a binary, happy/sad, good versus evil framing of happy meat? This dualistic framing tends to oversimplify the reality of both farmers and animals and can perpetuate a kind of othering where agents are polarized as either objects of disgust or idealized creatures.[15] Farm animals are either depicted as idyllic, unconfined creatures leading "natural" lives or suffering victims of abuse in factory farms. Similarly, farmers can be either idealized as "good" actors working outside the industrial system or "bad" actors who prioritize profit over animal welfare and sustainability. These binaries obscure two crucial aspects: 1) the inherent aliveness of farm animals, their agency, and their complex needs beyond mere freedom from confinement, and 2) the nuanced and often challenging relational work of caring for farm animals, which involves balancing their welfare with practical considerations and economic realities.

To better understand the first factor, which involves the aliveness and liveliness of farm animals encountered in daily farm work, we turn to political theorist Jane Bennett's concept of vitality in her book *Vibrant Matter*.[16] Bennett encourages us to perceive the material world, including animals and other elements like trash, metal, or food, not as passive or inert but as possessing vitality—the inherent capacity to act and shape events and other beings. This aligns with a new materialist perspective that recognizes the physical world as an active, dynamic force that interacts with both human and nonhuman actors. This shift toward acknowledging the agency of the natural world, including animals, is a crucial corrective to a traditional mechanistic view that often frames the nonhuman world as passive and inert. It allows us to better appreciate the ways in which animals act and exercise a kind of "proto-agency."[17] Animals are not merely passive objects acted upon by humans; they have their own drives, desires, and behaviors that influence their environment and interactions. Animals have abilities and instincts that they can follow in the service of managing their needs and vulnerabilities. This is particularly important in the context of meat and animal agriculture, where animals are often viewed through the relatively static lens of idyllic happiness or abject victimhood. By recognizing farm animal vitality, we open ourselves up to a more complex and nuanced understanding of the ethical meatscape, one that acknowledges and investigates the agency of the animals involved. This farm animal vitality is precisely what we aim to illustrate in the pages below.

The second factor that is obfuscated in a happy/sad meat binary is the challenging relational work of caring for animals. In a binary, happy/sad way of thinking, farmers are either villains overseeing animal cruelty or romanticized heroes. This oversimplified view of farm labor fails to acknowledge the complex reality of raising animals and disregards the role that animals play in shaping farmers' everyday realities, emotions, and identities.[18] Furthermore, it disregards the agency of animals and the profound impact they have on farmers' lives, emotions, and identities. As sociologists Colin Jerolmack and Iddo Tavory emphasize, nonhuman actors are not merely passive objects; they actively shape our social selves and *relationships*.[19] In the context of meat production, the happy/sad meat dichotomy tends to overlook the intricate, often emotional interactions between farmers and animals. Farm animals, with their own proto-agency and vitality, can disrupt the most well-intentioned farming strategies, evoking a range of emotions in farmers, from frustration and annoyance to affection and deep attachment. This emotional dimension is a crucial part of farm life, where human-animal relationships are central to the work of raising animals for food.[20] Farms are, in essence, hybrid spaces where humans and animals coexist, organized to produce meat more efficiently and reliably than hunting animals in the wild. The complex dynamics of these relationships, overlooked in simplistic narratives, are crucial for understanding the ethical considerations of meat production.

Learning from Producers

To ground these theoretical concepts—animal vitality and human-animal relationships—in the lived experiences of farmers, we turn to our interviews and site visits with ethical meat producers across Canada. These producers, raising "happy" pigs, chickens, and cattle, offer valuable insights into the complexities of balancing animal welfare with the practicalities of farming. In this chapter and the next, we discuss what we learned during our interviews with happy meat producers, most of which took place at their farms. The visits to the farms were extremely useful for learning more about how animals are raised. We could see the spaces where animals lived and how they were cared for. Being in the same spaces as the animals provoked many questions, which we were able to pose to producers and that would otherwise never have occurred to us to ask.

To be clear, our goal is not to prescribe specific guidelines for raising happy animals, nor to definitively measure their happiness. Instead, we aim to illuminate the nuanced realities of ethical animal husbandry, showcasing the perspectives of producers and the undeniable agency of the animals themselves. By examining the spectrum of practices within the ethical meat sector, we move beyond the simplistic binary of "happy" versus "sad" animals, revealing the diverse ways that farmers navigate the challenges of providing a good life for farm animals while also meeting the demands of production and consumer expectations. Further, we explore how animal vitality shapes relationships with producers—and also prevents farmers from giving animals the life of unfettered freedom imagined by some consumers.

As meat eaters ourselves, we are not immune to the cultural narratives that frame farm animals and meat within a happy/sad binary. Like many consumers, we began this research with limited knowledge of how animal vitality shapes the work of meat producers and a simplified understanding of the complexities of animal agriculture. In the following pages, we reveal some of our own learning process, sharing how our perspectives evolved as we engaged with farmers and their animals. For each animal, we acknowledge areas of ignorance and ambiguity, observations that are offered in the spirit of researcher reflexivity. We also aim to avoid creating a false dichotomy between "omniscient researchers" and "clueless consumers," or between romanticized rural producers and dimwitted urbanite eaters.

Our time spent with meat producers revealed a significant truth: the need for greater transparency in meat production. While not necessarily versed in academic food studies, the producers we spoke with were deeply concerned about the implications of consumer alienation from food production. They believe that consumers need a clearer understanding of how animals are raised for food. Farmers are keenly aware that most consumers know little about food production, especially animal products, and they shared many stories highlighting this disconnect. For instance, chicken farmers often had to explain that a "grass-fed" chicken would be malnourished, as chickens are omnivores requiring a diverse diet that includes grains and insects. Another farmer recalled a shopper at a farmers market asking if the lambskin on the table had "hurt the animal," to which the farmer replied, "No, because the animal is dead." Other farmers described the general frustration they experience at farmers markets when consumers often complain about food prices or haggle for a deal, a pattern that made them feel deeply devalued. These and other stories illustrate the frustrations farmers experience when faced with consumer ignorance and lack of appreciation for the complexities of their work.

A common refrain among the producers we interviewed was the importance of consumer education about the realities of raising animals for food. When asked about improving the food system, farmer responses emphasized the value of direct connections between consumers and farmers: "get to know a farmer" or "visit a farm." These answers make intuitive sense. Despite increased concern about factory farms, most consumers know little about the practicality of raising farm animals. This lack of understanding can lead to misconceptions about farmers' choices, such as those regarding animal confinement, and an underestimation of the challenges involved in producing ethical meat at scale. For example, many urban consumers might not appreciate how a farmer needs to keep pigs in a barn so that they don't root up and destroy a valuable pasture. Consumers might like to imagine a pig or a chicken roaming free, making it hard to appreciate how factors like long winters, slim profit margins, and fluctuating commodity prices necessitate housing animals indoors—even on farms committed to "natural" methods. Before embarking on this research, we too were unaware that "naturally raised" or organic chickens and pigs often spend most, if not all, of their short lives enclosed in a barn due to these economic and environmental pressures—and we were shocked to learn how short these lives are (six to eight weeks for chickens raised for meat).

As urbanites residing in large, congested cities, we recognize that expecting a significant portion of consumers to visit farms and establish meaningful relationships with farmers is unrealistic. As such, our aim is to help bridge this knowledge gap by sharing some of the stories and experiences of the farmers we interviewed. We explore the realities, struggles, and contradictions of farm life, highlighting the labor, emotional investment, and difficult choices involved in raising animals for food. These details might seem trivial from the perspective of a well-fed city dweller, but we believe that animal-specific details are an essential element of appreciating the challenges posed by the ethical meatscape—challenges of scale, access, affordability, and labor. When we visited farms, we saw many animals roaming freely, but we also saw many farm animals in pens—animals that are in some ways fragile, difficult to raise, and in need of expensive inputs (e.g., organic feed), huge amounts of farm labor (e.g., moving chicken pens), and significant reserves of emotional labor (e.g., the stress of discovering dead animals). Expanding knowledge of these complexities and challenges is an important part of reshaping our collective consciousness of meat consumption and challenging the problematic, ubiquitous assumption that meat should be cheap, plentiful, pain-free, and always available. Happy meat has a high price tag for consumers, but it also incurs a high cost for farmers, who must invest significant capital, labor, and emotional energy to raise animals.

In the spirit of reducing our collective alienation from meat production, in the following pages we present key findings on the realities of raising animals. We center the animals in our presentation, highlighting their distinctive attributes and characteristics. Beginning with pigs, then moving to chickens and cattle in the next chapter, we remain attentive to each animal's species-specific vitality and the varying care requirements they demand from farmers. For each animal, we provide context on their value as a commodity, share personal observations from our fieldwork, and most importantly, amplify the voices of farmers themselves. Our focus is on stories that showcase animal vitality as well as the important human-animal relationships required to raise happy meat.

The Vitality of Pigs and the Caring Work of Pig Farmers

Fieldwork Reflection: Sadness, Satisfaction, and Meaning

All of us grew up eating bacon (except Emily) and never questioned the normalcy of eating pork. One of the big surprises of our research was the charisma of pigs and their piggy tendencies. They literally like to make a mud pit and then lie around in the mud. In fact, their powerful tendency to dig and root can lead to problems with pasture management, as they can quickly turn a grassy patch of land into an uprooted mess. We were also struck by pigs' intelligence and the strong bonds they make with their caregivers, coming over for scratches and rubs. We will never forget the image of one pig playing with a toy ball, as a farmer fed grape leaves to his pig friends.

This farmer also described how he liked to set up a sprinkler on hot days for the pigs to run through.

Baby pigs are particularly adorable. We have fond memories of cuddling Pickles, a sickly piglet that one farmer, Kim, cared for in a box in her kitchen. Another farmer, Melissa, spoke about how she tucked a fragile newborn piglet into her nightgown to keep it warm and alive, and later became deeply attached to that pig. She would drive around with the pig on her Gator (a small John Deere farm vehicle). She was devastated when, one day, the pig fell off and was crushed under the wheels of the Gator. Melissa teared up while telling us this story.

When baby pigs grow into adults, caring for them takes more work, and they can become intimidating—especially the boars—to farm kids and adults. On Sheila and Derek's family farm in Alberta, the kids told us about how happy they were on slaughter day. Finally, they could send the pigs to market and be rid of their time-intensive chores! Through this fieldwork, we were struck by the satisfaction that comes with raising pigs, but also the challenges of raising a smart animal that will weigh hundreds of pounds when it is time to go to the slaughterhouse.

Pork production has steadily increased since the 1960s, peaking in 2021 at over 120 million tons globally. A significant portion of these animals are raised in China, which produced over 452 million pigs in 2023 and where pigs are raised in multi-story buildings that look, from the outside, like office buildings.[21] The vast majority of global pork production occurs in industrial settings around the world, operations that are a far cry from the small-scale farms we visited.[22] The stark contrast between industrial facilities and the farms we observed highlights a crucial point: only a tiny fraction of the world's pork comes from small-scale farms where pigs are raised outdoors. Beyond this contrast in scale lies a stark difference in emotional responses to pigs and pork production. Juxtaposed with the grim scenes of large numbers of pigs confined in barns, scenes that consumers frequently evoke when imagining industrial pork production, in our fieldwork we saw pigs lying in the mud, playing with balls, rooting in the dirt, and walking over to get scratches. This section explores the complexities of raising happy pigs, mapping out some of the challenges and rewards of working with this particular animal.

FIGURE 5.1: These heritage breed pigs were raised entirely outdoors.

Source: Author photo.

Indoor/Outdoor Pigs

Consumers often envision a carefree outdoor existence for all farm animals, including pigs. While most producers we interviewed believed that pigs *could* live outdoors, not all agreed that this was the most beneficial or practical approach. Frank, a producer of niche pork products highly prized by urban chefs and foodies, offered a unique perspective. He had experience raising both commodity and heritage pigs (e.g., Berkshires, Tamworths, wild boars) in different environments. Frank firmly believed that traditional pink commodity pigs were ill suited for outdoor life, stating, "They'll get a sunburn. You can't put them outside."[23] Frank raised his commodity pigs in an enclosed barn, which he considered a significant improvement over conventional hog production.[24] For approximately six months, these pink pigs lived out their lives in an enclosed space on slatted floors. Frank explained that his set-up allowed for small groupings of animals that could socialize and avoid aggression. He described it as a "familiar environment," and his wife, Ingrid, noted that it was created from an old barn: "It's not just steel and stuff like that, or plastic. So, they're not feeling totally out of character when they're there." Frank's perspective on animal ethics centered on "humanely raising animals in an environment where they thrive," which for him did not necessitate outdoor access.

Other farmers we spoke with, disagreeing with Frank's approach, raised a wide variety of pigs (including pink commodity pigs) outdoors or with outdoor access. However, this wasn't always straightforward due to challenges like pasture management, weather conditions, and land access. The complexities of raising pigs outdoors were evident in our interview with Dale and Sandra, ecologists and dedicated environmentalists. Their mixed farm prioritized land conservation and regeneration, with plans to establish diverse perennial grasses and trees for livestock feed, including a chestnut forest for pigs. However, during our winter visit, their pigs were housed in a barn. When asked about pasture management, Dale and Sandra admitted that they were struggling to integrate pigs into their farm system due to their natural rooting behavior. Dale explained, "They do tear up a lot of stuff. And sometimes it's instantaneous . . . maybe they'll munch on pasture for a week, and then they sort of get bored, and they start to turn it up." This destructive potential led them to avoid using their best pastures for pigs and highlighted the ongoing challenge of balancing pig welfare with sustainable land management. Dale concluded, "We haven't figured it out, because [pigs] can be *really* destructive."

The vitality of pigs—their unpredictable nature and their rooting behavior—posed a significant challenge, even for farmers like Dale and Sandra who had extensive experience in sustainable agriculture. This challenge was amplified on farms with limited pasture, especially in areas with expensive land. Consequently, many farmers we visited opted to keep pigs in barns or shelters with limited outdoor access, often in muddy enclosures rather than grassy fields. While technically offering outdoor access, these setups don't align with the "pasture-raised" label, as the pigs aren't integrated into a farm's pasture and grazing system. It was, however, clear to us that, aside from a few bucolic examples, the living conditions of most pigs we saw did not readily conform to the stereotypes presented by the happy/sad binary.

Free-Living Bush Pigs

Raising pigs on pasture requires a balance between the number of pigs and the available land. This is a balance we observed on only a few farms, like Sheila and Derek's in an area of central Alberta where land prices are relatively low. These "bush pigs" are raised with relative independence on a vast expanse of uncultivated land. Their story of raising bush pigs illustrates the complexities of raising pigs in the open air, showcasing the animals' vitality as they interact with the natural environment.

Sheila started the story by telling us how they would buy "weaners" from a neighbor and introduce them to the outdoors in the spring. She laughingly clarified that "weaners" meant newly weaned piglets—not "wieners," or hot dogs. Initially, they employed Joel Salatin's portable pen method, a popular technique that involves movable pens that provide animals access to fresh pasture while naturally fertilizing the land as the animals move.[25] Unfortunately, these pigs contracted pneumonia, which their vet guessed came from exposure to bacteria carried by birds scavenging at a nearby industrial farm's "dead pile." The necessary use of antibiotics to save the pigs compromised their "naturally raised" status and reduced their market value, prompting Sheila to exclaim, "We're supposed to be antibiotic-free, so we're like, 'Well, this kind of screws up our whole mantra!'"[26]

As a new strategy, Sheila and Derek decided to forgo the labor-intensive portable pens and grant the pigs more autonomy, allowing them to essentially "sink or swim" out in the bush. They transitioned to raising heritage breeds using a "farrow to finish" model in which the pigs lived and reproduced outdoors, finding shelter from the harsh Alberta winters in a straw bale structure.

As Sheila's said, "In the middle of January, they farrow [give birth] out there in a big straw stack. They do their thing. We give them the space to do it. And then we catch the babies and eat them. [Laughter.]" While this strategy worked for their family and their farm, it required ample land and presented unique challenges. Sometimes pigs could not be easily caught, creating problems of varying pig size due to unsynchronized births. Additionally, they reported that larger, older pigs are difficult or even dangerous to catch and transport for slaughter. Sheila and Derek's reliance on a single restaurant specializing in whole animal butchery was crucial, as the chef could accommodate the non-standard pig sizes they were delivering.

Another element of animal vitality that Sheila and Derek had to manage was the timing of boar slaughter. To avoid the trauma of castration and un-desirable "boar taint," which imparts an unpleasant flavor to the meat (a taste that Sheila described as reminiscent of "armpit"), they aimed to slaughter boars young, before they reached puberty. However, if a boar matured, they would keep it for personal consumption, with Sheila humorously noting, "We've had a few that were a little rank. I'm like, 'Good thing we didn't send that one [to the restaurant].'"

In sum, while the bush pigs on Sheila and Derek's farm enjoyed relative freedom compared to CAFO pigs, their unique model, requiring vast land and a niche market for nonstandard pigs, is not easily replicated. This approach, with its reliance on ample space and a flexible chef loyal to their product, oper-ates at a small scale. At the time of our interview, they had fifteen pigs on their land. This is a far cry from larger operations we visited that raised hundreds of pigs annually—let alone the tens of thousands of pigs raised in industrial set-tings. The story of the Alberta bush pigs underscores the appeal of this niche product but also highlights the limitations and tradeoffs associated with rais-ing small numbers of relatively free animals.

Raising Happy Pigs in a Barn?

The larger-scale pig farmers we interviewed found it impractical to raise an-imals on pasture, opting instead for barn-based systems. One such example was Trent's West Coast pig barn, frequently praised by chefs, butchers, and fellow producers for its exemplary practices. When we visited Trent's pig barn, we were struck by how spacious and clean it was; it had openable side panels so that the pigs could experience the wind, fresh air, and natural light. Despite these positive aspects, it's important to acknowledge that these pigs still spent the majority of their lives confined in a semi-enclosed barn. Trent explained that raising his entire herd of pigs on pasture was unfeasible due to limited land access and the pigs' natural rooting behavior. Our observations across various farms suggested that while raising pigs entirely outdoors is possible, it's often limited to small-scale operations raising dozens, rather than hundreds or thousands, of pigs. Even Trent's operation, considered larger by our standards, is a very minor player in the market. In Trent's words, "We're very small. [The province] has got quite a few people [raising pigs]. We're selling very little pork in the context of how much pork is consumed every day." Trent was acutely aware of the challenges of scaling up pork operations to meet broad consumer demand but felt his current scale allowed him to prioritize animal welfare and responsible farming practices.

The different practices for raising "happy pigs" invites the question of how to determine a reasonable amount of confinement. Who decides how much freedom a pig needs to be considered a happy pig? Our observations suggest that outside of formal certification systems, farmers have significant discretion. Their judgment, resources, and relationships with the animals influence the degree of freedom and movement allowed. Trent, for instance, had a personal philosophy guiding his practices. He prioritized limited outdoor access for young, energetic pigs, who liked to run "around like racehorses out there," while accepting confinement for older ones he described as "fat and lazy." Although Trent loved to see young pigs running freely in the field, he was not bothered by confining the older pigs in the barn. For Trent, the ideal, as far as animal welfare was concerned, "would be getting everybody outside at some point in their life. And not too squished."

Trent was aware of official animal welfare guidelines and strived to exceed the space requirements set by the British Columbia SPCA. However, he opted out of any formal certification processes, disagreeing with their top-down approach and its limitations. Instead, he preferred to determine what constituted a humane life for his pigs based on his own judgment and experience. This involved a degree of trial and error, as he learned to adapt to the pigs' vitality and preferences. Trent told us a story that illustrated the dynamic nature of the relationship he had with the animals. In his words, "We went through a thing not that long ago where I had too many in one pen. Oh, my God." He explained that because of the increased crowding, the pigs' "behavior really changes. Like the barn was noisier. We would go in there to clean out these feeders and waters and make sure everything's working, and they were biting

us. . . . We went over some tipping point of confinement." Trent's approach illustrates the dynamic and evolving nature of ethical animal husbandry. Conditions for animals can vary considerably, even on the same farm at different
times. His story also highlights the importance of farmers' individual judgment, ongoing learning, and responsiveness to the animals' needs in creating
a happy life for pigs, even within the confines of a barn.

Others Forms of Confinement and the Issue of Piglet Squish

Not all producers share Trent's perspective on the necessity of giving pigs
some amount of outdoor access. Some, like Frank, believe commodity pigs are
better suited for indoor living to limit sun exposure and prevent disease. Jenn,
another Ontario farmer with a background in conventional pig farming, also
holds this view. Adapting to evolving market demands, Jenn now operates
three barns: a conventional pig barn, a certified humane barn, and an organic
barn system. While each barn features distinct infrastructure and costs (e.g.,
straw bedding in the certified humane barn versus slatted floors in the conventional barn), Jenn views them all as integral to the food system, each offering unique advantages and disadvantages. She doesn't see any of these systems
as inherently inhumane; rather, she recognizes them as different approaches
to confinement, each with its own merits and drawbacks.

Jenn's pragmatic perspective on pig farming was shaped by her lifelong
experience on farms as well as her understanding of animal behavior. She surprised us by explaining that she believed that the "certified humane" system,
which allows sows more freedom to move during farrowing, to be potentially
less humane than the conventional system due to the increased risk of piglet
crushing: "When you give a sow . . . more freedom to move around, she's going
to squish more piglets." Jenn defended the use of farrowing crates, arguing
that they are a temporary measure to protect piglets and ensure their survival.
She attributed consumer opposition to farrowing crates to a lack of firsthand
experience with the realities of pig farming, stating, "Probably most consumers on their Saturday mornings don't pick up dead piglets out of pens, so they
don't see and feel the difference." Her perspective highlights the disconnect
between consumer ideals and the practical challenges farmers face balancing
animal welfare with production goals.

Other farmers we interviewed echoed Jenn's story about the vitality of
mother pigs and their tendency toward "piglet squish." Many spoke openly
and pragmatically about preventing piglet deaths. Some, like Jenn, used

FIGURE 5.2: Pigs living in an enhanced barn with more space, natural light, and air than the typical pig barn.

Source: Author photo.

temporary crates to protect piglets, but others, like Kim, avoided crates because they didn't seem right to her. However, Kim admitted that her decision to avoid crates forced her to make other tough choices, like turning a "terrible mom" into sausage. Kim told this story: "I started with my two sows. And the one sow is a phenomenal mother and the other was a terrible mother. She would just sit on her piglets. Just a terrible mother." Kim explained that after four litters, she said, "'Sorry, Sneeze [name of pig]. You've been given the opportunity to grow into being a mom, but you birth fourteen piglets and you kill half of your litter.'" She concluded, "We expect a couple to go," but Sneeze killed too many piglets, "so she became sausage." Despite her joking tone throughout the story, Kim concluded on an emotional note: "There was still a moment of grief for me, saying goodbye." Kim struck us as eminently kind and thoughtful, as an animal lover. That she could both joke about a pig as a "bad mother" while also feeling genuine grief illustrates the kind of emotional work and maturity needed to do this kind of farming. It also highlights the

FIGURE 5.3: Heritage pigs in a semi-enclosed barn. Some pigs in this barn were seen as "good" moms and others were seen as "bad" moms that squished an unreasonable number of their piglets.

Source: Author photo.

complex ethical considerations inherent in balancing animal welfare with the practicalities of farm management.

Judy, a small-scale farmer in British Columbia, took a more cerebral approach in answering our questions about her pigs and offered a nuanced perspective on pig confinement. While willing to house farrowing sows inside a barn, she drew the line at using farrowing crates. Judy encouraged consumers to think beyond the simple binary of "inside" or "outside" when considering animal welfare and instead ask, "*How* are these animals housed"? In her case, sows are brought into a barn to give birth and are given ample space in a 10-by-20-foot stall. Judy acknowledges the reality of piglet squish in open stalls: "We do lose some to squishing. . . . It happens. But not that often, and frankly, my sows have extras." While she tries to be present for the births to try and prevent piglet squish, she also considers piglet death "natural," especially given the sow's limited number of nipples and the inherent variability in piglet strength and survival instincts: "If they make it through the first twenty-four hours, they're generally gonna make it. But it's usually with the smaller ones and the weaker ones and the stupider ones that get squished, so that's kind of nature, right?"

Judy's perspective might sound harsh to urbanites, with her reference to squished piglets as expendable "extras." However, this view reflects her understanding of animal vitality and her relationship with the pigs. Acknowledging the limitations of her own physical and emotional energy, Judy recognizes and even appreciates the agency of the creatures she raises. She sees sows as part of "nature," playing a significant role determining which of their piglets survive.

Rethinking Confinement: Farmer-Animal Relationships and Pig Vitality

Our time spent visiting pig farms challenged our preconceived notions about animal confinement and welfare. The idyllic image of pigs frolicking in open pastures often clashes with the reality we observed: raising pigs outdoors in Canada's challenging environment is a costly and logistically complex endeavor, often at odds with the scalability demanded by the modern food system. Prior to this research, we had little understanding of pigs' vitality— their own baked-in inclinations, patterns, and behaviors. We quickly learned that pigs are active agents on the farm; their actions can destroy fields, squish piglets, and even create dangerous working conditions. Pigs' vitality led farmers to employ various strategies to confine them and restrict their movement in barns, pens, and other enclosed spaces. While the ideal of free-roaming pigs is appealing, it's not always feasible or even desirable in every context, and this kind of farming system could only be used for a very small percentage of the pork consumed in North America.

Our conversations with farmers revealed a spectrum of approaches to pig farming, each with its own ethical considerations and practical constraints. Producers saw confinement of various types and degrees as an ethical middle ground, a necessary choice to balance pigs' comfort and happiness alongside other constraints—like producing an appealing product, staying financially viable, and feeling good about their relationship with living and dead pigs. While living conditions varied across the sites we visited, our farm visits emphasized the dynamic interplay between human and animal agency and challenged a simplistic binary of "happy" and free versus "sad" and confined. As we explore the world of chicken farming and cattle-ranching in the next chapter, we'll see how the theme of animal vitality and the complexities of ethical farming continue to unfold.

SIX   Producing Happy Meat at Scale: Managing Vital Animals and Thinking Sustainably

CONSUMERS CRAVE ETHICAL CHOICES, yet popular meats like chicken and beef present conflicting dilemmas. Can the environmental footprint of cattle ever align with sustainable food systems? Is happy meat even possible when billions of chickens are slaughtered each year? In this chapter we continue our discussion of meat production, focusing on the ethical dilemmas involved in raising the "happy" chickens and cows that ultimately become the fried chicken sandwiches and burgers on consumers' plates.

Building on the previous chapter, we aim to transcend a simplistic happy/sad meat binary and to develop a more nuanced understanding of ethical meat production. This chapter continues our focus on two key ideas: the vitality of farm animals (their agency, needs, and preferences) and the relationships between animals and their caretakers. We examine the challenges farmers face raising animals ethically while navigating demands on their resources—both material and emotional. Through the firsthand accounts of chicken and beef producers, this chapter offers insights into ethical frameworks, environmental impacts, and animal welfare realities, ultimately illuminating the challenges of scaling up happy meat production.

The contrasting cases of chickens and cows epitomize the complex and evolving dynamics in the ethical meatscape. Chicken's popularity has soared, with global production accounting for approximately 40% of all meat, dwarfing beef's 20% share.[1] In 2023, the average American consumed 35.7 kg of chicken—significantly more than the 25.8 kg of beef consumed, on average.[2] These trends are not about simple shifts in market demand but reflect deeper cultural, environmental, and moral tensions within the ethical meatscape. For many, chicken is the last "safe" choice in an ethically fraught meatscape. We vividly recall an undergraduate student who refused to eat beef due to environmental concerns, found pork repulsive ("pigs are too smart"!), yet passionately declared her love for chicken, even identifying as a "chicken-etarian." It's important to make clear, however, that the chicken most people consume, including our student, originates from industrial indoor operations, not the small-scale farms we visited for this book. Exploring the complex and unpredictable work of raising chickens on smaller farms makes clear why it is unrealistic to expect such operations to ever meet the immense global appetite for poultry.

At first glance, chickens seem like ideal candidates for ethical meat production. Their rapid growth cycle and minimal resource demands result in a smaller environmental footprint compared to other livestock. Chickens boast the lowest feed conversion ratio among conventional meat animals, converting 1.5 kg of feed into 1 kg of body weight. However, this efficiency comes at a cost that clashes with the idyllic image of happy chickens that many consumers desire. Most commercially raised chickens spend their short lives in large, crowded barns. While efficient, these operations clash with bucolic scenes of free-range chickens pecking at bugs and grass in the fresh air. This dissonance is further amplified by the sheer scale of production required to meet global demand. Over 200 million chickens are slaughtered daily to meet global demand, totaling 74 billion annually—a figure roughly ten times the current human population.[3] In 2022, world production was just over 139 million tons.[4] The sheer magnitude of global chicken consumption casts doubt on the feasibility of transitioning to entirely free-range or pasture-based systems, given the immense logistical challenges and vast land requirements involved.

Despite being overshadowed by chicken in terms of production volume, beef remains a major player in the global meat market, with 72 million tons produced in 2023.[5] Although beef's share of global meat production has dropped considerably from the 1960s, cattle remain one of the top three meats worldwide. Beef holds particular significance in the ethical meatscape due to its substantial environmental impact. Cattle (including meat and dairy) are estimated to contribute a staggering 62% of livestock sector emissions, translating to roughly 9.5% of all global greenhouse gas emissions.[6] This out-sized impact stems from cattle's methane-producing digestion, their extensive land requirements for grazing and feed production, and the energy-intensive process of growing grain for feed. Cattle have the highest feed conversion ratio (5–10 kg of feed per 1 kg of body weight) among conventional livestock, further amplifying their resource consumption and emissions over their longer lifespans. Despite the potential for well-managed grazing operations to provide environmental benefits,[7] including utilizing marginal grazing areas and land restoration, the vast majority of North American cattle are raised in intensive systems, spending their last months in feedlots consuming large amounts of grain.[8]

The stark contrasts between chickens and cattle highlight the tensions between efficiency, animal welfare, and environmental sustainability in the ethical meatscape. Chickens, with their rapid growth and low resource requirements, offer an efficient and environmentally appealing option, particularly regarding the inputs needed to produce 1 kg of meat. However, their short, confined lives probably clash with many consumers' vision of a good life for a farm animal. In contrast, most beef cattle spend a significant portion of their 18-to-24-month lifespan grazing on pasture. This aligns more closely with consumers' perceptions of "natural" or "happy" animals, and fewer individual deaths are required to meet consumer demand (about 330 million cattle are killed per year).[9] However, as described above, this pastoral existence comes at a significant environmental cost. Producers striving for ethical meat production must navigate these competing priorities, balancing animal welfare considerations, sustainability, economic viability, and consumer expectations. This intricate balancing act underscores the nuanced nature of ethical meat production, revealing the vast gray areas that exist beyond a reductive "happy/sad" binary.

To better understand the gray areas within the ethical meatscape, we need to listen to the voices of those on the front lines: the farmers themselves. In the following sections, we'll share stories gathered through our fieldwork and interviews with small-scale chicken and cattle producers. We first examine the explosive growth of chicken production, exploring the ethical tensions between efficiency and animal welfare. Then we turn to beef, exploring its environmental impact and the potential for sustainable practices.

Our research challenged our own preconceptions as meat eaters and urbanites, and we begin our discussion of chicken and cows with a reflection on our evolving understanding. By centering farmers' voices and experiences, we aim to illuminate the nuanced realities of raising animals for happy meat. By examining the realities of raising chickens and cows on small-scale farms, we shed light on why scaling up these models to meet global demand presents a tremendous challenge, and why understanding these limitations is crucial for informed discussions about the future of meat.

Chickens

Fieldwork Reflections

> Even though two of us (Josée and Emily) grew up raising chickens, we all admit that our preconceptions of chickens were naïve. Raising chickens seemed straightforward. These flightless bird-brains should be easy to control and provide for, or so we thought. People don't get emotionally attached to chickens— or do they?
>
> Our fieldwork revealed that chickens are not as simple or predictable as we had initially assumed. Their behaviors and needs are complex, surprising, and sometimes bewildering. We learned that chickens can form alliances and relationships within their flocks. They can be aggressive, even cannibalistic, but they can also be cooperative and form attachments to their caretakers. We clearly underestimated the variety of relationships people form with these birds. While some farmers maintained a degree of emotional detachment, this was far from universal. One British Columbia farmer, Mitchell, had such a profound connection to the birds that he decided to stop raising meat birds altogether, focusing exclusively on laying hens. Mitchell's commitment to his hens led him to defy conventional practices, offering sanctuary to older hens rather than culling them. This approach translated into higher-priced eggs (more expensive than any we had ever seen!), but they consistently sold out at the local farmers market. Ultimately, our conversations with farmers revealed not only the challenges and labor-intensive nature of chicken farming but also the often-unexpected emotional depth and complexity involved in raising chickens on a small scale.

Raising Happy Outdoor Chickens: Limitations on Scale and Supply

The happy meat narrative often conjures a bucolic scene of chickens roaming freely outdoors, pecking at the ground and basking in the sunshine. During our farm visits, producers candidly shared the challenges of raising chickens in these open pasture environments, underscoring the difficult work of raising

FIGURE 6.1: Chalkboard image taken in an independent restaurant serving locally sourced happy meat and eggs.

Source: Author photo.

chickens as well as the logistical hurdles involved in scaling up production to meet the massive consumer demand for chicken. Here we explore some of the limitations of raising an idyllic, happy chicken—limitations presented by the chickens themselves as well as by climate, land, consumer budgets, and farmers' capacities.

Like other farm animals, chickens have vitality, meaning that they have "trajectories, propensities, and tendencies of their own."[10] They are not passive bundles of feathers. While farmers would not use the academic term *vitality,* we frequently observed how they intuitively understood chicken farming as a dynamic process, considering chicken tendencies and preferences when making farm decisions. For producers, the happy chicken ideal involves some degree of respect for chickens' preferences, including a desire to be warm, dry, and safe and to move around. A compelling articulation of this ideal was voiced by Mitchell, the farmer mentioned above who had tremendous empathy for his hens: "If you consider animals as a living body with feelings and thoughts, which they do have . . . they need to be able to have freedom to come and go pretty well, as they please. Within limits, obviously."

What were some of the limits constraining idyllic chicken life? We soon learned that one significant factor are the chickens' own preferences. Contrary to our romantic image of free-roaming chickens, we learned that chickens don't necessarily *want* to spend all their time outdoors. Farmers suggested that chickens needed early exposure to get them used to being outside, while others strategically positioned feed outside to force chickens out of the barn. Farmers' observations about chicken preferences led us to wonder how many chickens marketed as "naturally raised" actually venture outdoors, especially when the outside is unfamiliar, the temperature uncomfortably hot or cold, and their sustenance indoors.

Chicken genetics present another unexpected limitation to the consumers' idealized image of happy free-range chickens. Many farmers expressed concerns about the vulnerabilities of conventional breeds like the Cornish cross (signifying Cornish crossbreed), noting their timid nature and susceptibility to health problems, including disease, heart attacks, and broken legs. This contrasts sharply with consumer expectations of active, healthy chickens thriving in open-air environments. While the Cornish cross's rapid growth (6–8 weeks) and meaty, breast-heavy body make it popular in commercial operations, its lack of vigor and reluctance to venture outdoors present significant challenges for farmers.

Jane, an Ontario farmer running a biodynamic chicken and sheep operation, stated, "I'm not happy with any of the genetics currently available," leading her to raise only laying hens rather than meat birds. Despite Mitchell's affection for chickens, he described Cornish cross birds as "gross animals" that are prone to health issues due to their rapid growth: "They're not pleasant to have around. They get too big, and then they will have a heart attack." Mitchell contrasted these birds with heritage breeds, which are generally healthier and more active. However, heritage chickens that spend significant time outdoors develop less breast meat and more tough, dark meat due to increased physical activity. This presents a dilemma for farmers: while heritage breeds align better with the image of a "happy chicken," the Cornish cross produces the type of meaty carcass consumers expect, despite being ill suited for an outdoor lifestyle.

The concept of an idyllic, happy chicken life is further complicated by environmental factors that shape farming practices. The natural world's vitality extends beyond chickens to encompass weather systems, plant availability, and the diverse ecosystem of birds and animals coexisting with farms. These elements often necessitate indoor housing for chickens, particularly with extreme weather. Staying inside is not only what some chickens prefer but is also a practical necessity in many locations. Jane, quoted above, explained, "Chickens do need to be inside in the winter, just for practicality. I can't pasture them in the snow." Even in milder climates, like Vancouver Island, farmers confirmed that outdoor chicken raising is not feasible. This led to a significant personal realization (for Shyon and Josée): the "naturally raised" fresh chicken we purchased in Toronto in winter was raised entirely indoors. Consumers must either embrace frozen options if they aim to strictly eat pastured chicken year-round or accept the seasonal limitations of fresh, outdoor-raised chicken.

While we underestimated the impact of weather on chicken production, farmers like Russell, who operates one of the largest farms we visited, were acutely aware of the challenges. With over one hundred thousand certified organic birds and fifty employees, Russell initially described his operation as a straightforward business: "There's not a lot of difficulties. You give 'em great feed, good feed, making sure they have water, and spacing, and environment, and if all those are met, animals will do very, very well on their own." However, as our discussion progressed, the complexities of navigating nature's unpredictability became apparent. In the summer months, Russell's chickens have outdoor access, but in the winter they must stay indoors. Russell emphasized the importance of animal welfare during cold months, instructing his staff, "Can you sleep in here overnight, when you go into a barn? If you can sleep there overnight, you can feel satisfied that those birds are being looked after." This personalized approach was unexpected, given the scale of the operation and Russell's businesslike demeanor. Equally surprising were the challenges presented by extreme heat, even in Canada. Russell explained that high summer temperatures not only affected chicken comfort but also degraded the feed and damaged the health of young broods. He also detailed ongoing threats like omphalitis (and egg incubation infection) and other disease, admitting, "There's always something there that you're worrying about." Russell's narrative illuminates the dynamic interplay between chicken vitality, weather variables, and disease management. The unfolding narrative contradicted his initial portrayal of simplicity, revealing instead a complex, ever-evolving operation balancing consumer expectations of happy outdoor-raised chickens with the reality of raising birds in demanding conditions.

Russell's emphasis on the simplicity of his large-scale poultry operation may have been a way of downplaying the contentious nature of raising happy chickens at such high volumes. As with pig farming, opinions diverged regarding the ethics of high-volume or fully indoor animal operations. Russell dismissed "hobby farmers" who weren't able to scale up, while his large operation faced criticism from farmers like Carol, who questioned the ethics of large confinement barns. Carol is far from a hobby farmer and manages a diverse operation with 1,000 cattle, 450 pigs, and 300 chickens. While open to supplying grocery stores, she highlighted the challenges niche producers face to meet consumer demand and supermarket expectations. She remarked, "I don't have endless supplies of one particular product," referring to premium cuts of steak or chicken breast. Carol struggled to envision a relationship with mass-market retailers where "their store shelf is never allowed to be empty." She also expressed skepticism about the organic chicken supply in chain stores:

> Anybody that's supplying Costco with an organic chicken, how many chickens are they growing? Because they're selling them fresh additionally. Wow! That must be a lot of chickens. And are they being raised sustainably? Not likely, I'm afraid. They're probably being raised in huge confinement barns. And organic, what does "organic" mean? Most consumers think it means the chicken is running around outside. Well, you know, that's not the truth [chuckling]. It's not the way it is."

Carol questioned whether consumers understand the origin story of the rows of organic chicken available in large chain stores like Costco. They might want to believe that the chicken lived outside, but she laughs at the naïveté of this assumption. Russell's large barn operation addresses the demand for large volumes of chicken and the expectation of fully stocked store shelves, but it opens him to criticism regarding the sustainability and ethics of his approach. This contrast between Russell's and Carol's perspectives highlights an important tension in the ethical meatscape: balancing scale with ethical practices, especially given consumers' demand for abundant, affordable, always-available chicken.

For farmers like Carol, sustainable, "happy" chickens are inseparable from regenerative pasture management—a holistic approach that utilizes animals to enrich the land and foster a thriving ecosystem. This model challenges an

FIGURE 6.2: Movable pen used for chicken production.

Source: Author photo.

industrial approach, emphasizing the interconnectedness of animal welfare, environmental health, and long-term agricultural sustainability. Jim and Elaine, chicken farmers in British Columbia, echoed Carol's concerns about the challenge of scaling pastured poultry while maintaining a focus on land regeneration. Jim told us that in order to raise chickens year-round on a large scale, "you have to rely on the barns. You can't be on the pasture." They employed Joel Salatin–style movable pens for their pastured poultry, a labor-intensive technique that requires regularly moving pens and access to pasture. Although Jim and Elaine's operation raised around 1,200 chickens in spring and summer, this scale paled in comparison to industrial operations.[11] Space and weather constraints limited their production, as they had only so many good growing months and acres of land.[12]

To remain profitable, Jim and Elaine charged over $40 per chicken, catering to a small niche of loyal customers willing to pay a premium. Echoing Jim, Elaine acknowledged that feeding more people (with fewer resources) would force us "to rely on barns. And that would be a challenge." Jim and Elaine are dedicated to an ecological farming model where animals fertilize the land as the portable pens are moved across pasture.[13] She explained, "We're all about soil. We raise our livestock on pasture. Joel Salatin says it best: 'I'm not a livestock farmer. I'm a grass farmer.'" This emphasis on soil health resonated with other farmers, one of whom remarked, "I started raising chickens so I could have my own manure."

Feeling Emotional: How Vitality (and Scale) Shape Animal-Human Relationships

For farmers like Elaine and Jim, raising chickens on pasture cultivates a strong sense of identity as somebody who cares for the land. However, it also means contending with the vitality of non-farm animals, like the hawks, foxes, coyotes, and badgers that live alongside chickens. Unlike farmers who rely on barns, Elaine and Jim must be mindful of predators who see chickens as an easy meal. During our interview, an eagle circled above us in the clear blue sky. As we admired the bird, Jim sighed as he explained that this majestic raptor was a constant threat. Although Jim and Elaine found deep meaning in raising high-quality sustainable chickens, they spoke feelingly about the sacrifices and constraints: "You can't just go away for the whole day and have [chickens] outside like that. You can come back in the evening, and maybe the raccoons have walked in, or the eagles just decided that they were going to have dinner at your place." Losses from predators were accepted as an inherent risk of raising chickens outdoors, but Jim's words and demeanor revealed the emotional toll of these incidents.

Carol, the Alberta farmer, shared a similar story from her first year of farming that brought her "face to face" with death:

> My first loss was my beautiful Golden Laced Wyandotte hens that I absolutely loved. I had a badger come in and kill thirty-six in one night. Yeah. So, I was pretty choked about that. So that was my first real, "Oh, boy," you know, "What am I gonna do? Am I gonna shoot the badger?" Well, she [the badger] had two little babies, you know? She was just doing what a badger does. But it really upset me because I was really attached to a few of those hens!

This experience forced Carol to grapple with the emotional, ethical, and practical challenges of managing death in animal agriculture, prompting her to ask herself tough questions: "What is my place in the natural world, and how do I respond to death?" Respect, she realized, was the guiding principle: "Respect is the key and most important part of it all. And not losing sight of what that means with regard to the whole." She strove to respect the whole environment, including the badger, while also keeping in mind the financial viability of the farm. This delicate balancing act highlights the ethical gray areas faced by farmers, often misunderstood by urban eaters. In Carol's words: "People don't have to go out and pull a carrot out of the ground or chop the head off a chicken and pluck it for supper. . . . It's no longer a part of their natural psyche. . . . People are disconnected from the natural cycle, and . . . their disconnected ideas of life and death for animals [aren't] always accurate."

Another vital element of raising chickens not readily apparent to urban consumers is the threat of disease. Outdoor chickens, especially commercially dominant breeds, seem especially vulnerable. This introduces a microscopic level of vitality: the germs, bacteria, and viruses that threaten the short lives of these birds. Jim explained, "These kinds of birds, their immune systems are weak and so they come [as chicks] with a vaccine, and once that vaccine is gone, they're very susceptible to dying." He went on to say, "They do get fever, and they die in bigger numbers than you find in a barn. Because in most cases [in a commercial barn], they are using medicated feed." Since Jim and Elaine raise chickens outdoors, rather than a controlled barn environment, they "do have higher losses."

This fragility significantly shapes the relationships between chickens and humans. Disease contains a kind of proto-agency, significantly influencing farmers' thoughts, behaviors, and emotions. Jim described the emotional toll of chicken fragility: "To me, my biggest stress is going out there and I'll find a whole bunch of dead birds." Elaine agreed, noting that when birds die in large numbers, Jim "just is depressed." Jim clarified that his sadness is not about the loss of revenue, but "it's just the way you feel about it. You can't help them. What can you do? We try natural remedies" like apple cider vinegar, garlic, and oregano oil. As Jim acknowledged, "It helps, but it's not antibiotics." (Remember that antibiotics are off-limits insofar as consumers expect that "ethical" meat is antibiotic-free.) The paradox of outdoor, natural chicken operations is that they can involve more emotional distress for farmers and higher rates of mortality compared to controlled indoor barn environments, even as they more closely align with consumer expectations of ethically raised meat.

The contrast between large-scale and small-scale chicken farming reveals stark differences in emotional attachment to the birds. This dichotomy is exemplified by the contrasting experiences of Russell, the large chicken producer, and Mitchell, who managed the small flock of laying hens. An indoor barn with medicated feed can create a certain steadiness in a farm chicken's life; even as it limits their freedom, it leads to lower mortality rates, resulting in less emotional uncertainty for the humans who interact with these birds. Russell responded brusquely to our question about emotional relationships with animals: "No, no. We went past that, the emotional." He elaborated, "These animals are being raised for a certain purpose, to feed people, and we've gotta realize that . . . when you have five thousand laying hens, you're not picking out a certain personality, okay?" Raising a large volume of animals limits the relationship that farmers can have with their chickens, as Russell and other large operators clearly communicated to us.

Conversely, smaller-scale farmers like Mitchell, who had a flock of four hundred laying hens, can develop deeper relationships with their flocks, recognizing individual personalities and behaviors.[14] This emotional investment can lead to greater empathy and concern for animal welfare, but it also comes with the potential for greater emotional distress when faced with illness or loss. Mitchell and his wife initially raised meat birds, or broilers, but the emotional burden of taking them to slaughter led them to shift exclusively to egg production: "We kind of got attached to them, particularly the turkeys," he explained. "Then you kind of bundle them up and take them to slaughter. . . . It felt like, you weren't the guilty party, you weren't doing the actual slaughter, but you set them up for it. So, we just didn't like it." Although Mitchell was "not anti-meat," his close contact and emotional investment in his birds' well-being dramatically shaped his farming decisions. Recognizing the lack of a viable market for older hens, Mitchell was committed to letting them live out their lives on his farm. "We have an area called 'palliative care.' We keep them until they die," he shared. However, this ethical stance came with economic consequences. Fluctuating egg production from an aging flock made it difficult to consistently meet demand: "Right now, we have [multiple] stores waiting for our eggs. And they don't like that. . . . And we will lose [the contract] that way. But we do that." Describing how they keep the chickens until they die, Mitchell summed it up thus: "Economically, it's not a wise thing to do. Ethically, I think we're okay."

Mitchell's prioritization of ethics over profits led to lost contracts with retailers who required a steady supply of eggs. Mitchell also acknowledged his pricey, sought-after eggs were "really hot sellers in the affluent areas" but harder to sell in less wealthy areas. While Mitchell had a devoted customer base—many of whom claimed that his eggs helped overcome allergies and other health issues—the high price point and small supply limited accessibility. This highlights a crucial dilemma of Mitchell's happy chicken model: while ethically commendable, it struggles to balance economic viability with broader market reach, making it hard to scale up. Russell's critique of hobby farmers, particularly those relying on external income to subsidize niche products, applies here. Mitchell openly admitted that his egg business doesn't provide much of an income, especially given the high cost of organic feed. He relies on his pension income, and in our interview he openly wondered who would take over his beloved, yet minimally profitable operation. While we were deeply impressed by Mitchell's devotion to his chickens and sustainability more broadly, we left our visit to his farm with a sobering thought: the happy chicken ideal, as embodied by his small-scale operation, will remain out of reach for most consumers unless we fundamentally rethink our food system, making ethical and sustainable practices both scalable and affordable.

The happy chicken ideal encompasses not only the relationship between farmer and fowl but also the dynamics within the flock itself. Chickens, it turns out, sometimes need protection from other chickens, an aspect of chicken behavior we were mostly unfamiliar with.[15] This unexpected aspect of chicken vitality became strikingly clear during our interview with Sheila and Derek, Alberta farmers we interviewed at their dining room table. Throughout our conversation, their deep commitment to sustainability and natural animal husbandry shone through, a commitment they'd successfully applied to bush pigs (See Chapter 5) and cattle. Yet chickens presented unique behaviors and preferences that caught them off-guard.

Sheila's story began with their initial flock of Cornish cross chickens: "We started with two hundred chickens, and we were, like, 'This is easy! Let's do a thousand!'" However, scaling up proved difficult, even disastrous. "The next year when we did a thousand chickens, we discovered just how sensitive chickens are to stressors," she explained. "We screwed everything up that you could screw up." They had started the chicks in a heater enclosure known as a brooder, "hand-feeding all these lovely little chicks and everything's perfect." When they moved the hens outdoors, looking to fulfill their vision of free-range poultry, the results were devastating: "Within a day or two, they started to kill each other, just eating each other, pecking each other. You'd walk out there, and their guts would just be pulled out." Far from the idyllic happy meat imaginary, Sheila said, "There's these cute chickens just ripping each other to shreds." Even when placed on grass, "It wouldn't stop. They just kept going and going. They won't stop once they start. We lost six hundred birds to cannibalism that year." The moral of the story for Sheila and Derek came back to scale: "We're like, 'Okay, we need to scale back,' and then we *eventually* learned . . . chickens have to establish their pecking order" in smaller groups.[16]

After the disastrous "year of the cannibalism," Sheila and Derek experimented with different methods. They tried dividing chickens into large pens of five hundred birds, but aggression persisted. Sheila vividly recalled her frustration: "They can be nasty little creatures. You just feel the rage boiling up inside you when you see them eating their pen mates . . . it was terrible!" Next, they attempted smaller flocks in an open area, only to face a new threat: predators. "Hawks and something else flew in and wiped out a pile of them in one night," Sheila lamented, adding, "We're like, 'Oh, come on!'" Despite the humor in her storytelling, it was clear that these experiences evoked a range of intense emotions, from rage to sadness to frustration. Their final experiment involved heritage breeds, including roosters, in a forested area. The hope was that this "natural environment" would offer refuge from aggression. However, it resulted in incessant crowing and numerous escapees.[17] The vital character of wilder breeds was difficult to manage: "Because they were heritage breeds, they actually had a little bit of bird left in them. So, between the crowing, and the flying . . . we probably got some ostrich-sized feral birds in the backyard somewhere because so many of them disappeared. We don't know where they went." This experiment, too, ended in failure, leading Sheila and Derek to conclude, "You know what? Forget chickens. We'll just raise them for ourselves."

Sheila and Derek's experience with chickens illuminates the complex realities of raising happy meat, even for empathetic, experienced farmers. Their story, like others we heard, reveals a web of interconnected challenges that complicate the idealized notion of ethically raising outdoor chickens. Managing the vitality of chickens—birds with strong preferences, occasional flightiness, and a capacity for aggression—while contending with predators like hawks and badgers is no simple feat. These challenges were compounded by limited labor, especially for farmers like Sheila and Derek who were running the farm operation, raising kids, and bringing in off-farm income. The tension between scaling up to meet consumer demand and upholding ethical standards highlights the tremendous practical and economic pressures farmers face. Crucially, our research underscores the profound effect of these challenges on farmers' emotions and self-perceptions. The work required to raise happy, financially viable chickens can result in depressed, stressed, and worn-out farmers, demonstrating the impact chicken vitality has on the lives and emotions of those who care for them. Sheila and Derek's humbling chicken experiment underscored a broader truth: scaling up ethical animal farming is fraught with complexity and unforeseen challenges. These challenges extend beyond poultry and are equally present in the case of cattle, a species with a significant environmental impact and a unique need to be out on pasture.

Cattle

Fieldwork Reflections

To gain a holistic understanding of happy meat, we felt we needed to witness the transformation of an animal into food. This led us to a small-scale slaughterhouse, an essential yet often overlooked link in the chain of happy meat production. Arranging such a visit proved difficult. Hygiene and safety concerns, coupled with the dwindling number of small abattoirs in North America due to increased corporate concentration in meat processing (e.g., only three plants handle 85 percent of all federally inspected beef in Canada) presented significant barriers.[18] This scarcity impacted numerous producers we interviewed, who struggled to find nearby facilities capable of processing nonstandard sizes and types of animals.[19] Our journey took us to a family-owned abattoir in the middle of the Canadian prairies. This operation specialized in cattle but also offered services for hunters. It was integrated with the family's own cattle business, which followed a holistic management grazing philosophy and was committed to sustainability.

The slaughterhouse represents the final chapter in the extended life of cattle. Unlike short-lived pigs and chickens, cows spend an extended amount of time grazing on open pastures—a life that, to many, seems idyllic. Still, the stark reality of their end in a slaughterhouse is inescapable. As farmers often say, the animals "have one bad day." The bad day we witnessed was efficient yet visceral. Cattle were held in an outdoor pen before being led inside one by one. A chain was looped around a back leg, followed by a shot to the head. The animal was hoisted high and its throat slit to allow for bleeding. The overwhelming, nauseating smell of blood filled the air, serving as a powerful sensory reminder of the death we were witnessing.

Even in a slow-moving, non-industrialized setting that was staffed with experienced workers, the brutal reality of animal slaughter was inescapable. The experience was so impactful that it led one of us (Josée) to reconsider eating meat. It laid bare the inherent ethical complexities of consuming animals, even those raised humanely on a small scale. Witnessing the moment of death revealed the stark tension between the idyllic image of happy animals and the unavoidable, bloody endpoint shared by all creatures destined for the dinner table. This experience left us grappling with questions about the ethics of North America's high level of meat consumption, the transparency of our food systems, and the disconnect between consumers' enjoyment of meat and the often harsh realities of its production. Throughout our research, this visceral slaughterhouse encounter served as a sobering touchstone, grounding our exploration of happy meat in the undeniable realities of the animal-to-meat transformation.

The Long Life of a Happy Cow

At first glance, cattle appear to best embody the happy meat ideal. Unlike pigs and chickens, which can be exclusively raised indoors, beef cattle enjoy considerable freedom, open space, and long lives.[20] For their first six to nine months, calves graze alongside their mothers in small-scale cow-calf operations. This idyllic period creates a positive impression. During our fieldwork, we witnessed cows grazing contentedly, calves frolicking in open fields with their mothers as well as herds engaging in natural social behaviors. In the initial stage of our research, beef seemed the *most* ethical meat choice, given the

FIGURE 6.3: This cow had given birth to her calf just minutes earlier, out in the field. She was part of a herd that grazed rotationally across fields.

Source: Author photo.

relatively high quality of life experienced by cattle, especially compared to the relatively cramped, short lives of chickens and pigs.

However, cattle's pastoral beginning doesn't tell the full story. After weaning, some remain on the farm, while others move to specialized operations to gain weight through a combination of feed and pasture. Ultimately, the vast majority of cattle end up in feedlots for final fattening before slaughter at around eighteen months, weighing 1,000 to 1,400 pounds. Moreover, a happy cow does not necessarily equate to a sustainable one. Our initial, intuitive ethical assessment of happy meat centered on humane treatment and prioritizing open air, free movement, and sunshine didn't factor in less visible ecological factors. Cattle's low reproductive rates and slow growth demand vast amounts of land, water, and grain when finished in feedlots. This resource intensity, easily overlooked when focusing on animal welfare, contributes significantly to beef's status as the meat most linked to greenhouse gas and nitrogen emissions—a fact widely acknowledged by consumers but sometimes contested by producers we spoke with.[21] This illustrates a central paradox in the happy meat story: while cattle are perhaps the freest of the farm animals, they are highly resource-intensive.[22] In the remainder of this chapter, we explore this contradiction, examining how cattle are both free-moving and constrained, sustainably managed on individual farms yet collectively impactful. As with chickens, we also address questions of scale and the implications of widespread consumption of grass-finished beef.

Eating Grass, Managing Pasture

The image of a cow happily grazing isn't merely a romanticized consumer notion; it reflects the essential nature of cattle as ruminants, biologically adapted to thrive on grasslands. This natural diet not only promotes their health, reducing the need for antibiotics and medical interventions, but also yields healthier meat for human consumption, with lower antibiotic residues and increased omega-3 fatty acids.[23]

Managing cattle sustainably is much more complex than simply letting cattle out on an open field to find their dinner. Specialized pasture management techniques, such as rotational grazing (often referred to as holistic management), are essential to prevent overgrazing, enrich topsoil, foster biodiversity, and sequester carbon.[24] This approach, popularized by figures like Allan Savory and publications like *The Stockman Grass Farmer*, was commonly discussed in our interviews and involves strategically moving cattle through a series of paddocks using flexible fencing.[25] This allows them to graze naturally, fertilizing the land as they go, while preventing overgrazing and promoting healthy grassland ecosystems.

When asked what differentiated her cattle operation from a conventional approach, Alberta rancher Kerri didn't hesitate: "It's mostly the way we manage our grazing and our land, actually—with the different pastures and moving them and giving the grass a chance to recover." For ranchers like Kerri, cattle are not merely commodities but integral partners in improving grasslands' health and fertility. This philosophy led many of the producers we interviewed to identify as "grass farmers" rather than simply cattle ranchers. Soil health is a topic that inspires passionate discussion among ranchers, and it is difficult to overstate how central this goal was to their identity and livestock practices.

While rotational grazing involves fencing, it provides cattle with ample freedom of movement and space to roam compared to confined feeding operations. Technically, it could be considered a form of confinement, but given the expansive outdoor spaces involved, most consumers would be slow to object. In fact, during our field observations, cattle seemed eager to move between pastures, enticed by the promise of fresh forage. This enthusiastic grazing behavior closely aligns with the idealized image of happy farm animals evoked in our focus group discussions. One memorable moment solidified this impression: we arrived at a farm just as a cow had given birth in the field, her newborn calf nestled beside her as she licked it clean. This starkly contrasted with the more confined conditions we had witnessed for mother pigs (Chapter 5).

Despite being raised in open spaces, cattle still receive considerable care and attention from farmers, fostering significant human-animal relationships. A young Alberta rancher, Robyn, provided a compelling example:

> I've got a cow, Number 60, and she had an injured leg. We still don't know exactly what happened, but she had severe lameness in one leg when she was out on pasture and a huge swollen area, and could barely walk, but she had a calf on her side so we brought her home, where she didn't have to walk. And I nursed that leg back to health, putting her in the squeeze, squishing out the pus, you know, giving her antibiotics, wrapping it with hot poultices and everything.

Though Robyn refers to the cow by her numerical tag number rather than a name, her story highlights the significant relational work involved in raising cattle. Farmers like Robyn must be attuned to individual animals' well-being and prepared to provide individualized care, even as they think broadly about how to manage the sustainability of the farm as a whole.

Despite a general consensus on the importance of soil health and grass management, farmers diverged on optimal practices for ensuring cattle well-being. As with pigs and chickens, the debate centered on the degree of confinement considered humane, ethical, and sustainable. Opinions diverged on whether outdoor access directly correlated with an animal's well-being and what level of freedom constituted a good life for cows. While some farmers, like Robyn, utilized confinement in barns or smaller pastures for specific purposes such as assisting with calving, monitoring calf development, or addressing health concerns, others challenged the notion that outdoor access was essential for happy cows.

Dean, an Ontario cattle farmer with a small slaughterhouse operation, challenged the happy cattle idyll, stating, "Well, it's kind of tough. In today's world, everybody likes to think that animals should be outside on pasture." He acknowledged, "I agree that they [cattle] like it out on pasture," but he staunchly defended his barn-based operation, arguing that a controlled indoor environment allowed him to provide excellent care:

> I believe that it's very possible to have a very comfortable environment inside. Because we all like to go inside where the AC is turned on in the summer. The barns we run have fans in them, so they'll have moving air, they're in the shade, and they're very comfortable. Another thing is to make sure they've got lots of bedding, they're cleaned out often enough. Make sure they have good and fresh water, and good quality feed.

Dean offers a nuanced view of animal welfare that emphasizes comfort and care within a controlled environment. He highlighted the importance of adapting farming practices to individual circumstances, especially when access to affordable pasture is limited. For Dean, the indoor environment allowed for a high degree of control, enabling him to mitigate extreme weather conditions and promptly address health concerns. In his view, leaving animals exposed to the elements without shelter was inhumane. Dean also elaborated on his efforts to ensure ample space and a healthy social environment for the cattle, managing groupings to "try to keep them [the] same size as the others, so they don't harass each other." While Dean acknowledged that his approach diverged from conventional ideas of what makes cattle happy, his firm belief illustrates the nuanced spectrum between the often-oversimplified dichotomy of happy/free versus sad/confined.

This complexity was echoed by other farmers, like Brent, a farmer in southern Ontario who raised various livestock, including cattle, heritage chickens, and pasture-raised pigs. While utilizing a rotational grazing system for his cattle, Brent did not consider barn-based operations inherently inhumane or even unsustainable. In fact, he noted a growing trend toward indoor cow-calf operations, particularly in areas with high land values like southern Ontario. Brent even pointed out the benefits of indoor systems, such as efficient manure management that could be used to improve soil fertility. While Brent was deeply familiar with the environmental benefits of rotational grazing, he maintained that with proper care and attention, farmers could create humane conditions for cattle in barns.

Feedlot Cattle: Developing a Critical but Nuanced Storyline

The practice of confining cattle is perhaps most salient on feedlots, where financial imperatives drive physical restriction. In Canada and the United States, the vast majority of cattle (around 95%) are "finished" in these intensive facilities, consuming a grain-heavy diet designed to maximum growth and fat content before slaughter.[26] This practice has drawn significant criticism due to its impact on animal welfare, human health, and sustainability, contributing to the negative perceptions many consumers hold regarding industrialized beef production.[27] While a comprehensive critique of feedlots is beyond our scope, some key concerns warrant highlighting. A crucial distinction exists between "grass-fed" and "grass-finished": while all cattle start life consuming grass, only those that complete their entire lifespan on a grass diet are considered "grass-finished." Feedlot-finished cattle consume a predominantly grain-based diet, leading to accelerated growth and earlier slaughter, yielding the tender, marbled beef favored by many consumers. This preference is evident in grading systems where "prime" beef, with its high intramuscular fat, commands premium prices.[28]

Feedlot efficiencies come at a cost. Mirroring the consolidation seen in slaughterhouses, feedlots have shifted toward larger operations, some housing as many as one hundred thousand cattle simultaneously.[29] This scale intensifies concerns about overcrowding, animal welfare, and waste management. Moreover, grain-heavy diets, which are more difficult for cattle to digest, often necessitate routine use of antibiotics and steroids to maintain health and maximize growth. This practice contributes to a startling statistic: livestock consume roughly 80 percent of antibiotics sold in the United States, raising concerns about antibiotic resistance and potential impacts on human health.[30] Additionally, the high saturated fat content of feedlot beef can contribute to chronic health issues like cardiovascular disease, raising additional public health concerns.

Environmental concerns are equally pressing. Because feedlots generate vast quantities of manure, they present a significant risk of water contamination. They also rely heavily on intensively cultivated cereal crops (e.g., corn) that require significant inputs of chemical inputs, exacerbating broader environmental issues like soil degradation, water pollution, and greenhouse gas emissions. While the feedlot system is deeply entrenched in North American beef production, these mounting concerns have sparked awareness and criticism in public discourse, which we observed firsthand in our focus groups.[31]

Some feedlot critics come from within the beef industry itself. Jeremy, an Alberta farmer and small slaughterhouse operator, offered a stark critique of the industry's focus on growth and marbling. He describes "prime" beef as coming from "morbidly obese" cattle, often "days away from a heart attack or a blown liver." Jeremy recounts disturbing instances of cows dying from heart attacks while walking up the ramp to the slaughterhouse. The industry goal, he suggests, is to fatten the animal as much as possible, pushing them to the brink of death before slaughter.

Jeremy's firsthand observations paint a grim picture of a system focused on growth and fat accumulation. He describes blown livers, excessive visceral fat surrounding organs, and a stark contrast to leaner, grass fed animals like bison: "In a finished feedlot fat animal, there's 35 to 40 pounds around each kidney of fat. . . . Their stomachs are covered in fat," he explains. In one notable example, he recounts how in the slaughterhouse they, "cut a heart open on a really fat beef recently, and it had marbling inside the muscles of the heart!" While intramuscular marbling produces the tender meat North Americans enjoy, Jeremy laments the waste and potential health issues resulting from excessive fat—fat that he cannot utilize in his small operation: "inside the cavity of the beef is 140 pounds of pure white fat. . . . It irks me to throw that away all the time. It's limitless." Despite his evident disgust with these practices, Jeremy acknowledges the market reality driving them: "Consumers love well-marbled meat."

While grass-finished cattle appear to be an obvious, healthier, more sustainable alternative to feedlot beef, the issue is complex and is not easily reduced to a simple story of "good" grass-finished cattle versus "bad" feedlot villains. The first level of complexity involves questions of scale and sustainability.[32] Due to their longer lifespans, grass-finished cattle produce more methane. Although effective pasture management and carbon sequestration can partially mitigate this issue, it remains a concern.[33] Additionally, grass-finished cattle typically yield less meat per animal, requiring more cattle to satisfy current demand. One estimate suggests that a 30% increase in the U.S. cattle herd would be necessary if all cattle were grass-finished, yet American grasslands can only support 27% of the existing cattle population.[34] This discrepancy highlights the environmental challenges of transitioning to a purely grass-fed system, without simultaneously interrogating the overall quantity of meat consumed.

Indeed, the prevalence of feedlots in North America has created a reliance on imports for grass-finished beef. Despite being the world's largest beef producer, the United States sources 75%–80% of grass-finished beef from countries like Australia and Brazil.[35] While feedlots starkly contrast with idyllic images of cattle grazing freely, a wholesale shift toward local, grass-finished beef presents complex challenges. It would necessitate either a massive expansion of both pastureland and cattle herds (an unlikely scenario, given the land constraints) or a significant reduction in beef consumption, particularly in high-demand countries like the United States.

The second layer of complexity in the feedlot narrative involves economic considerations, particularly for farmers without direct-to-consumer opportunities. Niche producers of grass-finished beef take immense pride in their product, which they see as a tangible symbol of their environmental stewardship and care for animals. However, they face challenges marketing leaner meat that doesn't align with mainstream preferences for fatty, marbled cuts. This misalignment between beef characteristics and consumer expectations creates hurdles for producers seeking to transition away from feedlots.

One Ontario rancher, Barry, captured this tension when he voiced his disdain for the term "finishing," referring to feeding cattle in a feedlot for the final months of their lives rather than letting them continue to eat grass on pasture. He calls it a euphemism for adding unnecessary fat: "It's a bullshit word. 'Finishing' means you're adding fat." Barry emphasized the need to educate consumers about the unique qualities of grass-finished beef, emphasizing that with proper cooking techniques like slow braising, leaner cuts can be tender and flavorful. Barry acknowledged the challenge for consumers: "We do ask something of our customers. They have to learn to cook better. They have to learn to be more thoughtful." Despite the challenges, he remained optimistic that once consumers understood the benefits of grass-finished beef, they would become "hooked."

While Barry's success was inspiring to witness, this model doesn't appear easily replicable for most cattle ranchers we spoke with. Few possessed his unique combination of charisma, keen business acumen, and access to a loyal customer base willing to embrace the culinary challenges of leaner cuts and pay higher prices. Geographic distance from urban centers, where such markets are more prevalent, further compounded the challenges for many ranchers, making direct marketing an impractical or financially unviable option. This explains why even many ranchers who prioritized sustainability incorporated grain finishing or sold cattle to feedlots, despite understanding the benefits of grass-finishing. This seemingly contradictory practice stemmed from the harsh realities of the market: the economic pressures to maintain a viable farm business as well the need to cater to mainstream consumer preferences for fattier, marbled meat, which is typically achieved through grain-based diets.

Several producers, like Kerri in Alberta, told us they had always held back a few cattle for grass-finishing for their own consumption. When we asked her why she didn't try and sell this beef locally, she laughed and said: "Nobody in this [rural] area eats grass-finished beef. You can't do it." Roy, another Alberta rancher, echoed this sentiment. He also kept a few cattle for grass-finishing and spoke at great lengths about the health benefits for his family. He proudly showed us steaks from his personal freezer, pointing out the yellow veins of fat while also emphasizing the superior flavor. Yet, like Kerri and all of their rural Alberta peers we interviewed, economic realities dictated that most of Roy's cattle were destined for feedlots.

These examples illuminate the complex interplay of ideals, pragmatism, and economic realities that shape ranchers' decisions. While many acknowledge the benefits of grass-finished beef, market forces and consumer preferences often compel them to adopt practices that may not fully align with their personal values. This tension was evident in our conversation with Darren, a respected Alberta rancher deeply knowledgeable about holistic management and a passionate advocate for sustainable grazing's carbon sequestration potential.

Despite his expertise and convictions, Darren candidly acknowledged that his own cattle ultimately met the conventional fate of finishing in a feedlot.

"We've tried a little bit of [direct] marketing, but it just didn't work very well," he admitted, encapsulating the difficulty many ranchers face in accessing niche markets for grass-finished beef. His succinct summary of the situation clearly captures the tension between ranchers' environmental ideals and the economic realities they face: "We raise them the way we want to raise them [sustainably] and then they go to a feedlot." When we gently probed this apparent contradiction, saying, "So you are taking care of the land, but . . . ," Darren frankly completed our thought: "We are looking after ourselves." This exchange underscores the difficult balance ranchers must strike. Darren had dedicated immense effort to responsible land stewardship, but he recognized the economic necessity of selling to feedlots, where cattle could reach their maximum weight and command higher prices.

Some farmers avoided feedlots but incorporated grain feeding on the farm to ensure a fattier final product to meet consumer demand. Ontario farmers Ray and Marissa shared their experience "dabbling" in grass-finished beef at the request of health-oriented customers. They described their dismay when they went to pick up the beef from the slaughterhouse: "when we went and got the meat, we looked at it, and it's just like, ugh. There's no marbling, right?." While the meat was suitable for hamburger, it fell far short for higher-priced cuts like steaks. They concluded, "We can't stand by this," and reverted to grain-finishing in their barn operation. This decision was driven by the realities of their consumer base, where chefs and discerning consumers expect a "nice big thick piece of fat" on their steaks. Ray and Marissa, who personally delivered their beef to an upscale urban steakhouse, felt that their hard-earned reputation was inextricably linked to meeting these expectations.

Despite their inability to maintain a fully grass-finished beef operation, Ray and Marissa emphasized their commitment to animal welfare, ensuring that cattle had ample space and ventilation in their barn to prevent the health issues associated with feedlots. They were keenly aware of the negative perceptions surrounding confined cattle and stressed the small-scale nature and cleanliness of their operation. Ray articulated their philosophy: "It doesn't make any sense to be abusive to your animals, because that's your investment, so why would you do that, right?" He acknowledged feedlots as a "real bone of contention" but delivered a heartfelt defense of their commitment to their animals: "'You care for them. You're with them every single day, essentially. You're making sure they are taken care of."

Ray's comments underscore the complex interplay between sustainable, humane cattle raising practices and the pressures of meeting consumer expectations for tender beef from happy cows. This tension emerged throughout our research, with many producers challenging dominant narratives about cattle production. Some even defended feedlots, emphasizing that mistreating animals is counterproductive to economic success, as healthy animals yield higher returns. Luke, a rancher with a master's of science in agronomy, highlighted the potential of new technologies to enhance animal comfort and well-being in feedlots, asserting that the level of care provided in modern feedlots is "really amazing." While our research didn't directly assess the experiences of animals in feedlots, it did reveal how farmers challenge the simplistic, often negative portrayals of industrialized meat production prevalent in consumer discourse. While some consumers might believe that animal neglect and abuse are employed to minimize costs and maximize profits, farmers like Ray articulated a common view: prioritizing animal welfare is not only ethical but is also a sound business strategy.

Our analysis reveals a significant disconnect between farmers' understanding of good animal care and prevailing consumer narratives surrounding beef production. These narratives often reduce animal welfare to a simplistic binary of "happy" free-range versus "confined" feedlot cows, overlooking the nuanced lived realities of farmers striving to raise cattle sustainably and humanely. While most farmers prioritize sustainable pasture management, others focus on maintaining healthy, comfortable conditions within more confined settings. Similarly, the idealized view of grass-finished beef as the sole ethical and sustainable option oversimplifies a complex issue, potentially alienating farmers who feel that their efforts to produce sustainable, humanely raised beef are overlooked. While grass-finished beef offers undeniable benefits, a wholesale transition to this model presents significant challenges, including increased cattle herds and more grazing land. This singular narrative not only risks maligning farmers who utilize other methods, it also stifles crucial conversations about balancing consumer expectations for abundant, marbled beef with the realities of sustainable agriculture.

Conclusions

The dominant narrative surrounding meat production paints a stark picture: idyllic, free-ranging animals on one side, confined and suffering animals on the other. While emotionally resonant with consumers, this polarized story

fails to capture the complex realities of raising animals for food. Our research into pork, chicken, and beef production reveals a landscape far more
nuanced, where animal welfare, sustainability, and economic viability often
collide. The idealized image of animals frolicking in open fields obscures
multifaceted challenges: unpredictable animal behaviors, environmental limitations, extreme weather, finite resources, consumer demand for abundant
tender meat, and the relentless economic pressures of running a farm. From
a farmer's perspective, the story of happy meat is never black-and-white. Take
cattle, for instance. While a grass diet is ideal, feedlots are a cornerstone of the
system, producing affordable, tender, and abundant beef and even providing
an outlet for ranchers who prioritize sustainability but lack the resources for
direct marketing. By exploring these complexities, we aim to move beyond
simplistic narratives and foster a more compassionate understanding of the
challenges facing farmers.

To showcase these challenges and illustrate the problematic nature of simplistic narratives, we relay a story shared by Alberta farmers Sheila and Derek.
Sheila, a natural storyteller, recounted a harrowing yet humorous incident
that underscored the unpredictable nature of animal behavior, even in their
well-managed pastured beef operation. While out for a walk, the preternat-
urally calm Derek said in a deadpan voice, "Dear, you need to run." Sheila
continued:

> Then Derek is, like, flying. And I'm running, and I tripped in a tractor tire
> rut, and I fell and my face hit the barbed wire fence. . . . It wasn't a deep cut,
> but it was bleeding. And I'm tucking and rolling and trying to get under
> the fence. [Derek] hurdles like an Olympian over the fence. Standing on the
> other side, he says, "Come on. You can do it. She's still coming!"

The couple narrowly escaped the charging cow, leaving Sheila deeply shaken:
"I'm like, 'I hate these cows!' I'm freaking out. And Derek is like, 'Sometimes
they do that' [in a deadpan voice]. That's all he says! [laughter]." Derek's la-
conic response, "Sometimes they do that," reflects a farmer's pragmatic understanding of animal unpredictability—a dangerous and upsetting reality
often overlooked in romanticized depictions of farm life.

After recounting this harrowing incident, we asked Sheila and Derek if
they thought consumers understood the risks involved in working with animals. Sheila responded with a laugh, "No, they think everything's a giant pet."
She continued, "People seem to think that either you're raising pets or you're

raising animals in a horror movie or something. It seems like there's these two extremes, and I'm like, there is a middle ground! I mean, not that we're anywhere near the horror movie. Well, other than the animals getting killed! [laughter]."

Sheila's words aptly capture the polarized perceptions we encountered throughout our research: an idealized vision of farm animals as beloved companions versus a grim narrative of systemic abuse. As Sheila pointed out, and as we have observed, there exists a vast middle ground between these extremes. While farmers did restrict animals' movement for various reasons, they also demonstrated tremendous care and concern for their well-being. Though not always aligning with the anthropomorphized notion of "happiness" ascribed to pets, the deep-rooted respect and attention to well-being defied negative stereotypes of ruthless, profit-driven industrial farming. Not surprisingly, farmers frequently expressed frustration with the negative stereotype that anchors these simplistic meat narratives. Ontario cattle rancher Ray said, "I know the one thing we hear lots about is animal abuse, and stuff like that," while his wife Marissa pointed to the stereotype of "farmers stripping the land and just doing whatever we can to make a profit." Marissa sought to emphasize the care and dedication she and her husband invested in their animals:

I think there's a misconception about what we do in general. And how much we put into it, and how much thought we put into it. . . . And it is, it's an odd thing, right? We work our butts off to give them the best care, and to provide for them, and to give them a good life. But then they're going to go to slaughter, right? I always kind of say, "Well, I wanna give them the best life for the time that they're here with us."

Marissa's reflections reveal the emotional weight and inherent contradictions that farmers grapple with as stewards of animal life. Her poignant acknowledgment of the "odd thing" that is animal agriculture—raising animals with care and dedication, only to ultimately send them to slaughter—challenges us to confront the complexities of our ethical relationship with animals and the meat that we eat. The path toward a scalable, sustainable meat system is far from certain, but we argue that it should begin with acknowledging these complexities, questioning simplistic narratives, and fostering open dialogue that includes the voices and experiences of those who raise our food, like Ray and Marissa. Only then can we hope to create a food system that balances human needs with respect for animal life and environmental sustainability.

PART IV   **The Boundary Work of Happy Meat**

SEVEN   Other People's Meat

DO YOU EVER FIND yourself in a grocery store line, looking—and perhaps sizing up—the meat somebody beside you is about to purchase? Who do you think buys meat on sale at a grocery store? What might you be able to assume about somebody who purchases meat directly from a local farmer? How do we judge someone who eats oysters versus a person who prefers a hot dog? Are there "good" hot dogs—or are all hot dogs a bit questionable? These questions all speak to the ways that meat consumption involves symbolic boundary work, helping us draw lines that connect us to some people and distance us from others.

The chapter is organized around two categories of meat that elicited strong boundary-drawing reactions in our focus groups: *cheap meat* and *happy meat*. We analyze these categories to illuminate how they enable people to forge connections between various types of meat and distinct social groups. In each category, we draw from our survey data to highlight relevant trends and then analyze focus group data to showcase salient intersectional distinctions. Before we turn to the topic of cheap meat versus happy meat, we provide some essential background on how sociologists understand the connections between class, culture, and food choices. This overview will explain the significance of connecting low-status food items, like hot dogs, with people of lower socioeconomic status.

Connecting Class, Culture, and Food Choices

The foods we eat (or don't eat), like meat, work to shape borders of belonging and exclusion. Dietary preferences can create invisible borders, categorizing individuals into distinct groups and sometimes leading to a sense of "otherness." This phenomenon is especially apparent to those who follow specific dietary restrictions, such as vegetarians or individuals adhering to halal or kosher practices. Scholars in the sociology of culture and consumption have long recognized this dynamic. A key lesson from the sociology of culture literature is that there are reciprocal influences between consumption choices, *social boundaries* (the ties or lack of ties we have to other people), and *symbolic boundaries* (the understandings we have about those we are similar to or different from, and how we evaluate people). For example, the upper class often shares social ties and expensive food preferences, reinforcing their sense of belonging and worthiness. This is an iterative or cyclical relationship: social groups influence consumption choices, which shapes how others perceive us (e.g., as sophisticated? or tacky?), further reinforcing social boundaries. While class is a clear example of this process, it can work with numerous other social categorizations, illustrating the complex interplay between food, identity, and social boundaries.

As most students of culture will know, many of these insights about social boundaries, consumption, and symbolic boundaries can be traced back to the famed French sociologist Pierre Bourdieu.[1] Bourdieu conducted extensive research showing how those in lower and higher social classes approached the world of consumer goods differently. Importantly, he demonstrated how this involved a process of class othering (although Bourdieu did not use that term) grounded in embodied taste preferences that reflect membership in a social class. An enduring culinary insight from Bourdieu's work is that lower-class individuals tend to value abundance in their food preferences—what Bourdieu called *tastes of necessity*. People in the upper classes are more drawn to the aesthetic properties of the foods they consume and have lower priority for quantity—an idea that Bourdieu labeled *tastes of freedom*. Such tastes allow them to apply an *aesthetic disposition* to the mundane world of food choices. Having an aesthetic disposition means being able to take an aestheticized perspective toward objects that might be seen only in practical or functional terms by others.

Of course, many eaters see their tastes as natural or intuitive, thinking, "This is just what I like to eat!" But Bourdieu convincingly argued that tastes

are shaped by our class upbringing and can operate in subtle ways to perpetuate class distinctions. A privileged person may come to develop a taste for
refined, high-class foods (e.g., foie gras, oysters) that allows them to move
comfortably in upper-class spaces, ordering a fine bottle of wine and feeling a sense of repulsion when confronted with cheap, low-quality food and
drinks. A lower-class person eating on a limited budget may develop a taste
for meals that feature large quantities of food (e.g., a heaping plate of barbecue
ribs), and they might be less comfortable enjoying menu items at a high-end
restaurant (e.g., a small serving of bone marrow). As we will explore below,
these preferences have important implications for boundary work processes
involving meat.

Many food scholars have productively used a Bourdieusian frame, showing that higher-status people are drawn to more culturally legitimated food
choices, are more likely to have an aesthetic disposition toward food, and tend
to seek out foods that provide social status and distinction.[2] Their embodied
taste preferences commonly align with foods and drinks that are culturally
valued. These privileged consumers can use their money and cultural knowledge to eat foods that both require and generate *cultural capital* or high-status
cultural knowledge and practices.[3] In the case of food, that means having
knowledge of high-status food trends, chefs, and dishes and possessing an
embodied taste that allows you to enjoy high-status foods (e.g., the taste of a
raw oyster). Cultural capital in food is socially constructed through discourse
in the food world, where influential people promote their ideas about how to
evaluate food.[4]

In contrast to privileged taste buds that seek out rarefied food experiences,
working-class food tastes tend to focus more on abundance.[5] For example,
in an analysis of Canadian families' diets, a team of social scientists noted
that working-class families valued the buffet as an ideal eating experience and
were less likely to pursue foodie characteristics of authenticity and exoticism.[6]
For working-class families, a buffet offers quantity and affordability, and it
was these characteristics of abundance and variety that raised the buffet experience to the level of a food ideal. In contrast to the buffet, upper-class families
in the study described the food they valued through reference to its fine details, noting the provenance of the ingredients, commenting on tasting notes,
and highlighting the importance of how the food was presented. For example, one higher-income family member described to the interviewer how they
would prepare a meal to impress a guest, saying that they would "probably

get those tiny little peppers instead of the regular big bell peppers, and place it differently, asymmetrically."[7] Examples like this draw attention to the significance of class in creating embodied taste preferences for the quantity and affordability of foods—or in distancing people from these considerations.

Food choices speak volumes about cultural capital, but they can also signal morals, ethics, and values. Food research has productively drawn on Michèle Lamont's contributions to the sociology of culture, which demonstrate the importance of *moral* boundary work for inscribing self-worth and drawing distinctions between in-groups and out-groups.[8] Our own food scholarship has built on Lamont's work to investigate the moral dimensions of aesthetically consecrated foods.[9] This research shows that people with the highest status tend to have a taste preference for aesthetically and morally consecrated foods.[10] In meat terms, high-status consumers seem more likely to order the organic rack of lamb at the butcher's rather than a factory-farmed side of pork ribs. This helps explain why ethical and refined protein choices—like pastured heritage pork, free-range chicken, and line-caught fish—are regular features on high-end menus: they are both aesthetically and morally consecrated.

Lower-income consumers certainly draw moral boundaries to make sense of their own food choices; for instance, buying less food at the grocery store can be framed positively as being less wasteful compared to affluent shoppers who thoughtlessly fill up their carts.[11] Even so, the ethical foodscape (e.g., organic, fair-trade, local, farmers markets) can feel painfully out of reach for low-income consumers.[12] These research patterns suggest that food scholars need to investigate both aesthetic and moral consecration to fully understand the ways that food and meat consumption relate to class boundary work. In the following sections, we take this advice to heart and examine how high-quality, happy, "good" meat (versus low-quality, sad, "bad" meat) operates as a cultural medium that is used to draw symbolic boundaries of inclusion and exclusion. We start with the cultural and moral boundaries drawn around cheap meat.

Cheap Meat (Is Bad Meat)

Through our survey data, we saw various ways that meat is associated with class. One question asked "Which of the following foods do you think people of high and low social status eat?" and provided a range of meats as the options to choose from. The results weren't necessarily surprising, but they are useful to confirm that there are broadly shared understandings of meat and status. Only 4% of respondents imagined a high-status person eating a hot dog, while 66% pictured a low-status person eating a hot dog. The figures for ground beef are similar: only 8.5% of survey respondents imagined a high-status eater eating ground beef while 45% imagined a low-status eater consuming the product. In contrast, 75% of respondents could picture high-status people eating foie gras, with a similar percentage (71%) perceiving oysters as a food for high-status people. In contrast, only 8% of those surveyed imagined low-status people eating foie gras or oysters.

While individuals of any social class may, in reality, enjoy any type of food, our survey findings highlight the powerful symbolic associations that exist between food choices and perceived social class. The way specific foods are linked with certain social statuses can have real-world consequences, shaping how people interact with one another and even perpetuating inequalities.[13] This is further complicated by the fact that not everyone has the same degree of agency when it comes to food choices. Low-income individuals lack the financial flexibility or resources to challenge the negative stereotypes attached to inexpensive foods like hot dogs. On the other hand, higher-status consumers have more freedom to manipulate the narrative surrounding their food choices due to their greater access to a variety of options. For instance, a high-status individual can elevate the perception of a hot dog by choosing an artisanal variety or pairing it with a craft beer, effectively distancing themselves from the food's low-status connotations.[14] Conversely, when a low-income person eats a hot dog, it is more likely to reinforce existing associations of the food with low cost and lower social status, regardless of their personal preferences.

To examine how symbolic associations between cheap meat and social status manifest in real-life conversations, we turn to our focus group data. These discussions solidified the notion that cheap meat carries powerful, negative, class-based connotations, often linked to prioritizing quantity over quality. Notably, many participants were reluctant to openly express potentially snobbish opinions about food, aligning with prior research on the aversion to food snobbery—and overt snobbery more generally.[15] However, despite this reluctance, many had visceral reactions to cheap meat, expressing concerns about its taste, quality, hygiene, and healthfulness, sometimes extending these concerns to those who purchase it. This finding can be interpreted through a Bourdieusian lens, suggesting that class dispositions and cultural capital manifest powerfully at a visceral level. Reactions against cheap meat are less likely to be explicit judgments and are more often experienced as embodied responses, specifically a felt sense of cheap meat as gross, disgusting, or distasteful.

People are often aware of the social acceptability of certain opinions, such as negative judgments about others' food tastes or a cultural aversion to blatant snobbery. This awareness requires a nuanced analysis of qualitative data, distinguishing between socially acceptable ("honorable") intentions and a deeper, more "visceral" emotional reaction about what is good and moral or bad and disgusting.[16] In focus groups, participants frequently articulated an "honorable" aversion to making class-based stereotypes, instead aiming to appear open to various cultures and ways of being. At the same time, participants' visceral reactions to cheap meat—often tinged with disgust and linked to stereotypes about specific stores or consumers—revealed a more complex and potentially contradictory set of feelings. These embodied responses highlight the importance of examining both explicit statements and underlying emotional reactions when interpreting qualitative data on food preferences.

These visceral associations with cheap most frequently emerged when the group discussed the meat options found in discount supermarkets or low-cost restaurants. For example, when describing the kinds of meat that she wouldn't feel comfortable eating, Hailey, a forty-two-year-old white woman who lives in Vancouver, brought up the example of hot dogs:

> I have to say I'm a bit picky when it comes to eating meat. . . . Like, I wouldn't get a hot dog off the street. [Group laughter.] I'm a bit OCD, and I always think about, like, the street vendors. I'm always like, "Where do they, where do they wash?" Like, it's not really bad, but I just like—I would rather go to a restaurant if I know there's good bathroom facilities. That sounds terribly awful, but I'm just not comfortable.

Hailey is reluctant to say that she is too snobbish to eat a hot dog from a street vendor, especially as the group laughs and teases her for her food snobbery. Reacting to this teasing, she blames her obsessive-compulsive tendencies that restrict her from eating a food she associates with dirtiness and unhygienic conditions—like unwashed hands after using the bathroom.

Displaying a similar disgust for cheap meat, we return to the case of Hope, a twenty-nine-year-old white woman who lives in Toronto. We learned about Hope's disgust toward grocery store meat in Chapter 3 when we explored the topic of factory farm disgust. Even though Hope's aversion to eating meat from a grocery store is socially awkward and she worries that it makes her look like a snob, she feels it difficult to overcome at an embodied level. This feeling of disgust emerges when her friends or family have prepared a dish using meat purchased at a grocery store. Hope feels disgusted by this kind of meat but knows she will look snobbish and judgmental if she refuses to eat it. Both Hailey and Hope worry they are appearing elitist but also find the grossness of these meats difficult to overcome.

Supermarket meat, especially from discount retailers, was dismissed as being suspiciously cheap. As Dan, a fifty-year-old U.K.-Canadian, said in a Vancouver focus group, "I just don't trust cheap meat." He elaborated, "I don't even shop at Costco, [Real Canadian] Superstore, or any of those big chain stores. I don't trust them. They're selling steak for three dollars? I don't think so." Greg, a fifty-seven-year-old white man, agreed with Dan, saying, "I've read stories where they inject red dye to make [the meat] go from brown back to red. Just dodgy stuff, that."

In a Toronto focus group, the subject of cheap grocery store meat elicited a discussion about the limits of the characteristic foodie disposition toward openness and aversion to snobbery. Loretta, a forty-four-year-old East Asian woman, expressed a classic foodie position, saying, "I really try never to be a snob about anything. Like coffee or booze. I'll eat anything—almost just as a statement." Len, a forty-year-old white man, disagreed on this point, saying:

> Unlike Loretta, I am a snob. [Laughter.] . . . We live next to two discount grocery stores. And I remember the last time I was at [one of them], in the end-bin, there were like a thousand striploins. I remember looking in and going, "Oh, what are those?" and on the side, it said "Grade D American Meat." And I was like, "Grade D?" Where does that fall in the chain of command? And then I remember going back home and realizing that Grade D is, like, not even what they're sending to the prisons in the States. So, for me, the discount chain. . . . I just won't buy meat from there.

Len then admits that he would "go to McDonald's and have a hamburger or chicken burger, like, at the drop of a hat" because "I guess I don't have to touch that meat" and therefore "it's not as gross," even though he considers cheap meat at the discount grocery store "too gross" to be edible.

Like Len and Hope, Garth, a fifty-year-old white man, finds cheap supermarket meat "gross" and hard to stomach: "I don't want to look at it. I don't want to participate in it. I don't want to smell it. I don't want to touch it. I don't want to take the maxipad at the bottom of the Styrofoam and throw it away. It's just gross." Despite being repulsed by supermarket meat, comparing the absorbent meat packaging to a sanitary pad, Garth, like Loretta, is wary of appearing snobbish. He describes in extensive terms how cheap meat can probably be transformed into something delicious—*if* somebody applies enough love and attention: "If you're some Italian *nonna* [grandmother] who makes her Sunday sauce and uses a bunch of pork from [the discount grocery store], I guarantee you that sauce is still going to be super wicked, even though that pork came from probably a terrible place." Speaking of higher-quality meat, Garth says, "It's also super expensive . . . and it can be weaponized as sort of this elitist thing. It's like, 'Oh, I don't want to eat that!' And I hate that. . . . I hate socioeconomic barriers to food." At the same time that Garth articulated honorable ideas about good food as a democratic right and cheap meat as something that can be transformed with loving preparation, he also had some of the most visceral reactions against cheap meat we observed in our focus groups. These reactions were etched into his facial expressions and visceral accounts of disgust. Garth, like many other focus group participants we spoke with, wants to be open-minded and generous to people who can't afford expensive meat purchases, but at an embodied taste level, he believes that expensive meat options simply "taste better."

Participants occasionally expressed negative associations between cheap meat and East Asian markets/restaurants. While appreciating the variety and low prices, they voiced visceral reactions against purchasing meat from these spaces due to perceived hygiene concerns. These comments were often made with hesitation, as participants recognized the potential for their remarks to be perceived as racially insensitive or even racist. These instances showed participants struggling to balance their visceral reactions with a desire for cultural inclusivity. For example, Rochelle, a sixty-four-year-old white woman from Toronto, mentioned enjoying East Asian markets for their variety but because of her concerns about cleanliness, she avoids buying meat there:

> I just don't see [East Asian supermarkets] as clean. This could be me. I don't—maybe they're just as good if not better [than the butcher]? I have no idea. But I have the option [to shop elsewhere]. I wouldn't go there and buy even short ribs. Say I'm going to make, you know, a Korean short rib stew. I did that the other day. But I bought my short ribs from [an organic butcher] instead and paid five times as much for them, probably. [Laughs.] But you know, whatever, right? [Laughs.]

Rochelle's uncertainty about the "dirty" quality of cheap meat at an East Asian supermarket, suggesting that "maybe they're just as good if not better," contrasts with her visceral reaction against it. While striving to express an honorable opinion, she ultimately chooses the more expensive organic butcher for its perceived higher quality and cleanliness.

As demonstrated in the example of Rochelle's Korean short rib stew, a visceral skepticism toward cheap meat at East Asian supermarkets can be accompanied by an attempt to articulate a more honorable sentiment of social openness and non-judgment toward Asian food spaces. This honorable/visceral balancing was evidenced in a focus group exchange on the topic of East Asian markets and food hygiene involving Ella, a thirty-year-old white woman, and Priya, a thirty-year-old South Asian woman living in Toronto. Ella tells the group about two places she finds meat questionable: No Frills (a discount grocery store) and a Korean grocery store. Although she enjoys shopping at the Korean grocery store, which she describes as a "great, great grocery store," she notes that "there is something very unappetizing about the meat there." Priya follows Ella's remark by bringing up "food hygiene" and says this plays a "big role" for her, as shopping at places where the meat "doesn't look right, you automatically tend to sort of, you know, repel away from it." Priya notes that her in-laws "buy their fish from Chinatown" and admits that the fish is "fresh" and "cheaper" than the boutique meat market where she likes to shop. However, despite the lower prices in Chinatown, Priya claims she "can't buy my fish [and meat] from the place" because it might make her sick or might be contaminated. Two other members of the focus group join in to agree with Priya, suggesting that it *might* be okay to buy animal protein in Chinatown, but it would involve an element of risk. Ella makes the following analogy to Priya's concern about meat in a Chinatown store: "To me, it's in line with eating at a restaurant where it's visibly unclean. I may do it anyway. But I have to just kind of say, 'I know there has been no handwashing of any kind in any of these [cooking] processes today, and I hope I don't get sick tonight.'"

Like Hailey's aversion to a street hot dog, Ella and Priya connect cheap meat—and, in this case, East Asian food—with unsanitary conditions, like lack of handwashing. The connection between meat that is dirty and cheap, East Asian markets, and anti-Asian racism is further suggested by Ella's sharply contrasting positive description of a southern European butcher. While this butcher is seen as operating outside of standard hygiene practices,

Ella perceives it as clean and safe. Speaking about Italian and Portuguese butchers in the city, Ella links nonstandard hygiene practices to a "refreshing" commitment to high food quality provided outside of the industrial system:

> I actually sometimes find it a little bit refreshing when immigrant grocers follow certain practices that may not be seen as, like, Canadian ones. But where it's still clean. Like [a local Italian butcher] is one of those examples and [a local Portuguese butcher] is another one. I'm amazed that this place has not been shut down, because they're slaughtering meat, like, two feet from where I'm paying! That's against the rules, but I'm like, 'everything is fine. . . . No one's getting sick from it.' And I almost feel encouraged by that to some degree, because I'm just like—they're selling me good meat, they're doing their own practices that are working just fine. . . . What we see is sanitary.

This positive depiction of a Portuguese butcher flouting regulations starkly contrasts with the visceral reaction against East Asian meat sources.

We observed a similar association between East Asian meat markets and poor hygiene in a Vancouver focus group when the topic of Chinatown emerged in the conversation. Kaitlynn, a thirty-eight-year-old white woman, says of her visits to Vancouver's Chinatown:

> So, if you're sort of walking down the street and [the meat] is sort of displayed in the window and it's just this piece of meat that's been hanging there all day . . . you're kind of going, "I don't know if I really want to eat that." Because it's been in the sun all day long, and it's not sort of preserved in that sense. I think it's just, again, it's culture-wise [culturally specific]. It's not how I would hang my meat. Not that I hang my meat. [Group laughter.]

As the group laughs at the idea of Kaitlynn hanging meat in her window, her friend Mindy, a fifty-one-year-old Filipino woman, chimes in and says, "Yeah, that [practice] is really gross." Although Kaitlynn wants to preserve an honorable intention of allowing different groups to adhere to their own cultural practices, for her and others in the group, this specific practice is seen as dirty, gross, and unhygienic. This skepticism and association toward cheap meat sold in East Asian supermarkets and restaurants was commonly but not exclusively voiced by white focus group participants, as we saw above in groups with participants of various ethnocultural backgrounds (e.g., South Asian, Filipino). In another Vancouver focus group, Max, a thirty-nine-year-old white man, said: "This is going to sound borderline racist, but I'm very skeptical about the [meat] in Chinese restaurants sometimes." His friend, Palmer, 34, who is mixed-race (his mother is from Laos), joins the conversation and says, "No, fair enough. I get it, for sure." The consistent pattern of these reactions is precisely what suggests the presence of a schema, or framework, of thinking that operates at a broad cultural level. The overarching schema contrasts high-value meat (expensive, ethical) with low-value meat (cheap, often ethnically East Asian) and can be engaged with by white and nonwhite eaters, sometimes in distinct ways.

We observed the presence of this cheap meat schema clearly in a focus group involving Hayun, a twenty-four-year-old Korean-Canadian woman. Hayun was aware that ethical meat represented a "very white space," as one might find in a pricey organic butcher. At the same time, Hayun felt that the matter of cheap meat was more complex than white versus nonwhite. Like other racial minority participants in our study, Hayun saw herself as part of a larger cultural movement demanding alternatives to factory farming. She described how her Korean parents started out buying meat at Chinese supermarkets when they first immigrated to Canada and money was tight. They felt like they had finally "arrived" when they could afford to buy meat at Costco, especially the organic Costco chicken her mother remains adamant about purchasing. Hayun says:

> I remember the first time my dad was able to get a Costco membership and buy us meat from Costco. It was such a key moment for all of us. Because it was understood that it was like, a step up. . . . And I remember anytime we would have meat that was not bought at a Chinese grocery store, [my dad] would make it known to everyone that it's a "Costco meat night" versus going to the Chinese butcher and getting cheaper meats, which was seen as just an everyday option.

Hayun's story makes clear that buying expensive meat, like organic chicken from Costco, can serve as a schematic symbol of high-value, high-status meat for groups of varied ethnocultural backgrounds, as they are able to move away from the negative perceptions of the cheap meat schema associated with East Asian food stores.

Having explored the cultural, class, and ethno-racial associations of cheap meat, we turn next to the people who purchase cheap meat—how are they understood and what moral boundaries are drawn? Our focus group participants' views captured a tension between seeing cheap meat eaters as choosing poorly and seeing them as relatively constrained in the types of meat they can buy.

This tension in perceptions of cheap meat eaters came out clearly in the case of Cameron, a thirty-five-year-old mixed-race chef who lives in Vancouver. Cameron began the focus group by drawing a moral boundary between the higher-quality meat he eats (from a butcher or ideally from an animal that he had hunted) and the meat available at a discount supermarket: "A meat that I don't eat would basically be something that you would buy at a Walmart, so it's basically the most unethical, the most probiotic, whatever you want to call it, [factory] fed animal. I try to avoid that." Later in the focus group, the topic of cheap meat comes up, and Cameron tells a story about encountering cheap chickens in Walmart:

> I live near a Walmart, so every so often I'll go in there and get toilet paper and whatnot and then I'll kind of cruise through the food aisle just to check it out. And I see whole chicken specials sometimes for maybe, like, six dollars a chicken. And I see this energy in people's eyes that are just like, "Let's go for it." [Cameron makes an animated, crazed face.] And for me, I'm personally horrified. And it's literally, it's a no-label chicken just wrapped up basically. I wouldn't touch it with a ten-foot pole, but there's a large majority of the population and they think they're getting a deal because it's like, "Oh, I'm getting a six-dollar chicken."

His friend, Max, cuts in at this point to say, "Well, they *are* getting a good deal!" and the group laughs. Cameron continues to make his point about conscientious meat consumption versus thoughtless bargain-hunting, even as he acknowledges that there is an element of judgment in his story:

> These people [buying a six-dollar chicken] aren't thinking about where it's coming from! So, for me, on the other side of things, and I hate to . . . talk bad about people. Like, talk bad and judge. But I have no choice but to [judge] because I'm like, "Guys!" This is a part of our society that these people are blinded by! Well, I will not touch that [chicken] because I know that I'm shopping at Walmart. Wherever this [chicken] came from, is probably one of the worst places a chicken can grow.

When the group turns to discuss what kind of person would buy a six-dollar chicken, Cameron states, "That person is, um, what do you call it? I'm not finding my words here. I don't want to call them non-intelligent. . . ." His friend, Palmer, suggests, "Unconscious?" Cameron replies, "Exactly! They're unconscious consumers that maybe have come from a family that doesn't care about food or what have you. . . . They just only see finding a deal as probably the most important thing." Max interrupts again to say, "Maybe they're just poor!" and Cameron responds, "Yeah, but the thing is, even if I'm poor, I'm still going to find an ethical way to . . . I'm not going to feed my kid shitty food." Max retorts, "That's easy to say when you're not poor." Cameron responds defensively, saying, "What about an uneducated individual? That's the word I was looking for," and then points to his friend Palmer, who grew up in a low-income household. Cameron says, "I know someone like you [Palmer], you wouldn't buy that [Walmart] meat, would you?" By bringing Palmer into the discussion, Cameron suggests that a poor person can spend responsibly *and* avoid cheap meat. Reacting to Max's challenge, Cameron works to balance his visceral reaction against cheap Walmart chickens, and the people who enthusiastically buy them, with a more honorable perspective that acknowledges the limits of shopping while poor.

Focus group participants often expressed an honorable orientation toward poor food consumers, acknowledging the constraints shaping their choices. This finding resonates with previous research showing that there is broad discursive recognition of the structural obstacles shaping low-income food decisions.[17] Ellen, a twenty-four-year-old white woman, described a typical cheap meat shopper as "a parent with three kids running around that just cannot handle anything else." While these discussions displayed sympathy, they also suggested a persistent association between cheap meat and poor, uneducated people with many children who don't prioritize good food.

Roberta, a forty-five-year-old Filipino woman living in British Columbia, says that she didn't want to "stereotype" but that she imagines the typical cheap meat consumer as follows:

People who are lower-income. . . . I imagine those people who are drug users and people who are low-income and can hardly make ends meet. . . . I think they have too much on their plate to even think about buying ethical meat, or people who have a lot of children. I'm almost imagining the people, like the Duggars, who have '19 kids and counting' [citing the name of the reality show the Duggars are on]. . . . People who have a lot of kids and are just really busy or just really have a lot of problems or people that are just trying to make ends meet.

Akash, a thirty-six-year-old Punjabi-Canadian, agrees with Roberta's depiction and affirms the notion that low-income people do not care as much about high-quality meat or making healthy food choices for their kids. He also adds that he thinks of "refugees and newer immigrants" as well as working-class families like his own parents: "I don't think my dad or my mom would say, 'This is ethically raised meat.' They wouldn't care." Akash and other focus group participants are critical of cheap meat as a choice, but they also view the people who make that choice with some sympathy, as seen here in Akash's reference to his parents.

While many participants, like Cameron, worked to distinguish themselves from the schema of the uncaring, uneducated cheap meat consumer, some participants felt they operated *within* the cheap meat schema. Those participants described the emotional toll that results from crossing a symbolic boundary and entering the negative domain of cheap meat. It can feel painful to not be able to buy the more ethical, expensive meat option, and people expressed feelings of guilt for not making the "right" choices.

Selena, a thirty-year-old woman in Toronto, describes feeling guilty when buying "cellophane on Styrofoam" meat from a discount supermarket due to its questionable status "hygiene-wise." Fiona, a fifty-four-year-old mother in Vancouver with six kids, acknowledges that ethical meat is better for the environment but prioritizes affordability. She buys meat at a discount supermarket, choosing organic only when it's "reduced price." Amanda, a thirty-two-year-old low-income mother, agrees, to which Fiona adds, "I don't really care what type of meat it is . . . so long as it's organic *and* reduced price."

Roberta, introduced earlier, poignantly describes the tension she feels as a teacher who was trying to educate her four children about the environment and then failing to make sustainable meat choices:

> There's a bit of guilt because, you know, it's like, "Okay, this is not good for the environment. This is not really good meat. It's also not that healthy with all the toxins, all the antibiotics, all the hormones." But living in British Columbia [is expensive]. I've got to do it. There's just simply—I cannot feed my family if I'm constantly buying eighteen-dollar packs of meat, for just chicken thighs. I saw four chicken thighs at Whole Foods was eighteen dollars! [Group members gasp with disbelief.]

People felt guilty for not being able to be "good" consumers and purchase ethical meat, especially on tight budgets. Roberta linked buying cheap meat with emotional pain and guilt, feeling she wasn't meeting societal expecta-tions: "It's the value that is dominant in society now. . . . If you don't believe in it [buy expensive ethical meat], it's like you're considered not really doing good for the community, right?"

Focus group participants demonstrated a keen awareness of the negative connotations surrounding cheap meat. While some made honorable attempts to not judge people who buy it, cheap meat invoked a reaction of visceral disgust and was also linked with racialized, and sometimes racist, mental schemas. Feelings of guilt, shame, and disappointment were common when participants found themselves buying cheap meat due to financial constraints, unable to consistently afford happy meat alternatives. This internal conflict—a desire to appear open-minded while struggling with budgetary limitations and ingrained aversions—underscores the multifaceted, often contradictory emotions elicited by cheap meat consumption. We now turn to the boundary work processes surrounding happy meat.

Happy Meat (Is Good Meat)

In our survey, "healthy" and "moral" were the top traits selected to describe ethical meat eaters.[18] This suggests a powerful link between ethical meat choices and perceptions of personal virtue and well-being, a stark contrast to the negative connotations surrounding cheap meat. However, these asso-ciations are far from straightforward. In the following pages, we'll explore the complex ways social class and gender intersect with these perceptions, demonstrating that the boundary work accomplished by ethical meat is far more nuanced than a simple equation of "happy meat = good person."

Similar to the discussions around cheap meat, focus group participants were generally hesitant to explicitly link ethical meat consumption with moral superiority. People often expressed discomfort with making judgments based on diet, acknowledging the significant role of income shaping these decisions. Despite recognizing the presence of moralizing judgments around diet, par-ticipants expressed unease with the idea that moral worth could be purchased. However, Vancouver focus group involving participants deeply invested in ethical meat eating and the health benefits of all-meat diets revealed some stark instances where moral boundaries were drawn based on food choices.

The Vancouver focus group was hosted by Bonnie, a thirty-seven-year-old whose family owns the butcher shop she manages. Bonnies draws a clear moral boundary between her own ethical meat diet and "people who don't know how to eat." She is critical of those who charged that happy meat was an "an elitist thing," and says that with careful planning, a diet of ethical meat is possible even on a limited budget. Repeating a logic that is common in ethical food discourse, Bonnie argues, "If you use the bones—you make bone broths—and fats, you're going to get all the proteins and the fats that you need." She imagines herself debating a low-income shopper who says they can't afford ethical meat and insists that this diet is accessible with mindful choices. Bonnie continues, "You're not going to be eating steak, but even if all you can afford is three dollars a day worth of bones to make broth, and fats, you're still going to get everything you need [from a nutrition perspective]." In short, Bonnie claims, "It's all affordable. There's no excuse."

For Bonnie and the other participants in her focus group, a low income is "no excuse" to eat cheap meat, because the benefits of ethical meat cannot be replaced by cheap or conventional meat. Markus, a twenty-year-old man who works at Bonnie's butcher shop, says that spending a great deal on high-quality meat was a priority for him: "I'd say it's number one. It's what I put the most of my money into besides rent and things." Markus attributes his improved mental health this high-meat diet, stating, "It's the reason I'm a lot less depressed and anxious than I was a few years ago." Aaron, who is thirty-four-years-old, agrees, saying that spending money on good food had been a priority for him as he struggled to heal from a chronic health issue: "It's definitely my primary cost. I spend more on food than rent. If I had to choose between a roof over my head and a proper diet, I'd be homeless and eat well, no question."

Bonnie adds that she believes the main reason her kids never get sick is because they eat ethical meat. When asked to explain why her children's classmates got sick, she says, "I think they probably eat a lot of carbs, lots of things like pasta and breads and things like that. Not properly prepared food. Like the mom is not—or the dad, whomever—are not bothering to open a book and read." In contrast to a diet high in happy meat, her children's sickly classmates are eating food that is "coming out of a tin or no effort, no effort, just minimal time invested in making food for the families."

The moral boundary work we saw in Bonnie's focus group was uncommonly explicit compared with our other focus group discussions. We foreground this case because it so sharply illustrates how health discourse can be used to draw a moral boundary around happy meat. Bonnie and her co-participants conveyed a clear sense that the person who buys ethical meat is someone who cares about their health and the health of their family.

While Bonnie's perspective emphasizes a strong moral boundary around ethical meat, our focus group and survey data reveal a broader range of perceptions regarding happy meat consumption. In our survey, although more people described ethical meat eaters as healthy and moral, one-fifth of respondents selected "wealthy" as an adjective. This speaks to a sense that ethical meat can be prohibitively expensive, despite Bonnie's exhortations about the affordability of buying bones and fat. In focus group discussions, most participants resisted explicitly judging a poor family who doesn't have enough to eat or who makes seemingly unhealthy dietary choices due to financial constraints. Indeed, wealth and education were commonly listed as driving factors explaining who purchased ethical meat. When asked who buys ethical meat, Mahir, a thirty-one-year-old blue-collar worker in Vancouver, responds simply, "Probably somebody rich."

Ivan, a fifty-two-year-old business owner, acknowledges that although he tries to buy ethical meat, not everyone can: "Anything that is organic or free-range or whatever, the price tag is substantially higher. It does knock out a major part of society, because they simply can't afford it." Akash, who includes himself among those who can't effortlessly afford happy meat, speaks almost wistfully about the lifestyle an ethical meat eater enjoys: "They're probably a higher income, $150,000-plus. They have a lot of disposable income. . . . They probably own their own house as well! [Laughs.]"[19] It is worth pointing out that this accurately describes Bonnie's financial position.

Many of our participants conveyed a general sense that happy meat is a high-status food option and expressed frustration that an ethical choice should be a status marker. We saw this when Heather, a sixty-eight-year-old woman living in Toronto, argues that it is "a luxury to say, 'Do I have to think about sustainability? Do I have to think about ethical?' For a family who is struggling, or a large family, or a single parent family—they just want to get [their food]." The rest of the focus group participants agreed with Heather and nodded sympathetically.

Because people perceived ethical food as a luxury, they were hesitant to draw moral boundaries around happy meat and the people who eat it. In one focus group with Toronto professionals in their twenties, the conversation involved a significant and extended critique of the wealth and privilege that allowed people to access happy meat. This critique intensified to a point where the group, who were sharply critical of class privilege but were also heavily invested in foodie culture, reached a surprising conclusion: happy meat could not be seen as truly ethical due to the inherent elitism of applying such a term to such an expensive food.

This discomfort with the exclusivity of "ethical" was voiced by Hayun, a participant who had earlier shared her commitment to Korean cultural food-ways, including bone broths. She notes that "the whole idea of ethical as a label and as a practice, at this point, I feel like largely it's still used to exclude . . . because it's just not accessible." When asked who the typical happy meat consumer is, Felipe draws a paradoxical picture of privilege and education combined with cluelessness and trendiness: "Privileged, usually. Well-educated, well-funded people that are food-literate enough to be making those decisions. But also, they just kind of trust blindly in what they're buying, because they have the money." Amber agrees with Felipe's paradoxical depiction of wealthy consumers who buy happy meat because they know about good food and because they are sheep following the herd of status-conscious food trends. Amber spoke at length about how it is a "privilege to be able to afford the ethical meat." She critiques a "privileged perception" that involves "a real element of shaming," which suggests that "people are just choosing to buy shittier or less ethical meat because they're ignorant, or they don't care about the environment, or they're lazy."

Although the framing of happy meat as so expensive it becomes *unethical* was a relatively extreme position unique to this young professional focus group, an awareness of the privilege associated with happy meat was a recurring theme in discussions with participants of varying ages and backgrounds. Jason, a sixty-one-year-old Toronto resident committed to ethical buying and shopping practices, is also conscious of how doing so involved an element of social status. Jason sees happy meat as involving "an aspect of conspicuous consumption." He suggests that some people are drawn to upscale meat options because "that is what they think they should be doing, and it's what their friends do. . . . I think there's outward pressure—I think it's a little bit of 'keeping up with the Joneses.'" This idea of status-driven consumption was also articulated in a Vancouver focus group, where Kaitlynn critiqued a social class of people who bought ethical meat as a flavor of stylized, West Coast consumption: "I'm looking at this demographic of people who really have nothing to want. . . . It's like the healthy people, living on the water and in the mountains and everything." She described this group as saying, "'We're going to make a conscious effort. We are going to be sustainable and ethical.' And not that I don't think that they actually truly believe it, but I think that it's very, I don't want to say *trendy*, but kind of." While acknowledging their potential sincerity, Kaitlynn also noted a "trendy" aspect to these choices, suggesting that happy meat consumers are not solely driven by ethical concerns.

Participants grappled with the class implications of happy meat on both an honorable intellectual level as well as a more emotional, visceral level. Alongside "honorable" critiques of elitism and concerns for those with limited food choices, raw emotions like guilt and shame bubbled to the surface, revealing people's awareness of their own privileged positions within a stratified food system. When Jason talked about the "keeping up with the Joneses" aspect of happy meat, his fellow focus group participant Anne, forty-six years old, emphatically agreed. Anne spoke at length about a particular upscale butcher she liked to frequent and her discomfort with her own participation in a class-segregated food system. She said, "There is definitely a privilege that comes with that [kind of meat consumption], being able to care that my butcher has worked with local farmers, and you know, dedicate more of my income to that." This participation came at an emotional cost, as Anne remarked, "There's a bit of tension there for me. It does feel bad that not everybody has access to this amazing level of meat." As Anne spoke about this privilege, the tenor of the conversation grew somewhat somber as the group agreed that it was a privilege to be able to shop at these boutique butchers.

Jason broke the serious tone by shifting the focus back to another visceral element of happy meat: the sheer pleasure of eating meat from ethical butchers. He said, "Well, it comes down to taste and quality. If you cook and you prepare and then eat that food, the [deliciousness] comes out on the plate. I don't want to sound, you know, as Anne pointed out, part of the privileged class, but I guess I am! [Group laughter.]" Jason insisted that if you "bought something as simple as ground beef" from a high-quality, ethical butcher, "there's a remarkable difference at the end of the day as to how it tastes." Jason's emphasis on the sensory pleasures of meat resonated with the group, offering a reprieve from the discomfort surrounding the topic of their class privilege. However, this focus on pleasure didn't entirely dispel the lingering unease about the socioeconomic barriers to accessing his kind of quality meat. For participants in Jason and Anne's focus group, there remained a visceral tension between the uncomfortable guilt they associated with a privileged product and the pleasure they experienced consuming delicious, ethically sourced meat.

Participants across other focus groups echoed these visceral connections between happy meat and the pleasures of eating. Xin, a woman in her twenties, articulates a common theme in happy meat discussions, emphasizing quality and deliciousness over quantity: "I'm very much 'flavor first.' So, I'd much rather have a really good steak once a month than an okay steak every week." Xin contrasts the aesthetic properties of this meat from conventional meat: "Tons of people buy their meat at Walmart, so clearly, you're not—it's not like you're gonna die if you eat it. But I find there is a big difference in flavor when you buy cheaper meat." Here, Xin draws a subtle but symbolic boundary. While acknowledging that conventional meat is safe, she implies that consumers who prioritize flavor and quality—those who are "flavor first"—possess a higher level of culinary discernment and, by extension, a certain social status. By making these more considered meat choices, they can reap the symbolic benefits associated with choosing a "really good steak," even it involves eating meat less frequently. This subtle form of class-based distinction reflects a broader pattern in focus group discussions, where the visceral pleasure of consuming happy meat became intertwined with a sense of consecrated taste and elevated social standing yet coexisted with an aversion to overt class judgments of those who make different dietary choices.

The Lululemon Lady: Gender, Race, and the Stereotypical Ethical Meat Eater

As a character, the meat eater has long been imagined in masculine terms, a finding demonstrated in diverse cultural settings where meat is linked to masculinity and large bodies, both fat and muscled.[20] In our survey data, we found that the adjectives people most frequently associated with conventional meat eaters were *traditional, healthy, muscular,* and *masculine.* However, a different picture emerged for ethical meat eaters. As noted above, in our survey data healthy meat was strongly associated with the words *healthy* and *moral,* suggesting a distinct set of values and a more feminine association. In our focus groups, this gendered dimension of ethical meat consumption became even more apparent. The figure of the thin, often white, woman emerged as the archetypal ethical meat eater—a conscientious environmentalist, yet paradoxically viewed as superficial, trendy, and excessively judgmental.[21]

For example, we asked participants in a focus group to describe the figure they had in mind when they imagined an ethical meat eater. Loretta, previously introduced, responded quickly, saying, "I imagine Gwyneth

Paltrow—her exact gendered body type and income level." Fellow participant Garth, quoted earlier, agreed, commenting, "It's funny, but yes, I as well
have a very thin, rich, white woman [in my mind]." Ibon, a twenty-six-year-
old Black man, imagined "a very skinny white lady in exercise gear . . . yeah,
she is jogging around the supermarket." In one Vancouver focus group, this
question elicited a collective shout-out of responses, including "Lululemon,"
"got your yoga mat in your backpack," and "maybe a little dog." In another
Vancouver focus group, Peter described a person who "does a boot camp,
shops at Whole Foods, and blogs about their cleansing diet," while Ivan
added, "and eats kale!" Roberta pictured a person who likes "go to Whole
Foods" and is "wearing the Lululemon clothes, long hair, everything is
trendy." In the same focus group, Joanna, who is forty-six years old, agreed,
saying, "people who are conscious of health, who ask, 'What kind of food am
I taking and how will it impact my health?'" to which Roberta added, "Yes,
body-conscious, yes."

This prototypical ethical meat-eating lady is subject to mockery and de-
rision. One of the most memorable negative depictions of a feminine happy
meat eater involved a story told by Kaitlynn. To illustrate her understanding
of an ethical meat eater, Kaitlynn recounts a "ridiculous story" about a woman
she encountered through work in a "white Lululemon outfit" with a turmeric
latte:

> She came home and, oh my, she was just having the worst day in the entire
> world because she put [the latte] on her white marble top and, of course, the
> turmeric latte went everywhere, and she had to remind herself that people
> were starving in the world. [Laughter] . . . And like, I remember myself and
> my friend just sitting there going, "I don't know what to say to you, 'cause I
> cannot say I'm sorry." [Laughter.]

Thinking about what motivates this "ridiculous" woman in her "white Lululemon outfit" to choose ethical meat, Kaitlynn wonders if she was "consciously thinking" about what she is buying, or whether it is simply a trend she
can afford because "you have the money and disposable income and it doesn't
matter." Sandra, a thirty-four-year-old white woman, comments, "I think it
only bothers me when people look down on other people who don't live that
way," to which Kaitlynn responds, "Exactly. Yeah. Which again, the turmeric
latte that goes on the white Carrara marble . . . they're kind of the people that
look down on the people that can't, unfortunately."

Our survey data confirmed this perception, revealing that people associate the trait "judgmental" with ethical-meat eaters far more than with conventional meat eaters. This image of the white-Lululemon-pants-wearing, turmeric-latte-sipping woman epitomizes the judgmental ethical eater, as Kaitlynn's story suggests. Kaitlynn effectively draws a moral boundary, framing this feminine figure as more concerned with trends and appearances than with genuine ethical concerns regarding the environmental impact of eating meat.

The ethical meat-eating figure was occasionally described in masculine terms, especially as a bearded hipster type. Len, who reported that he did most of the cooking in his household, counters Loretta's description of the ethical eater as Gwyneth Paltrow by saying, "I wasn't thinking . . . it wasn't a tall white lady. It was kind of a tall white man. I kind of had in mind—I thought of a hipster guy who's going to the Healthy Butcher [an upscale Toronto butcher shop] and spending thirty-five dollars on a steak." Len introduces this character mockingly: "He lets everybody know that he is an ethical person, and he bought an expensive steak, and he probably cooked the shit out of it and ruined it." Len recognizes that he is, in fact, in the same lineup as this character and admits, "Maybe I'm a little bit like that. . . . I'm the tall white hipster dad buying a bunch of meat!" Although these masculine happy meat figures sometimes appeared in focus group discussions, the ethical meat-eating character was more frequently depicted as feminine and associated with thinness, wellness culture, a superficial focus on appearances, and health concerns.

When pressed further on connections with gender, participants often attributed the femininity of the ethical meat eater to women's greater responsibilities for foodwork and family health. Ellen says that she "pictures women, just because, I think it's still predominantly women who are doing the grocery shopping." Felipe, introduced earlier, agrees, saying, "I feel like that [gender] transcends race and class. It is the gender norm." David, a man in his seventies, also felt that ethical meat eaters are more likely to be feminine because "women are more conscious." Heather followed up on David's point, connects this consciousness to women's roles as mothers: "Women are more conscious, because they are the ones, by and large, who are going to prepare the meal for those children before they go to school. By and large. I'm not talking about everyone." Amber, a thirty-year-old white woman, said that she wanted to resist gender norms but noted that women are still doing "an overwhelming amount of the grocery shopping for their household. So, the chances that it would be a woman [buying ethical meat] are statistically higher."

The ethical meat eater is not only gendered but often explicitly depicted as white, as in Garth and Ibon's comments. While the schematic ethical meat eater is seen as white, our diverse focus group participants were clear that they did not consider ethical eating to be only a food priority for white people. Peter, who is Korean, says that he thought of ethical meat eaters as a "beautiful Caucasian couple with no children" but then also situates himself and his wife in happy meat discourse. He jokes that he and his wife started their parenting journey with happy meat ideals—"we're never going to feed her anything but [ethical] filet mignon that's been ground down"—but then "ended up just like, 'Let's just eat mac and cheese and chicken nuggets. I'm so tired.'" Peter's store highlights how the ethical meat schema is associated with whiteness but is not exclusive to it, as diverse individuals struggle to integrate ethical food ideals into their daily food routines.

Similarly, in other discussions, participants debated the extent to which racial minority communities could or would participate in ethical meat consumption. In a Vancouver focus group, a debate arose over the demographics of the customers at a Vancouver ethical butcher. Oliver, a thirty-year-old white man, described the butcher as serving "predominantly white people." Max, also white, counters by saying "Welll, it's very Chinese" in that area. Palmer, who is mixed-race and Asian, disagreed, asserting that "it's mostly white people" buying meat at these kind of upscale butcher shops. Cameron, who is also mixed-race, then jumped in, suggesting that "Chinese and Iranians" were also customers at ethical butcher shops. Palmer pushed back, stating, "There's a lot of Chinese and Iranians over there [in that neighborhood], but they're not going" to ethical meat outlets, like this butcher or to ethical chains like Whole Foods Market. This focus group exchange suggests some discomfort with the idea of drawing a firm moral boundary around ethical eating as the purview of white people because it risks framing other ethno-racial groups as not interested in eating ethically.

The issue of race and ethical eating also sparked a lively discussion in an Ontario focus group. Heather, a Black participant, jokingly remarked, "Well, I don't want to say too much" on the topic of race, meat, and ethical eating, which caused the group to explode in laughter and Namita, a sixty-one-year-old South Asian woman, to say, "Now you have opened up a big kettle of fish!" In this conversation, Heather clarified her intention not to perpetuate stereotypes about ethical eating being solely a white concern. At the same time, Heather wanted to acknowledge how racialized poverty can limit access to happy meat for some minority groups:

> You know, immigrants do not have a large percentage of disposable income. Or opportunities. Or income. They probably have larger families. There are women, even established [in Canada], who have more daily struggles [and don't have the luxury to think of about ethical meat]. Race and ethnicity also goes along with economics to a large degree.

Heather's remarks and these broader conversations highlight the complex interplay of race, class, and cultural identity in shaping ethical food choices, challenging simplistic assumptions about who can and does aspire to eat ethical meat. While the ethical meat eater is schematically associated with white, affluent women, participants frequently troubled the notion that happy meat is, or should be, exclusively reserved for white wealthy consumers.

Conclusion

Are you a bad person if you buy a package of discounted steak from a grocery store clearance bin? Most people would deny drawing such an explicit moral boundary, especially if the shopper is a low-income parent trying to put food on the table. On the flip side, are you a good person if you buy an expensive cut of grass-fed, aged ribeye from a local farmer who slaughters their own grass-finished cattle? Because most people see this kind of meat as good but also expensive, they are reluctant to straightforwardly valorize this consumption choice. Indeed, our meat-related research documents a persistent aversion to explicit, food-related moral boundaries. This validates previous research showing an aversion to foodie snobbery as well as some empathy to the limitations of grocery shopping on a limited budget.[22]

Most people will avoid explicitly judging you for picking up that cheap steak, and you might not receive many fawning shout-outs for your expensive grass-fed ribeye. But does this mean that meat is *not* used to draw symbolic and moral boundaries? In short, the answer is no. Meat consumption is deeply entangled with symbolic and moral boundary work, especially around two salient categories of meat: cheap meat and happy meat.

In the case of cheap meat, boundaries are evidenced at a visceral level and reveal a pervasive sense of disgust alongside associations of dirtiness, lack of hygiene, and health risks. The visceral boundary work of cheap meat spilled into racialized othering. A racist schema of cheap meat emerged in our focus groups that was associated with East Asian grocery stores, which are depicted as purveyors of cheap, unhygienic, and risky meat. We also observed an othering process involving uneducated, low-income consumers who are largely (although not exclusively) viewed with sympathy but are also seen as too preoccupied with more immediate concerns to make ethical, healthy meat-eating a priority.

The happy meat consumer presented a more complex picture involving numerous points of contention around negative and positive boundaries. On the negative side, the wealthy consumer of happy meat is viewed suspiciously as a feminine trend-follower who is judgmental, vain, and focused on leisure pursuits like yoga. The negative boundaries drawn around privileged, clueless consumers and happy meat showed ample evidence of class consciousness and class critique. Happy meat boundary work also demonstrated a degree of sexism, as the ethically oriented meat consumer, in contrast to the traditional masculine meat consumer, was seen as feminine, superficial, trendy, and overly invested in appearances—like a white marble countertop or a pair of white yoga pants.

Yet the happy meat consumer was not always framed in negative terms. Many described them positively: conscientious, appreciative of quality over quantity, concerned for animal welfare, careful about what their children eat. This "moral glow" surrounding happy meat reinforces its appeal as a status symbol but makes clear how this "happy object" can also be weaponized to shame those unable or unwilling to make similar choices—especially when an individualizing health discourse is invoked. (e.g., lauding the thrifty shopper who makes their own bone broth to prevent chronic disease.) Ultimately, while explicit moral judgments around meat may be avoided, especially as many consumers avoid overt class-based food shaming, our findings reveal a complex landscape of subtle distinctions and visceral reactions. Within this cultural landscape, happy meat still largely seen as the most morally and aesthetically palatable option, even if it is not an option accessible to everyone.

EIGHT

Meat Makes Us Healthy and Whole— and Can Even Heal the Planet

MINDY IS A MEMORABLE focus group participant, standing out for her sense of humor and her candid—but complicated—commentary on meat. Mindy grew up on a farm in the Philippines but didn't like to eat the animals her family raised because, "I see them every day." But Mindy likes meat: "Pork—I love pork! And anything that has pork in it, I'm there. [Laughter]." Mindy is proud of the quality of the meat her family sold and that her family's customers "come to our farm because the meat tastes fresher and they see that it's being killed that day so they can get it right away." They say, "'The meat tastes better.'"

Although Mindy loves eating meat, her dietary habits were radically disrupted by a health crisis. This scare "made me decide that I should stop eating pork and go for leaner meats and more vegetables. . . . I still eat meat, but not that much. And I haven't given up chicken, but the beef and pork. Pork I totally cut down, and then beef, just a little bit." Since cutting back on meat, Mindy has started noticing how common pork and beef are in Filipino cuisine: "My Filipino friends, every time we have a gathering, you'll see three, four, five dishes. They're all meat. They're all pork dishes. Or beef. And there will be one or two fish and one or two vegetables." In short, "The meat dominates the table." Mindy laughs as she says, "I feel like I want to buy my own food and bring it," so she can avoid the pork and beef that feel risky to her health.

Mindy also worries about meat's impact on the planet. She says, "I just read the news lately about the Amazon, and that really got to me. It was like, I should not eat a lot of meat just because they're burning the Amazon jungle to make way for the cows." Even though Mindy's tone in the focus group is jokey and lighthearted, she gets emotional talking about this issue: "They said that now the world wants to eat more meat. They have a lot of demand. So Brazil is now burning the Amazon jungle, which is like, they're choking the earth. . . . And it really, really hits me hard. I mean, it's like, 'Come on guys, this is our home! Why are you doing this?'"

Later in the focus group, we ask everyone what kind of person they picture as a conventional meat eater who never buys ethical meat. Mindy tells the group, "You're looking at her," and laughs. She has bought some ethically marketed meats at the supermarket, but it's expensive and she is not sure it tastes better: "If you buy everything organic, if you buy everything, you know, ethical food, then I won't be able to buy anything else." Before her health scare, Mindy says she rarely thought about ethical meat. Now, ethical meat is an ideal but one that is out of reach. She explains, "Because it's my health, so I want to eat, you know, healthier stuff, but I can't afford it every time. So that's how it is."

Mindy's meat story is one of being forced to give up something she loves because she thought it was killing her. Although she still pines for meat-based meals, Mindy feels healthier now and has even started liking the taste of vegetables, which she hated before. She thinks differently about meat these days: "Now that I've cut down on meat, I think it's not as healthy as I thought because of the changes that I've experienced when I switched [to] eating more vegetable-based food as opposed to just eating meat with very, very little vegetables." Because of how she feels now, Mindy knows that "if you eat a lot of meat, then it's not good."

Now consider Aaron, a thirty-four-year-old white man who was another memorable participant in our focus groups. Early on, Aaron explains that he eats only raw meat, once per day. Like Mindy, he made a drastic change in his diet because of a health condition. He explains, "I'm trying to heal from chronic illness, and that's one of my main motivators." Aaron finds that eating only raw meat each morning has been beneficial for his health: "I've been finding great benefit from this diet. I'm attracted to it; my body seems to crave it." Now, Aaron will only purchase ethical beef because he wants meat that was raised and killed in a way that emulates life in the wild. His logic is, "To take an animal not only out of its natural environments [but also] away from its natural diet is not only a disadvantage to the animal but [also] to the person or animal consuming that animal." More specifically, Aaron says, "A less healthy animal means less nutrients, [and more] toxins being distributed from that animal then to you. It's just bad for everything involved." Aaron spends a lot of money on his diet, laughing as he says, "Ask Bonnie. She can tell you!" Bonnie, whose family owns the butcher shop where Aaron buys his meat and in whose home the focus group is gathered, affirms: "It's a lot." But, Aaron attests, this is a choice he would make "even if [he] were homeless." Eating pasture-raised meat is the cornerstone of Aaron's healthy lifestyle and identity. He believes it is good for his body and good for the environment. Aaron tells us that the link between meat and climate change is "exaggerated in the media," especially since cows "also replenish the land." He contends that emissions from cattle is "nothing compared to industry emissions or cars," and quips, "You know who else produces methane gas? People. [Laughs.] I guess we should take them out, too."

While Mindy and Aaron both love the taste of meat, their attitudes toward the environmental and health impacts of meat-eating couldn't be more different. Mindy is worried about the impact that meat-eating has on planetary health and believes that people should eat less meat, with a focus on the leaner cuts of white meat recommended by health experts. Aaron is skeptical about the connection between meat and climate change and questions standard health advice to limit red meat consumption. Aaron's diet is a result of "self-experimentation," and he believes that if our palettes were untainted by refined sugars and processed foods, we would instinctively choose the foods our bodies need. Aaron and Mindy both experienced a health risk that caused them to make drastic shifts impacting the place of meat in their diet, and they both feel healthier as a result. Aaron's journey led him to eat exclusively red meat, while Mindy's led her to almost eliminate beef and pork from her diet and to eat more vegetables. When Mindy gave up pork and beef, she was surprised to learn that she liked vegetables. But Aaron has "never liked vegetables in my life. . . . I've always been attracted to meat." For Aaron, this confirms the wisdom of his carnivorous diet: "Why would our tongue guide us toward something or actually dissuade us from eating something that's supposed to be so good for us?"

Mindy's and Aaron's stories showcase the confusion surrounding the link between meat and personal and planetary health. Advocates of high-meat diets (Paleo, keto, carnivore diet) tout grass-fed meat's benefits, while vegans urge complete avoidance—and both groups work to marshal evidence to support their claims. This chapter explores the consumers' understanding of information about meat, the environment, and health, highlighting the uncertainty surrounding its impact and the complexity of information about meat. We then examine the rise of happy meat as a response to consumers' concerns, while also revealing the challenges and dilemmas consumers face navigating the ethical meatscape.

Meat's Power to Heal—and to Harm

We begin by contextualizing why health is such an important topic for consumers. As sociologists emphasize, health isn't just physical; it has normative and ideological dimensions. Health is described as a *super value*, an ideal state to which we should all aspire, which ultimately casts unhealthy food (and people) as morally inferior to healthy food (and people).[1] In short, the labels *healthy* and *unhealthy* are imbued with moral weight—as we explore further below.

While health is commonly framed as a universal goal, scholars argue that it is also replete with dilemmas.[2] The meat paradox frequently manifests as a tension between disgust and deliciousness, but dilemmas of healthfulness and health risk also exist in a paradoxical state. Healthy meat-based diets can be challenging to define and maintain. What kind of meat is best? How much should we eat? As Mindy and Aaron illustrate, people can navigate these dilemmas using wildly different strategies: Aaron embraces red meat as healthy and sustainable, while Mindy is actively working to moderate her meat consumption.

Although our primary focus is on the health dilemmas of meat consumption, these often intertwine with environmental concerns and questions about animal welfare. The narrative of happy meat is that it is health-promoting for humans, animals, public health, and the planet. Bonnie and Aaron, for example, express frustration with the promotion of plant-based diets, believing that this misrepresents the sustainability of grass-fed animal agriculture. As Bonnie noted, "There's people who are taking proper care of the land and the animals, which [is] technically a sustainable way to [raise meat], because it's the way nature intended." Their belief in the sustainability of meat overlaps with their view of meat as a positive and healthy food. Aaron even (inaccurately) depicted cultures with reduced meat consumption as unhealthy and morally vulnerable: "That's why they promoted vegetarianism in India. It makes people frail. It makes people weak. It makes people more complacent." Aaron also believed that vegans are "generally very aggressive and very irrational, very emotional" and (also inaccurately) linked these negative traits to health deficiencies: "The [dietary] lack of B vitamins. There are actually biochemical reactions. The brain actually shrinks."[3]

Aaron's ideas about meat-eating represent extreme perspectives in our focus group discussions. However, the idea that meat was good for health was commonplace, affirmed by focus group and survey data. Let's explore how people understand meat in relation to individual and planetary health.

Is Meat Healthy? Yes, But It's Complicated

Our data reveal a firm belief that meat is a cornerstone of a healthy diet, associated with strength, muscle growth, and weight management. Nearly 75 percent of our survey respondents agreed that meat beats other types of foods when it comes to supporting muscle growth, supporting the commonplace idea that we need to eat muscle to make muscle. Meat is also seen as a tool for combatting excess body fat, with over 80 percent of survey respondents agreeing that a diet that includes meat is helpful for maintaining a healthy weight.

Focus group participants frequently emphasized meat's role in delivering protein, satiety, muscle building, and weight control. Xin, a woman in her twenties raised as a vegetarian, explained her decision to shift her diet to include meat for athletic performance:

> The sport I did was rock climbing, so obviously you want to be building a lot of muscle. . . . My eating was informed by that. . . . If I'm not eating meat, I'm not getting enough iron. I tried having legumes and a lot of plant-based leafy greens, and I find it's not the same. I still need more. . . . For me, I have to eat beef.

Xin believed meat provided superior protein for muscle building and iron levels (other female participants also commented on iron). Sarah, a forty-seven-year-old woman living in Toronto, agreed with Xin: "[In the] times in my life where I've eaten less meat, I just didn't feel like I got the same nutrition." Beyond protein, participants, especially those who were middle-aged, identified eating meat as a strategy for satiety and weight management.

Although Xin and Sarah mentioned plant-based protein, for many participants "protein" simply meant "meat." In an Ontario focus group discussion that gave significant attention to weight management, Jane, a woman in her forties, described following a high-protein (meaning high-meat) diet with her husband to alleviate his health problems:

> He was insulin-resistant, so next step was pre-diabetic and his sugars were out of whack, and so I decided, as a very crazy person, that I would support him in this process and eat a similar, like more of a low-carb diet but very, very high on protein. . . . So I do. . . . I buy massive quantities of meat. I think I'll just leave it at that. [Group laughter.]

Jane, like others, acknowledged the environmental impact of meat but felt supporting her husband's health by eating a high-meat diet was extremely important. She also connected this diet to her own well-being: "I find that I feel the healthiest when I'm eating lean proteins [meats], vegetables, and a nice healthy carb. But the protein [meat] for me is key in just feeling satiated for one and just having the energy that my body and my brain requires to function at the level I expect for myself." Financial constraints limited Jane to affordable meat from conventional stores: "I will out myself as a Costco meat shopper." The other focus group participants did not pass judgment and instead affirmed the perceived benefits of a high-meat diet. Anne, also a woman in her forties, shared a similar experience: "I live with a very insecure heterosexual man who tries lots of different diets [Group laughter]." Like Jane, she had landed on a high-meat diet to manage middle-aged weight gain and feel healthy. Anne continued,

> The ketogenic, high-protein, lots of leafy greens diet was very healthy, and I would say I felt pretty good. When I was eating that way, for me, that felt really healthy, so meat was a big part of that, of course, because you can't be ketogenic, as you know, without lots of protein [meat].

Jane and Anne's experiences highlight the centrality of meat in perceptions of a healthy diet and a healthy (read: thin) body. For the consumers we studied, meat's health value stemmed primarily from its satiating protein content. As Jason, a man in his sixties, summarized, "I think meat is very healthy. At my age, it's got to be one of many different foods that are part of my diet." Over half of our survey respondents identified meeting protein needs as the biggest obstacle to reducing meat consumption. These findings suggest that many consumers see meat as essential for a healthy diet, a source of protein, and a tool for building muscle and managing weight.[4]

Alongside a perception of meat as a convenient and efficient source of protein is a perception of meat as a health dilemma. Published research on meat and illness paints a complex picture, challenging the "meat is healthy" narrative. In the past decade, this tension has grown, especially since a high-profile 2015 report from the World Health Organization identified processed meats as carcinogenic and red meat as probably carcinogenic.[5]

We found that consumers often acknowledge the health risks of eating specific kinds, and high volumes, of meat. Indeed, over 60% of our survey respondents had reservations about eating meat. When respondents had reservations, it was most often for health-related reasons, with 42% of respondents with reservations linking red meat to cancer risk and 65% identifying smoked and cured meats as carcinogenic. In a Vancouver focus group, Peter, a Korean-Canadian father, illustrated the tension between meat as both healthy and risky:

> Peter: I know the consumption of red meat is the main contributor to stroke and heart disease. Especially as I'm getting older. I think I'm more sluggish day after day. Yes, I really like red meat, so it's very hard. I know I need to reconcile those things, but yes, I know that too much consumption, it will lead to higher risk of heart [disease] and stroke.
> Jun: Colon cancer, too.
> Peter: Yes. Colon cancer.

Both Peter and Jun enjoyed meat but worried about its impact on their health and the health of their families. Jun, for example, struggled with his teenage kids' desire for fast food—and his own temptation to eat the food he bought for them: "Children, all they know is about hamburgers and stuff. We go to McDonald's, getting them a chicken nugget. They're happy. I try to not eat it. But at the end of the drive, I say, 'Can I have a little bit?' [Group laughter]." Later, Peter discussed trying to balance his desire to make his daughter happy by purchasing fast food with the uncomfortable knowledge that meat was bad for health and the planet:

> If my daughter says, "Dad, I want a hamburger!" it's like, "Yes, we are going to get a hamburger today. We're going to get those chicken nuggets. That's going to be my mission today." I know that's not sustainable. It's not good for our health. It's not sustainable for the earth. It's hard to balance the

immediacy of now with what seems like the ether of the future. I don't know. I know I should I make better choices for myself and my family.

For Peter and Jun, the health risks of meat became part of a larger conflict between personal goals, family happiness, and long-term health for themselves, their children, and the planet.

The notion that "meat is healthy" is further complicated by the issue of quantity. Consumers often associate high meat intake with fatness, sloth, or sluggishness.[6] Meat *can* be healthy, but it is mainly seen as healthy when consumed in moderation. For example, nearly three-quarters of our survey respondents agreed that reducing meat is healthier for most people and over one-third said that people should generally eat less meat.[7] In a Vancouver focus group, Ivan, a fifty-two-year-old British-Canadian man interested in fitness, summarized a common view: "I'm going to say yes [meat is healthy]. I know there's a lot of people saying, 'No, it's bad for your health,' but by nature, we're omnivores. Obviously, don't gorge yourself with meat all the time. Balance it out."

Concerns about meat overconsumption were also linked to environmental health. Benjamin, a thirty-five-year-old father and tradesperson, connected serving size to personal and planetary well-being: "I think from a sustainability perspective, yes. The average Canadian does eat too much meat. If everyone ate like us in the world, we wouldn't have much of a world left." Malwina, a sixty-two-year-old woman who grew up in rural Poland, agreed with Benjamin, and observed that overconsumption is a recent phenomenon, concentrated in the Global North: "Humans [are] eating today, especially now in North America, eating too much meat, eating meat every day. It was not like this before." Malwina associated past trends of meat consumption with a healthier physique, using her father as an example: "My father was fantastic, muscular, a wonderful-looking man, like Schwarzenegger."

For Malwina and others, overeating meat is linked to negative environmental and health outcomes and represents a symbolic marker of cultural and moral decline. This perception of meat reinforces the idea of health as a *super value*—an overarching value that everyone should strive for—and highlights the important symbolic role that meat plays in the construction of this value.[8] The moral weight of meat is not necessarily linked to whether you eat meat but how much meat you eat. Although meat and health are morally charged, as we will see in the next section, navigating the vast and often conflicting information about meat's health impacts can be a bewildering experience for many consumers.

Understanding Meat: Navigating Conflicting and Complex Information

We begin our exploration of meat and information by looking to Akash, a thirty-six-year-old IT analyst living in Vancouver. Akash, who is highly educated, found it hard to pin down the health status of meat. He said, "The older I get, I am more skeptical of everything online." He looked for reputable sources of information on nutrition but found that "it's really hard to just sort of keep track of all the things that are happening in nutrition. One day egg yolks are good; the next day egg yolks are bad. I do feel overwhelmed when it comes to health." When it comes to meat specifically, it's hard for Akash to sort out the health from the hype:

> Maybe we're all designed to eat meat. I've also heard the vice versa, where I have a friend who is Buddhist, and she swears by *not* eating meat. She feels that our teeth are designed in a way where we're supposed to only eat plants. I don't know. I just find sometimes it's really hard to not feel overwhelmed to make the best decisions for your body.

Benjamin also spoke to diverging ideas about meat's health status. After watching the pro-vegan documentary *The Game Changers* on Netflix, he temporarily switched to a vegetarian diet. But Benjamin then recounted "listening to Joe Rogan talking about one of his guests and how awesome the carnivore diet was," and he found that perspective equally convincing. These contrasting views led Benjamin to conclude: "You got to just do what works for you and figure out what's best for your body. And from there, how you can make the . . . [biggest] difference to the world and . . . make the smallest impact." Akash and Benjamin's remarks share common themes: sharply contrasting ideas on the status of meat, uncertainty about whom to trust, and a desire to make the "best decisions for your body" and the planet. Feeling overwhelmed and uncertain is reasonable given that health-related information about meat is abundant and often contradictory.

To get a sense of the scope of the information landscape, we searched Google to identify news content related to meat and health. The search produced "about 148,000" articles. A cursory scan of the headlines showed that orientations toward meat ranged from strongly against to strongly for, with many articles purporting to make sense of the messy middle. These articles come from sources that are known for reputable journalism and sources that are not so reputable. For anyone trying to glean a clear answer about whether eating meat is healthy or not, reading the news would be confusing.

Take, for example, a 2022 *Newsweek* article. It begins by citing the International Agency for Research on Cancer's 2015 report linking processed meats to cancer and red meat to probable cancer but then introduces conflicting research: "While some studies show a clear association between high meat consumption and poor health, others show no such link."[9] This contradictory information is not uncommon. Headlines often portray meat consumption as unhealthy, yet numerous articles counter these claims. A study analyzing meat and health claims in *The Daily Mail* over fifteen years found blatantly contradictory information within the tabloid itself.[10] Despite questionable journalistic practices, *The Daily Mail* reaches an estimated 24 million monthly readers.[11]

Conflicting information about meat's health benefits extends beyond tabloid newspapers. A 2019 *New York Times* article discussed a set of four peer-reviewed, comprehensive studies concurrently published in *Annals of Internal Medicine*.[12] The studies were "among the largest such evaluations ever attempted."[13] According to the *New York Times,* this research found that calls to eat less meat are not supported by strong scientific evidence on health. Notably, reports advocating for reduced meat consumption *and* those challenging such claims emphasize the strength of their underlying evidence. And the conflicting information is not constrained to meat, as there is also conflicting information about the healthfulness of plant-based proteins. There has been a lot of critical attention paid to the health implications of processed foods, and many plant-based proteins (e.g., Impossible Meat products) are highly processed, raising questions about their health advantages over meat.[14] The ever-changing information landscape and multitude of voices in public discussions on meat and health make for a challenging space for most people to navigate.

The complexity of scientific research also presents communication challenges in news media. For instance, we encountered news coverage of a study published in the well-regarded journal *Nature Scientific Reports*. This longitudinal study of over forty thousand participants was nuanced and detailed.[15] The researchers observed a reduced risk of type 2 diabetes when red or processed meat was replaced with fruits and cereals but, surprisingly, *not* with legumes or vegetables. And interestingly, this effect was only statistically significant in men. Perhaps due to the study's complexity, the news coverage was limited. However, we did find headlines like "Replacing Red and Processed Meat with Plant-Based Food Could Lower the Risk of Type 2 Diabetes."[16] While this tagline mischaracterizes the results (researchers found benefits with cereals and fruits but not all plant-based options and only for men), it's not entirely inaccurate. This example highlights the difficulty of translating complicated scientific evidence into clear, informative, and digestible news content for the public.

In this environment of conflicting information, it's unsurprising that consumers struggle to find reliable sources. As *New York Times* reporter Gina Kolata noted, studies supporting meat's health benefits "add to public consternation over dietary advice that seems to change every few years."[17] Indeed, many participants, like Akash, expressed frustration with divergent expert reports and skepticism about shifting dietary advice. Research suggests this lack of clear guidance leads to decreased trust in experts, increased reliance on dubious sources like advertisements and social media, and reduced commitment to healthy eating habits.[18]

Can You Trust Governments and Scientists? It Depends.

Building on Chapter 4's exploration of trust in butchers and farmers, we now examine consumer trust in government and scientific sources regarding meat. Unlike the consistent and strong trust in those who raise and sell meat, views on scientific and governmental advice were less positive. Our survey found that while nearly half (48%) of respondents trusted government recommendations on meat consumption, a higher percentage (58%) reported trusting their instincts over scientific advice when making dietary choices.[19]

In the focus groups, consumers' trust in government and scientific advice on meat varied—a theme that was particularly apparent around discussions of Canada's food guide. Food guides have been criticized for emphasizing increased consumption and prioritizing meat and dairy.[20] However, the 2019 version of Canada's food guide surprised many by promoting plant-based protein and eliminating the dedicated dairy category.[21] Some participants saw this as the government moving in the right direction. In a Toronto focus group, Karsten, a thirty-two-year-old manager, described it as a "positive step," and his friend Minel agreed, praising it for "re-imagin[ing] what we think of as protein" and encouraging plant-based sources. To be clear, this group wasn't entirely uncritical. They mocked the old guide's unscientific and culturally biased advice, including its emphasis on dairy and stereotypical imagery like "photos of a milk jug" and "two white people running on the cover [laughter]."

While this focus group praised the revised food guide's emphasis on plant-based protein, participants in another focus group saw it differently. Grant, a fifty-year-old white man, voiced skepticism over the government's motives for the changes, stating, "I can't trust it!" Building on this sentiment, Dan, another participant, agreed and argued that the guide was a product of "manufactured legitimacy," suggesting collusion between government and industry. Grant chimed in, adding, "What they are legitimizing is that heavy lobbying works." Even though the revised guide appeared to align with their dietary preferences, they still saw it as evidence of untrustworthy lobbying influencing government recommendations.

Dan and Grant's comments illustrate the confusion and skepticism surrounding the abundance of dietary advice from various government sources and scientific experts. With so much conflicting information, keeping up with the latest science and identifying reliable experts is a challenge. Some participants, like Roberta, identified criteria like "peer-reviewed" and "well-researched" for evaluating information quality. Others, like Danielle, a twenty-nine-year-old Toronto woman, valued "balanced" and non-sensational information. Danielle expressed a preference for "a well-researched article from someone who does eat meat" and avoids extreme viewpoints on both sides.

Although a "well-researched" article that sticks to the science of meat and avoids political extremes is seen as the ideal, various participants recognized the difficult of directly accessing this kind of information. Piotr, a thirty-five-year-old administrative assistant, exemplified this struggle:

> I should probably aspire to read scholarly articles about vegetarianism and I should probably read books. Like physical books written by doctors and research their names to find out if they're reputable authors. What I usually end up doing in practice is just whatever I stumble upon online, like an article from some random website.

Although not everybody was as candid as Piotr about the imperfect, random nature of their information sources, our discussions (unsurprisingly) revealed that few people read academic research. Instead, they rely on accessible sources like personal contacts, documentaries, and social media. For example, Max was reading a diet and nutrition book that he chose largely because someone he knows wrote it.

Some participants shared Cameron's viewpoint, wanting to "go the extra mile to research" the origins and ethical practices behind their meat purchases. He told the group he would go to "the store's website" or "the butcher's website" to verify their claims regarding happy meat. When his friend Palmer questioned the reputability of store websites, Cameron conceded, "I appreciate that it's all propaganda in the end." Still, he believed "you can kind of balance that out" with more research. This exchange highlights a common theme among participants: a recognition of the imperfect and potentially biased nature of information sources, coupled with a belief in the empowering potential of "doing your own research." Although the sources of information people accessed seemed varied and scattershot (e.g., butchers' websites, books, social media, friends), we observed a common refrain of individual responsibility articulated by diverse participants. This theme is distilled in Cameron's directive statement to the group: "Do your own research. You can educate yourself."

The ubiquitous mantra "do your own research" appeared to stem from a lack of trust in scientific and government nutrition advice, viewed as potentially corrupted by industry influence. This skepticism did not reflect a wholesale rejection of scientific data but rather reflected a complicated, contradictory relationship with science. For example, Aaron, introduced earlier as an avid meat eater, named both "scientific studies" and "anecdotal evidence" as important sources for learning about dietary choices. Despite this apparent trust in science, Aaron then proceeded to describe scientific research in disparaging terms: "Science is funded. . . . Scientists can be bought. So don't forget about your instincts in the process, you know, how you feel, experimentation." When pressed on his mistrust in science, Aaron countered, "Not 'mistrust' . . . I just don't see it as the end-all. Science is continually evolving and growing every few months. 'We were wrong about this.' 'This new study concludes this.'" Aaron's conflicted relationship with science was echoed in another Vancouver focus group, where Elaine asked, "When you think about science, is it even something that you can 100% trust? . . . How do you tell between trustworthy and untrustworthy information?" People like Aaron and Elaine both valued and mistrusted science and found it challenging to

discern reliable information in a sea of conflicting claims. This sentiment resonated with many participants, who acknowledged navigating a cacophony of
voices—scientists, corporations, farmers, butchers, government agencies, and
their own bodily experiences—when making food decisions.

Many recognized the difficulty of navigating this cacophony. Jun, one
of the few participants who described going to the library to read scientific
sources, said, "You cannot just go to Google first. . . . You do have to spend
some time—trust me." Sarah, who had a background in journalism, agreed
on the importance of research and empathized with consumers: "I mean, I
love the internet, but I'm also a proficient internet researcher. There's a lot of
misinformation out there." Even those who valued research acknowledged its
inherent challenges.

The abundance of information felt like a burden for many participants.
Max argued that too much information leads to cynicism, particularly when
information is conflicting or untrustworthy. He remarked, "We get cynical
because we have so much information, we can't do anything right." Max's
solution to figuring out if meat is healthy? Trust yourself. He concluded, "You
can't trust anybody but yourself, pulling the bullet, to kill that elk." While
an extreme solution, his fellow participants agreed there is a connection between information overload and growing cynicism. Oliver lamented, "The day
I started paying more attention is the day I became more cynical because I realized just how much we've all been hoodwinked." Cameron reminisced about
a simpler time: "Let's face it, it was our grandparents who had it the best. . .
. Ignorance is bliss. Then our parents were like, 'Eat meat every day. Let's go
to McDonald's. It doesn't hurt you!' . . . Now we're left to pick up the pieces."
These reflections highlight the challenges of navigating a foodscape saturated
with information, where trust in traditional sources of authority has eroded,
leaving individuals to grapple with complex issues and often contradictory
dietary advice.

We Can Trust Our Bodies

In a world of conflicting information and corporate influence, taste and intuition emerged as surprisingly influential factors in meat-eating decisions.[22]
Like our survey respondents, who trusted their instincts over scientific advice,
many focus group participants reported that they prioritized their instincts
over scientific advice. Mindy, for example, relied on labels and taste to define

healthy meat. When asked why she trusted health claims from A&W, Mindy said: "Because I tasted it, and it's good!"

Trusting their bodies also influenced participants' decisions on meat consumption versus vegetarianism. Mary, a woman in her sixties who had deep concerns about conventional meat, felt vegetarianism wasn't an option because of how it made her feel:

> I can go along and have a plant-based diet for a while and then I crave meat and I miss it in my diet and I have to have it. I don't consume it on a daily basis, but it is important to me. I like the protein. It makes me feel stronger. And I don't get that feeling when I eat greens and salads and grains. I don't feel the same. I feel lighter, but I don't feel maybe as strong.

Sarah agreed: "When I've gone periods without eating meat, I do miss it. I do feel it's nourishing. I don't find that I'm as satisfied when I eat completely plant-based diets."

Trusting your body was also seen as a way to navigate information overload. Cameron described constant diet trends as overwhelming: "We'll see the new Netflix documentary. . . . We'll jump on that. And then, oh fuck, we do this [other thing], and then we'll forget about it. And then something else will come up. . . . There's so much information." Max responded by saying, "Your body's going to tell you. If you feel like crap, if you don't have any energy, it's probably an indicator that you're lacking something." Palmer chimed in, "It's like a body diary!" This resonated with the group, suggesting body signals are a vital strategy for managing information overload.[23]

Let's return to Aaron's story. We left off with Aaron distrusting scientific information. So how does he decide what's healthy? "Research and experience," he explains, emphasizing taste and how his body feels. He meticulously tracks his food intake and has been "food journaling for over a year straight and tracking everything." This is what led him to his all-meat diet. While this may not be for everyone, it highlights a trend: over 20 percent of our survey respondents agreed that "people should eat meat because that's the way our ancestors ate." The ancestral link strengthens Aaron's trust in his instincts. His advice? "Just take research with skepticism, look at many different sources, be open-minded and self-experiment. Trust in your own instincts is key and paramount." Aaron's story, along with the focus group discussion, shows how exposure to conflicting information can lead people to distrust experts and rely on alternative forms of evidence, especially their own intuition and body signals.

Is Meat Bad for the Environment?

While our primary focus has been on human health, consumers often link health concerns to environmental ones. What are the environmental issues surrounding meat production? Compared with the complexities of health research, the scientific evidence on environmental impacts is clearer. Meat production contributes heavily to climate change, with livestock generating roughly 14.5% of global greenhouse gases annually.[24] The livestock industry is also a major water consumer, accounting for an estimated one-third of Earth's freshwater usage.[25] These impacts are out of proportion to the caloric value of meat: meat and dairy use 83% of the planet's farmland and generate 60% of agriculture's greenhouse gas (GHG) emissions but provide only about 18% of global calories.[26] Within the broad category of livestock, beef produces the largest carbon footprint because of the methane cattle release and the land required to grow feed for and graze cattle.

Research supports the environmental benefits of eliminating or reducing animal-based foods. One study found vegans have a 25% lower carbon footprint compared to high meat eaters.[27] The authors argue that to meet sustainability targets, "most high-income countries [need] to radically reduce consumption of animal-based foods."[28] However, there is significant debate about whether it's possible to mitigate these impacts through regenerative agriculture and holistic pasture management (see Chapter 6). Grazing ruminants can help return nutrients to the soil, and the soil sequestration from effective pasture management can offset the emissions from grazing animals.[29] It's not clear, though, that regenerative animal agriculture can occur at scale given current meat consumption levels. Additionally, these practices require more land to generate the same volume of meat, and cows in pastured systems produce more methane.[30] Chicken production, while less resource-intensive, raises animal welfare concerns due to the high volume of birds raised intensively indoors.[31]

While earlier research observed limited public awareness of the impacts of meat on climate change, our participants were acutely aware of environmental issues.[32] Three-quarters of our survey respondents agreed on the need for government action to achieve a sustainable food system. And focus group participants readily acknowledged the link between meat production and climate change. For example, Ellen, a woman in her mid-twenties who works for a health-focused catering company, stated simply, "Meat definitely contributes to climate change." However, some outliers existed. Max, who was reading a book on vegetarianism, surprised his focus group by saying, "I am a climate change denier." Yet even Max acknowledged meat's contribution to GHG emissions, although he downplayed its severity, a theme that also emerged in some interviews with meat producers.[33] Still, nobody in our focus groups outright denied a connection between meat and climate change, underscoring twenty-four-year-old Xin's assessment: "I think denying the fact that eating meat contributes to climate change doesn't really make sense at this point because we do know it does [laughing]." Fiona, who works as a nurse and has six children, bluntly summed up the situation on "intensive beef farming": "It can't carry on like this."

Not only did our participants regard meat production as a driver of GHG emissions, they also identified specific causal factors. Mindy linked climate change to deforestation caused by "the space [needed] to grow these animals," while Cameron pointed to methane emissions and resource consumption throughout the meat supply chain. He lists these impacts: "The water that's used to feed the wheat to feed the cows . . . the transportation [with] diesel trucks. The plastic packaging." Overconsumption was also a common concern. Nearly all focus group participants and 40 percent of survey respondents agreed that people should eat less meat.[34] In Toronto, Hope argued, "We probably shouldn't be eating it every day" while noting that "the average person doesn't consider it a meal unless there is meat in it." Finally, focus group participants distinguished between conventional (cheap) meat and ethical meat, perceiving the latter as less damaging, as we discuss below.

Happy Meat Is Healthy and Sustainable

As we have seen, meat consumption is a dilemma. It's a source of pleasure and enjoyment but concerns linger about health risks, environmental impacts, and the murkiness of health information. Enter happy meat, a solution promising higher-welfare meat production as a way to address these issues. The core message, echoed by both producers and consumers in our study, is simple: eat less meat and eat better meat.[35] Happy meat offers the possibility of a happy ending—a meat-based diet that is good for animals, farmers, eaters, and the environment.[36]

As we have noted throughout this book, happy meat's focus on ethics and quality offers consumers a potential pathway for reconciling the contradictions of the meat paradox. Bonnie's account of speaking with a vegan protester outside her family's butcher shop exemplifies this narrative's potential for a happy ending. After noticing a vegan protesting meat consumption outside her shop (which sells locally sourced, sustainable meats), she asked him why he wouldn't instead target one of the "at least 200 businesses selling factory farmed conventional meat." She told the group that the protester replied, "Because you're the problem. You're offering people an alternative. It's easy enough to scare people off the conventional meat, but you're offering an alternative, and we want them to be vegan.'" Bonnie felt the exchange was clarifying: "That's why they're going to come after ethical meat way more than they're going to come after conventional meat. Because it offers a solution." This story illustrates the positioning of happy meat as a solution to the ethical concerns of meat consumption, allowing consumers to indulge in animal protein without compromising their values.[37]

Participants in our survey and focus groups conveyed a belief that the risks associated with conventional meat are transformed into rewards for those who consume happy meat. Many linked happy meat to positive outcomes for health and the environment. Happy meat is generally perceived as a healthy choice, allowing meat eaters to indulge without the guilt associated with environmental impact and animal welfare concerns (explored in Chapter 3). The logic goes that a healthier (and tastier) animal is one that lived outdoors, moving around, eating grass, and living a natural life. Over 75 percent of our survey respondents agreed that eating pasture-raised meat is better for you than eating grain-fed meat. Focus group conversations echoed this sentiment, with Aaron stating, "The healthier the animals, the healthier the land. The healthier the land, the healthier the animals."

The ethical and environmental benefits of happy meat did not represent the only factor exerting an influence on our participants. Taste also played a crucial role in their assessment, with many echoing the sentiment voiced by Dan, a fifty-year-old social worker, who declared that ethically sourced meat might cost more, but "it tastes better actually." This perception of superior taste was further explored in the Vancouver focus group with Cameron and his friends, as they compared sustainable meat to cheap options. They stressed that while not everyone will notice the taste and texture, for them, the difference was obvious:

Max: There's a difference in taste, though.
Cameron: The taste, the texture [are better]. But when you actually think about the taste, I feel like someone at Walmart probably doesn't think

about the taste. They probably just eat mac and cheese and slap some barbecue sauce on it [the meat].

Max: They slather it in HP [sauce].

Cameron: Yeah, HP. Exactly! So, I think taste is nothing to them. But we would notice the taste, you know?

Similarly, Rochelle, a sixty-four-year-old with a background in marketing and film, told us that by "learning about the practices that are out there for industrially raised animals and how badly they treat them," she came to prioritize eating ethically raised animals, and that this choice has a clear taste payoff: "I think the taste is completely different, and I prefer the taste of free-range, grass-fed."

Happy meat is also seen as a more sustainable option, with some participants going so far as to argue that ethical meat could help to heal the planet. For example, Rochelle argued that conventionally raised animals produce more methane and that "the [animals] that are on regenerative farming, they restore that area back to its lush and vital nature and bring back all the everything that contributes to better, whatever, betterness [laughing]." While Rochelle laughingly acknowledged the difficulty in clearly articulating the ecological benefits of regenerative agriculture, a general sense of environmental "betterness" was associated with happy meat production. Rochelle further clarified her belief that ethically raised animals can ameliorate climate change, in stark contrast to "unethically treated animals [that] contribute to the climate change that we're experiencing now." Sarah echoed the importance of reducing overall meat consumption but saw promise in happy meat as a sustainable option. She acknowledged that "eating less beef is important. And eating beef that comes from regenerative farming practices is important" especially since "*not* eating beef is never going to be something that human beings are okay with." For Sarah, happy meat offers a way to enjoy beef without compromising environmental values, avoiding the more radical step of eliminating it from her diet entirely.

While some participants disentangled the health and environmental benefits of happy meat, our conversations revealed many instances where they were intertwined. Rochelle's malapropism "betterness" showcases how happy meat is surrounded by generally positive, yet somewhat undefined, emotional associations. These positive associations encompass both personal well-being and environmental benefits, as highlighted in our conversation with Akash, as he gave a free-flowing response to a question about meat's health status. Akash began: "The older I get, the more I realize that some meat, a lot of meat, isn't maybe the most healthiest option" and "the more I'm concerned about the environment and mass production of meat and how it is raised, ethically." After acknowledging the health and environmental problems associated with industrial meat, he then moved to an observation linking cheap meat with excess body fat, which he associated with poor health: "I find people who are vegetarians tend to be way more healthier, and they're in better shape. They have less BMI." Akash then mentioned his own negative feelings of guilt and skepticism about cheap meat, saying, "I think for unethical meat, I know I feel guilty. . . . For the love of God, sometimes I wonder, how are they able to sell a hamburger for a dollar?"

In contrast, Akash spoke of happy meat emotionally positive terms, saying that with organic or "grass-fed [meat], you feel a little less guilty." He concluded by emphasizing the higher cost of happy meat, but justified the expense as an investment in personal and environmental well-being, arguing, "Yes, you're paying [more], but you know that it's organic and it's the top of the line. You feel like you're doing your body good, I guess." Akash's complex response to the question "is meat healthy?" reveals the contrasting associations of cheap industrial meat and happy meat. Negative feelings like guilt, environmental concerns, and associations with poor health are linked to cheap meat, while happy meat evokes less guilt, a sense of individual responsibility, and a belief that it benefits both personal and planetary health.

Happy Meat Creates Its Own Dilemmas

Although consumers in our study saw happy meat as a solution to the health and environmental problems created by industrial meat, it remains a food with inherent challenges. The positive health and environmental associations surrounding happy meat did not completely dispel their anxieties. In particular, participants frequently voiced concerns about the affordability of ethically sourced meat and the challenge of verifying claims about animal welfare and production practices.

Accessibility Issues in the Ethical Foodscape

While participants generally agreed that ethical meat production offers a sustainable alternative, most spoke about a significant hurdle—affordability.

In many focus group conversations, participants worried that widespread adoption of ethical practices would raise meat prices, putting it out of reach for many consumers. Tom, a thirty-three-year-old who works in marketing in Toronto, suggested that this could be "a good thing," since it would reduce meat consumption overall. However, his partner, Danielle, countered this viewpoint, "That's a good thing? That only rich people can afford meat?" Danielle's response captures the core dilemma: ethical production methods often translate to higher prices. As she says, "You have to pay farmers more to have them produce meat to not be in shitty circumstances. . . . That's going to isolate people who don't have as much money." As a solution, happy meat puts two ideals in conflict: meat prices should reflect the true cost of production, and people have a right to eat good food.

In addition to the inequity in accessing high-quality meat, our participants also worried about the collective impacts that results from products like happy meat becoming trendy. Roberta articulates this concern clearly: she acknowledges that ethical consumption of products like happy meat is "the value that is dominant in society now." And she is critical of its associations with wealthy celebrities who have the power to establish what is "cool." As she says, "It's so trendy. You see a lot of the stars, the movie stars, they have hobby farms. Like Jennifer Garner, I don't know if you know her, she's an actress. She's on Instagram, and she's running around with her chickens!" She further notes how celebrities like Meghan Markle contribute to the perception that "buying cheap meat or meat that's not humane or not free-range, not organic, it's not as cool." Roberta's critique highlights a concern about social pressure and the marginalization of those who can't afford happy meat. She argues that buying ethical and sustainable meat is not an option for everyone and feels it is being "pushed down our throats" by wealthy celebrities and media narratives that "are always talking about global warming."

One exception to the prevalent concerns about happy meat's affordability and accessibility emerged in the Vancouver focus group with high-meat consumers. This group insisted that ethical meat was attainable for anyone who prioritized it. Bonnie, for example, argued that affordability hinged on shopping and cooking savvy: "people don't know how to eat," a view she contrasted with her own knowledge of how to shop and cook carefully, where to find cheaper cuts, and how to use all the nutrients in bones.

While happy meat offered some a path to alleviate guilt about meat consumption, people still harbored anxieties about inequalities and sustainability crises. Roberta's thought-provoking query—"Are we doing enough so that we can sustain our world to where we can make enough meat, we can make enough vegetables, plants, *for everybody*?"—underscored these concerns. She even expressed a fear of a dystopian future resembling the uninhabitable Earth of the Disney movie *WALL-E,* sharing her worry that "we're going to end up destroying the earth." Akash made a similarly dark postulation: "I feel like meat will just eventually be reserved for wealthy elites, and we'll be left eating like [laughs] insects or other unmentionables." In sum, happy meat may offer partial respite from the guilt associated with meat consumption, for some, but does not alleviate larger concerns about global food access and looming environmental crises.

Trust Issues in the Ethical Foodscape
In contrast to participants' confidence in the quality and ethics of happy meat sourced from a farmer, most of the people we spoke with were skeptical of corporate messaging about meat and sustainability. Indeed, food corporations were the most distrusted group among our participants. Only a few, typically with lower cultural and/or economic capital (see Chapter 4), expressed trust in corporate claims.

This lack of trust stemmed from a general concern with corporate power and profit-driven motives. For example, Cameron believed that large food corporations couldn't be trusted, since they "have the world on their pinky" and are only motivated by "greed." Fiona was explicit in her distrust of corporate brands: "I don't like anything that's sponsored by supermarkets, or when you see the ads at prime-time television with someone bringing out a plate of burgers or something, I don't really like that." While participants like Kaila, a thirty-seven-year-old in the same Vancouver focus group as Grant and Dan, acknowledged the possibility of ethical meat from corporations, she doubted its authenticity: "I think big corporations *can* sell ethical meat, but I'm way more likely to be suspicious of whether it's really ethical meat." Kaila suspected that corporations would focus on a single aspect, like antibiotic-free meat, "and really promote it, but not really take other things into consideration," thinking specifically about animal welfare issues. Kaila's friend Greg agreed, adding, "You've got to think money's the bottom line for those corporations,

right? So I don't know. I kind of don't trust them." This deep suspicion sometimes led people to extreme perspectives, like Joanna's belief that she should
avoid eating fast food because she "heard from sources that they are not really
a real meat. . . . The beef patty, I heard it's not made of real meat, ground beef."
While this may seem outlandish, Joanna's claim reflects a broad pattern of
consumer distrust of corporate corruption.[38]

Ideally, regardless of where meat is sold, food labels would provide a clear
distinction between ethically raised, healthy meat and its less desirable coun-
terpart. However, many of our participants expressed a deep distrust of corporate labels due to concerns about transparency. For instance, in a Toronto
focus group, Ellen, who works for a catering company, said simply, "I don't
really like labels because I don't trust them." This resonated with others, as
Felipe added, "I was going to say, why should I believe them?" For Felipe, the
lack of traceability was a major issue, since he couldn't verify who had certified the labels or track the animals' origin and the practices used to raise
them. His comment, "I don't really know how they do that [certify animal
products]," reflects the feeling of insecurity many consumers have about the
accuracy and trustworthiness of labels.

While many participants looked for terms like "free-range" and "grass-fed,"
it was also common for participants to question whether these labels truly reflected their ideals of happy meat. Even those who felt confident deciphering
labels expressed doubt about when they signified a meaningful certification
process and when they reflected clever marketing. Jun, who actively researched
meat's health risks, captured this experience: "I think even those certified labels
are important to me, but in general, sometimes it's a little hard to distinguish
if this is an infomercial or this is actually something else they're trying to do."
The shopping experience could exacerbate this distrust. Len, a new parent who
works as an architect, described scrutinizing labels at a large chain grocery store
that sells both ethical and conventional meat. In this setting, he is used to seeing
meat that just has "a picture of a farmer on the package of chicken thighs," concluding that "it just seems like a scam." Likewise, Benjamin said of the "free-
from" brand of chicken at the same chain: "It doesn't say how they were raised,
what their environments were. They're grain-fed. Was the grain organic? They're
supposed to be eating insects, for God's sakes!" Benjamin criticized consumers
who might think "free-from" meant everything was good, urging them to consider where the meat came from, its environmental impact, and the entire production process—factors notably absent from labels and packaging.

Conclusion: Happy Meat's Solutions and Challenges

While happy meat offers a potential solution to the ethical and environmental concerns surrounding industrial meat production, it also presents a new set of challenges. Those who could afford to buy happy meat appreciated the emotional rewards it offers but also worried about the significant barriers preventing widespread access. The moral implications of a solution inaccessible to most households created tension and struggle for most of our participants. They also had difficulty imagining how small-scale, ethical producers could ever meet global meat demand. Our participants were caught between the desire for a sustainable solution and the limitations of current ethical meat production. Although many believed happy meat had ecologically regenerative properties, participants also expressed concern about how emerging environmental crises would impact how the long-term viability of this approach.

The challenges of happy meat extend beyond big-picture environmental issues. Consumers are bombarded with upsetting and often conflicting information about meat's health impacts, and this can create a sense of confusion and mistrust. The science of meat's health impacts is constantly evolving, and this is mirrored in news coverage. To be fair, researchers face significant challenges in providing definitive answers to complex questions. But when confronted with new or contradictory answers to questions about meat and health, even from reputable sources, many people struggle with trust and uncertainty. This leads some people to adopt less-than-ideal methods to navigate the shifting informational landscape, like gut instincts and unconfirmed information. Trusting personal intuition over scientific evidence can lead to bewildering dietary beliefs and choices. It remains true, nonetheless, that *following* scientific advice in the past—e.g., the 1980s advice to cut out all fat from your diet to reduce your weight and the risk of heart disease—has also led people to make choices that look misguided from today's perspective.

It's easy to critique consumers' choices—for eating meat, for not eating the "right" kind of meat, or for abstaining altogether. There are pros and cons to all these positions. Simplistic judgments fail to capture the nuanced reality of food decision-making. We hope that we have shown that consumers are in a difficult spot. We've found that stereotypical portraits—of snobs, gluttons, puritans, or scolds—are hard to find. Instead, we have encountered consumers sincerely grappling with contradictions and complexities, attempting to balance moral considerations, personal health, family preferences, and the simple enjoyment of food. They strive to make informed decisions amidst a landscape of conflicting information and competing ethical frameworks. The science of meat is truly complicated, and translating complex research into actionable advice is challenging—even for us as researchers.

We see in our research that consumers are striving to check a lot of boxes at the same time; they try to follow their moral compass, do what they think is wise and informed, care for themselves and their family, and eat enjoyably. Consumers are struggling daily with a question that remains highly debatable, even at the end of our research journey: can we find a way to satisfy our appetites while substantively addressing the ethical, social, and environmental costs of meat production and consumption? Ultimately, this research challenges us to move beyond judgmental binaries of "good" and "bad" meat-eating and instead recognize the thoughtful deliberations, practical struggles, deep skepticism, and diverse perspectives that characterize the contemporary experience of meat eating.

CONCLUSION

How Can We Eat Ethically When Meat Is Murder?

WE END THIS BOOK with a question that has loomed large since we began this research: How is it possible to be an ethical omnivore when meat is murder? The term *murder* is undeniably dramatic and will likely annoy many meat-eating readers. However, it does reflect an obvious and unavoidable facet of meat-eating—it involves killing animals. Currently, we kill farm animals at an astronomical rate each year: about 70 billion chickens, well over one billion pigs, and hundreds of millions of cows globally.[1] As we saw in Chapter 2, rates of vegetarianism and veganism are relatively low and are not significantly expanding. Despite the increased attention paid to plant-based diets in popular culture, we wondered how we could sociologically make sense of the continued persistence of meat-eating. Many vegetarian voices continue to remind meat eaters that meat involves taking a life, but by and large people continue to eat meat.

This is not a simple story of ignorance, denial, or indifference to animal welfare. As we saw in our focus group conversations, many concerned meat eaters care about animals, recognize that meat is an animal product, and express myriad negative feelings about the industrial meat system. The happy meat story provides a way to keep eating meat, while minimizing heartache and maximizing good feelings. Happy meat superimposes an ethical framework on a food product that inevitably involves killing animals. It offers a pathway to move away from the bad feelings involved with taking a life and generates the good feelings that come with supporting farmers, frequenting local butchers, promoting sustainability, and eating delicious food. Happy meat provides an important cultural answer to the question of how to be an ethical meat eater.

While our focus has been on meat as a "happy object", to use Sara Ahmed's term, it is important to emphasize that the ethical meatscape is not just about feelings.[2] It also contains tangible material alternatives to the environmental and ethical concerns raised by industrialized meat production. While questions of scalability persist, as explored in Chapters 5 and 6, the efforts of ethical producers to prioritize animal welfare and sustainability, especially within the constraints of small- and medium-scale farming, are significant and warrant further attention and support.

We conclude this book by highlighting the diverse ways individuals navigate the complexities of ethical meat consumption and the meanings they derive from their choices. This journey is fraught with challenges, especially given the material ambiguities surrounding ethical meat—including corporate greenwashing, the environmental impacts of animal agriculture, and the inherent tension between animal welfare and the reality of slaughter. The ethical meatscape is also complicated by the cultural tendency toward polarization, simplistic binaries like "happy/sad meat," and stigmatizing moral judgments. Our aim has been to add nuance, resist these polarities, and unpack the subtle distinctions embedded in these boundary-making processes. To further this aim in our final, concluding chapter, we begin by reviewing what we have learned, offering a short synopsis of the key concepts that allow us to understand the complexity of happy meat as a partial solution to the contemporary problems of meat-eating. In the second section, we review the concept of the *meat paradox*, which forms the core of this book, and speak to some of the dangers of binary thinking. In the final section of this chapter, we acknowledge the dynamic nature of the concept of *happy meat*. It is not a fixed notion but a component of a constantly changing ethical meatscape. We conclude by outlining how we would like to nudge this evolving discourse.

Lessons from the Field

We experienced many surprises and "aha" moments doing this research. There are too many significant revelations to list them all here, but a select few are worth highlighting, as they speak to the myriad paradoxes embodied in the project of eating meat ethically and to some of the key concepts we developed or contributed to through our research.

The first paradox that surprised us was the deep and abiding desire consumers had to continue eating meat, even as they simultaneously worried about its health implications, its environmental impact, and the mistreatment of animals. Psychologists have documented the importance of "animal reminder disgust" when it comes to eating animals (e.g., eaters easily eat a piece of bacon but may feel reluctant to approach a whole roast pig). Through our sociological approach, we documented a significant degree of what we termed "factory farm disgust"—a phenomenon that involves feelings of repulsion, horror, and avoidance that relate to awareness of industrialized animal agriculture (e.g., not wanting to eat supermarket meat that presumably comes from a factory farm).

As eaters, we are complicated creatures, capable of juggling a high degree of cognitive dissonance when we make our food choices. Our psychological and cultural ability to manage dissonance helps us better understand *meat moralization*—a process first identified in 1997 by psychologist Paul Rozin and colleagues.[3] Moralization involves the association of a product, like meat, with moral qualities that complicate its hedonic appeal and prompt different modes of evaluation. Indeed, we can confidently state that meat no longer occupies neutral terrain in the public sphere and has been thoroughly moralized, even though this has not stimulated a widespread conversion to vegetarianism. Happy meat is an important part of the meat moralization story. We observed that the same consumers who are deeply concerned about meat's negative social and environmental implications can be deeply enthusiastic about the ways that local farmers, small butchers, and happy animals address the problems associated with industrialized meat. In a context where industrial meat is the norm, the availability of happy meat might serve as a preferable alternative to meat reduction (or vegetarianism) as a response to meat moralization.

A second set of surprises came from our farm visits. We were continually astounded at the hard work involved with raising animals for food and farmers' wide-ranging concerns for sustainability.[4] We were also struck by the deep affection that many producers expressed for their animals. This reflects a true, albeit not particularly novel, paradox: *animal lovers can raise animals to be killed for food.*[5] The stories we heard from producers revealed the importance of animal-human relationships as well as the complex ways that farm animals express vitality. They are living creatures that are forceful, agentic, and sometimes unpredictable. For example, a farmer might not be able to predict why one sow squishes half her piglets and another doesn't.

Given the hard work that producers put into raising animals and caring for the land, it is not a surprise that many feel misunderstood and under-valued and complain about consumers' lack of understanding. Examples of consumer myopia are peppered throughout our data and our personal lives. Indeed, as we were wrapping up this research, we asked an undergraduate student how long they thought it took for a chicken to reach maturity, and they ventured, "One year?" (The answer is six to eight weeks.) Indeed, while consumers are aware in general terms of some of the practices of industrial-ized agriculture, the full implications of these practices are far from clear. All the work that goes into raising a "happy chicken" that takes longer to raise (8–12 weeks) and might cost $40 is hard for a consumer to fully appreciate—or afford. The happy meat imaginary involves relatively small operations (e.g., dozens of chickens roaming outdoors versus tens of thousands of chickens in a barn) that could never come close to meeting the current demand for meat. As food scholars, consumer fetishization of meat was not a total surprise to us. However, the size of the gap between farmers' everyday realities and consum-ers' knowledge of the meat system was a troubling discovery.

The final set of surprises that we highlight here centers on stories. Al-though there is much we could say on this topic, in the interest of brevity we focus on the power of stories for understanding what seem to be contradictory consumption choices. There are thousands of articles written on the so-called attitude-behavior gap.[6] Put simply, people often say one thing matters to them but then do the opposite. For example, we spoke with and surveyed people who said their health was a priority for them, that they believed eating red meat was a risk for heart disease, and that they regularly ate red meat. A stan-dard solution to this sort of contradiction is to look to social context: what are the norms at play? What is the person's level of knowledge or income, and so on?[7] We found that an additional factor of importance is the stories people tell. Many of the people we spoke with made statements that would logically conclude with eliminating meat from their diet: stories about watching videos of factory farms and documentaries about the vagaries of industrial meat production or tales of seeing animals slaughtered at a young age. Yet, these people ate meat, and often in considerable quantities. We can make sense of this apparent contradiction by looking at the other powerful stories people told about meat. Three particularly common storylines are worth mentioning:

first, the story that a healthy body (read: thin, muscular) is a meat-eating body; second, the many stories showcasing the centrality of meat to a valued cultural identity (e.g., meat dishes connected to nationality or ethnicity); and, third, the story of happy meat—meat from animals that led fulfilled lives, raised by caring and contented farmers who are attentive to sustainability. To understand ongoing meat consumption in the face of the many reasons to not eat meat, we need to be cognizant of the meaningful storylines that support continued meat-eating.

Eating Meat Is a Paradox, Not a Happy/Sad Binary

Psychologists define the *meat paradox* as the seeming contradiction that occurs when people hold a strong love for animals alongside high rates of meat consumption. Our research sought to build on this concept by incorporating a sociological lens, capturing the structural critique of the meat industry that often accompanies this paradox. Our participants not only expressed concern for animal welfare, their own health, and the environment but also perceived the dominant mode of meat production as exploitative, dangerous, and unjust. This condemnation of industrial meat creates a space for alternative, more virtuous, happier options to emerge.

However, when the vast majority of consumers purchase meat without direct knowledge of its origins, it can be extremely challenging to meaningfully identify ethical meat options. In this context, we witnessed consumers resorting to simplistic distinctions, such as differentiating between "disgusting cheap meat" and "ethical happy meat," often accompanied by judgments about the type of people who buy each. As explored in Chapter 7, these perceptions range from the stereotype of the uninformed, low-income shopper grabbing discounted chickens at Walmart to the image of the affluent, white woman self-righteously purchasing happy meat at a farmers market.

While these happy/sad meat binaries might provide a heuristic for navigating a complex marketplace, they oversimplify the nuanced realities of meat production and consumption. As we saw in Chapter 7, these emotionally laden binaries—like disgusting meat versus feel-good meat—can become the basis for inaccurate or even harmful storylines. These deeply felt stories may feel true, but they are not necessarily based on a rigorous empirical assessment of various meat options. For instance, a local Portuguese butcher shop may be perceived as safe and charming, while a nearby Chinese supermarket selling cheaper meat might be unfairly associated with risk and suspicion. The take-away is that while emotional responses and simplified narratives can work to guide consumer choices, they may be based on deeply ingrained biases and stereotypes rather than a rigorous assessment of the actual conditions of meat production.

These cognitive shortcuts are understandable, given the challenges consumers face in conducting thorough investigations of meat produc-tion practices, especially when faced with budgetary and time constraints. Throughout our focus groups, we heard so much uncertainty about how to tell when meat is happy, ethical, or sustainable. There are a few iconic mo-ments of clear meat happiness, such as when Ella ate a delicious burger in California across the road from a pasture of freewheeling cattle. But these moments are rare in contrast to the many instances where consumers draw from rudimentary heuristics, glancing at photographs of happy cows or images of wholesome farmers and then hoping for the best. Ella has an ideal happy-meat touchstone to connect to, but she also told us about shopping at a local mom-and-pop butcher and hoping that they source their meat from animals that lead good lives. The few consumers who conveyed minimal uncertainty, fear, and guilt about their meat tended to spend a lot of money at selective butcher shops or places like Whole Foods Market that use ex-plicit criteria to categorize their products as humane. This reinforces the perception that ethical meat is a luxury good, accessible to those who are willing—and able—to pay a premium. While consumers frequently equate expensive meat with ethical meat, our research suggests that ethical meat is difficult to identify in a retail landscape lacking clear signposts and relying on feel-good imagery.

What is lost when we think in binary terms about happy meat versus "sad" meat? First, it is an empirically inaccurate conceptualization that obfuscates the many gray areas involved with raising happy animals (see Chapters 5 and 6). Second, thinking about a dualism of happy/sad meat can work to crowd out perspective-taking and instead encourage harsh judgment and polarized attitudes.

To illustrate the empirical inaccuracy limitation, think back to Chapter 2, where we shared our survey data. These data show that it is too simplis-tic to assume that people who don't eat meat hate it and people who eat it love it. Instead, we found that many vegetarians, vegans, and pescatarians enjoy the taste of meat: 46 percent of vegans agree that meat can be delicious!

Further, many meat eaters have significant reservations about meat. As our focus groups revealed, it is common for meat eaters to feel a great deal of guilt, discomfort, and anger about the environmental impacts of meat. Indeed, our survey data show that nearly one-third of omnivores report sometimes being grossed out by meat, and a similar proportion believes that the way meat is produced is a big problem. Overall, all of these data points illustrate that dichotomizing meat-loving omnivores and meat-hating vegetarians is inaccurate and misses common ground.

The second limitation of binary thinking relates more broadly to our cohesiveness as a society that needs to collectively reckon with serious environmental and social problems in the food system—problems ranging from rampant food insecurity and chronic health issues to animal welfare and the climate crisis. Dividing consumers, producers, and other actors into good and bad limits emotional nuance, subjectivity, and empathy. Chapter 7 describes the boundary work that meat enables, detailing the way in which meat can be seen as dirty, thereby contaminating those who eat it in ways that tend to stigmatize ethnic minorities and people with low incomes. At the same time, ethical, happy meat can communicate sanctimoniousness and reproduce class privilege. Whether we are describing meat itself in binary terms, or the people whose work puts meat on the table, or the people who eat it, when we use a binary, it often results in a ranking of one over the other. Sorting the social world into such dualistic categories makes social inequalities feel justified and thereby more entrenched.

In our focus groups, we heard significant empathy for people who had to shop on a limited budget—a reason for hope. But we also listened to people judge cheap meat as gross, risky, and racialized—even as they were aware of the inaccuracy and harshness of such judgments. Expensive, ethical meat was seen as a superior way of eating meat, but it invoked feelings of guilt and shame for those who were not able to consistently eat this way. Peter from Vancouver stated, "I'm not a bad person. I eat meat sometimes, but I'm really not a bad person," signaling his awareness that contemporary moralization processes typically cast meat-eating in a negative light. Happy meat offers meat eaters the promise of enjoying the deliciousness of meat and identification as a good person, but many of the people we spoke with sensed that the rules of the game in the ethical meatscape are constantly changing and hard to keep up with, especially on a limited budget. We shift to this topic for the last section of this conclusion.

The Conversation around Happy Meat Is in Flux

The ethical meatscape has both material and discursive dimensions, and both dimensions are changing for happy meat. When we started this project, around 2016, the ethical meatscape was not new, but it looked quite different from how it looks today in terms of its scope and its reception by consumers. Since that time, awareness of the problems with conventional meat has grown, and the number of ethical meat options (and plant-based meat alternatives) has expanded. The climate crisis has deepened, and the horrifying, and sometimes fatal, working conditions in meat-packing plants during the COVID-19 pandemic became a major news story. The cultural context of meat production has shifted, especially awareness of the environmental and human consequences of industrial meat. At the same time, changes have emerged from within the meat industry at the happy meat end of the field. For example, in May 2023, the U.S. Supreme Court upheld a California law that requires any pork sold in the state to come from sows that are housed with at least twenty-four square feet of space and the ability to move freely.[8] Because of these changes from both inside and outside the meat industry, the conversation around happy meat is in flux.

Given this evolution, we end by reflecting on the state of the happy meat storyline. How would we like to edit this story? How can we make this story more nuanced, more inclusive, and more honest about the need for most consumers to cut back on their meat consumption? To answer this question, we think that more clarity around the material realities of happy meat is required to address the problems of consumer confusion and corporate obfuscation. We hope that this book can be one small part of that effort. Obviously, most consumers will not read an academic book to illuminate their consumption choices. For a larger impact, we need policymakers and producers, both large- and small-scale, to participate in creating and disseminating information about the conditions under which livestock are raised and the material consequences of meat consumption. The phrase "less meat, better meat"—often touted by activists and farmers to promote a move away from industrial meat—is informed by material considerations about meat and gives us a clear direction for action. At the same time, "better meat" is an easier direction to follow for many people than "less meat," but one without the other is really missing the point.

The ethical meatscape is not sealed off from other parts of the foodscape; there is an ongoing dialogue with mutual influence, and North Americans can learn from debates and practices elsewhere. Although we have focused on the North American meatscape, the ethical meatscape draws on actors and discourses from around the globe. For example, one significant evolution within the meatscape has been the End the Cage Age movement in Europe. Concerns over the inhumane conditions of animal confinement were the impetus for this initiative, which collected 1.4 million signatures and led members of the European Parliament to vote to work toward a ban on the use of cages in animal agriculture.[9] It is not hard to see how these ideas are crossing borders, especially as consumers and policymakers grapple with the challenges of the global climate crisis. For this reason, the ethical meatscape's future direction can and should be influenced by larger forces than individual consumers or local producers.

There are serious reasons to be skeptical of individual consumer solutions to structural problems in the meatscape. We cannot assume that shoppers will each solve the environmental, labor, and animal welfare problems of industrial meat by consuming conscientiously and with perfect information. At the same time, the ethical meatscape's direction will inevitably be shaped by the consumers it is meant to serve. We don't want to be structural determinist nihilists who insist that individual food choices don't matter and that individuals can't make a difference. Certainly, our survey respondents are not so nihilistic: 55% of them agree with the statement that "shopping is a powerful source for social and environmental change," while only 8% disagree! We were surprised to see that these results are consistent across age, gender, and racial groups. Some consumers are looking for a different way to eat meat to address the tension of the meat paradox and to make a positive change in the world. Consumer demand will likely continue to shape how the ethical meatscape evolves in scope and in its material and discursive emphases.

With a growing global population, a changing climate, and deforestation that can be seen from space, it is clear that our prodigious meat consumption cannot continue indefinitely. In this context, an unavoidable question is how to align global meat production and consumption with known ecological limits. With the rise of flexitarianism came the prospect that more people would reduce their meat consumption ("less meat, better meat"); however, that is far from a guaranteed outcome. Indeed, a 2024 industry report, entitled

"The Power of Meat," notes that "the number of households that purchase meat (98%) remains steady from 2023, while the number seeking to decrease meat consumption has fallen by 20% since 2020."[10]

How can we encourage flexitarians, conscientious consumers, and the average concerned omnivore to eat less meat? Accomplishing a significant decrease in meat eating in our current context will be extremely challenging for two major reasons. One major obstacle lies in the rise and emotional resonance of happy meat itself. By offering a seemingly ethical and delicious alternative to industrial meat, happy meat provides an appealing salve for the concerned meat eater, assuaging guilt and aligning with values of animal welfare, sustainability, and health. Simply put, if people feel good about the meat they are eating, they are less inclined to reduce their consumption, especially given the significant pleasures associated with meat (as explored in Chapter 3). This emotional satisfaction aligns with Sara Ahmed's analysis of "happy objects," which highlights how such objects—in this case, happy meat—are imbued with positive cultural meanings and can reinforce certain values and lifestyles.[11] In the case of happy meat, this emotional resonance can hinder consumers from questioning the assumed positive outcomes of their ethical consumption habits as well as the underlying environmental and ethical problems of massively scaled meat production.

A second challenge associated with reducing meat consumption centers on the confusing, complex, and often contradictory information about meat. While vegetarian and vegan eaters face their own challenges when it comes to finding plant-based products, the choices facing an ethical carnivore are even more complex, and certainly less clearly labeled.[12] Consumers perusing the different meat options in a grocery store or butcher shop may reasonably ask themselves, was this meat *really* produced in a sustainable, humane way? The answer is often hard to determine, even for the authors of this book after having devoted years to the study of this topic.

The health discourse surrounding meat further muddies the waters. While consumers are increasingly aware of the health risks associated with high meat consumption, especially red and processed meats, the dominant cultural narrative still portrays meat as a nutritional powerhouse, essential for muscle growth and maintaining a healthy body weight. This dominant storyline powerfully amplified by industry messaging. As Meat Institute president and CEO Julie Anna Potts noted, "When shoppers hear 'protein' they think 'meat,' and the Meat Institute is actively working to maintain and grow Americans' confidence about meat's role in healthy, balanced diets."[13]

Our research affirms the commonplace equation between protein and meat, as well as the often positive association between meat and health. Moreover, as we saw in Chapter 8, when people feel overwhelmed with information, especially contradictory information, they often turn back to their own bodily cues for information on what to eat. And many people believe that they just *feel* better when they eat meat, even as they feel that this might not be the best choice for animals or the planet. These factors, combined with the emotional and cultural significance of meat, make widespread reductions in meat consumption unlikely within the current North American cultural context. However, by identifying and defining these challenges, we aim to inspire future scholars to generate solution-driven research that addresses the question of how to achieve an alignment between the amount of meat people eat and what the planet can support.

Methods Appendix

IN THIS APPENDIX, WE describe how we collected and analyzed our data. This book is a multi-method project, meaning that we rely on several forms of data. Collecting different kinds of data increased the work required but allowed us to address a wider array of issues. We review each data collection effort in turn.

Focus Groups with Consumers

We hosted sixteen focus groups with 67 participants in Toronto and Vancouver between 2019 and 2022. We held eight focus groups in each city. We aimed to have four participants in each focus group, but some focus groups had three while others had five. The focus groups were labeled according to the province (ON and BC) in which they were held (e.g., BC01 is the name given to the first Vancouver focus group). We selected these two cities to provide geographic and cultural variation within Canada.

We sought to have a sample that was roughly representative of the population of ethical meat shoppers. Key details are summarized in the table below, but some factors are worth noting. There was a relatively equal portion of male and female participants, with a slight overrepresentation of females—a distribution that makes sense given that women do more food shopping than men. Also, the sample was racially and ethnically diverse. With only six exceptions, all participants were employed, and most participants were highly educated, holding either a bachelor's or a postgraduate degree.

The focus groups began before the COVID-19 pandemic (2019–2020) and, as such, the first groups (BC01–BC04 and ON01–ON04) were in-person

TABLE A.1

Focus Group Demographics (n = 67)						
Sex	Age	Sexuality	# of Children	Race	Highest Educational Credential	Income
Female = 38	20 – 29 = 10	Heterosexual = 56	0 = 38	White = 41*	High school = 11	Less than $25K = 2
Male = 29	30 – 39 = 23	Gay = 0	1 = 12	Visible	Bachelor's = 35	$25-$50K = 10
	40 – 49 = 12	Lesbian = 0	2 = 12	Minority = 26	Post-graduate = 21	$50-$100K = 17
	50 – 59 = 9	Bisexual = 4	3 = 3			$100-$150K = 22
	60 – 69 = 8	Queer = 3	4 = 1			$150-$200K = 11
	70 – 79 = 1	MD = 4	5 = 0			$200K+ = 5
	80 – 89 = 1		6 = 1			
	MD = 3					

MD = Missing data.
*This includes "white," "Caucasian," "British," "European," "English," and "Anglo."

gatherings. For in-person focus groups, we provided snacks and drinks and aimed to establish a friendly, informal, nonjudgmental atmosphere. The in-person focus groups took place in the home of one of the participants or in the home of a researcher. When it was clear that the pandemic was leading to a prolonged period of lockdowns and social distancing, we resumed focus groups online (2021–2022) using Zoom (BC05–BC06 and ON05–0N08). For online focus groups, participants took part via synchronous video and audio stream, with some participants additionally responding using the chat function of the online platform. When pandemic social distancing wound down in the summer of 2022, we held two final in-person focus groups (BC07–BC08) in Vancouver. For both in-person and online focus groups, we facilitated discussion using a semi-structured interview guide that assessed what kinds of meat participants enjoy; where they regularly shop for meat; what their attitudes and emotions toward meat (pleasure, disgust, etc.) were; and how they feel about "bigger picture" meat issues, such as the impacts of intensive meat production on climate change.

We recruited participants using a variety of techniques, starting with word-of-mouth snowball sampling but expanding to online ads, flyers posted in butcher shops and farmers markets as well as ads in community newspapers and online newsletters. All our recruitment materials explicitly referenced meat. Surprisingly, in a handful of focus groups, a few vegetarians signed up to participate, interpreting "meat" to include not only livestock products, but also vegan and vegetarian substitutes, such as tofu, Beyond Meat products, and veggie burgers. Given this outcome, we adopted a flexible interviewing approach, modifying questions as needed to meet the needs and interests of participants. For example, we reframed questions that dealt with disgust around handling whole animal products to capture a range of emotional responses to preparing "meat," as defined by participants. A flexible interviewing approach allowed us to capture novel themes and consumer issues; to facilitate comparisons between consumers who used traditional definitions of meat and those who provided more expansive understandings; and to ensure that our final analyses emerged from participant understandings, not extant research.

Immediately after interviews, the team wrote memos that included a description of the focus group site and subject(s), post-focus group thoughts and reflections, and a working set of emerging themes. Subsequent memos were informed, but not constrained by, earlier memos in terms of the list of emerging themes. The interviews were transcribed and coded in qualitative data analysis software. The coding process began with sensitizing concepts based on the research questions and prior literature. As the codes were applied, they were refined and revised to allow them to capture the most salient patterns, balancing the need for data reduction strategies with the desire to represent the nuances and details of the participants' conversations. All participants quoted in the book are presented using pseudonyms that attempt to signal their self-described ethnicity.

In-Person versus Online Focus Groups

In-person focus groups had the advantage of allowing for face-to-face camaraderie, free-flowing conversation, and snacks. In general, in-person focus groups featured a higher degree of joking, laughter, and casual interactions than online focus groups. That said, the latter also had their strengths. Consistent with prior research comparing online and traditional focus groups, we observed several benefits of the online method.[1] In addition to reducing barriers to participation, the online format enabled us to capitalize on the rich group interactions characteristic of traditional focus groups, while offering participants enhanced privacy and autonomy. The online space sometimes appeared to curb the "groupthink" tendency of in-person, face-to-face focus groups.[2] Rather than shying away from controversial topics and conforming to a single perspective, some online participants openly discussed contentious issues relating to meat and meat abstention, perhaps feeling more socially free than they might have felt in an in-person setting. In several groups, meat avoiders and meat eaters discussed, and reported benefiting from hearing, one another's alternative perspectives on the ethics of meat consumption and the costs and benefits of shopping conscientiously. While online focus groups had the disadvantage of curbing spontaneous conversations, they also created a more orderly conversational flow that seemed to give more space for shy participants to contribute.

Interviews with Producers

We carried out interviews with meat producers in Western Canada (primarily Alberta and British Columbia with a handful of interviewees working in Saskatchewan) and Ontario between 2017 and 2022. The geographic range allowed us to access a diversity of perspectives that were not constrained to the specific environmental and regulatory conditions of a single region or province. The average age of interviewees was forty-six, and our sample included a fair number of female interviewees, especially considering the farming sector is traditionally a masculine realm. We frequently interviewed married couples who managed their businesses together. In one case, in Alberta, we held a group interview with a holistic ranching group that had worked together for several decades.

Most participants were heterosexual, but some did not answer the question and two participants described themselves as fluid. Almost all interviewees self-identified as white or Caucasian; exceptions included three participants who described themselves as Cree, Chinese-Canadian, and Jewish, respectively.

TABLE A.2

Interview Demographics (n = 76)			
	# of People	Sex	Average Age
Alberta and Saskatchewan	28	Female = 11 Male = 17	44
British Columbia	15	Female = 5 Male = 10	51
Ontario	33	Female = 14 Male = 19	44

Although the Canadian government does not collect data on the race of farmers, this trend reflects broad patterns of dominant whiteness in land ownership that are also observed in the United States. This pattern has its roots in the colonial history of North America, intergenerational land transfer within farming families, and potentially cultural ideas and beliefs about who farmers ideally are.

We targeted producers of beef, pork, and/or chicken, although many also worked with other animals (e.g., lamb, ducks) and with plant crops. In most cases, we conducted interviews at workplaces—mainly farmhouses but also butcher shops, pastures, farm-to-table restaurants, and two slaughterhouses. Site visits greatly increased the amount of information we gained, and we were often able to observe everyday aspects of farm life and pose additional questions related to what we were observing. A small proportion of our interviewees were referred to us by earlier interviewees. Some referrals were to producers who were not personally known to earlier interviewees but were known by reputation. Interviews lasted between 30 minutes and 4.5 hours, but most were around two hours long.

Immediately after interviews, we wrote memos that included a description of the interview site and subject(s), post-interview thoughts and reflections, and a working set of emerging themes. Subsequent memos were informed, but not constrained by, earlier memos in terms of the list of emerging themes. All the interviews were recorded, transcribed, and coded for themes, and interviewees were assigned a pseudonym that attempts to signal their ethnicity. The coding process began with a set of concerns and ideas based on past research and our major research questions. The codes were refined during the coding process as new concerns and new distinctions became apparent. When codes were refined or new codes were created, we recoded transcripts according to the updated codes.

Because we are not experts in farming or raising livestock, we asked a farmer with significant experience raising livestock outside the industrial meat system to review our chapters on raising animals. This reading provided a check against the unwitting introduction of inaccuracies or serious omissions regarding the day-to-day practicalities of raising livestock.

National Survey

In mid-2019, we developed a set of survey questions based on our reading of the literature on meat consumption, with the goal of establishing a base of knowledge about "typical" beliefs, feelings, and behaviors related to meat-eating. We

TABLE A.3

Descriptive Statistics for Major Demographics of our Survey Sample (n = 2,328)

	N	Weighted % or Mean
Gender		
Female	1326	49.9%
Male	994	49.8%
Other	8	0.3%
Age (Mean)	-	47.3
Race		
White	1839	73.4%
Indigenous	113	7.0%
Black	27	1.5%
Asian/Arab	294	12.3%
Other	55	3.8%
Education		
High School or Less	833	35.2%
Moderate Education	839	36.3%
High Education	656	28.5%
Household Income		
Less than $15,000	150	6.4%
$15,000 to $29,999	292	11.4%
$30,000 to $44,999	311	12.6%
$45,000 to $59,999	322	12.3%
$60,000 to $79,999	329	13.8%
$80,000 to $99,999	265	11.1%
$100,000 to $149,000	427	17.7%
$150,000 to $199,000	152	7.9%
$200,000 or more	80	6.8%

also included questions that we saw as relevant to filling gaps in prior research regarding important distinctions between different kinds of meat-eating, different motivations for both eating and avoiding meat, and the social contexts in which people make choices about meat-eating. In addition to questions about demographic background, political orientation, and other social characteristics, our survey included almost 70 questions related to thoughts, feelings, and behaviors related to meat consumption.

The survey was administered online from September to November of 2019 through a contract with Qualtrics, which maintains connections to panel members who can take surveys for remuneration. Panelists were screened based on gender, race, income, education, age, and Canadian province of residence to develop a sample that was representative of Canadian national distributions for these six variables. Because not all variables could be matched exactly with Canadian national distributions, we developed a sample weighting to correct for these differences and apply the weight in the calculations we report in the book. To enhance data quality, responses were screened based on speed of survey completion and lack of variation in responses, with responses below our quality thresholds discarded. We paused data collection after the first 100 responses to verify that respondents were interpreting our questions as intended.

Further Reading

There is a rich trove on scholarly materials from multiple disciplines on the topic of meat-eating and vegetarianism. For readers seeking a deeper understanding grounded in research and analysis, we've identified a selection of particularly insightful academic books from various fields. These are texts that we have found useful in our own thinking about meat and works that seem important to the evolution of this field of scholarship.

Singer, Peter. *Animal Liberation.* **New York: HarperCollins, 1975.** Working from a specifically philosophical paradigm, Singer's book has been foundational in thinking about the ethics of how humans interact with animals. Singer challenges the concept of "speciesism," arguing that discrimination against other species simply because they are not human is unethical. Singer exposes the harsh realities of factory farming and product-testing procedures, arguing that these practices are not only profoundly unethical but also environmentally and socially detrimental. While he does not equate animal rights with human rights, he advocates for rights appropriate to animals' level of sentience. In many ways, this work got people thinking about the problems with industrial meat that then led to the alternative of happy meat (although Singer would not be satisfied with that outcome).

Joy, Melanie. *Why We Love Dogs, Eat Pigs, and Wear Cows: An Introduction to Carnism.* **San Francisco: Conari Press, 2010.** As the title indicates, many people have contradictory relationships to different animals. Joy introduces the term *carnism* as she explores the psychological and cultural mechanisms that enable people to eat meat while caring for some animals as pets. These discrepancies in our approaches to different animals facilitate the growth and maintenance of factory farming and its attendant cruelties, labor hazards, and environmental harms. Many of us consume the products of factory farming even as we see ourselves as animal lovers. This inconsistency arises through a process of social conditioning, and it is not inevitable. As a social psychologist, Joy argues that becoming aware of our food choices, and the implicit system of beliefs that influence them, can lead to personal empowerment and social transformation.

Pachirat, Timothy. *Every Twelve Seconds: Industrialized Slaughter and the Politics of Sight*. **New Haven: Yale University Press, 2011.** Pachirat's ethnographic study of an industrial slaughterhouse provides a powerful account of the social and ethical dimensions of industrial meat production. The book gives us an insider's perspective on industrialized killing, including the realities of slaughterhouse work and the implications for workers. Pachirat describes how, as complex, large-scale organizations, slaughterhouses employ practices and routines that obscure some information while intensively monitoring and tracking other information, all in the service of maximizing the efficiency and scale of slaughter. The book also examines how societies keep unpleasant institutions invisible from the consuming public.

Adams, Carol J. *The Sexual Politics of Meat: A Feminist-Vegetarian Critical Theory*. **New York: Continuum, 1990.** Adams explores the connections between the oppression of women and the oppression of animals, presenting a feminist-vegetarian perspective on meat consumption and animal welfare. She argues that both women and animals are subjected to similar forms of oppression in patriarchal societies. Using an analytic approach that emphasizes semiotics, Adams demonstrates symbolic parallels between the farming and consumption of animals on the one hand and the objectification and subjugation of women on the other. Like with many of the other books here, this book challenges readers to consider the ethical implications of their food choices. What is unique about Adams's work is the symbolic connections she makes between the domination and exploitation of both animals and women, showing how broad patterns of hierarchy can implicitly reinforce one another.

Blanchette, Alex. *Porkopolis: American Animality, Standardized Life, and the Factory Farm*. **Durham, N.C.: Duke University Press, 2020.** Blanchette's book is a comprehensive ethnographic study of industrialized pork production in the United States. His research focuses on a large-scale pork processing facility in the Midwest. The findings from his research site can speak to issues that are salient throughout the industry. Blanchette examines the intricate relationships between humans and pigs, revealing how the commodification and mechanization of animal life affect both species. This examination highlights the ways in which labor, biology, and technology are brought together to maximize productivity and profit. Through detailed accounts of workers' experiences and the transformation of pigs from living beings into standardized commodities, Blanchette critiques the broader implications of industrial agriculture on human-animal relations and the environment, urging a rethinking of contemporary practices in animal husbandry and food production.

Schatzker, Mark. *Steak: One Man's Search for the World's Tastiest Piece of Beef.* **New York: Penguin Group, 2010.** Schatzker's book embarks on a rigorous exploration of the pursuit for the world's finest steak, blending culinary adventure with investigative journalism. Schatzker traverses diverse landscapes, from the wide-open pampas of Argentina to the severe Australian outback, engaging with dedicated ranchers, scientists, and culinary experts. His narrative is imbued with vivid descriptions of environments and flavors, uncovering the intricate interconnections between genetics, diet, and environmental factors that contribute to the quality of beef. *Steak* examines not only the sensory attributes of this prized meat but also its cultural and historical significance. The message of *Steak* is important to remember as we consider happy meat—for many people, beef, and particularly steak, is a profound gastronomic experience that people feel strongly connected to.

Pollan, Michael. *The Omnivore's Dilemma: A Natural History of Four Meals.* **New York: Penguin Press, 2006.** This book is a little strange to include here, since it is not mainly about meat. However, we include it because it has become a classic and was responsible for setting the trajectory for the public discourse about food politics in the twenty-first century. Pollan is an obvious food lover who cares about human welfare, social justice, public health, and the food system. The critiques of the food industry and the corporatization of food production and distribution apply equally, and perhaps especially, to meat specifically. Pollan exposes many myths and common misunderstandings about how food is produced. He also provides informed ideas about how people can address the dilemmas we all face as eaters who must navigate the industrial food system.

Katz-Rosene, Ryan M., and Sarah J. Martin, eds. *Green Meat? Sustaining Eaters, Animals, and the Planet.* McGill-Queen's University Press-MQUP, 2020. An edited volume from diverse contributors, this book raises important questions about meat eating and its environmental impacts. The chapters collectively take an eclectic epistemological approach, and they do not hew closely to any single philosophical or political perspective. The contributors include academics from disciplines such as geography, political science, food studies, and environmental studies. The question mark in the title represents both the commitment to explore whether and how meat eating can be sustainable and the reality that the answer to that question remains uncertain.

Percival, Rob. *The Meat Paradox: Eating, Empathy, and the Future of Meat.* New York, London: Pegasus Books, 2022. Percival covers a lot of ground—he talks to diverse constituencies, reviews historical and anthropological scholarship, visits many sites along the meat commodity chain, and assesses contemporary health science about meat eating. He does this work to write in a balanced and nuanced way about the psychology of the meat paradox. His efforts to gather as many viewpoints and as much information as possible about the complexities of the meat paradox pay off, making the book a rich and entertaining consideration of the psychological reactions, maneuvers, and dissonance inherent to eating meat.

Rodgers, Diana, and Robb Wolf. *Sacred Cow: The Case for (Better) Meat: Why Well-Raised Meat is Good for You and Good for the Planet.* Dallas: BenBella Books, 2021. Unlike our own book, this book is concerned solely with beef as meat-eating, and also unlike our own book, this book is primarily concerned with providing an answer to the question of whether eating meat is a good idea for individuals, for societies, and for the world. Rodgers and Wolf have the goal of bucking the dominant paradigm of meat-eating as a major social problem. They review, and critique, a large amount of scientific research relating to health, to animals, and to the environment. They offer an alternative perspective to what we usually see, one that is more optimistic and focused on finding the benefits eating beef. They make the case for "better" meat and the role that cattle can play when raised on grassland with practices geared toward maximizing soil health. Although their takes will be controversial for some readers, there is no doubt that some of the perspectives they advance inspire many consumers of happy meat.

Notes

Introduction

1. *Portlandia*, season 1, episode 1, "Farm," directed by Jonathan Krisel, written by Fred Armisen et al., featuring Fred Armisen and Carrie Brownstein, aired January 21, 2011.

2. Marco Springmann et al., "Options for Keeping the Food System within Environmental Limits," *Nature* 562 (2018): 519–25, https://doi.org/10.1038/s41586-018-0594-0.

3. Xia Wang et al., "Red and Processed Meat Consumption and Mortality: Dose-Response Meta-Analysis of Prospective Cohort Studies," *Public Health Nutrition* 19, no. 5 (2015): 893–905, https://doi.org/10.1017/S1368980015002062; John N. Sofos and Ifigenia Geornaras, "Overview of Current Meat Hygiene and Safety Risks and Summary of Recent Studies on Biofilms, and Control of *Escherichia Coli* O157:H7 in Nonintact, and *Listeria Monocytogenes* in Ready-to-Eat, Meat Products," *Meat Science* 86, no. 1 (2010): 2–14, https://doi.org/10.1016/j.meatsci.2010.04.015. The United States Center for Disease Control estimates that one in six Americans gets sick each year from foodborne pathogens. For a list of the top ten food pathogen risks (seven of which are related to animal foods), see Michael B. Batz, Sandra Hoffman, and J. Glenn Morris Jr., *Ranking the Risks: The 10 Pathogen-Food Combinations with the Greatest Burden on Public Health* (Gainesville: Emerging Pathogens Institute, University of Florida, 2011), https://folio.iupui.edu/bitstream/handle/10244/1022/72267report.pdf?sequence=1.

4. Fred Gerr, "Meatpacking Plant Workers: A Case Study of a Precarious Workforce," *Journal of Occupational and Environmental Hygiene* 18, no. 4–5 (2021): 154–58, https://doi.org/10.1080/15459624.2021.1895997. Sarah E. Dempsey, Heather M. Zoller and Kathleen Hunt, "The Meatpacking Industry's Corporate Exceptionalism: Racialized Logics of Food Chain Worker Disposability during the COVID-19 Crisis," *Food Culture and Society* 26, no. 3 (2023): 571–90, https://doi.org/10.1080/15528014.2021.2022916.

5. For example, see Elin Kubberød et al., "Attitudes Toward Meat and Meat-Eating Among Adolescents in Norway: A Qualitative Study," *Appetite* 38, no. 1 (2002): 53–62, https://doi.org/10.1006/appe.2002.0458; Jonas R. Kunst and Christian Andrés Palacios Haugestad, "The Effects of Dissociation on Willingness to Eat Meat Are Moderated

by Exposure to Unprocessed Meat: A Cross-Cultural Demonstration," *Appetite* 120 (2018): 356–66, https://doi.org/10.1016/j.appet.2017.09.016.

6. "Meat Consumption," OECD, accessed December 13, 2022, https://doi.org/10.1787/fa290fd0-en.

7. Hank Rothgerber, "Meat-Related Cognitive Dissonance: A Conceptual Framework for Understanding How Meat Eaters Reduce Negative Arousal from Eating Animals," *Appetite* 146 (2020): 6, https://doi.org/10.1016/j.appet.2019.104511.

8. "Meat Consumption," OECD.

9. "Projected per Capita Meat Consumption Worldwide from 2020 to 2032, by Country Group (in Kilograms of Retail Weight)," *Statista*, Statista Inc., 7 Jun 2023, https://www.statista.com/statistics/1270102/meat-consumption-worldwide-per-capita/.

10. "Meat Consumption," OECD.

11. Merin Oleschuk, Josée Johnston, and Shyon Baumann, "Maintaining Meat: Cultural Repertoires and the Meat Paradox in a Diverse Sociocultural Context," *Sociological Forum* 34, no. 2 (2019): 337–60, https://doi.org/10.1111/socf.12500.

12. Jared Piazza et al., "Rationalizing Meat Consumption. The 4Ns," *Appetite* 91 (2015): 114–28, https://doi.org/10.1016/j.appet.2015.04.011.

13. Adrienne Rose Johnson, "The Paleo Diet and the American Weight Loss Utopia, 1975–2014," *Utopian Studies* 26, no. 1 (2015): 101–24, https://doi.org/10.5325/utopianstudies.26.1.0101; Víctor de la O et al., "Scoping Review of Paleolithic Dietary Patterns: A Definitional Proposal," *Nutrition Research Reviews* 34, no. 1 (2021): 78–106, https://doi.org/10.1017/S0954422420000153. Manvir Singh, "Is an All-Meat Diet What Nature Intended?" *New Yorker,* October 22, 2023.

14. Steve Loughnan, Nick Haslam, and Brock Bastian, "The Role of Meat Consumption in the Denial of Moral Status and Mind to Meat Animals," *Appetite* 55, no. 1 (2010): 156–59, https://doi.org/10.1016/j.appet.2010.05.043.

15. Carl Jung, *Collected Works* (Princeton, N.J.: Princeton University Press, 1969), 417.

16. Paula Arcari, *Making Sense of "Food" Animals: A Critical Exploration of the Persistence of 'Meat'* (Singapore: Palgrave Macmillan, 2020).

17. Sara Ahmed, *The Promise of Happiness* (Durham, N.C.: Duke University Press, 2010).

18. See Arcari, *Making Sense of "Food" Animals*; Alex Blanchette, *Porkopolis* (Durham, N.C.: Duke University Press, 2020).

19. For examples of scholars who take a similar approach, see Ryan Katz-Rosene and Sarah J. Martin, *Green Meat? Sustaining Eaters, Animals, and the Planet.* (Montreal: McGill-Queen's University Press, 2020); Christine Jeske, "Re-Enchanting Meat: How Sacred Meaning-Making Strengthens the Ethical Meat Movement," *Agriculture and Human Values,* 2023, https://doi.org/10.1007/s10460-023-10477-9.

20. For a seminal text on the ethics of eating animals see Peter Singer, *Animal Liberation* (New York: Random House, 1975). For a more recent review see Candace Croney and Janice Swanson, "Is Meat Eating Morally Defensible? Contemporary Ethical Considerations," *Animal Frontiers* 13, no. 2 (2023): 61–71.

21. Although Arcari takes a different approach that is explicitly opposed to meat-eating and rooted in a Foucauldian method, her research with ethical meat producers and consumers in Australia also leads her to argue that increased transparency around meat production does not impact the perceived edibility of animals and does not decenter eaters' understandings of animals as food. Arcari, *Making Sense*, ch. 9.

22. See, for example, Timothy Pachirat, *Every Twelve Seconds* (New Haven: Yale University Press, 2013); Alex Blanchette, *Porkopolis: American Animality, Standardized Life, and the Factory Farm* (Durham, N.C.: Duke University Press, 2020).

23. Psychologists use the term *meat paradox* to refer specifically to the disconnect between caring about animals while also eating them, a topic that is the subject of much psychological research. See Brock Bastian and Steve Loughnan, "Resolving the Meat-Paradox: A Motivational Account of Morally Troublesome Behavior and Its Maintenance," *Personality and Social Psychology Review* 21, no. 3 (2017): 278–99, https://doi.org/10.1177/1088868316647562. Some psychologists use a broader term, *meat-related cognitive dissonance* (MRCD), to refer to the meat paradox as well as a wider class of meat-related inconsistencies. In this book, we use the term *meat paradox* as a general master category—to refer to the broad phenomena of paradoxical outcomes generated by the contemporary cultural politics of meat-eating and involving multiple instances of cognitive dissonance. See Rothgerber, "Meat-Related Cognitive Dissonance," 2.

24. *Okja*, directed by Bong Joon-ho (Los Angeles: Plan B Entertainment, 2017); *Cowspiracy*, directed by Kip Anderson and Keegan Kuhn (A.U.M. Films & First Spark Media, 2014).

25. The meat paradox is a generalized version of what is known as the *attitude behavior gap*. This term refers to a common tendency for people to express a set of values that does not align with their behaviors and practices around these values. See Iris Vermeir and Wim Verbeke, "Sustainable Food Consumption: Exploring the Consumer 'Attitude—Behavioral Intention' Gap," *Journal of Agricultural and Environmental Ethics* 19 (2006): 169–94, https://doi.org/10.1007/s10806-005-5485-3. For example, most people consider climate change to be a pressing issue, but few substantively mitigate their high greenhouse gas-emitting behaviors. See Robert Gifford, "The Dragons of Inaction: Psychological Barriers That Limit Climate Change Mitigation and Adaptation," *American Psychologist* 66, no. 4 (2011): 290–302, https://doi.org/10.1037/a0023566; Janet A. Lorenzen, "Going Green: The Process of Lifestyle Change," *Sociological Forum* 27, no. 1 (2012): 94–116, https://doi.org/10.1111/j.1573-7861.2011.01303.x; Saffron O'Neill and Sophie Nicholson Cole, "'Fear Won't Do It': Promoting Positive Engagement With Climate Change Through Visual and Iconic Representations," *Science Communication* 30, no. 3 (2009): 355–79, https://doi.org/10.1177/1075547008329201. The meat paradox can be seen as a close cousin of the attitude behavior gap in that they share similar cultural features (i.e., people don't do exactly what they say they believe in), but the meat paradox more specifically tackles the empirical puzzle of eating animals.

26. Rothberger, "Meat-Related Cognitive Dissonance," 1.

27. For example, see Rothgerber, "Meat-Related Cognitive Dissonance," 6; Daniel L. Rosenfeld, "The Psychology of Vegetarianism: Recent Advances and Future Directions," *Appetite* 131 (2018): 125–38, https://doi.org/10.1016/j.appet.2018.09.011; Bronwyn Mariana Antonia Monteiro et al., "The Carnism Inventory: Measuring the Ideology of Eating Animals," *Appetite* 113 (2017): 51–62, https://doi.org/10.1016/j.appet.2017.02.011.

28. See Hank Rothgerber, "'But I Don't Eat That Much Meat': Situational Underreporting of Meat Consumption by Women," *Society and Animals* 27, no. 2 (2019): 150–73, https://doi.org/10.1163/15685306-12341468.

29. For full details of this experimental study, see Loughnan, Haslam, and Bastian, "Role of Meat Consumption," 156. See also Brock Bastian et al., "Don't Mind Meat? The Denial of Mind to Animals Used for Human Consumption," *Personality and Social Psychology Bulletin* 38, no. 2 (2012): 247–56, https://doi.org/10.1177/0146167211424291; James A. Serpell, "Having Our Dogs and Eating Them Too: Why Animals Are a Social Issue," *Journal of Social Issues* 65, no. 3 (2009): 642, https://doi.org/10.1111/j.1540-4560.2009.01617.x.

30. Research shows that apologetic dissociations are commonplace among eaters, as psychologists believe that most consumers simply don't think, and don't want to think, very much about where their meat comes from. See Hal Herzog, *Some We Love, Some We Hate, Some We Eat: Why It's So Hard to Think Straight about Animals* (Toronto: Harper Perennial, 2010), 188; Rothgerber, "Meat-Related Cognitive Dissonance," 4.

31. Lotte Holm and Mette Møhl, "The Role of Meat in Everyday Food Culture: An Analysis of an Interview Study in Copenhagen," *Appetite* 34, no. 3 (2000): 280, https://doi.org/10.1006/appe.2000.0324.

32. See Rothgerber, "'But I Don't Eat That Much Meat'"; Rothgerber, "Meat-Related Cognitive Dissonance," 4.

33. This is explained more fully in Rothgerber, "'But I Don't Eat That Much Meat,'" 7.

34. See Rothgerber, "'But I Don't Eat That Much Meat,'" 7; Rothgerber, "Meat-Related Cognitive Dissonance," 6; Melanie Joy, *Why We Love Dogs, Eat Pigs, and Wear Cows: An Introduction to Carnism* (San Francisco: Red Wheel/Weiser, 2010).

35. See Piazza et al., "Rationalizing Meat Consumption"; Joy, *Why We Love Dogs, Eat Pigs, and Wear Cows.*

36. Rothgerber, "Meat-Related Cognitive Dissonance," 8.

37. Carol J. Adams, *The Sexual Politics of Meat: A Feminist-Vegetarian Critical Theory* (New York: Bloomsbury, 1990).

38. Rothgerber, "'But I Don't Eat That Much Meat,'" 8.

39. For example, see Rothgerber, "'But I Don't Eat That Much Meat'"; Hank Rothgerber, "Real Men Don't Eat (Vegetable) Quiche: Masculinity and the Justification of Meat Consumption," *Psychology of Men and Masculinity* 14, no. 4 (2013): 363–75, https://doi.org/10.1037/a0030379; Matthew B. Ruby, "Vegetarianism: A Blossoming Field of Study," *Appetite* 58, no. 1 (2012): 141–50, https://doi.org/10.1016/j.appet.2011.09.019. Elin Kubberød, Elin, Øydis Ueland,

Gunvor Irene Dingstad, Einar Risvik, and Inge Jan Henjesand, "The Effect of Animality in the Consumption Experience—A Potential for Disgust," *Journal of Food Products Marketing*, 14 no. 3 (2008): 103–24, https://doi.org/10.1080/10454440801985985. Elin Kubberød, Øydis Ueland, Einar Risvik, and Inge Jan Henjesand, "A Study on the Mediating Role of Disgust with Meat in the Prediction of Red Meat Consumption Among Young Females," *Journal of Consumer Behaviour* 5, no. 4 (2006): 281–91, https://doi.org/10.1002/cb.180.

40. Rothgerber, "'But I Don't Eat That Much Meat,'" 1.

41. See Nina Hestermann, Yves Le Yaouanq, and Nicolas Treich, "An Economic Model of the Meat Paradox," *European Economic Review* 129 (2020): 103569, https://doi.org/10.1016/j.euroecorev.2020.103569.

42. For more on consumers with inelastic demands for meat, see Eryn Bell, F. Bailey Norwood, and Jayson Lusk, "Are Consumers Willfully Ignorant About Animal Welfare?" *Animal Welfare* 26, no. 4 (2017): 399–402, https://doi.org/10.7120/09627286.26.4.399. For research on how messaging about the harmful effects of meat can actually reinforce meat-eating, see Hestermann et al., "Economic Model of the Meat Paradox."

43. Richard W. Bulliet, *Hunters, Herders, and Hamburgers: The Past and Future of Human-Animal Relationships* (New York: Columbia University Press, 2005).

44. Bulliet, *Hunters, Herders, and Hamburgers*, 3.

45. Cecilie A. H. Thorslund and Jesper Lassen, "Context, Orders of Worth, and the Justification of Meat Consumption Practices," *Sociologia Ruralis* 57, no. 1 (2017): 836–58, https://doi.org/10.1111/soru.12143.

46. Robert Magneson Chiles, "Hidden in Plain Sight: How Industry, Mass Media, and Consumers' Everyday Habits Suppress Food Controversies," *Sociologia Ruralis* 57, no. S1 (2017): 791–815, https://doi.org/10.1111/soru.12152.

47. Tyler Bateman, Shyon Baumann, and Josée Johnston, "Meat as Benign, Meat as Risk: Mapping News Discourse of an Ambiguous Issue," *Poetics* 76 (2019): 101356, https://doi.org/10.1016/j.poetic.2019.03.001.

48. For a more robust discussion of the routine nature of consumption choices as it relates to ethical consumption, see Ethan D. Schoolman, "Completing the Circuit: Routine, Reflection, and Ethical Consumption," *Sociological Forum* 31, no. 3 (2016): 619–41, https://doi.org/10.1111/socf.12266; Alan Warde, *The Practice of Eating* (Malden, Mass.: Polity Press, 2016).

49. For some of the published findings, see Oleschuk, Johnston, and Baumann, "Maintaining Meat"; Josée Johnston, Shyon Baumann, and Merin Oleschuk, "Capturing Inequality and Action in Prototypes: The Case of Meat-Eating and Vegetarianism," *Poetics* 87 (2021): 101530, https://doi.org/10.1016/j.poetic.2021.101530.

50. Michèle Lamont, *Money, Morals, and Manners: The Culture of the French and the American Upper-Middle Class* (Chicago: University of Chicago Press, 1992); Ann Swidler, "Culture in Action: Symbols and Strategies," *American Sociological Review* 51, no. 2 (1986): 273–86, https://doi.org/10.2307/2095521; Ann Swidler, *Talk of Love: How Culture Matters* (Chicago: University of Chicago Press, 2001).

51. Swidler, *Talk of Love*.

52. Swidler's conceptualization of culture as a flexible tool kit, rather than a set of fixed values, has been profoundly influential in sociology as well as food studies. On the use of repertoires in sociology, see Sarah B. Garrett, "Foundations of the Cultural Repertoire: Education and Social Network Effects Among Expectant Mothers," *Poetics* 55 (2016): 19–35, https://doi.org/10.1016/j.poetic.2015.12.003; David J. Harding, "Cultural Context, Sexual Behavior, and Romantic Relationships in Disadvantaged Neighborhoods," *American Sociological Review* 72, no. 3 (2007): 341–64, https://doi.org/10.1177/000312240707200302. For food-specific illustrations, see Josée Johnston, Michelle Szabo, and Alexandra Rodney, "Good Food, Good People: Understanding the Cultural Repertoire of Ethical Eating," *Journal of Consumer Culture* 11, no. 3 (2011): 293–318, https:// doi.org/10.1177/1469540511417996; Brenda Beagan et al., *Acquired Tastes: Why Families Eat the Way They Do* (Vancouver: UBC Press, 2014).

53. Oleschuk, Johnston, and Baumann, "Maintaining Meat," 8.

54. Health scholars continue to debate the myriad linkages between body fat and ill health, with some research pointing toward an obesity paradox, whereby individuals (especially elderly individuals) with elevated body fat may have lower morality. See, for example, Carl J. Lavie, Richard V. Milani, and Hector O. Ventura, "Obesity and Cardiovascular Disease: Risk Factor, Paradox, and Impact of Weight Loss," *Journal of the American College of Cardiology* 53, no. 21 (2009): 1925–32, https://doi.org/10.1016/j.jacc.2008.12.068. A useful survey of critical social scientific perspectives on fat can be found in Esther Rothblum and Sondra Solovay, eds., *The Fat Studies Reader* (New York: NYU Press, 2009).

55. This paradoxical figure of the unhealthy fat man is in keeping with prior research showing the diversity of masculine ideals and masculine prototypes associated with meat-eating. See Johnston, Baumann, and Oleschuk, "Capturing Inequality and Action in Prototypes."

56. This finding aligns with past work showing how the cultural repertoire concept is a powerful tool for understanding how people develop and maintain ethnic identities and boundaries. See Michèle Lamont, *The Dignity of Working Men: Morality and the Boundaries of Race, Class, and Immigration* (Cambridge, Mass.: Harvard University Press, 2000).

57. Michiel Korthals, "Taking Consumers Seriously: Two Concepts of Consumer Sovereignty," *Journal of Agricultural and Environmental Ethics* 14, no. 2 (2001): 201–15, https://doi.org/10.1023/A:1011356930245.

58. Josée Johnston, "The Citizen-Consumer Hybrid: Ideological Tensions and the Case of Whole Foods Market," *Theory and Society* 37, no. 3 (2008): 229–70, https://doi.org/10.1007/s11186-007-9058-5; Norah MacKendrick, *Better Safe Than Sorry: How Consumers Navigate Exposure to Everyday Toxics* (Berkeley: University of California Press, 2018), 123.

59. On our methods, see the appendix.

60. Natália Otto, Josée Johnston, and Shyon Baumann, "Moral Entrepreneurialism for the Hamburger: Strategies for Marketing a Contested Fast Food," *Cultural Sociology* 16, no. 2 (2022): 190–211, https://doi.org/10.1177/17499755211039932.

61. See Oleschuk, Johnston, and Baumann, "Maintaining Meat"; Johnston, Baumann, and Oleschuk, "Capturing Inequality and Action in Prototypes."

62. We think the term *concerned omnivore* is a more accurate label for our focus group participants than *conscientious omnivore*, a term used by scholars to describe eaters who only eat meat that has met specific ethical standards. See Hank Rothgerber, "Can You Have Your Meat and Eat It Too? Conscientious Omnivores, Vegetarians, and Adherence to Diet," *Appetite* 84 (2015): 197, https://doi.org/10.1016/j.appet.2014.10.012. Much to our surprise, our call for meat-eating participants also attracted a handful of people with semi-vegetarian or vegetarian diets who wanted to talk to us about the harmful nature of the meat industry. While these participants brought unintended heterogeneity to our sample, we kept them in our study because their presence worked to inspire lively and dynamic focus group discussions about the ethics of meat-eating and the possibilities and limitations of happy meat.

63. "No Sign of Greenhouse Gases Increases Slowing in 2023," *NOOA Research*, National Oceanic and Atmospheric Administration, April 5, 2024, https://research.noaa.gov/no-sign-of-greenhouse-gases-increases-slowing-in-2023/#.

Chapter 1

1. Australian research finds that eggs play a central role in consumers' understandings of ethical animal-based products; happy, cage-free chickens are associated with eggs that are more "natural," higher in quality, and healthier for consumers. Compared to other ethical animal products (e.g., chicken, beef), eggs can be seen relatively straightforward, as they offer consumers a clear choice between caged or cage-free. See Heather J. Bray and Rachel A. Ankeny, "Happy Chickens Lay Tastier Eggs: Motivations for Buying Free-Range Eggs in Australia," *Anthrozoös* 30, no. 2 (2017): 213–26, https://doi.org/10.1080/08927936.2017.1310986.

2. Chickens that are bred for high productivity might exhibit poor social behavior and have been known to engage in feather pecking and aggression that leads to injuries and death. Mara Miele, "The Taste of Happiness: Free-Range Chicken," *Environment and Planning A* 43, no. 9 (2011): 2081, https://doi.org/10.1068/a43257.

3. As Miele notes, the "happy," free-range chicken is assumed to offer "a better chance of good welfare," but may experience higher welfare risks when compared to their conventional brethren. Miele, "Taste of Happiness," 2080.

4. By *cultural politics*, we refer to struggles for power, meaning, and legitimacy surrounding meat-eating in the twenty-first century. This draws on critical scholarship examining power dynamics in everyday life, particularly under global capitalism. It views politics beyond state-citizen relations, encompassing webs of power relations in daily life. Complementing this, sociological thought argues cultural conceptions of the good life (and good eating) are socially constructed, not inherent. Contemporary studies recognize diverse power structures and intersecting oppressions at global and local scales. See Kate Nash, "The 'Cultural Turn' in Social Theory: Toward a Theory of Cultural Politics," *Sociology* 35, no. 1 (2001): 77–92, https://doi.org/10.1017/S0038038501000050.

5. Miele, "Taste of Happiness," 2080.

6. We return to this argument in more detail in Chapters 6 and 7 when we discuss the ideals surrounding farm animal agriculture and what it means to raise happy animals outdoors.

7. Note that these questions also invoke literature on the social construction of nature. In *American Zoo,* sociologist David Grazian uses zoos to illustrate the ideas people have about what counts as "natural" when it comes to animals and their habitats. Regardless of how true these ideas might be, they come to shape how people understand animals and their relationships with them. David Grazian, *American Zoo: A Sociological Safari* (Princeton, N.J.: Princeton University Press, 2015).

8. See Paul Ricoeur, *Time and Narrative* (Chicago: University of Chicago Press, 1984); Francesca Polletta, *It Was Like a Fever: Storytelling in Protest and Politics* (Chicago: University of Chicago Press, 2006); Arlie Russell Hochschild, *Strangers in Their Own Land: Anger and Mourning in the American Right* (New York: The New Press, 2016); Harold R. Johnson, *The Power of Story* (Ottawa, Ont.: Biblioasis, 2022).

9. Raul Lejano, Mrill Ingram, and Helen Ingram, *The Power of Narrative in Environmental Networks* (Cambridge: The MIT Press, 2013), 6.

10. Lois Presser, *Why We Harm* (New Brunswick, N.J.: Rutgers University Press, 2013), 55.

11. Lejano, Ingram, and Ingram and Presser both make this point. See Lejano, Ingram, and Ingram, *Power of Narrative*; Presser, *Why We Harm*, 52–57.

12. For the point that not all elements are required for a narrative, see Lois Presser, *Inside Story: How Narratives Drive Mass Harm* (Berkeley: University of California Press, 2018), 58. Contrast Lejano, Ingram, and Ingram, *The Power of Narrative*; and Polletta, *It Was Like a Fever.*

13. Others have argued this as well. See Polletta, *It Was like a Fever,* x; Presser, *Inside Story,* 68; Hochschild, *Strangers in Their Own Land.*

14. Johnson, *Power of Story,* 20.

15. See Polletta, *It Was like a Fever,* 166.

16. Christopher George Takacs, "Becoming Interesting: Narrative Capital Development at Elite Colleges," *Qualitative Sociology* 43, no. 2 (2020): 269, https://doi.org/10.1007/s11133-020-09447-y.

17. Lejano, Ingram, and Ingram, *Power of Narrative,* 58.

18. Polletta, *It Was Like a Fever,* 172–74.

19. Wendy Griswold, "The Fabrication of Meaning: Literary Interpretation in the United States, Great Britain, and the West Indies," *American Journal of Sociology* 92, no. 5 (1987): 1077–1117.

20. Polletta, *It Was Like a Fever,* 7, 24; Presser, *Inside Story,* 2; Presser, *Why We Harm,* 28.

21. Polletta, *It Was Like a Fever,* 83.

22. Presser, *Inside Story,* 2, 19.

23. Polletta, *It Was Like a Fever,* 14, 16–17.

24. Lejano, Ingram, and Ingram, *Power of Narrative,* 7.

25. Hochschild, *Strangers in Their Own Land*, 16.

26. Hochschild, *Strangers in Their Own Land*, 16.

27. This point about the superfluous relationship between stories and facts is also central to Grazian's analysis of the social construction of the "natural" in zoos. See Grazian, *American Zoo*.

28. *The Scarecrow*, directed by Brandon Oldenburg and Limbert Fabian (Los Angeles: CAA Marketing, 2013), 3:13, https://www.adforum.com/creative-work/ad/player/34489969/the-scarecrow/chipotle-mexican-grill.

29. For further discussion on the roles of the villain, see Lejano, Ingram, and Ingram, *Power of Narrative*, 66; Polletta, *It Was Like a Fever*, 9–10.

30. *Chicken Run*, directed by Peter Lord and Nick Park (Universal City, Calif.: DreamWorks Pictures, 2000).

31. Presser, *Why We Harm*; Presser, *Inside Story*.

32. Presser, *Inside Story*, 51.

33. Presser, *Why We Harm*, 65.

34. Presser, *Why We Harm*, 50–51; Presser, *Inside Story*, 51.

35. Presser, *Why We Harm*, 55–57.

36. Carol J. Adams, *The Sexual Politics of Meat: A Feminist-Vegetarian Critical Theory* (New York: Bloomsbury, 1990).

37. Presser, *Why We Harm*, 50–51.

38. Presser, *Why We Harm*, 117.

39. Presser, *Why We Harm*, 55–57.

40. Presser, *Why We Harm*, 57–63; Lois Presser and William V. Taylor, "An Autoethnography of Hunting," *Crime, Law, and Social Change* 55, no. 5 (2011): 483–94, https://doi.org/10.1007/s10611-011-9299-0.

41. Presser, *Inside Story*, 24.

42. Buddle and Bray's study of Australian media representations of farm animal welfare identifies a central consumer-focused media frame: consumer responsibility for addressing farm welfare through ethical consumption choices. Emily Buddle and Heather J. Bray, "How Farm Animal Welfare Issues are Framed in the Australian Media," *Journal of Agricultural and Environmental Ethics* 32, no. 3 (2019): 357–76, https://doi.org/10.1007/s10806-019-09778-z.

43. Presser, *Why We Harm*, 65.

44. Presser, *Why We Harm*, 65.

45. Merin Oleschuk, Josée Johnston, and Shyon Baumann, "Maintaining Meat: Cultural Repertoires and the Meat Paradox in a Diverse Sociocultural Context," *Sociological Forum* 34, no. 2 (2019): 337–60, https://doi.org/10.1111/socf.12500; Emily Buddle, "Meet Your Meat! How Australian Livestock Producers Use Instagram to Promote 'Happy Meat,'" in *Food Instagram*, edited by Emily J. H. Contois and Zenia Kish (Chicago: University of Illinois Press), ch. 10; Bray and Ankeny, "Happy Chickens."

46. Polletta, *It Was Like a Fever*; Presser, *Why We Harm*, 28.

47. Polletta, *It Was Like a Fever*, 19.

48. Presser, *Why We Harm*, 80.

49. For an extensive, multidisciplinary review of the term *foodscape*, see Simon Vonthron, Coline Perrin, and Christophe-Toussaint Soulard, "Foodscape: A Scoping Review and a Research Agenda for Food Security-Related Studies," *PLoS One* 15, no. 5 (2020): e0233218, https://doi.org/10.1371/journal.pone.0233218. The term *foodscape* first appeared in food studies scholarship in 1995 and its presence increased dramatically in English-speaking publications after 2010.

50. Josée Johnston and Michael K. Goodman, "Spectacular Foodscapes: Food Celebrities and the Politics of Lifestyle Mediation in an Age of Inequality," *Food, Culture, and Society* 18, no. 2 (2015): 205–22, https://doi.org/10.2752/175174415X14180391604369; Josée Johnston and Shyon Baumann, *Foodies: Democracy and Distinction in the Gourmet Foodscape*, 2nd ed. (New York: Routledge, 2015); Norah MacKendrick, "Foodscape," *Contexts* 13, no. 3 (2014): 16–18, https://doi.org/10.1177/1536504214545754; Bent Egberg Mikkelsen, "Images of Foodscapes: Introduction to Foodscape Studies and Their Application in the Study of Healthy Eating Out-of-Home Environments," *Perspectives in Public Health* 131, no. 5 (2011): 209–16, https://doi.org/10.1177/1757913911415150.

51. Johnston and Goodman, "Spectacular Foodscapes," 207; MacKendrick, "Foodscape."

52. Michael K. Goodman, Damian Maye, and Lewis Holloway, "Ethical Foodscapes? Premises, Promises, and Possibilities," *Environment and Planning A* 42, no. 8 (2010): 1782, https://doi.org/10.1068/a43290.

53. Kevin Morgan, "Local and Green, Global and Fair: The Ethical Foodscape and the Politics of Care," *Environment and Planning A* 42, no. 8 (2010): 1854, https://doi.org/10.1068/a42364. See also Goodman, Maye, and Holloway, "Ethical Foodscapes," 1782.

54. See David Goodman, E. Melanie DuPuis, and Michael K. Goodman, *Alternative Food Networks: Knowledge, Practice, and Politics* (New York: Routledge, 2012).

55. Miele argues that at the start of the twenty-first century, European consumers began to recognize and appreciate animal emotions, similar to how children's emotions were first discovered and valued in the early 1900s. Miele, "Taste of Happiness," 2075; On rising European interest in animal welfare standards, see also Henry Buller, and Emma Roe, *Food and Animal Welfare* (London: Bloomsbury Academic, 2018); Henry Buller, "Animal Welfare: From Production to Consumption," in *Improving Farm Animal Welfare*, edited by Harry Blokhuis, Mara Miele, Isabelle Veissier, and Bryan Jones, 49–69 (Wageningen, Netherlands: Wageningen Academic Publishers, 2013.)

56. Miele, "Taste of Happiness," 2087.

57. Jamie Waldron and Angela England, *Home Butchering Handbook: Enjoy Finer, Fresher, Healthier Cuts of Meat from Your Own Kitchen* (New York: Alpha, 2013), 3.

58. The hyper-efficient process of turning pigs' bodies into hundreds of constituent commodity parts is carefully documented in Alex Blanchette's ethnography of a factory farm, where he observes that even vegetarians may find themselves inadvertently consuming the products of pigs' bodies in everyday life. See Blanchette, *Porkopolis: American Animality, Standardized Life, and the Factory Farm* (Durham, N.C.: Duke University Press, 2020).

59. Blanchette's research leads him to question an instrumentalist system that ruthlessly extracts value from animals' bodies (and the humans who work in the factory). He wants to revalue small-scale systems that "nurture animals in a fashion whereby every moment of their lives, and every microgram of their bodies, is not saturated by economic value." Indeed, Blanchette ultimately argues for a "positive politics of inefficiency" when it comes to meat production. Blanchette, *Porkopolis*, 236–37.

60. Ifat Zur and Christian A. Klöckner, "Individual Motivations for Limiting Meat Consumption," *British Food Journal* 116, no. 4 (2014): 630, https://doi.org/10.1108/BFJ-08-2012-0193.

61. See Oleschuk, Johnston, and Baumann, "Maintaining Meat"; Hank Rothgerber, "Can You Have Your Meat and Eat It Too? Conscientious Omnivores, Vegetarians, and Adherence to Diet," *Appetite* 84 (2015): 196–203, https://doi.org/10.1016/j.appet.2014.10.012; Daniel L. Rosenfeld, "The Psychology of Vegetarianism: Recent Advances and Future Directions," *Appetite* 131 (2018): 125–38, https://doi.org/10.1016/j.appet.2018.09.011. McKendree, Croney, and Widmar conducted a survey of 798 American households and found that almost half of respondents (46%) were somewhat to extremely concerned about the welfare of livestock animals in the United States. See Melissa G. S. McKendree, Candace Croney, and Nicole J. O. Widmar, "Effects of Demographic Factors and Information Sources on United States Consumer Perceptions of Animal Welfare," *Journal of Animal Science* 92, no. 7 (2014): 3164, https://doi.org/10.2527/jas.2014-6874.

62. Mara Miele et al., "Changes in Farming and in Stakeholder Concern for Animal Welfare," in *Improving Farm Animal Welfare: Science and Society Working Together: The Welfare Quality Approach*, edited by Harry Blokhuis et al. (Wageningen, Netherlands: Wageningen Academic Publishers, 2013), 39, https://doi.org/10.3920/978-90-8686-770-7_2.

63. Emily Huddart Kennedy and Darcy Hauslik, "The Practice of Green Consumption," in *Environment and Society: Concepts and Challenges*, edited by Magnus Boström and Debra J. Davidson (Cham: Palgrave Macmillan, 2018), 187–206, https://doi.org/10.1007/978-3-319-76415-3_9.

64. Rothgerber, "Can You Have Your Meat and Eat It Too?," 198.

65. Miele, "Taste of Happiness," 2087.

66. Rothgerber, "Can You Have Your Meat and Eat It Too?"; Michael Pollan, "An Animal's Place," *New York Times Magazine*, November 10, 2002, https://www.nytimes.com/2002/11/10/magazine/an-animal-s-place.html.

67. Pollan, "Animal's Place."

68. Michael Pollan, "Power Steer," *New York Times Magazine*, March 31, 2002, https://www.nytimes.com/2002/03/31/magazine/power-steer.html.

69. Pollan, "Animal's Place."

70. Michael Pollan, *The Omnivore's Dilemma: A Natural History of Four Meals* (New York: Penguin Books, 2006).

71. For a critique of Michael Pollan's prominent role in public conversations about the food system, see Julie Guthman, "Commentary on Teaching Food: Why I Am Fed

Up with Michael Pollan et al.," *Agriculture and Human Values* 24, no. 2 (2007): 261–64, https://doi.org/10.1007/s10460-006-9053-x.

72. Paul DiMaggio, Manish Nag, and David Blei, "Exploiting Affinities Between Topic Modeling and the Sociological Perspective on Culture: Application to Newspaper Coverage of U.S. Government Arts Funding," *Poetics* 41, no. 6 (2013): 570–606, https://doi.org/10.1016/j.poetic.2013.08.004. On our methods, see the appendix.

73. Catherine Friend, *The Compassionate Carnivore: Or, How to Keep Animals Happy, Save Old MacDonald's Farm, Reduce Your Hoofprint, and Still Eat Meat* (Boston: Da Capo Press, 2008).

74. Christine Jeske, "Re-Enchanting Meat: How Sacred Meaning-Making Strengthens the Ethical Meat Movement," *Agriculture and Human Values*, June 22, 2023, https://doi.org/https://doi.org/10.1007/s10460-023-10477-9.

75. Berlin Reed, *The Ethical Butcher: How Thoughtful Eating Can Change Your World* (Berkeley: Soft Skull Press, 2013).

76. Reed, *Ethical Butcher*, 11.

77. Reed, *Ethical Butcher*, 12, 20.

78. Josée Johnston, "The Citizen-Consumer Hybrid: Ideological Tensions and the Case of Whole Foods Market," *Theory and Society* 37, no. 3 (2008): 229–70, https://doi.org/10.1007/s11186-007-9058-5.

79. Waldron and England, *Home Butchering Handbook*.

80. Waldron and England, *Home Butchering Handbook*, 3.

81. Waldron and England, *Home Butchering Handbook*, 5–6.

82. Dan Barber, *The Third Plate: Field Notes on the Future of Food* (New York: Penguin Press, 2014). 17.

83. Barber, *Third Plate*, 17–18, emphasis added.

84. See Joop de Boer, Hanna Schösler, and Harry Aiking, "'Meatless Days' or 'Less but Better'? Exploring Strategies to Adapt Western Meat Consumption to Health and Sustainability Challenges," *Appetite* 76 (2014): 121, https://doi.org/10.1016/j.appet.2014.02.002.

85. Mark Schatzker, *Steak: One Man's Search for the World's Tastiest Piece of Beef* (New York: Viking, 2010).

86. Schatzker, *Steak*, 253.

87. Schatzker, *Steak*, 256.

88. Schatzker, *Steak*, 265.

89. A minor exception to this trend is Michael Pollan's essay, which uses the life of a cow, "Steer 534," as a literacy device to illustrate the environmental and animal welfare challenges of industrial beef production. Pollan, "Power Steer," *New York Times Magazine*, March 31, 2002, 44–52.

90. This is not to say that the happiness of an animal is always a central theme in the ethical meatscape. For example, Bray and Ankeny argue that the consumers they spoke with about "happy chickens" in Australia "largely viewed the happiness of the chicken as 'good' because of its influence on the eggs produced by them, rather than as 'good for the chicken.'" Bray and Ankeny, "Happy Chickens Lay Tastier Eggs."

91. Schatzker, *Steak*, 250–52.

92. Schatzker, *Steak*, 252.

93. Lejano, Ingram, and Ingram, *Power of Narrative*, 147.

94. Lejano, Ingram, and Ingram, *Power of Narrative*, 156–57.

95. Lejano, Ingram, and Ingram, *Power of Narrative*, 171.

96. Lejano, Ingram, and Ingram, *Power of Narrative*, 160–61, 170.

97. Hochschild, *Strangers in Their Own Land*.

98. This is not to diminish the efforts to empirically study and regulate farm welfare conditions to ensure the well-being of animals. For an account of how this works in the case of regulating and measuring happy chickens, see Miele, "Taste of Happiness," 2082–86.

99. Sara Ahmed, *The Promise of Happiness* (Durham, N.C.: Duke University Press, 2010).

100. Goodman, Dupuis, and Goodman, *Alternative Food Networks*.

101. We deliberately employed the ethnic and racial labels that participants used to describe themselves. For example, we used the term "Latinx" if it was used by the participant to describe themselves. Compared to race, ethnic identity inductively arose as a more predominantly salient feature in our participants' relationships with meat. While we acknowledge the importance of analyzing the relationship between "happy meat" and concepts like whiteness, our data does not allow us to adequately address this complex issue. Future research could productively build on existing work exploring the intersection of whiteness and alternative food networks to investigate this further. See Rachel Slocum. "Whiteness, Space, and Alternative Food Practice," *Geoforum* 38, no. 3 (2007): 520–33; Alison Hope Alkon and Christie Grace McCullen, "Whiteness and Farmers Markets: Performances, Perpetuations. . . Contestations?" *Antipode* 43, no. 4 (2011): 937–59.

Chapter 2

1. *Anthony Bourdain: No Reservations*, directed by Tom Vitale et al., written by Anthony Bourdain, featuring Anthony Bourdain, aired 2005 to 2012, in broadcast syndication, Cable News Network, Inc.; Anthony *Bourdain: Parts Unknown*, directed by Tom Vitale et al., written by Anthony Bourdain, featuring Anthony Bourdain, aired 2013 to 2018, in broadcast syndication, Cable News Network, Inc.

2. Catherine Bremer, "Don't Say Nay to Horsemeat: French Eaters," Reuters, February 12, 2013, https://www.reuters.com/article/us-france-horsemeat-idUSBRE91B0RX20130212.

3. Amy Finley, "Concerned about Climate? You Should Be Eating Rabbit," *Gastronomica* 22, no. 4 (2022): 90–92, https://doi.org/10.1525/gfc.2022.22.4.90.

4. Mathieu Ferry, "What's India's Beef with Meat? Hindu Orthopraxis and Food Transition in India Since the 1980s," *Sociological Forum* 35, no. 2 (2020): 511–34, https://doi.org/10.1111/socf.12592.

5. When we use the term *practice*, we are referring to embodied, habitual human activities that are mediated by material objects and social contexts. Practices are

experienced individually but are socially constituted. On practice theory in relation to food, see Alan Warde, *The Practice of Eating* (Malden, Mass.: Polity Press, 2016).

6. Matthew B. Ruby, "Vegetarianism: A Blossoming Field of Study," *Appetite* 58, no. 1 (2012): 141–50, http://dx.doi.org/10.1016/j.appet.2011.09.019; Daniel L. Rosenfeld, "The Psychology of Vegetarianism: Recent Advances and Future Directions," *Appetite* 131 (2018): 136, https://doi.org/10.1016/j.appet.2018.09.011; Johannes Simons, Carl Vierboom, Jeanette Klink-Lehmann, Ingo Härlen, and Monika Hartmann, "Vegetarianism/Veganism: A Way to Feel Good," *Sustainability* 13, no. 7 (2021): 1–19, https://doi.org/10.3390/su13073618. See also Elizabeth Cherry, "I Was a Teenage Vegan: Motivation and Maintenance of Lifestyle Movements," *Sociological Inquiry* 85, no. 1 (2015): 55–74, https://doi.org/10.1111/soin.12061; Eric C. Anderson et al., "Vegetarians' and Omnivores' Affective and Physiological Responses to Images of Food," *Food Quality and Preference* 71 (2019): 96–105, https://doi.org/10.1016/j.foodqual.2018.06.008; Nick Fox and Katie Ward, "Health, Ethics, and Environment: A Qualitative Study of Vegetarian Motivations," *Appetite* 50, no. 2–3 (2008): 422–29, https://doi.org/10.1016/j.appet.2007.09.007; Lenka Malek and Wendy J. Umberger, "Distinguishing Meat Reducers from Unrestricted Omnivores, Vegetarians and Vegans: A Comprehensive Comparison of Australian Consumers," *Food Quality and Preference* 88 (2021): 104081, https://doi.org/10.1016/j.foodqual.2020.104081.

7. But see, for example, Hank Rothgerber, "Can You Have Your Meat and Eat It Too? Conscientious Omnivores, Vegetarians, and Adherence to Diet," *Appetite* 84 (2015): 196–203, http://dx.doi.org/10.1016/j.appet.2014.10.012; Josée Johnston, Shyon Baumann, and Merin Oleschuk, "Capturing Inequality and Action in Prototypes: The Case of Meat-Eating and Vegetarianism," *Poetics* 87 (2020): 101530, https://doi.org/10.1016/j.poetic.2021.101530; Mara Miele et al., "Changes in Farming and in Stakeholder Concern for Animal Welfare," in *Improving Farm Animal Welfare: Science and Society Working Together: The Welfare Quality Approach*, edited by Harry Blokhuis et al. (Wageningen, Netherlands: Wageningen Academic Publishers, 2013), 38, https://doi.org/10.3920/978-90-8686-770-7_2; Daniel L. Rosenfeld, "The Psychology of Vegetarianism: Recent Advances and Future Directions," *Appetite* 131 (2018): 132, https://doi.org/10.1016/j.appet.2018.09.011; Joop de Boer, Hanna Schösler, and Harry Aiking, "'Meatless Days' or 'Less but Better'? Exploring Strategies to Adapt Western Meat Consumption to Health and Sustainability Challenges," *Appetite* 76 (2014): 120–28, https://doi.org/10.1016/j.appet.2014.02.002; Lotte Holm and Mette Møhl, "The Role of Meat in Everyday Food Culture: An Analysis of an Interview Study in Copenhagen," *Appetite* 34, no. 3 (2000): 277–83, https://doi.org/10.1006/appe.2000.0324.

8. Rothgerber, "Can You Have Your Meat and Eat It Too?" 203. Sanchez-Sabate and Sabaté also conclude that "meat-reducers have received scant attention" in academic studies. Ruben Sanchez-Sabate and Joan Sabaté, "Consumer Attitudes Toward Environmental Concerns of Meat Consumption: A Systematic Review," *International Journal of Environmental Research and Public Health* 16, no. 7 (2019): 2, https://doi.org/10.3390/ijerph16071220.

9. On the prevalence of vegetarianism, see Mirjana Valdes et al., "Plant-Based Dietary Practices in Canada: Examining Definitions, Prevalence and Correlates of Animal Source Food Exclusions Using Nationally Representative Data from the 2015 Canadian Community Health Survey-Nutrition," *Public Health Nutrition* 24, no. 5 (2021): 777–86, https://doi.org/10.1017/S1368980020003444; James Waters, "A Model of the Dynamics of Household Vegetarian and Vegan Rates in the U.K.," *Appetite* 127 (2018): 364–72, https://doi.org/10.1016/j.appet.2018.05.017. For an overview of motivations underlying vegetarian and vegan diets, see Ruby, "Vegetarianism."

10. Strong empirical support for the tripartite model exists, demonstrating that understanding people's attitudes toward individuals, groups, issues, or objects requires attending to their feelings and beliefs about, and perceptual responses toward, the attitude-object. See Steven J. Breckler, "Empirical Validation of Affect, Behavior, and Cognition as Distinct Components of Attitude," *Journal of Personality and Social Psychology* 47, no. 6 (1984): 1191–1205, https://doi.org/10.1037/0022-3514.47.6.1191; Thomas M. Ostrom, "The Relationship Between the Affective, Behavioral, and Cognitive Components of Attitude," *Journal of Experimental Social Psychology* 5, no. 1 (1969): 12–30, https://doi.org/10.1016/0022-1031(69)90003-1; Milton J. Rosenberg and Carl I. Hovland, "Cognitive, Affective, and Behavioral Components of Attitude," in *Attitude Organization and Change: An Analysis of Consistency Among Attitude Components*, edited by Milton J. Rosenberg et al. (New Haven: Yale University Press, 1960), 1–14.

11. What is an example of the *tripartite model of attitude*? In 1984, the psychologist Steven J. Breckler published a now widely cited study of people's responses to snakes. Breckler presented research subjects with a live snake and took numerous measurements to describe their attitudes. These measures included the amount of contact people were willing to have with the snake (behavior), beliefs about snakes (cognition), and participants' responses to a checklist of positive and negative moods after being near a snake (affect). See Breckler, "Empirical Validation of Affect, Behavior, and Cognition as Distinct Components of Attitude."

12. A clear explanation of identity as it relates to food can be found in Warren Belasco, *Food: The Key Concepts* (New York: Berg, 2008).

13. To learn more about different kinds of eaters and vegetarians, see Johnston, Baumann, and Oleschuk, "Capturing Inequality and Action in Prototypes."

14. We, too, live with inconsistencies between identity and practices. After researching the industrial meat system, we like to think of ourselves as prioritizing ethical meat-eating but have certainly found ourselves eating foods (e.g., ball-park hot dogs) that don't match up to that self-conception.

15. For the full study details, see Waters, "Model of the Dynamics."

16. For American data, see "Nutrition and Food," Gallup, accessed May 27, 2021, https://news.gallup.com/poll/6424/Nutrition-Food.aspx. For Canadian results, see Valdes et al., "Plant-Based Dietary Practices in Canada."

17. Ruby, "Vegetarianism."

18. See Holm and Møhl, "Role of Meat in Everyday Food Culture."

19. Genaro C. Miranda-de la Lama et al., "Mexican Consumers' Perceptions and Attitudes Toward Farm Animal Welfare and Willingness to Pay for Welfare Friendly Meat Products," *Meat Science* 125 (2017): 106–13, https://doi.org/10.1016/j.meatsci.2016.12.001.

20. See Sanchez-Sabate and Sabaté, "Consumer Attitudes."

21. Sanchez-Sabate and Sabaté, "Consumer Attitudes," 3.

22. Gallup, "Nutrition and Food."

23. It is worth noting that affect and emotion are overlapping but not identical concepts. *Affect* is a general term that refers to a subjective sense or experience of feeling and can range from positive to negative to neutral. *Emotion* is a more specific term. Emotions are socially shaped categories of feeling, like happiness, guilt, rage, and disgust. We do not explore the distinction between affect and emotion in this book, but we aim to use these terms accurately, which is why we have defined them for our readers.

24. For a more detailed account of the importance of measuring affect concerning meat, see Mariëtte Berndsen and Joop van der Pligt, "Ambivalence Toward Meat," *Appetite* 42, no. 1 (2004): 71–78, https://doi.org/10.1016/S0195-6663(03)00119-3; Mariëtte Berndsen and Joop van der Pligt, "Risks of Meat: The Relative Impact of Cognitive, Affective, and Moral Concerns," *Appetite* 44, no. 2 (2005): 195–205, https://doi.org/10.1016/j.appet.2004 .10.003. See also Marlyne Sahakian, Laurence Godin, and Irène Courtin, "Promoting 'Pro,' 'Low,' and 'No' Meat Consumption in Switzerland: The Role of Emotions in Practices," *Appetite* 150 (2020): 104637, https://doi.org/10.1016/j.appet.2020.104637.

25. See Elisa Becker and Natalia S. Lawrence, "Meat Disgust Is Negatively Associated with Meat Intake—Evidence from a Cross-Sectional and Longitudinal Study," *Appetite* 164 (2021): 105299, https://doi.org/10.1016/j.appet.2021.105299; Fabienne Michel, Christina Hartmann, and Michael Siegrist, "Consumers' Associations, Perceptions, and Acceptance of Meat and Plant-Based Meat Alternatives," *Food Quality and Preference* 87 (2021): 104063, https://doi.org/10.1016/j.foodqual.2020.104063.

26. See Janis H. Zickfeld, Jonas R. Kunst, and Sigrid M. Hohle, "Too Sweet to Eat: Exploring the Effects of Cuteness on Meat Consumption," *Appetite* 120 (2018): 181–95, https://doi.org/10.1016/j.appet.2017.08.038.

27. See Jonas R. Kunst and Sigrid M. Hohle, "Meat Eaters by Dissociation: How We Present, Prepare, and Talk about Meat Increases Willingness to Eat Meat by Reducing Empathy and Disgust," *Appetite*, 105 (2016): 758–74, https://doi.org/10 .1016/j.appet.2016.07.009.

28. This is a topic we explore further in Chapter 3.

29. For information about how affect relates to behavior more broadly, see Amanda Rivis, Paschal Sheeran, and Christopher J. Armitage, "Expanding the Affective and Normative Components of the Theory of Planned Behavior: A Meta-Analysis of Anticipated Affect and Moral Norms," *Journal of Applied Social Psychology* 39, no. 12 (2009): 2985–3019, https://doi.org/10.1111/j.1559-1816.2009.00558.x. For an inspirational example of feeling-oriented sociological analysis, see Arlie Russell Hochschild, *Strangers in Their Own Land: Anger and Mourning in the American Right* (New York: The New Press, 2016).

30. The first Vegetarian Society appeared in England in 1847. James Gregory, *Of Victorians and Vegetarians: The Vegetarian Movement in Nineteenth Century Britain* (London: Tauris Academic Studies, 2007), 1.

31. As we note in Chapter 1, some scholars link the rise of conscientious omnivores to the publication of Michael Pollan's influential 2002 *New York Times* essay "An Animal's Place." See Rothgerber, "Can You Have Your Meat and Eat It Too?"

32. The options respondents chose from were *omnivore* (my diet includes meat); *flexitarian* (I try to limit my meat consumption); *pescatarian* (I don't eat meat, but I do eat fish); *vegetarian* (I don't eat meat or fish, but I do eat eggs and/or dairy); and *vegan* (I don't eat meat, fish, eggs, or dairy).

33. Josée Johnston, Shyon Baumann, and Merin Oleschuk, "Capturing Inequality and Action in Prototypes: The Case of Meat-Eating and Vegetarianism," *Poetics* 87 (November 2020): 101530, https://doi.org/10.1016/j.poetic.2021.101530.

34. For instance, in contrast to some claims that the adoption of a vegetarian diet is becoming more and more frequent in Western societies, other studies measuring consumption practices report specific and consistently low levels of vegetarianism and veganism in Western countries. For examples of these divergent findings, see Géraldine Dorard and Sasha Mathieu, "Vegetarian and Omnivorous Diets: A Cross-Sectional Study of Motivation, Eating Disorders, and Body Shape Perception," *Appetite* 156 (2021): 104972, https://doi.org/10.1016/j.appet.2020.104972; Valdes et al., "Plant-Based Dietary Practices in Canada."

35. In addition to the literature reviewed that examines whether people identify as vegetarian or vegan, recent research has introduced survey measures that seek to generate a continuum of plant-based diets, ranging from flexible to strict adherents. Tamara M. Pfeiler and Boris Egloff, "Examining the 'Veggie' Personality: Results from a Representative German Sample," *Appetite* 120 (2018): 246–55, https://doi.org/10.1016/j.appet.2017.09.005. A promising new direction in this body of literature is to look beyond vegetarian diets to understand how multiple dimensions of attitudes compare for omnivores, flexitarians, vegetarians, and vegans. Lenka Malek and Wendy J. Umberger, "Distinguishing Meat Reducers from Unrestricted Omnivores, Vegetarians and Vegans: A Comprehensive Comparison of Australian Consumers," *Food Quality and Preference* 88 (2021): 104081, https://doi.org/10.1016/j.foodqual.2020.104081.

36. See Merin Oleschuk, Josée Johnston, and Shyon Baumann, "Maintaining Meat: Cultural Repertoires and the Meat Paradox in a Diverse Sociocultural Context," *Sociological Forum* 34, no. 2 (2019): 337–60, https://doi.org/10.1111/socf.12500.

37. Kate Cairns and Josée Johnston, "On (Not) Knowing Where Your Food Comes from: Meat, Mothering and Ethical Eating," *Agriculture and Human Values* 35, no. 3 (2018): 569–80, https://doi.org/10.1007/s10460-018-9849-5.

38. The tendency to minimize meat consumption has been noted by other scholars. Rothgerber's experimental design showed that women tend to minimize their meat consumption more than men when exposed to a challenging PETA video. Hank Rothgerber, "'But I Don't Eat That Much Meat': Situational Underreporting

of Meat Consumption by Women," *Society and Animals* 27, no. 2 (2019): 150–73, https://doi.org/10.1163/15685306-12341468.

39. For details about the survey design and administration, see the appendix.

40. While, in theory, we could have also offered a *carnivore* label, we didn't expect to find many, or even any, respondents who identified as following a meat-only diet. This type of diet, sometimes called the "lion diet," went from near obscurity to a cultural talking point after it was popularized by the psychologist and right-wing media pundit Jordan Peterson, who claimed that it helped him and his daughter solve various psychological and physical health issues. See James Hamblin, "The Jordan Peterson All-Meat Diet," *The Atlantic*, August 28, 2018, https://www.theatlantic.com/health/archive/2018/08/the-peterson-family-meat-cleanse/567613/.

41. We explore this in more detail in Chapter 3.

Chapter 3

1. *Cowspiracy*, directed by Kip Andersen and Keegan Kuhn (West Hollywood: Appian Way Productions, 2014).

2. Rhee and colleagues review how the study of moralization has shifted and how to best define and conceptualize the concept. Joshua J. Rhee, Chelsea Schein, and Brock Bastian, "The What, How, and Why of Moralization: A Review of Current Definitions, Methods, and Evidence in Moralization Research," *Social and Personality Psychology Compass* 13, no. 12 (2019): e12511, https://doi.org/10.1111/spc3.12511.

3. The nonlinear nature of moralization is not a major feature of the psychological literature, which tends to focus on individual-level processes. An important exception is work by Rozin and colleagues. They describe a social process of *amoralization* whereby socially held moral values are transformed into individual preferences that lack a moral charge—as they suggest is the case for divorce or smoking marijuana. See Paul Rozin, Maureen Markwith, and Caryn Stoess, "Moralization and Becoming a Vegetarian: The Transformation of Preferences into Values and the Recruitment of Disgust," *Psychological Science* 8, no. 2 (1997): 67–73, https://doi.org/10.1111/j.1467-9280.1997.tb00685.x. The retreat of ethical considerations for individuals has also been studied as a form of *ethical fading* where individuals can deceive themselves about the moral implications of their actions. Ann E. Tenbrunsel and David M. Messick, "Ethical Fading: The Role of Self-Deception in Unethical Behavior," *Social Justice Research* 17, no. 2 (2004): 223–36, https://doi.org/10.1023/B:SORE.0000027411.35832.53. The push and pull factors of moralization for individuals—where the imperative to do the right thing operates in tension with hedonic motivations—has been studied by Feinberg and colleagues. They point to the possibility of *unmoralization*, where previously moralized issues lose their moral relevance. See Matthew Feinberg et al., "Understanding the Process of Moralization: How Eating Meat Becomes a Moral Issue," *Journal of Personality and Social Psychology* 117, no. 1 (2019): 50–72, https://doi.org/10.1037/pspa0000149.

4. Melanie Joy, *Why We Love Dogs, Eat Pigs, and Wear Cows* (San Francisco: Red Wheel/Weiser, 2010).

5. Jared Piazza et al., "Rationalizing Meat Consumption. The 4Ns," *Appetite* 91 (2015): 114–28, https://doi.org/10.1016/j.appet.2015.04.011.

6. Piazza and colleagues find that the 4Ns account for 83% of the justifications given for meat-eating. The largest category of justification is that meat is necessary (42%), followed by meat is natural (23%), meat is nice (16%), and meat is normal (10%). See Piazza et al., "Rationalizing Meat Consumption," 117.

7. Emma J. Lea and Anthony Worsley, "Influences on Meat Consumption in Australia," *Appetite* 36, no. 2 (2001): 127–36, https://doi.org/10.1006/appe.2000.0386.

8. Daniel L. Rosenfeld and A. Janet Tomiyama, "Taste and Health Concerns Trump Anticipated Stigma as Barriers to Vegetarianism," *Appetite* 144 (2020): 104469, https://doi.org/10.1016/j.appet.2019.104469.

9. Hal Herzog, *Some We Love, Some We Hate, Some We Eat: Why It's So Hard to Think Straight about Animals* (Toronto: Harper Perennial, 2010); Anthony L. Podberscek, "Good to Pet and Eat: The Keeping and Consuming of Dogs and Cats in South Korea," *Journal of Social Issues* 65, no. 3 (2009): 615–32, https://doi.org/10.1111/j.1540-4560.2009.01616.x.

10. Mary Douglas, *Purity and Danger: An Analysis of Concepts of Pollution and Taboo* (London: Routledge and Kegan Paul, 1966).

11. Merin Oleschuk, Josée Johnston, and Shyon Baumann, "Maintaining Meat: Cultural Repertoires and the Meat Paradox in a Diverse Sociocultural Context," *Sociological Forum* 34, no. 2 (2019): 337–60, https://doi.org/10.1111/socf.12500.

12. Oleschuk, Johnston, and Baumann, "Maintaining Meat."

13. Oleschuk, Johnston, and Baumann, "Maintaining Meat," 13.

14. Piazza et al., "Rationalizing Meat Consumption"; Rosenfeld and Tomiyama, "Taste and Health Concerns."

15. Shyon Baumann, Emily Huddart Kennedy, and Josée Johnston, "Moral and Aesthetic Consecration and Higher Status Consumers' Tastes: The 'Good' Food Revolution," *Poetics* 92 (February 2022), https://doi.org/10.1016/j.poetic.2022.101654.

16. Oleschuk, Johnston, and Baumann, "Maintaining Meat."

17. Michèle Lamont and Virág Molnár, "The Study of Boundaries in the Social Sciences," *Annual Review of Sociology* 28 (2002): 167–95, https://doi.org/10.1146/annurev.soc.28.110601.141107.

18. For example, a 2019 study by Feinberg et al. found that the emotions surrounding meat (e.g., disgust, guilt, shame) are a powerful predictor of who will come to moralize the issue of meat-eating. See Feinberg et al., "Understanding the Process of Moralization."

19. Jonathan Haidt et al., "Body, Psyche, and Culture: The Relationship between Disgust and Morality," *Psychology and Developing Societies* 9, no. 1 (1997): 112, https://doi.org/10.1177/097133369700900105; Paul Rozin, Jonathan Haidt, and Clark McCauley, "Disgust," in *Handbook of Emotions*, edited by Lisa Feldman Barrett, Michael Lewis, and Jeannette M. Haviland-Jones (New York: Guilford Press, 2016), 820.

20. Rozin and colleagues came up with a four-part typology of disgust, of which animal reminder disgust is one component. See Rozin, Haidt, and McCauley, "Disgust."

21. As discussed in the introduction, this is termed an "apologetic" strategy. See Hank Rothgerber, "'But I Don't Eat That Much Meat': Situational Underreporting of Meat Consumption by Women," *Society and Animals* 27, no. 2 (2019): 150–73, https://doi.org/10.1163/15685306-12341468.

22. Jonas R. Kunst and Sigrid M. Hohle, "Meat Eaters by Dissociation: How We Present, Prepare and Talk About Meat Increases Willingness to Eat Meat by Reducing Empathy and Disgust," *Appetite* 105 (2016): 758–74, https://doi.org/10.1016/j.appet.2016.07.009.

23. A significant limitation of existing research is its focus on the Western world, as highlighted by Rozin and colleagues: "almost the entire literature on disgust comes from the approximately 6% of the world in which English is the native language." Rozin, Haidt, and McCauley, "Disgust." Generating cross-cultural data is critical. As psychologist Hal Herzog notes, culture is "the most important influence on whether we find a food delicious or disgusting," Herzog, *Some We Love, Some We Hate, Some We Eat*. See also Janis H. Zickfeld, Jonas R. Kunst, and Sigrid M. Hohle, "Too Sweet to Eat: Exploring the Effects of Cuteness on Meat Consumption," *Appetite* 120 (2018): 181–95, https://doi.org/10.1016/j.appet.2017.08.038.

24. Catarina Possidónio et al., "An Appetite for Meat? Disentangling the Influence of Animal Resemblance and Familiarity," *Appetite* 170 (2022): 105875, https://doi.org/10.1016/j.appet.2021.105875.

25. Rozin, Haidt, and McCauley, "Disgust," 824; Rothgerber, "'But I Don't Eat That Much Meat,'" 10.

26. Rozin, Haidt, and McCauley, "Disgust," 820.

27. Eduardo Bericat, "The Sociology of Emotions: Four Decades of Progress," *Current Sociology* 64, no. 3 (2016): 495, https://doi.org/10.1177/0011392115588355.

28. Arlie Russell Hochschild, "Ideology and Emotion Management: A Perspective and Path for Future Research," in *Research Agendas in the Sociology of Emotions*, edited by Theodore D. Kemper (Albany: State University of New York Press, 1990), 117.

29. Rozin, Markwith, and Stoess, "Moralization and Becoming a Vegetarian."

30. Rozin, Markwith, and Stoess, "Moralization and Becoming a Vegetarian," 68.

31. Rozin and colleagues suggest that cigarette smoking has been moralized—transformed from a simple individual taste preference into an activity that involves collective associations of immorality. A more contemporary example is marijuana consumption, which has experienced a process of *demoralization*, delinking the practice from traits of moral deficiency. Rozin, Markwith, and Stoess, "Moralization and Becoming a Vegetarian," 67.

32. We are not alone in this belief. See Rhee, Schein, and Bastian, "The What, How, and Why of Moralization."

33. Benjamin Buttlar and Eva Walther, "Escaping from the Meat Paradox: How Morality and Disgust Affect Meat-Related Ambivalence," *Appetite* 168 (2022): 105721, https://doi.org/10.1016/j.appet.2021.105721.

34. Buttlar and Walther, "Escaping from the Meat Paradox."

35. This connection between moralization and the loss of hedonic pleasure is affirmed by research by Feinberg and colleagues. They find that the pull of hedonic motivations is a central driver operating in a dialectic with the push of moralization. Feinberg et al., "Understanding the Process of Moralization."

36. Thomas J. Scheff, "Shame and the Social Bond: A Sociological Theory," *Sociological Theory* 18, no. 1 (2000): 85, https://doi.org/10.1111/0735-2751.00089.

37. Lotte Holm and Mette Møhl, "The Role of Meat in Everyday Food Culture: An Analysis of an Interview Study in Copenhagen," *Appetite* 34, no. 3 (2000): 277–83, https://doi.org/10.1006/appe.2000.0324; Steve Loughnan, Nick Haslam, and Brock Bastian, "The Role of Meat Consumption in the Denial of Moral Status and Mind to Meat Animals," *Appetite* 55, no. 1 (2010): 156–59, https://doi.org/10.1016/j.appet.2010.05.043; Hank Rothgerber, "Meat-Related Cognitive Dissonance: A Conceptual Framework for Understanding How Meat Eaters Reduce Negative Arousal from Eating Animals," *Appetite* 146 (2020): 6, https://doi.org/10.1016/j.appet.2019.104511; Rothgerber, "'But I Don't Eat That Much Meat.'"

38. Men and women have different meat consumption patterns: women eat 42% less beef than men. Susanna Klassen and Sean Patrick Kearney, "The 'Irony' of Gendered Meat Consumption," *Medium*, March 7, 2019, https://medium.com/the-nature-of-food/the-irony-of-gendered-meat-consumption-15371feocfcd. In a 2002 paper, Elin Kubberød and co-authors report than men have much more favorable attitudes toward meat than women. Elin Kubberød et al., "Gender Specific Preferences and Attitudes Toward Meat," *Food Quality and Preference* 13, no. 5 (2002): 285–94, https://doi.org/10.1016/S0950-3293(02)00041-1. In 2021, Rosenfeld and Tomiyama used survey data to demonstrate that women who conform to traditional gender roles are more likely to express willingness to adopt a vegetarian diet. Rosenfeld and Tomiyama, "Taste and Health Concerns."

39. We are not claiming that all consumers will experience factory farm disgust. Psychological research suggests a segment of consumers will resist moralized meat messaging and continue to enjoy eating industrialized meat. Feinberg and colleagues used an intervention to introduce moral issues around meat production and found more people reacted *against* the moralized meat messaging than accepted it. As they explain, "Direct and intense moral appeals can work on some people, but backfire on others." Feinberg et al., "Understanding the Process of Moralization," 66.

40. In the case of the German veg* eaters that Simon studied, the nightmarish vision of factory farming included images of concentration camps and a blurred boundary between the harm done to human and nonhuman beings. Johannes Simons, Carl Vierboom, Jeanette Klink-Lehmann, Ingo Härlen, and Monika Hartmann, "Vegetarianism/Veganism: A Way to Feel Good," *Sustainability* 13, no. 7 (2021): 19, https://doi.org/10.3390/su13073618.

41. Julia Kristeva, *Powers of Horror: An Essay on Abjection*, trans. Leon Roudiez (New York: Columbia University Press, 1984).

42. Theories of the abject reference a paradoxically attractive element to disgust that earlier theorists of boundaries like Mary Douglas did not fully appreciate. See Deborah Lupton, "Purity and Danger," in *The Blackwell Encyclopedia of Sociology*, edited by George Ritzer (Malden, Mass.: Wiley-Blackwell, 2016), 1–3, https://doi.org/10.1002/9781405165518.wbeos0729.

43. Natália Otto, Josée Johnston, and Shyon Baumann, "Moral Entrepreneurialism for the Hamburger: Strategies for Marketing a Contested Fast Food," *Cultural Sociology* 16, no. 2 (2022): 190–211, https://doi.org/10.1177/17499755211039932.

44. See Piazza et al., "Rationalizing Meat Consumption." A reminder to readers that the 4 Ns of meat consumption involve seeing meat as nice, normal, natural, and necessary.

45. Rozin, Markwith, and Stoess, "Moralization and Becoming a Vegetarian."

46. Feinberg et al., "Understanding the Process of Moralization," 53.

Chapter 4

1. Sara Ahmed, *The Promise of Happiness* (Durham, N.C.: Duke University Press, 2010).

2. Ahmed, *Promise of Happiness*, 49.

3. The idea that consuming ethical meat allows meat eaters to feel that they deserve happiness is adapted from Ahmed's concept of the happiness promise. Ahmed, *Promise of Happiness*.

4. Although some small-scale artisanal butcher will prioritize sourcing from small local farms, most butchers source meat from multiple sources, including local farmers and ranchers, but also from corporate wholesalers and meatpacking plants.

5. The suggestion that seeing a whole, dead animal is "too real" aligns with another argument from Ahmed's *The Promise of Happiness*. For Ahmed, the political significance of challenging happiness narratives is as a form of resistance and a pathway to awareness of system injustice. Just as the sadness and anger that the "affect alien" expresses about immigration sheds light on the injustice that animates migration flows, the inevitability of death as part of a meat-based meal can illuminate the trouble with a food system that demands the death of millions of animals every day. See "How Many Animals Get Slaughtered Every Day," 2023, *Our World in Data,* last modified September 26, 2023, https://ourworldindata.org/how-many-animals-get-slaughtered-every-day.

6. Shyon Baumann, Michelle Szabo, and Josée Johnston, "Understanding the Food Preferences of People of Low Socioeconomic Status," *Journal of Consumer Culture* 19, no. 3 (2019): 316–39, https://doi.org/10.1177/1469540517717780.

7. For a review of the cultural capital associations associated with upscale butchers and the people that work at them, see Richard Ocejo, *Masters of Craft: Old Jobs in the New Urban Economy* (Princeton, N.J.: Princeton University Press, 2017).

8. We speculate that our participants' cultural backgrounds (e.g., growing up in South Asia) could inform how they place trust in meat retailers and food brands, as well as brands more broadly. Future research could pursue this question.

9. Brenda Beagan et al., "'It's Just Easier for Me to Do It': Rationalizing the Family Division of Foodwork," *Sociology* 42, no. 4 (2008): 664, https://doi.org/10.1177/0038038508091621.

10. Kate Cairns and Josée Johnston, *Food and Femininity* (London: Bloomsbury Academic, 2015); Sarah Bowen, Joslyn Brenton, and Sinikka Elliott, *Pressure Cooker: Why Home Cooking Won't Solve Our Problems and What We Can Do About It* (New York: Oxford University Press, 2019).

11. Some of our other research points to how this tension can operate beyond the level of the family and into ethnocultural communities. In communities where meat-eating reflects a connection to one's ethnocultural identity or religion, reducing or eliminating meat risks being perceived as disrespecting or rejecting that heritage. See Merin Oleschuk, Josée Johnston, and Shyon Baumann, "Maintaining Meat: Cultural Repertoires and the Meat Paradox in a Diverse Sociocultural Context," *Sociological Forum* 34, no. 2 (2019): 337–60, https://doi.org/10.1111/socf.12500.

Chapter 5

1. Johannes Simons, Carl Vierboom, Jeanette Klink-Lehmann, Ingo Härlen, and Monika Hartmann, "Vegetarianism/Veganism: A Way to Feel Good," *Sustainability* 13, no. 7 (2021): 9, https://doi.org/10.3390/su13073618.

2. *Okja*, directed by Bong Joon-ho (Los Angeles: Plan B Entertainment, 2017).

3. *Okja*.

4. Simons et al., "Vegetarianism/Veganism," 9.

5. *Babe*, directed by Chris Noonan (Universal City, Calif.: Universal Pictures, 1995).

6. E. B. White, *Charlotte's Web* (New York: Harper & Brothers, 1952).

7. Miele notes that while these marketing images emphasize freedom, they say little about other significant elements of animals' lives, like "mortality and health, absence of hunger or thirst, absence of injuries, absence of stress, and good human-animal relationships" that might not necessarily be improved in a free-range system of production. Mara Miele, "The Taste of Happiness: Free-Range Chicken," *Environment and Planning A* 43, no. 9 (2010): 2080, https://doi.org/10.1068/a43257.

8. Sara Ahmed, *The Promise of Happiness* (Durham, N.C.: Duke University Press, 2010), 26.

9. Bridging the gap between producers and consumers is a central and persistent challenge of food studies—and a challenge we take seriously in this section of the book. See David Goodman and E. Melanie DuPuis, "Knowing Food and Growing Food: Beyond the Production–Consumption Debate in the Sociology of Agriculture," *Sociologia Ruralis* 42, no. 1 (2002): 5–22, https://doi.org/10.1111/1467-9523.00199.

10. Wendell Berry, *What Are People For? Essays* (Berkeley: Counterpoint, 2010), 145.

11. To read an analysis extending Karl Marx's theory of alienation to dairy cattle, see Diana Stuart, Rebecca L. Schewe, and Ryan Gunderson, "Extending Social Theory to Farm Animals: Addressing Alienation in the Dairy Sector," *Sociologia Ruralis* 53, no. 2 (2013): 201–22, https://doi.org/10.1111/soru.12005. To read a general historical account of how urban dwellers have become distanced from farm animals, see Richard

W. Bulliet, *Hunters, Herders, and Hamburgers: The Past and Future of Human-Animal Relationships* (New York: Columbia University Press, 2005). For a more recent exploration focussed on how ethical meat systems aim to connect consumers with meat, and "re-enchant" their relationship with food animals and the natural world, see Christine Jeske, "Re-Enchanting Meat: How Sacred Meaning-Making Strengthens the Ethical Meat Movement," *Agriculture and Human Values,* June 22, 2023, https://doi.org/10.1007/s10460-023-10477-9

12. Warren Belasco, *Food: The Key Concepts* (New York: Berg, 2008), 4.

13. Tyler Bateman, Shyon Baumann, and Josée Johnston, "Meat as Benign, Meat as Risk: Mapping News Discourse of an Ambiguous Issue," *Poetics* 76 (2019): 1–13, https://doi.org/10.1016/j.poetic.2019.03.001; Robert Magneson Chiles, "Hidden in Plain Sight: How Industry, Mass Media, and Consumers' Everyday Habits Suppress Food Controversies," *Sociologia Ruralis* 57, no. S1 (2017): 791–815, https://doi.org/10.1111/soru.12152.

14. Miele, "Taste of Happiness," 2080.

15. See Tzvetan Todorov, *The Conquest of America: The Question of the Other* (Norman: University of Oklahoma Press, 1999).

16. Jane Bennett, *Vibrant Matter: A Political Ecology of Things* (Durham, N.C.: Duke University Press, 2010).

17. This does not mean that there is a consensus on exactly or precisely how nonhumans can act. Debate exists on the degree of action that a nonhuman can hold and whether nonhumans can possess *agency.* As Jerolmack and Tavory write, "actor-network theorists seem to forget" that "agency can never be equally distributed between humans and nonhuman actors. Rather, there is a spectrum of agency, with doors and yarmulkes occupying one end, humans the other, and cocks, pigeons, and dogs somewhere in the middle." Colin Jerolmack and Iddo Tavory, "Molds and Totems: Nonhumans and the Constitution of the Social Self," *Sociological Theory* 32, no. 1 (2014): 74, https://doi.org/10.1177/0735275114523604.

18. For a thoughtful account of this relationship and how it relates to rituals surrounding farm animal death, see Jeske, "Re-Enchanting Meat."

19. Jerolmack and Tavory, "Molds and Totems."

20. For a clear and comprehensive account of animal domestication, as well as an ethnographic exploration of human-animal relationship on farms, see Rhoda Wilkie, *Livestock/Deadstock: Working with Farm Animals from Birth to Slaughter* (Philadelphia: Temple University Press, 2010).

21. For specific figures and comparisons to other regions, see Mahsa Shahbandeh, "Number of Pigs Worldwide in 2023, by Leading Country (in Million Head)," Statista, accessed August 21, 2023, https://www.statista.com/statistics/263964/number-of-pigs-in-selected-countries/#:~:text=Unsurprisingly%2C%20China%20is%20the%20oleading,and%20importers%20oof%20pork%20worldwide. For research into pig farming in China, see Michael Standaert and Francesco De Augustinis, "A 12-Storey Pig Farm: Has China Found the Way to Tackle Animal Disease?" *The Guardian,*

September 18, 2020, https://www.theguardian.com/environment/2020/sep/18/a-12-storey-pig-farm-has-china-found-a-way-to-stop-future-pandemics-.

22. For a fascinating and nuanced scholarly inside-view of industrial big production, see Alex Blanchette, *Porkopolis: American Animality, Standardized Life, and the Factory Farm* (Durham, N.C.: Duke University Press, 2020).

23. Although many farmers in our study disagreed with Frank, the conventional pork industry certainly agrees with him. See Blanchette, *Porkopolis*, 228.

24. To be clear, we are not in position to evaluate whether Frank's pigs' living conditions were a significant step up from conventional production conditions. However, even if we were in such a position, our focus here is on producer perceptions and producer choices, not an assessment of the objective quality of animals' conditions.

25. Many of our producers mentioned or made use of the portable pen method, an innovation developed to raise chickens by the charismatic and controversial farm figure Joel Salatin. Although moveable pens can vary in size, this kind of pen can contain many animals and is usually big enough that the animals are not crowded. The pen allows them to feed on grass in (and to fertilize) a set area. When pigs need more fresh grass, the pen is moved and the cycle repeats. See Joel Salatin, "Our Production Models—Polyface Farms," accessed August 1, 2021, http://www.polyfacefarms.com/production/; Tom Philpot, "Joel Salatin's Unsustainable Myth," *Mother Jones*, November 19, 2020, https://www.motherjones.com/food/2020/11/joel-salatin-chris-newman-farming-rotational-grazing-agriculture/.

26. It is worth mentioning that this conundrum was expressed by many of the farmers we interviewed. They were committed to raising animals in the most natural and humane ways they could, which usually would mean that antibiotics are not necessary. However, just like with people, sometimes animals get sick and need medicine. When faced with the choice of being committed to an "antibiotic-free" label and letting their animals die on the one hand, or medicating their animals and allowing them to fully grow to become food on the other, most farmers found the medication route a better choice. They were not comfortable—morally or financially—with needless animal deaths.

Chapter 6

1. See *Our World in Data*, which uses data from the UN Food and Agriculture Organization. See Hannah Ritchie, Pablo Rosado, and Max Roser, "Meat and Dairy Production," *Our World in Data*, last modified December 2023, accessed June 28, 2024, https://ourworldindata.org/meat-production#meat-production-by-type.

2. "Meat consumption," OECD, https://www.oecd.org/en/data/indicators/meat-consumption.html, accessed June 28, 2024.

3. Max Roser, "How Many Animals Get Slaughtered Every Day?" *Our World in Data*, last modified September 26, 2023, https://ourworldindata.org/how-many-animals-get-slaughtered-every-day.

4. See "OECD-FAO Agricultural Outlook 2023–2032," accessed June 28, 2024, https://data-explorer.oecd.org/vis?pg=0&bp=true&snb=3&df[ds]=dsDissemin

ateFinalDMZ&df[id]=DSD_AGR%40DF_OUTLOOK_2023_2032&df[ag]=
OECD.TAD.ATM&df[vs]=&lc=en&pd=2010%2C2032&dq=W.A.CPC_EX_PT. . .&to
[TIME_PERIOD]=false&vw=tb.

5. "OECD-FAO Agricultural Outlook 2023–2032."

6. Food and Agriculture Organization of the United Nations, *Pathways Towards Lower Emissions—A Global Assessment of the Greenhouse Gas Emissions and Mitigation Options from Livestock Agrifood Systems*, Rome, 2023, https://doi.org/10.4060/cc9029en.

7. Paulo César de Faccio Carvalho et al., "Reconnecting Grazing Livestock to Crop Landscapes: Reversing Specialization Trends to Restore Landscape Multifunctionality," *Frontiers in Sustainable Food Systems* 5, October 2021, https://doi.org/10.3389/fsufs.2021.750765.

8. César de Faccio Carvalho et al., "Reconnecting Grazing Livestock." See also James M. MacDonald and William D. McBride, "The Transformation of U.S. Livestock Agriculture: Scale, Efficiency, and Risks," Economic Information Bulletin No. 43, United States Department of Agriculture, Economic Research Service, January 2009.

9. Roser, "How Many Animals Get Slaughtered Every Day?"

10. Jane Bennett, *Vibrant Matter: A Political Ecology of Things* (Durham, N.C.: Duke University Press, 2010), viii.

11. By contrast, a typical industrial chicken production facility would raise around 350,000 chickens. See Janet Perry, David Banker, and Robert Green, *Broiler Farms' Organization, Management, and Performance* (Washington, D.C.: Resource Economics Division, Economic Research Service, U.S. Department of Agriculture, 1999), https://www.ers.usda.gov/webdocs/publications/42203/13408_aib748_1_.pdf?v=8118.4.

12. The provincially regulated, supply management chicken and egg quota systems also limit how many chickens and eggs ethical producers can legally sell. In British Columbia, for example, producers who produce 2,000-plus chickens must own a quota and report to the British Columbia Chicken Marketing Board. See British Columbia Chicken Marketing Board, "Getting into Broiler Chicken Farming in BC," accessed August 1, 2023, https://bcchicken.ca/getting-into-broiler-chicken-farming-in-bc/.

13. Not all producers agreed that the Salatin method was the only way to use animal fertilizer to maintain soil fertility, as some noted it was possible for farmers to move animal waste out of a barn or enclosure onto the field.

14. Technically, Mitchell reported that he had 399 hens. To have 400 hens, he would have to purchase a quota and register with the provincial egg marketing board.

15. One exception: During her childhood, Josée recalled incidents where they mistakenly placed a runaway chicken back in the wrong movable pen, only to find that it was attacked (and sometimes killed) by the other chickens who perceived it as a foreign intruder.

16. Other farmers we spoke to had different experiences with raising chickens, and countered the idea that chickens are always aggressive when raised in large groupings. We heard that including bone meal in chicken feed helps reduce or prevent chicken aggression, since chicken cannibalism could be about nutritional needs. We also

heard that chickens are often raised in much larger flocks and so the outcomes of flock size experienced by Sheila and Derek are not necessarily generalizable.

17. Regarding the problem of roosters crowing, we heard from other farmers that roosters that are old enough to crow constantly have reached sexual maturity. They are commonly slaughtered before this age, so many farmers do not experience this problem.

18. Jake Edmiston, "Three Meat-Packing Plants Turn Out 85% of Canada's Beef. How Did This Happen?" *Financial Post*, May 6, 2020, https://financialpost.com/commodities/agriculture/why-only-three-meat-packing-plants-process-the-vast-majority-of-canadas-beef.

19. In Ontario, as elsewhere, the number of provincially inspected slaughterhouse facilities that service small producers has declined significantly, from 300 in 1995 to 122 in 2023 (as of August 2023). Mary Baxter, "Does Ontario Have Enough Slaughterhouses?" *TVO Today*, August 28, 2019, https://www.tvo.org/article/does-ontario-have-enough-slaughterhouses; "All Abattoirs," Ontario Ministry of Agriculture, Food, and Rural Affairs, last modified October 5, 2023, https://data.ontario.ca/dataset/provincially-licensed-meat-plants/resource/3256ec2b-2c49-4d57-98f3-4e2293738d3e.

20. Two important exceptions are dairy and veal operations, which are generally located within barns. Also, when land is expensive and scarce, it is possible to have cow/calf operations that use barns. This is something that producers said that they increasingly observed. One respondent remarked that a neighbor down the road has "fifty Angus cows inside a barn of sorts with an acre pasture they go out once awhile to stretch their legs."

21. Gidon Eshel et al., "Land, Irrigation Water, Greenhouse Gas, and Reactive Nitrogen Burdens of Meat, Eggs, and Dairy Production in the United States," *Proceedings of the National Academy of Sciences of the United States of America* 111, no. 33 (2014): 11996–12001, https://doi.org/10.1073/pnas.1402183111. For more information on producers' perceptions, see Josée Johnston, Anelyse Weiler, and Shyon Baumann, "The Cultural Imaginary of Ethical Meat: A Study of Producer Perceptions," *Journal of Rural Studies* 89 (2022): 192–93, https://doi.org/10.1016/j.jrurstud.2021.11.021.

22. Pierre J. Gerber et al., "Environmental Impacts of Beef Production: Review of Challenges and Perspectives for Durability," *Meat Science* 109 (2015): 2–12, https://doi.org/10.1016/j.meatsci.2015.05.013.

23. Cynthia A. Daley et al., "A Review of Fatty Acid Profiles and Antioxidant Content in Grass-Fed and Grain-Fed Beef," *Nutrition Journal* 9, no. 10 (2010): 1–12, https://doi.org/10.1186/1475-2891-9-10.

24. Darrell J. Bosch et al., "Farm Returns to Carbon Credit Creation with Intensive Rotational Grazing," *Journal of Soil and Water Conservation* 63, no. 2 (2008): 91–98, https://doi.org/10.2489/jswc.63.2.91; Elizabeth J. Jacobo et al., "Rotational Grazing Effects on Rangeland Vegetation at a Farm Scale," *Rangeland Ecology and Management* 59, no. 3 (2006): 249–57, https://doi.org/10.2111/05-129R1.1.

25. Alan Savory and Jody Butterfield, *Holistic Management: A Commonsense Revolution to Restore Our Environment*, 3rd ed. (Washington, D.C.: Island Press, 2016).

26. Matthew N. Hayek and Rachael D. Garrett, "Nationwide Shift to Grass-Fed Beef Requires Larger Cattle Population," *Environmental Research Letters* 13, no. 8 (2018): 1–8, https://doi.org/10.1088/1748-9326/aad401.

27. For a general critique of feedlots, see Environmental Working Group, "Animal Feeding Operations Harm Environment, Climate, and Public Health," Environmental Working Group, accessed July 6, 2024, https://www.ewg.org/research/animal-feeding-operations-harm-environment-climate-and-public-health; Eurogroup for Animals, "Cattle Feedlots: Environmental Impacts and Animal Welfare Concerns," accessed July 6, 2024, https://www.eurogroupforanimals.org/files/eurogroupforanimals/2021-12/2020_12_eurogroup_for_animals_cattle_feedlots.pdf. For an academic assessment of the animal welfare dimensions of intensive feedlot productions, see Temple Grandin, "Evaluation of the Welfare of Cattle Housed in Outdoor *Veterinary and Animal Science* 1–2 (2016): 23–28.

28. See Larry Meadows, "What's Your Beef—Prime, Choice or Select?" U.S. Department of Agriculture, January 28, 2013, https://www.usda.gov/media/blog/2013/01/28/whats-your-beef-prime-choice-or-select; "The Importance of the Grader and Grade Consistency," Canadian Beef Grading Agency, accessed May 31, 2023, https://beefgradingagency.ca/livestock-grading-in-canada/beef-grading/.

29. Before the 1960s, most cattle in the United States were finished in small, farmer-owned feedlots. Today, large feedlots dominate the market, with the largest operations feeding 100,000 cattle at a time. In 2024, a large majority of cattle in the United States (87%) were finished in feedlots with a capacity of at least one thousand head of cattle. J. M. MacDonald and W. D. McBride, "The Transformation of U.S. Livestock Agriculture: Scale, Efficiency, and Risks," Economic Information Bulletin No. 43, United States Department of Agriculture, Economic Research Service, 2009; AGDAILY Reporters, "U.S. Feedlot Inventory Shows Marginal Growth Year-Over-Year," *AGDAILY*, February 26, 2024, https://www.agdaily.com/livestock/u-s-feedlot-inventory-shows-marginal-growth-year-over-year/. {not in biblio?}

30. Michael J. Martin, Sapna E. Thottathil, and Thomas B. Newman, "Antibiotics Overuse in Animal Agriculture: A Call to Action for Health Care Providers," *American Journal of Public Health* 105, no. 12 (2015): 2409–10, https://doi.org/10.2105/AJPH.2015.302870.

31. One of the most notable public critiques of the beef feedlot system is Michael Pollan, "Power Steer," *New York Times Magazine,* March 31, 2002.

32. See Nancy Matsumoto, "Is Grass-Fed Beef Really Better for the Planet? Here's the Science," NPR, August 13, 2019, https://www.npr.org/sections/thesalt/2019/08/13/746576239/is-grass-fed-beef-really-better-for-the-planet-heres-the-science.

33. Paige L. Stanley et al., "Impacts of Soil Carbon Sequestration on Life Cycle Greenhouse Gas Emissions in Midwestern USA Beef Finishing Systems," *Agricultural Systems* 162 (2018): 249–58, https://doi.org/10.1016/j.agsy.2018.02.003.

34. Hayek and Garrett, "Nationwide Shift to Grass-Fed Beef."

35. "Back to Grass: The Market Potential for U.S. Grassfed Beef," *Stone Barns Center for Food and Agriculture*, April 2017, https://www.stonebarnscenter.org/wp-content/uploads/2017/10/Grassfed_Full_v2.pdf.

Chapter 7

1. Pierre Bourdieu, *Distinction* (Cambridge, Mass.: Harvard University Press, 1984).

2. Tony Bennett et al., *Culture, Class, Distinction* (New York: Routledge, 2009); Josée Johnston and Shyon Baumann, *Foodies: Democracy and Distinction in the Gourmet Foodscape*, 2nd ed. (New York: Routledge, 2015); Will Atkinson and Christopher Deeming, "Class and Cuisine in Contemporary Britain: The Social Space, the Space of Food and Their Homology," *Sociological Review* 63, no. 4 (2015): 876–96, https://doi.org/10.1111/1467-954X.12335.

3. Michèle Lamont and Annette Lareau, "Cultural Capital: Allusions, Gaps and Glissandos in Recent Theoretical Developments," *Sociology Theory* 6, no. 2 (1988): 153–68.

4. Johnston and Baumann, *Foodies*.

5. Shyon Baumann, Michelle Szabo, and Josée Johnston, "Understanding the Food Preferences of People of Low Socioeconomic Status," *Journal of Consumer Culture* 19, no. 3 (2019): 316–39, https://journals.sagepub.com/doi/10.1177/1469540517717780.

6. Brenda Beagan et al., *Acquired Tastes: Why Families Eat the Way They Do* (Vancouver: UBC Press, 2014); Baumann, Szabo, and Johnston, "Understanding the Food Preferences."

7. Baumann, Szabo, and Johnston, "Understanding the Food Preferences," 322.

8. Michèle Lamont, *Money, Morals, and Manners: The Culture of the French and the American Upper-Middle Class* (Chicago: University of Chicago Press, 1992).

9. *Consecration* is a term used to describe the approval given to certain cultural choices by people whose opinions are influential in a field. For example, a positive review in *The New York Review of Books* can contribute toward the aesthetic consecration of a novel. Similarly, organic certification by a recognized organization can contribute to the ethical consecration of a food.

10. Shyon Baumann, Emily Huddart Kennedy, and Josée Johnston, "Moral and Aesthetic Consecration and Higher Status Consumers' Tastes: The 'Good' Food Revolution," *Poetics* 92, Part B (2022): 101654, https://doi.org/10.1016/j.poetic.2022.101654.

11. Josée Johnston, Michelle Szabo, and Alexandra Rodney, "Good Food, Good People: Understanding the Cultural Repertoire of Ethical Eating," *Journal of Consumer Culture* 11, no. 3 (2011): 293–318, https://doi.org/10.1177/1469540511417996.

12. Johnston, Szabo, and Rodney, "Good Food, Good People."

13. Michèle Lamont, Stefan Beljean, and Matthew Clair, "What Is Missing? Cultural Processes and Causal Pathways to Inequality," *Socio-Economic Review* 12, no. 3 (2014): 573–608, https://doi.org/10.1093/ser/mwu011.

14. Technically speaking, this hybrid *omnivorous* form of consumption, where low-status items like hot dogs are mixed with high-status elements like artisanal ingredients, has become a defining, high-status mode of consumption. Omnivorousness

is an important element of food culture and helps explain a highly valued cultural orientation to appear open to varied forms of culture and cuisine, but it exceeds the scope of this chapter. See Johnston and Baumann, *Foodies*.

15. In our research on foodies, we found that people tended to reject or accept the term *foodie* for a similar reason—a resistance to snobbery. They either thought the term *foodie* was snobbish and rejected it, or they thought it was a relatively inclusive term and accepted it. Either way, nobody wanted to appear like a food snob. See Johnston and Baumann, *Foodies*. On the general cultural aversion to snobbery, see Dave O'Brien and Lisa Ianni, "New Forms of Distinction: How Contemporary Cultural Elites Understand 'Good' Taste," *Sociological Review* 71, no. 1 (2023): 201–20.

16. See Allison J. Pugh's analysis of the different interpretations that are possible with interview data. Pugh, "What Good Are Interviews for Thinking about Culture? Demystifying Interpretive Analysis," *American Journal of Cultural Sociology* 1 (2013): 42–68, https://doi.org/10.1057/ajcs.2012.4.

17. Merin Oleschuk, "'In Today's Market, Your Food Chooses You': News Media Constructions of Responsibility for Health through Home Cooking," *Social Problems* 67, no. 1 (2020): 1–19, https://doi.org/10.1093/socpro/spz006.

18. For full descriptive statistics, see the appendix.

19. In a context like Vancouver, where Akash lives, the average cost of a home is $1.4 million as of 2024.

20. Josée Johnston, Shyon Baumann, and Merin Oleschuk, "Capturing Inequality and Action in Prototypes: The Case of Meat-Eating and Vegetarianism," *Poetics* 87 (2021): 101530, https://doi.org/10.1016/j.poetic.2021.101530.

21. See Johnston, Baumann, and Oleschuk, "Capturing Inequality and Action in Prototypes," 10. We identify the presence of a prototypical thin, rich, often white woman that exists as a prototypical vegetarian, and which has many similarities with the ethical meat-eating figure we observed in this research.

22. Johnston and Baumann, *Foodies*; Oleschuk, "'In Today's Market.'"

Chapter 8

1. Robert Crawford, "Healthism and the Medicalization of Everyday Life," *International Journal of Health Services* 10, no. 3 (1980): 365–88, https://doi.org/10.2190/3h2h-3xjn-3kay-g9ny.

2. A dilemma refers to a situation in which a difficult choice must be made between two or more equally undesirable options. To describe health as dilemmatic is to understand it "in terms of the mutually incompatible goals involved, and in terms of the dilemmatic consequences involved in *any* of the available choices." Joseph E. McGrath, "Dilemmatics: The Study of Research Choices and Dilemmas," *American Behavioral Scientist* 25, no. 2 (1981): 179, https://doi.org/10.1177/000276428102500205.

3. Both the claim that Hinduism promotes vegetarianism as a strategy to make a population weak and complacent and the claim that vegans have smaller brains and poor emotional regulation are either demonstrably untrue or unsubstantiated. Vegetarian diets can meet all nutritional needs and are associated with health benefits.

Abderrahim Oussalah, Julien Levy, Clémence Berthezène, David H. Alpers, and Jean-Louis Guéant, "Health Outcomes Associated with Vegetarian Diets: An Umbrella Review of Systematic Reviews and Meta-Analyses," *Clinical Nutrition* 39, no. 11 (2020): 3283–3307. Also, there is no evidence linking the presence or absence of meat in diets to motivation or complacency. Likewise, vegans consume B vitamins through non-meat sources and there is no link between vegan diets and increased aggression. Isabel Iguacel, Inge Huybrechts, Luis A. Moreno, and Nathalie Michels, "Vegetarianism and Veganism Compared with Mental Health and Cognitive Outcomes: A Systematic Review and Meta-Analysis," *Nutrition Reviews* 79, no. 4 (2021): 361–81.

4. This view is pervasive, even though it is well established that people can get the protein they require from a plant-based diet and that protein deficiency in rich countries is essentially unheard of.

5. Véronique Bouvard et al., "Carcinogenicity of Consumption of Red and Processed Meat," *The Lancet Oncology* 16, no. 16 (2015): 1599–1600, https://doi.org/10.1016/S1470-2045(15)00444-1.

6. Josée Johnston, Shyon Baumann, and Merin Oleschuk, "Capturing Inequality and Action in Prototypes: The Case of Meat-Eating and Vegetarianism," *Poetics* 87 (2021): 101530, https://doi.org/10.1016/j.poetic.2021.101530.

7. It's not clear if people think *other* people are eating more meat than is healthy, while they are eating the right amount for *themselves*. If so, this could help explain why the vast majority of Canadians and Americans eat a lot of meat, especially in global terms (see the introduction).

8. Crawford, "Healthism and the Medicalization of Everyday Life," 379.

9. Pandora Dewan, "What Happens to Your Body When You Eat Meat and Dairy Every Day?" *Newsweek,* December 25, 2022, https://www .newsweek.com/newsweek-com-health-body-diet-meat-dairy-every-day-1769403.

10. Frédéric Leroy et al., "Meat in the Post-Truth Era: Mass Media Discourses on Health and Disease in the Attention Economy," *Appetite* 125 (2018): 345–55, https://doi.org/10.1016/j.appet.2018.02.028.

11. Dominic Ponsford, "Who Reads the Daily Mail? Why Biggest Print Title Still Has a Huge Influence," *Press Gazette*, March 10, 2023, https://pressgazette.co.uk/publishers/nationals/who-reads-the-daily-mail-circulation-and-readership/.

12. Gina Kolata, "The Perplexing Red Meat Controversy: 5 Things to Know," *New York Times*, September 30, 2019, https://www.nytimes.com/2019/09/30/health/red-meat-questions-answers.html.

13. Gina Kolata, "Eat Less Red Meat, Scientists Said. Now Some Believe That Was Bad Advice," *New York Times,* September 30, 2019, https://www.nytimes.com/2019/09/30/health/red-meat-heart-cancer.html.

14. Scott-Reid, Jessica, "'Ultraprocessed' Plant-Based Meat Isn't as Bad for You as the Meat Industry Wants You to Believe," *Toronto Star,* July 6, 2024,

https://www.thestar.com/opinion/contributors/ultraprocessed-plant-based-meat-isnt-as-bad-for-you-as-the-meat-industry-wants-you/article_7cd5cb1e-3944-11ef-98a3-630c7eb74f1d.html.

15. Mirkka Maukonen et al., "Partial Substitution of Red or Processed Meat with Plant-Based Foods and the Risk of Type 2 Diabetes," *Scientific Reports* 13, no. 5874 (2023), https://doi.org/10.1038/s41598-023-32859-z.

16. Nicole Axworthy, "Does Cutting Out Meat Help with Diabetes? New Study Says Yes," *VegNews*, April 25, 2023, https://vegnews.com/vegan-news/cutting-red-meat-diabetes-study.

17. Kolata, "Eat Less Red Meat."

18. Rebekah H. Nagler, "Adverse Outcomes Associated with Media Exposure to Contradictory Nutrition Messages," *Journal of Health Communication* 19, no. 1 (2014): 24–40, https://doi.org/10.1080/10810730.2013.798384.

19. Looking in the literature for other examples of where there is a strong discourse around trusting instincts over experts, we noted this is a prominent theme in some communities of mothers with infants. See Victoria O'Key and Siobhan Hugh-Jones, "'I Don't Need Anybody to Tell Me What I Should Be Doing': A Discursive Analysis of Material Accounts of (Mis)trust of Healthy Eating Information," *Appetite* 54, no. 3 (2010): 524–32, https://doi.org/10.1016/j.appet.2010.02.007. More recently, trusting instincts over experts is a theme in research on government mandates surrounding the COVID-19 pandemic. See Paul Cairney and Adam Wellstead, "COVID-19: Effective Policymaking Depends on Trust in Experts, Politicians, and the Public," *Policy Design and Practice* 4, no. 1 (2021): 1–14, https://doi.org/10.1080/25741292.2020.1837466.

20. For a classic elaboration of the influence of corporate lobbying on government food recommendations, see Marion Nestle, *Food Politics: How the Food Industry Influences Nutrition and Health* (Berkeley: University of California Press, 2002).

21. Ann Hui, "The New Canada's Food Guide Explained: Goodbye Four Food Groups and Serving Sizes, Hello Hydration," *Globe and Mail*, January 22, 2019, https://www.theglobeandmail.com/canada/article-new-canadas-food-guide-explained/.

22. The trend of "trusting your body" to make food choices can be linked back to a loss of trust in institutional sources of knowledge on nutrition and food. Although expanding on the topic exceeds the goals of this chapter, we note that the idea of trusting your body as a source of signals on satiety and wellness has been positively informed by a philosophy of *intuitive eating* pioneered by Evelyn Tribole and Elyse Resch as a way of resisting hegemonic diet culture. Some research supports intuitive eating as effective for achieving certain health goals. See Nina Van Dyke and Eric J. Drinkwater, "Relationships between Intuitive Eating and Health Indicators: Literature Review," *Public Health Nutrition* 17, no. 8 (2014): 1757–66, https://doi.org/10.1017/s1368980013002139.

23. Without using the term explicitly, Aaron, Max, and Cameron are each describing elements of *intuitive eating*. As already mentioned, evidence suggests intuitive eating can be an effective pathway to a healthy diet.

24. A carbon footprint is an estimate of the greenhouse gas emissions re-sulting from a range of consumption domains, including transportation, hous-ing, and eating. "We Need to Talk About Meat," United Nations Climate Change, May 19, 2021, https://unfccc.int/blog/we-need-to-talk-about-meat?gclid=CjoKCQj wkqSlBhDaARIsAFJANkhoGnnZH7qb1Iid2nwPAQZsbtQiREjpWLqrwb7-wS--7Qs_aodzAEUaAgKNEALw_wcB.

25. "We Need to Talk About Meat."

26. Joseph Poore and Thomas Nemecek, "Reducing Food's Environmental Im-pacts through Producers and Consumers," *Science* 360, no. 6392 (2018): 987–92, https://doi.org/10.1126/science.aaq0216.

27. Peter Scarborough et al., "Vegans, Vegetarians, Fish-Eaters, and Meat-Eaters in the UK Show Discrepant Environmental Impacts," *Nature Food* 4 (2023): 565–74, https://doi.org/10.1038/s43016-023-00795-w.

28. Scarborough et al., "Vegans, Vegetarians, Fish-Eaters, and Meat-Eaters," 566.

29. Paige L. Stanley et al., "Impacts of Soil Carbon Sequestration on Life Cycle Greenhouse Gas Emissions in Midwestern USA Beef Finishing Systems," *Agricul-tural Systems* 162 (2018): 249–58, https://doi.org/10.1016/j.agsy.2018.02.003. On the re-generative benefits of grazing ruminants, see "Managing the Complexities of Land and Livestock," Savory Institute, accessed September 1, 2023, https://savory.global/holistic-management/.

30. Christopher D. Lupo et al., "Life-Cycle Assessment of the Beef Cattle Pro-duction System for the Northern Great Plains, USA," *Journal of Environmental Quality* 42, no. 5 (2013): 1386–94, https://doi.org/10.2134/jeq2013.03.0101; Jason E. Rowntree et al., "Ecosystem Impacts and Productive Capacity of a Multi-Species Pastured Livestock System," *Frontiers in Sustainable Food Systems* 4 (2020): 544984, https://doi.org/10.3389/fsufs.2020.544984.

31. Maya B. Mathur, "Ethical Drawbacks of Sustainable Meat Choices," *Science* 375, no. 6587 (2022): 1362, https://doi.org/10.1126/science.abo2535.

32. Jennie I. Macdiarmid, Flora Douglas, and Jonina Campbell, "Eating Like There's No Tomorrow: Public Awareness of the Environmental Impact of Food and Reluctance to Eat Less Meat as Part of a Sustainable Diet," *Appetite* 96 (2016): 487–93, https://doi.org/10.1016/j.appet.2015.10.011.

33. In interviews with producers, we encountered the idea that current systems of meat production are sustainable, but this was a minority perspective, rooted in a distrust of science. In the words of one rancher, Dean, "What I would suggest [is that] in research [and] in science, you specialize, and you learn more and more about less and less. Until you know absolutely everything about nothing." His wife, Betty, agreed that scientists do not understand the environmental impact of beef production, adding, "Humans probably give off more methane gas than cows." Josée Johnston, Anelyse Weiler, and Shyon Baumann, "The Cultural Imaginary of Ethi-cal Meat: A Study of Producer Perceptions," *Journal of Rural Studies* 89 (2022): 193, https://doi.org/10.1016/j.jrurstud.2021.11.021.

34. The discrepancy between our focus group findings and our survey findings is attributable to our different sampling strategies for each. Whereas our focus groups sampling targeted people with an expressed interest in ethical meat, the survey attempted to create a sample that would represent the average consumer.

35. The "eat less meat, eat better meat" frame was the dominant perspective we heard in our interviews with ethical meat producers. According to this perspective, consumers should increase their consumption of meat sourced from sustainable, humane, and economically decentralized small or mid-scale operations. While acknowledging that such meat may come at a higher price compared to conventional options, these producers believe that consumers should prioritize ethical meat expenditures and make a conscious choice to de-link from large-scale industrialized operations. Johnston, Weiler, and Baumann, "Cultural Imaginary of Ethical Meat."

36. Other solutions include eating a plant-based diet but, as we show in Chapter 2, fewer than 5% of Canadians avoid meat. In recent years, lab-grown meat and insect protein have emerged as protein alternatives. Our survey data cast skepticism on their widespread adoption: just over five percent of respondents said they would be comfortable eating insect protein and less than ten percent said they would eat lab-grown meat.

37. The pattern of consumers turning toward ethical meat to address concerns about industrial meat has been demonstrated by existing research. For example, in a survey of Swiss households, Michael Siegrist and Christina Hartmann found that people who reported high levels of concern for their health were more likely to buy organic meat than their less health-concerned counterparts. Michael Siegrist and Christina Hartmann, "Impact of Sustainability Perception on Consumption of Organic Meat and Meat Substitutes," *Appetite* 132 (2019): 196–202, https://doi.org/10.1016/j.appet.2018.09.016.

38. Malwina, a sixty-two-year-old woman who was skeptical of meat, also expressed skepticism of the vegetarian and vegan products produced by large corporations: "I will never buy Beyond [Meat] Burger, because I heard some information . . . they're buying leftovers of children from abortion to put in this meat. I hear information like this. And even if it is just fake news or someone's joke, I prefer, just in case, not to touch this product anymore."

Conclusion

1. The Food and Agriculture Organization of the United Nations provides specific data by animal. See "Data," Food and Agriculture Organization of the United Nations, accessed August 1, 2023, https://www.fao.org/faostat/en/?#data. For data broken down by daily consumption rates see Roser, "How Many Animals Get Slaughtered Every Day?" *Our World in Data,* last modified September 26, 2023, https://ourworldindata.org/how-many-animals-get-slaughtered-every-day.

2. Sara Ahmed, *The Promise of Happiness* (Durham, N.C.: Duke University Press, 2010).

3. Paul Rozin, Maureen Markwith, and Caryn Stoess, "Moralization and Becoming a Vegetarian: The Transformation of Preferences into Values and

the Recruitment of Disgust," *Psychological Science* 8, no. 2 (1997): 67–73, https://doi.org/10.1111/j.1467-9280.1997.tb00685.x.

4. For a range of these perspectives on sustainability and meat, see Josée Johnston, Anelyse Weiler, and Shyon Baumann, "The Cultural Imaginary of Ethical Meat: A Study of Producer Perceptions," *Journal of Rural Studies* 89 (2022): 186–98, https://doi.org/10.1016/j.jrurstud.2021.11.021.

5. See, for example, Rhoda Wilkie, *Livestock/Deadstock: Working with Farm Animals from Birth to Slaughter* (Philadelphia: Temple University Press, 2010).

6. For just one example, see Thomas A. Heberlein and J. Stanley Black, "Attitudinal Specificity and the Prediction of Behavior in a Field Setting," *Journal of Personality and Social Psychology* 33, no. 4 (1976): 474–79, https://doi.org/10.1037/0022-3514.33.4.474.

7. See, for instance, Anja Kollmuss and Julian Agyeman, "Mind the Gap: Why Do People Act Environmentally and What Are the Barriers to Pro-Environmental Behavior?" *Environmental Education Research* 8, no. 3 (2002): 239–60, https://doi.org/10.1080/13504620220145401.

8. Adam Liptak, "Supreme Court Upholds California Law on Humane Treatment of Pigs," *New York Times*, May 11, 2023, https://www.nytimes.com/2023/05/11/us/supreme-court-california-pigs.html.

9. Antonia Noori Farzan and Quentin Ariès, "Europe Weights Banning Cages for Farm Animals," *Washington Post*, July 1, 2021, https://www.washingtonpost.com/world/2021/07/01/europe-cages-farming/.

10. North American Meat Institute, "19th Annual Power of Meat Report: Strong Meat Consumption, Evolving Consumer Trends," *North American Meat Institute*, accessed July 22, 2024, https://www.meatinstitute.org/press/19th-annual-power-meat-reports-strong-meat-consumption-evolving-consumer-trends.

11. Ahmed, *Promise of Happiness*.

12. Simon et al.'s study of vegetarian and vegan eaters in Berlin shows that even a simple rule to not eat meat can be difficult to implement in everyday life. Participants admitted breaking these rules (as we also documented in Chapter 2) and some experienced feeling guilty and weak as a result. Johannes Simons, Carl Vierboom, Jeanette Klink-Lehmann, Ingo Härlen, and Monika Hartmann, "Vegetarianism/Veganism: A Way to Feel Good," *Sustainability* 13, no. 7 (2021): 11, https://doi.org/10.3390/su13073618.

13. North American Meat Institute, "19th Annual Power of Meat Report."

Methods Appendix

1. See, for example, Cory R. Woodyatt, Catherine A. Finneran, and Rob Stephenson, "In-Person Versus Online Focus Group Discussions: A Comparative Analysis of Data Quality," *Qualitative Health Research* 26, no. 6 (2016): 741–49, https://doi.org/10.1177/1049732316631510.

2. Colin MacDougall and Frances Baum, "The Devil's Advocate: A Strategy to Avoid Groupthink and Stimulate Discussion in Focus Groups," *Qualitative Health Research* 7, no. 4 (1997): 532–41, https://doi.org/10.1177/104973239700700407.

References

Ahmed, Sara. *The Promise of Happiness*. Durham, N.C.: Duke University Press, 2010.

Alkon, Alison Hope, and Christie Grace McCullen. "Whiteness and Farmers Markets: Performances, Perpetuations . . . Contestations?" *Antipode* 43, no. 4 (2011): 937–59.

"All Abattoirs." Ontario Ministry of Agriculture, Food, and Rural Affairs. Last modified October 5, 2023. https://data.ontario.ca/dataset/provincially-licensed-meat-plants/resource/3256ec2b-2c49-4d57-98f3-4e2293738d3e.

Anderson, Eric C., Jolie Wormwood, Lisa Feldman Barrett, and Karen S. Quigley. "Vegetarians' and Omnivores' Affective and Physiological Responses to Images of Food." *Food Quality and Preference* 71 (2019): 96–105. https://doi.org/10.1016/j.foodqual.2018.06.008.

Andersen, Kip, and Keegan Kuhn, dirs. *Cowspiracy*. West Hollywood: Appian Way Productions, 2014.

Arcari, Paula. *Making Sense of "Food" Animals: A Critical Exploration of the Persistence of 'Meat'*. Singapore: Palgrave Macmillan, 2019.

Armisen, Fred, et al., writers. *Portlandia*. Season 1, episode 1, "Farm." Directed by Jonathan Krisel, featuring Fred Armisen and Carrie Brownstein. Aired January 21, 2011.

Atkinson, Will, and Christopher Deeming. "Class and Cuisine in Contemporary Britain: The Social Space, the Space of Food, and Their Homology." *Sociological Review* 63, no. 4 (2015): 876–96. https://doi.org/10.1111/1467-954X.12335.

Axworthy, Nicole. "Does Cutting Out Meat Help with Diabetes? New Study Says Yes." *VegNews*, April 25, 2023. https://vegnews.com/vegan-news/cutting-red-meat-diabetes-study.

"Back to Grass: The Market Potential for U.S. Grassfed Beef." *Stone Barns Center for Food and Agriculture*. April 2017. https://www.stonebarnscenter.org/wp-content/uploads/2017/10/Grassfed_Full_v2.pdf.

Barber, Dan. *The Third Plate: Field Notes on the Future of Food*. New York: Penguin Press, 2014.

Bastian, Brock, and Steve Loughnan. "Resolving the Meat-Paradox: A Motivational Account of Morally Troublesome Behavior and Its Maintenance." *Personality and Social Psychology Review* 21, no. 3 (2017): 278–99. https://doi.org/10.1177/1088868316647562.

Bastian, Brock, Steve Loughnan, Nick Haslam, and Helena R. M. Radke. "Don't Mind Meat? The Denial of Mind to Animals Used for Human Consumption." *Personality and Social Psychology Bulletin* 38, no. 2 (2012): 247–56. https://doi.org/10.1177/0146167211424291.

Bateman, Tyler, Shyon Baumann, and Josée Johnston. "Meat as Benign, Meat as Risk: Mapping News Discourse of an Ambiguous Issue." *Poetics* 76 (2019): 1–13. https://doi.org/10.1016/j.poetic.2019.03.001.

Batz, Michael B., Sandra Hoffman, and J. Glenn Morris Jr. *Ranking the Risks: The 10 Pathogen-Food Combinations with the Greatest Burden on Public Health*. Gainesville: Emerging Pathogens Institute, University of Florida, 2011. https://folio.iupui.edu/bitstream/handle/10244/1022/72267report.pdf.

Baumann, Shyon, Emily Huddart Kennedy, and Josée Johnston. "Moral and Aesthetic Consecration and Higher Status Consumers' Tastes: The 'Good' Food Revolution." *Poetics* 92, Part B (2022): 101654. https://doi.org/10.1016/j.poetic.2022.101654.

Baumann, Shyon, Michelle Szabo, and Josée Johnston. "Understanding the Food Preferences of People of Low Socioeconomic Status." *Journal of Consumer Culture* 19, no. 3 (2017): 316–39. https://doi.org/10.1177/1469540517717780.

Baxter, Mary. "Does Ontario Have Enough Slaughterhouses?" *TVO Today*, August 28, 2019. https://www.tvo.org/article/does-ontario-have-enough-slaughterhouses.

Beagan, Brenda, Gwen E. Chapman, Andrea D'Sylva, and B. Raewyn Bassett. "'It's Just Easier for Me to Do It': Rationalizing the Family Division of Foodwork." *Sociology* 42, no. 4 (2008): 653–71. https://doi.org/10.1177/0038038508091621.

Beagan, Brenda, Gwen E. Chapman, Josée Johnston, Deborah McPhail, Elaine M. Power, and Helen Valliantos. *Acquired Tastes: Why Families Eat the Way They Do*. Vancouver: UBC Press, 2014.

Becker, Elisa, and Natalia S. Lawrence. "Meat Disgust Is Negatively Associated with Meat Intake—Evidence from a Cross-Sectional and Longitudinal Study." *Appetite* 164 (2021): 105299. https://doi.org/10.1016/j.appet.2021.105299.

Belasco, Warren. *Food: The Key Concepts*. New York: Berg, 2008.

Bell, Eryn, F. Bailey Norwood, and Jayson Lusk. "Are Consumers Wilfully Ignorant About Animal Welfare?" *Animal Welfare* 26, no. 4 (2017): 399–402. https://doi.org/10.7120/09627286.26.4.399.

Bennett, Jane. *Vibrant Matter: A Political Ecology of Things*. Durham, N.C.: Duke University Press, 2010.

Bennett, Tony, Mike Savage, Elizabeth Bortolaia Silva, Alan Warde, Modesto Gayo-Cal, and David Wright. *Culture, Class, Distinction*. New York: Routledge, 2009.

Bericat, Eduardo. "The Sociology of Emotions: Four Decades of Progress." *Current Sociology* 64, no. 3 (2016): 491–513. https://doi.org/10.1177/0011392115588355.

Berndsen, Mariëtte, and Joop van der Pligt. "Ambivalence Towards Meat." *Appetite* 42, no. 1 (2004): 71–78. https://doi.org/10.1016/S0195-6663(03)00119-3.

Berndsen, Mariëtte, and Joop van der Pligt. "Risks of Meat: The Relative Impact of Cognitive, Affective, and Moral Concerns." *Appetite* 44, no. 2 (2005): 195–205. https://doi.org/10.1016/j.appet.2004.10.003.

Berry, Wendell. *What Are People For? Essays*. Berkeley: Counterpoint, 2010.

Blanchette, Alex. *Porkopolis: American Animality, Standardized Life, and the Factory Farm*. Durham, N.C.: Duke University Press, 2020.

Bosch, Darrell J., Kurt Stephenson, Gordon Groover, and Blair Hutchins. "Farm Returns to Carbon Credit Creation with Intensive Rotational Grazing." *Journal of Soil and Water Conservation* 63, no. 2 (2008): 91–98. https://doi.org/10.2489/jswc.63.2.91.

Bourdain, Anthony. *Anthony Bourdain: No Reservations*. Directed by Tom Vitale et al., featuring Anthony Bourdain. Aired 2005 to 2012, in broadcast syndication. Cable News Network, Inc.

——. *Anthony Bourdain: Parts Unknown*. Directed by Tom Vitale et al., featuring Anthony Bourdain. Aired 2013 to 2018, in broadcast syndication. Cable News Network, Inc.

Bourdieu, Pierre. *Distinction*. Cambridge, Mass.: Harvard University Press, 1984.

Bouvard, Véronique, Dana Loomis, Kathryn Z. Guyton, Yann Grosse, Fatiha El Ghissassi, Lamia Benbrahim-Tallaa, Neela Guha, Heidi Mattock, and Kurt Straif. "Carcinogenicity of Consumption of Red and Processed Meat." *Lancet Oncology* 16, no. 16 (2015): 1599–1600. https://doi.org/10.1016/S1470-2045(15)00444-1.

Bowen, Sarah, Joslyn Brenton, and Sinikka Elliott. *Pressure Cooker: Why Home Cooking Won't Solve Our Problems and What We Can Do About It*. New York: Oxford University Press, 2019.

Bray, Heather J., and Rachel A. Ankeny. "Happy Chickens Lay Tastier Eggs: Motivations for Buying Free-Range Eggs in Australia." *Anthrozoös* 30, no. 2 (2017): 213–26. https://doi.org/10.1080/08927936.2017.1310986.

Breckler, Steven J. "Empirical Validation of Affect, Behavior, and Cognition as Distinct Components of Attitude." *Journal of Personality and Social Psychology* 47, no. 6 (1984): 1191–1205. https://doi.org/10.1037/0022-3514.47.6.1191.

Bremer, Catherine. "Don't Say Nay to Horsemeat: French Eaters." Reuters, February 12, 2013. https://www.reuters.com/article/us-france-horsemeat-idUSBRE91B0RX20130212.

Buddle, Emily. "Meet Your Meat! How Australian Livestock Producers Use Instagram to Promote 'Happy Meat.'" In *Food Instagram: Identity, Influence, and Negotiation*, edited by Emily J. H. Contois and Zenia Kish, ch. 10. Chicago: University of Illinois Press, 2022.

Buddle, Emily A., and Heather J. Bray. "How Farm Animal Welfare Issues are Framed in the Australian Media." *Journal of Agricultural and Environmental Ethics* 32, no. 3 (2019): 357–76. https://doi.org/10.1007/s10806-019-09778-z.

Buller, Henry. "Animal Welfare: From Production to Consumption." In *Improving Farm Animal Welfare*, edited by Harry Blokhuis, Mara Miele, Isabelle Veissier, and Bryan Jones, 49–69. Wageningen, Netherlands: Wageningen Academic Publishers, 2013.

Buller, Henry, and Emma Roe. *Food and Animal Welfare*. London: Bloomsbury Academic, 2018.

Bulliet, Richard W. *Hunters, Herders, and Hamburgers: The Past and Future of Human-Animal Relationships*. New York: Columbia University Press, 2005.

Buttlar, Benjamin, and Eva Walther. "Escaping from the Meat Paradox: How Morality and Disgust Affect Meat-Related Ambivalence." *Appetite* 168 (2022): 105721. https://doi.org/10.1016/j.appet.2021.105721.

Cairney, Paul, and Adam Wellstead. "COVID-19: Effective Policymaking Depends on Trust in Experts, Politicians, and the Public." *Policy Design and Practice* 4, no. 1 (2021): 1–14. https://doi.org/10.1080/25741292.2020.1837466.

Cairns, Kate, and Josée Johnston. *Food and Femininity*. London: Bloomsbury Academic, 2015.

———. "On (Not) Knowing Where Your Food Comes From: Meat, Mothering, and Ethical Eating." *Agriculture and Human Values* 35, no. 3 (2018): 569–80. https://doi.org/10.1007/s10460-018-9849-5.

Carolan, Michael. "Affective Sustainable Landscapes and Care Ecologies: Getting a Real Feel for Alternative Food Communities." *Sustainability Science* 10, no. 2 (2015): 317–29. https://doi.org/10.1007/s11625-014-0280-6.

"Cattle Feedlots: Environmental Impacts and Animal Welfare Concerns." Eurogroup for Animals, accessed July 6, 2024. https://www.eurogroupforanimals.org/files/eurogroupforanimals/2021-12/2020_12_eurogroup_for_animals_cattle_feedlots.pdf.

Cherry, Elizabeth. "I Was a Teenage Vegan: Motivation and Maintenance of Lifestyle Movements." *Sociological Inquiry* 85, no. 1 (2015): 55–74. https://doi.org/10.1111/soin.12061.

Chiles, Robert Magneson. "Hidden in Plain Sight: How Industry, Mass Media, and Consumers' Everyday Habits Suppress Food Controversies." *Sociologia Ruralis* 57, no. S1 (2017): 791–815. https://doi.org/10.1111/soru.12152.

Crawford, Robert. "Healthism and the Medicalization of Everyday Life." *International Journal of Health Services* 10, no. 3 (1980): 365–88. https://doi.org/10.2190/3h2h-3xjn-3kay-g9ny.

Croney, Candace, and Janice Swanson. "Is Meat Eating Morally Defensible? Contemporary Ethical Considerations." *Animal Frontiers* 13, no. 2 (2023): 61–71.

Daley, Cynthia A., Amber Abbott, Patrick S. Doyle, Glenn A. Nader, and Stephanie Larson. "A Review of Fatty Acid Profiles and Antioxidant Content in Grass-Fed and Grain-Fed Beef." *Nutrition Journal* 9, no. 10 (2010): 1–12. https://doi.org/10.1186/1475-2891-9-10.

"Data." Food and Agriculture Organization of the United Nations, accessed August 1, 2023. https://www.fao.org/faostat/en/?#data.

de Boer, Joop, Hanna Schösler, and Harry Aiking. "'Meatless Days' or 'Less but Better'? Exploring Strategies to Adapt Western Meat Consumption to Health and Sustainability Challenges." *Appetite* 76 (2014): 120–28. https://doi.org/10.1016/j.appet.2014.02.002.

de la O, Víctor, Itziar Zazpe, J. Alfredo Martínez, Susana Santiago, Silvia Carlos, M. Ángeles Zulet, and Miguel Ruiz-Canela. "Scoping Review of Paleolithic Dietary Patterns: A Definitional Proposal." *Nutrition Research Reviews* 34, no. 1 (2021): 78–106. https://doi.org/10.1017/S0954422420000153.

Dempsey, Sarah E., Heather M. Zoller, and Kathleen P. Hunt. "The Meatpacking Industry's Corporate Exceptionalism: Racialized Logics of Food Chain Worker Disposability during the COVID-19 Crisis." *Food, Culture, and Society* 26, no. 3 (2023): 571–90. https://doi.org/10.1080/15528014.2021.2022916.

Dewan, Pandora. "What Happens to Your Body When You Eat Meat and Dairy Every Day?" *Newsweek,* December 25, 2022. https://www.newsweek.com/newsweek-com-health-body-diet-meat-dairy-every-day-1769403.

DiMaggio, Paul, Manish Nag, and David Blei. "Exploiting Affinities Between Topic Modeling and the Sociological Perspective on Culture: Application to Newspaper Coverage of U.S. Government Arts Funding." *Poetics* 41, no. 6 (2013): 570–606. https://doi.org/10.1016/j.poetic.2013.08.004.

Dorard, Géraldine, and Sasha Mathieu. "Vegetarian and Omnivorous Diets: A Cross-Sectional Study of Motivation, Eating Disorders, and Body Shape Perception." *Appetite* 156 (2021): 104972. https://doi.org/10.1016/j.appet.2020.104972.

Douglas, Mary. *Purity and Danger: An Analysis of Concepts of Pollution and Taboo.* London: Routledge and Kegan Paul, 1966.

Edmiston, Jake. "Three Meat-Packing Plants Turn Out 85% of Canada's Beef. How Did This Happen?" *Financial Post,* May 6, 2020. https://financialpost.com/commodities/agriculture/why-only-three-meat-packing-plants-process-the-vast-majority-of-canadas-beef.

Eshel, Gidon, Alon Shepon, Tamar Makov, and Ron Milo. "Land, Irrigation Water, Greenhouse Gas, and Reactive Nitrogen Burdens of Meat, Eggs, and Dairy Production in the United States." *Proceedings of the National Academy of Sciences of the United States of America* 111, no. 33 (2014): 11996–12001. https://doi.org/10.1073/pnas.1402183111.

Faccio Carvalho, Paulo César de, Pedro Arthur de Albuquerque Nunes, Arthur Pontes-Prates, Leonardo Silvestri Szymczak, William de Souza Filho, Fernanda Gomes Moojen, and Gilles Lemaire. "Reconnecting Grazing Livestock to Crop Landscapes: Reversing Specialization Trends to Restore Landscape Multifunctionality." *Frontiers in Sustainable Food Systems* 5 (October 2021). https://doi.org/10.3389/fsufs.2021.750765.

Farzan, Antonia Noori, and Quentin Ariès. "Europe Weights Banning Cages for Farm Animals." *Washington Post,* July 1, 2021. https://www.washingtonpost.com/world/2021/07/01/europe-cages-farming/.

Feinberg, Matthew, Chloe Kovacheff, Rimma Teper, and Yoel Inbar. "Understanding the Process of Moralization: How Eating Meat Becomes a Moral Issue." *Journal of Personality and Social Psychology* 117, no. 1 (2019): 50–72. https://doi.org/10.1037/pspa0000149.

Ferry, Mathieu. "What's India's Beef with Meat? Hindu Orthopraxis and Food Transition in India Since the 1980s." *Sociological Forum* 35, no. 2 (2020): 511–34. https://doi.org/10.1111/socf.12592.

Food and Agriculture Organization of the United Nations. *Pathways Towards Lower Emissions—A Global Assessment of the Greenhouse Gas Emissions and Mitigation Options from Livestock Agrifood Systems.* Rome, 2023. https://doi.org/10.4060/cc9029en.

Fox, Nick, and Katie Ward. "Health, Ethics, and Environment: A Qualitative Study of Vegetarian Motivations." *Appetite* 50, no. 2–3 (2008): 422–29. https://doi.org/10.1016/j.appet.2007.09.007.

Friend, Catherine. *The Compassionate Carnivore: Or, How to Keep Animals Happy, Save Old MacDonald's Farm, Reduce Your Hoofprint, and Still Eat Meat.* Boston: Da Capo Press, 2008.

Garrett, Sarah B. "Foundations of the Cultural Repertoire: Education and Social Network Effects Among Expectant Mothers." *Poetics* 55 (2016): 19–35. https://doi.org/10.1016/j.poetic.2015.12.003.

Gerber, Pierre J., Anne Mottet, Carolyn I. Opio, Alessandra Falcucci, and Félix Teillard. "Environmental Impacts of Beef Production: Review of Challenges and Perspectives for Durability." *Meat Science* 109 (2015): 2–12. https://doi.org/10.1016/j.meatsci.2015.05.013.

Gerr, Fred. "Meatpacking Plant Workers: A Case Study of a Precarious Workforce." *Journal of Occupational and Environmental Hygiene* 18, no. 4–5 (2021): 154–58. https://doi.org/10.1080/15459624.2021.1895997.

"Getting into Broiler Chicken Farming in BC." British Columbia Chicken Marketing Board, accessed August 1, 2023. https://bcchicken.ca/getting-into-broiler-chicken-farming-in-bc/.

Gifford, Robert. "The Dragons of Inaction: Psychological Barriers That Limit Climate Change Mitigation and Adaptation." *American Psychologist* 66, no. 4 (2011): 290–302. https://doi.org/10.1037/a0023566.

Goodman, David, and E. Melanie DuPuis. "Knowing Food and Growing Food: Beyond the Production-Consumption Debate in the Sociology of Agriculture." *Sociologia Ruralis* 42, no. 1 (2002): 5–22. https://doi.org/10.1111/1467-9523.00199.

Goodman, David, E. Melanie DuPuis, and Michael K. Goodman. *Alternative Food Networks: Knowledge, Practice, and Politics.* New York: Routledge, 2012.

Goodman, Michael K., Damian Maye, and Lewis Holloway. "Ethical Foodscapes? Premises, Promises, and Possibilities." *Environment and Planning* 42, no. 8 (2010): 1782–96. https://doi.org/10.1068/a43290.

Grandin, Temple. "Evaluation of the Welfare of Cattle Housed in Outdoor Feedlot Pens." *Veterinary and Animal Science* 1–2 (2016): 23–28.

Grazian, David. *American Zoo: A Sociological Safari.* Princeton, N.J.: Princeton University Press, 2015.

Gregory, James. *Of Victorians and Vegetarians: The Vegetarian Movement in Nineteenth Century Britain.* London: Tauris Academic Studies, 2007.

Guthman, Julie. "Commentary on Teaching Food: Why I Am Fed Up with Michael Pollan et al." *Agriculture and Human Values* 24, no. 2 (2007): 261–64. https://doi.org/10.1007/s10460-006-9053-x.

Haidt, Jonathan, Paul Rozin, Clark McCauley, and Sumio Imada. "Body, Psyche, and Culture: The Relationship between Disgust and Morality." *Psychology and Developing Societies* 9, no. 1 (1997): 107–31. https://doi.org/10.1177/097133369700900105.

Hamblin, James. "The Jordan Peterson All-Meat Diet." *The Atlantic.* August 28, 2018. https://www.theatlantic.com/health/archive/2018/08/the-peterson-family-meat-cleanse/567613/.

Harding, David J. "Cultural Context, Sexual Behavior, and Romantic Relationships in Disadvantaged Neighborhoods." *American Sociological Review* 72, no. 3 (2007): 341–64. https://doi.org/10.1177/000312240707200302.

Hayek, Matthew N., and Rachael D. Garrett. "Nationwide Shift to Grass-Fed Beef Requires Larger Cattle Population." *Environmental Research Letters* 13, no. 8 (2018): 1–8. https://doi.org/10.1088/1748-9326/aad401.

Heberlein, Thomas A., and J. Stanley Black. "Attitudinal Specificity and the Prediction of Behavior in a Field Setting." *Journal of Personality and Social Psychology* 33, no. 4 (1976): 474–79. https://doi.org/10.1037/0022-3514.33.4.474.

Heenan, Lisa, and Isaebella Doherty, dirs. *Polyfaces: A World of Many Choices.* Eppalock, Australia: Regrarians, 2015.

Herzog, Hal. *Some We Love, Some We Hate, Some We Eat: Why It's So Hard to Think Straight About Animals.* Toronto: Harper Perennial, 2010.

Hestermann, Nina, Yves Le Yaouanq, and Nicolas Treich. "An Economic Model of the Meat Paradox." *European Economic Review* 129 (2020): 103569. https://doi.org/10.1016/j.euroecorev.2020.103569.

Hochschild, Arlie Russell. "Ideology and Emotion Management: A Perspective and Path for Future Research." In *Research Agendas in the Sociology of Emotions*, edited by Theodore D. Kemper, 117–42. Albany: State University of New York Press, 1990.

———. *Strangers in Their Own Land: Anger and Mourning in the American Right.* New York: The New Press, 2016.

Holm, Lotte, and Mette Møhl. "The Role of Meat in Everyday Food Culture: An Analysis of an Interview Study in Copenhagen." *Appetite* 34, no. 3 (2000): 277–83. https://doi.org/10.1006/appe.2000.0324.

Hui, Ann. "The New Canada's Food Guide Explained: Goodbye Four Food Groups and Serving Sizes, Hello Hydration." *Globe and Mail,* January 22, 2019. https://www.theglobeandmail.com/canada/article-new-canadas-food-guide-explained/.

Iguacel, Isabel, Inge Huybrechts, Luis A. Moreno, and Nathalie Michels. "Vegetarianism and Veganism Compared with Mental Health and Cognitive Outcomes: A Systematic Review and Meta-Analysis." *Nutrition Reviews* 79, no. 4 (2021): 361–81.

"The Importance of the Grader and Grade Consistency." Canadian Beef Grading Agency, accessed May 31, 2023. https://beefgradingagency.ca/livestock-grading-in-canada/beef-grading/.

Jacobo, Elizabeth J., Adriana M. Rodríguez, Norberto Bartoloni, and Víctor A. Deregibus. "Rotational Grazing Effects on Rangeland Vegetation at a Farm Scale." *Rangeland Ecology and Management* 59, no. 3 (2006): 249–57. https://doi.org/10.2111/05-129R1.1.

Jerolmack, Colin. *The Global Pigeon*. Chicago: University of Chicago Press, 2013.

Jerolmack, Colin, and Iddo Tavory. "Molds and Totems: Nonhumans and the Constitution of the Social Self." *Sociological Theory* 32, no. 1 (2014): 64–77. https://doi.org/10.1177/0735275114523604.

Jeske, Christine. "Re-Enchanting Meat: How Sacred Meaning-Making Strengthens the Ethical Meat Movement." *Agriculture and Human Values* (2023). https://doi.org/10.1007/s10460-023-10477-9.

Johnson, Adrienne Rose. "The Paleo Diet and the American Weight Loss Utopia, 1975–2014." *Utopian Studies* 26, no. 1 (2015): 101–24. https://doi.org/10.5325/utopianstudies.26.1.0101.

Johnson, Harold R. *The Power of Story*. Ottawa, Ont.: Biblioasis, 2022.

Johnston, Josée. "The Citizen-Consumer Hybrid: Ideological Tensions and the Case of Whole Foods Market." *Theory and Society* 37, no. 3 (2008): 229–70. https://doi.org/10.1007/s11186-007-9058-5.

Johnston, Josée, and Shyon Baumann. *Foodies: Democracy and Distinction in the Gourmet Foodscape*, 2nd ed. New York: Routledge, 2015.

Johnston, Josée, Shyon Baumann, and Merin Oleschuk. "Capturing Inequality and Action in Prototypes: The Case of Meat-Eating and Vegetarianism." *Poetics* 87 (2021): 101530. https://doi.org/10.1016/j.poetic.2021.101530.

Johnston, Josée, and Michael K. Goodman. "Spectacular Foodscapes: Food Celebrities and the Politics of Lifestyle Mediation in an Age of Inequality." *Food, Culture, and Society* 18, no. 2 (2015): 205–22. https://doi.org/10.2752/175174415X14180391604369.

Johnston, Josée, Michelle Szabo, and Alexandra Rodney. "Good Food, Good People: Understanding the Cultural Repertoire of Ethical Eating." *Journal of Consumer Culture* 11, no. 3 (2011): 293–318. https://doi.org/10.1177/1469540511417996.

Johnston, Josée, Anelyse Weiler, and Shyon Baumann. "The Cultural Imaginary of Ethical Meat: A Study of Producer Perceptions." *Journal of Rural Studies* 89 (2022): 186–98. https://doi.org/10.1016/j.jrurstud.2021.11.021.

Joon-ho, Bong, dir. *Okja*. Los Angeles: Plan B Entertainment, 2017.

Joy, Melanie. *Why We Love Dogs, Eat Pigs, and Wear Cows: An Introduction to Carnism*. San Francisco: Red Wheel/Weiser, 2010.

Jung, Carl. *Collected Works*. Princeton, N.J.: Princeton University Press, 1969.

Katz-Rosene, Ryan, and Sarah J. Martin. *Green Meat? Sustaining Eaters, Animals, and the Planet*. Montreal: McGill-Queen's University Press, 2020.

Kennedy, Emily Huddart, and Darcy Hauslik. "The Practice of Green Consumption." In *Environment and Society: Concepts and Challenges*, edited by Magnus Boström and Debra J. Davidson, 187–206. Cham: Palgrave Macmillan, 2018. https://doi.org/10.1007/978-3-319-76415-3_9.

Klassen, Susana, and Sean Patrick Kearney. "The 'Irony' of Gendered Meat Consumption." *Medium*, March 7, 2019. https://medium.com/the-nature-of-food/the-irony-of-gendered-meat-consumption-15371feocfcd.

Kolata, Gina. "Eat Less Red Meat, Scientists Said. Now Some Believe That Was Bad Advice." *New York Times*, September 30, 2019. https://www.nytimes.com/2019/09/30/health/red-meat-heart-cancer.html.

———. "The Perplexing Red Meat Controversy: Five Things to Know." *New York Times*, September 30, 2019. https://www.nytimes.com/2019/09/30/health/red-meat-questions-answers.html.

Kollmuss, Anja, and Julian Agyeman. "Mind the Gap: Why Do People Act Environmentally and What Are the Barriers to Pro-Environmental Behavior?" *Environmental Education Research* 8, no. 3 (2002): 239–60. https://doi.org/10.1080/13504620220145401.

Korthals, Michiel. "Taking Consumers Seriously: Two Concepts of Consumer Sovereignty." *Journal of Agricultural and Environmental Ethics* 14, no. 2 (2001): 201–15. https://doi.org/10.1023/A:1011356930245.

Kristeva, Julia. *Powers of Horror: An Essay on Abjection*. Translated by Leon Roudiez. New York: Columbia University Press, 1984.

Kubberød, Elin, Øydis Ueland, Åsne Tronstad, and Einar Risvik. "Attitudes Towards Meat and Meat-Eating Among Adolescents in Norway: A Qualitative Study." *Appetite* 38, no. 1 (2002): 53–62. https://doi.org/10.1006/appe.2002.0458.

Kubberød, Elin, Øydis Ueland, Gunvor Irene Dingstad, Einar Risvik, and Inge Jan Henjesand. "The Effect of Animality in the Consumption Experience—A Potential for Disgust." *Journal of Food Products Marketing* 14 no. 3 (2008): 103–24. https://doi.org/10.1080/10454440801985985.

Kubberød, Elin, Øydis Ueland, Einar Risvik, and Inge Jan Henjesand. "A Study on the Mediating Role of Disgust with Meat in the Prediction of Red Meat Consumption Among Young Females." *Journal of Consumer Behaviour* 5, no. 4 (2006): 281–91. https://doi.org/10.1002/cb.180.

Kubberød, Elin, Øydis Ueland, Marit Rødbotten, Frank Westad, and Einar Risvik. "Gender Specific Preferences and Attitudes Towards Meat." *Food Quality and Preference* 13, no. 5 (2002): 285–94. https://doi.org/10.1016/S0950-3293(02)00041-1.

Kunst, Jonas R., and Christian Andrés Palacios Haugestad. "The Effects of Dissociation on Willingness to Eat Meat Are Moderated by Exposure to Unprocessed Meat: A Cross-Cultural Demonstration." *Appetite* 120 (2018): 356–66. https://doi.org/10.1016/j.appet.2017.09.016.

Kunst, Jonas R., and Sigrid M. Hohle. "Meat Eaters by Dissociation: How We Present, Prepare and Talk About Meat Increases Willingness to Eat Meat by Reducing Empathy and Disgust." *Appetite* 105 (2016): 758–74. https://doi.org/10.1016/j.appet.2016.07.009.

Lamont, Michèle. *The Dignity of Working Men: Morality and the Boundaries of Race, Class, and Immigration.* Cambridge, Mass.: Harvard University Press, 2000.

———. *Money, Morals, and Manners: The Culture of the French and the American Upper-Middle Class.* Chicago: University of Chicago Press, 1992.

Lamont, Michèle, Stefan Beljean, and Matthew Clair. "What Is Missing? Cultural Processes and Causal Pathways to Inequality." *Socio-Economic Review* 12, no. 3 (2014): 573–608. https://doi.org/10.1093/ser/mwu011.

Lamont, Michèle, and Annette Lareau. "Cultural Capital: Allusions, Gaps and Glissandos in Recent Theoretical Developments." Sociology Theory 6, no. 2 (1988): 153–68.

Lamont, Michèle, and Virág Molnár. "The Study of Boundaries in the Social Sciences." *Annual Review of Sociology* 28 (2002): 167–95. https://doi.org/10.1146/annurev.soc.28.110601.141107.

Latour, Bruno. *Reassembling the Social: An Introduction to Actor-Network-Theory.* Oxford: Oxford University Press, 2005.

Lavie, Carl J., Richard V. Milani, and Hector O. Ventura. "Obesity and Cardiovascular Disease: Risk Factor, Paradox, and Impact of Weight Loss." *Journal of the American College of Cardiology* 53, no. 21 (2009): 1925–32. https://doi.org/10.1016/j.jacc.2008.12.068.

Lea, Emma, and Anthony Worsley. "Influences on Meat Consumption in Australia." *Appetite* 36, no. 2 (2001): 127–36. https://doi.org/10.1006/appe.2000.0386.

Lejano, Raul, Mrill Ingram, and Helen Ingram. *The Power of Narrative in Environmental Networks.* Cambridge: MIT Press, 2013.

Leroy, Frédéric, Malaika Brengman, Wouter Ryckbosch, and Peter Scholliers. "Meat in the Post-Truth Era: Mass Media Discourses on Health and Disease in the Attention Economy." *Appetite* 125 (2018): 345–55. https://doi.org/10.1016/j.appet.2018.02.028.

Liptak, Adam. "Supreme Court Upholds California Law on Humane Treatment of Pigs." *New York Times,* May 11, 2023. https://www.nytimes.com/2023/05/11/us/supreme-court-california-pigs.html.

Lord, Peter, and Nick Park, dirs. *Chicken Run.* Universal City, Calif.: DreamWorks Pictures, 2000.

Lorenzen, Janet A. "Going Green: The Process of Lifestyle Change." *Sociological Forum* 27, no. 1 (2012): 94–116. https://doi.org/10.1111/j.1573-7861.2011.01303.x.

Loughnan, Steve, Nick Haslam, and Brock Bastian. "The Role of Meat Consumption in the Denial of Moral Status and Mind to Meat Animals." *Appetite* 55, no. 1 (2010): 156–59. https://doi.org/10.1016/j.appet.2010.05.043.

Lupo, Christopher D., David E. Clay, Jennifer L. Benning, and James J. Stone. "Life-Cycle Assessment of the Beef Cattle Production System for the Northern Great Plains, USA." *Journal of Environmental Quality* 42, no. 5 (2013): 1386–94. https://doi.org/10.2134/jeq2013.03.0101.

Lupton, Deborah. "Purity and Danger." In *The Blackwell Encyclopedia of Sociology,* edited by George Ritzer, 1–3. Malden, Mass.: Wiley-Blackwell, 2016. https://doi.org/10.1002/9781405165518.wbeos0729.

Macdiarmid, Jennie I., Flora Douglas, and Jonina Campbell. "Eating like There's No Tomorrow: Public Awareness of the Environmental Impact of Food and Reluctance to Eat Less Meat as Part of a Sustainable Diet." *Appetite* 96 (2016): 487–93. https://doi.org/10.1016/j.appet.2015.10.011.

MacDougall, Colin, and Frances Baum. "The Devil's Advocate: A Strategy to Avoid Groupthink and Stimulate Discussion in Focus Groups." *Qualitative Health Research* 7, no. 4 (1997): 532–41. https://doi.org/10.1177/104973239700700407.

MacKendrick, Norah. *Better Safe Than Sorry: How Consumers Navigate Exposure to Everyday Toxics*. Berkeley: University of California Press, 2018.

———. "Foodscape." *Contexts* 13, no. 3 (2014): 16–18. https://doi.org/10.1177/1536504214545754.

MacDonald, James M., and William D. McBride. "The Transformation of U.S. Livestock Agriculture: Scale, Efficiency, and Risks." Economic Information Bulletin No. 43. United States Department of Agriculture, Economic Research Service, January 2009.

Malek, Lenka, and Wendy J. Umberger. "Distinguishing Meat Reducers from Unrestricted Omnivores, Vegetarians and Vegans: A Comprehensive Comparison of Australian Consumers." *Food Quality and Preference* 88 (2021): 104081. https://doi.org/10.1016/j.foodqual.2020.104081.

"Managing the Complexities of Land and Livestock." Savory Institute, accessed September 1, 2023. https://savory.global/holistic-management/.

Martin, Michael J., Sapna E. Thottathil, and Thomas B. Newman. "Antibiotics Overuse in Animal Agriculture: A Call to Action for Health Care Providers." *American Journal of Public Health* 105, no. 12 (2015): 2409–10. https://doi.org/10.2105/AJPH.2015.302870.

Mathur, Maya B. "Ethical Drawbacks of Sustainable Meat Choices." *Science* 375, no. 6587 (2022): 1362. https://doi.org/10.1126/science.abo2535.

Matsumoto, Nancy. "Is Grass-Fed Beef Really Better for The Planet? Here's the Science." *NPR*, August 13, 2019, accessed October 7, 2021. https://www.npr.org/sections/thesalt/2019/08/13/746576239/is-grass-fed-beef-really-better-for-the-planet-heres-the-science.

Maukonen, Mirkka, Kennet Harald, Niina E. Kaartinen, Heli Tapanainen, Demetrius Albanes, Johan Eriksson, Tommi Härkänen, et al. "Partial Substitution of Red or Processed Meat with Plant-Based Foods and the Risk of Type 2 Diabetes." *Scientific Reports* 13, no. 5874 (2023). https://doi.org/10.1038/s41598-023-32859-z.

McGrath, Joseph E. "Dilemmatics: The Study of Research Choices and Dilemmas." *American Behavioral Scientist* 25, no. 2 (1981): 175–210. https://doi.org/10.1177/000276428102500205.

McKendree, Melissa G. S., Candace Croney, and Nicole J. O. Widmar. "Effects of Demographic Factors and Information Sources on United States Consumer Perceptions of Animal Welfare." *Journal of Animal Science* 92, no. 7 (2014): 3161–73. https://doi.org/10.2527/jas.2014-6874.

Meadows, Larry. "What's Your Beef—Prime, Choice, or Select?" U.S. Department of Agriculture, January 28, 2013. https://www.usda.gov/media/blog/2013/01/28/whats-your-beef-prime-choice-or-select.

"Meat Consumption." OECD, accessed December 13, 2022. https://doi.org/10.1787/fa290fd0-en.

Michel, Fabienne, Christina Hartmann, and Michael Siegrist. "Consumers' Associations, Perceptions, and Acceptance of Meat and Plant-Based Meat Alternatives." *Food Quality and Preference* 87 (2021): 104063. https://doi.org/10.1016/j.foodqual.2020.104063.

Miele, Mara. "The Taste of Happiness: Free-Range Chicken." *Environment and Planning A* 43, no. 9 (2011): 2076–90. https://doi.org/10.1068/a43257.

Miele, Mara, Harry Blokhuis, Richard Bennett, and Bettina Bock. "Changes in Farming and in Stakeholder Concern for Animal Welfare." In *Improving Farm Animal Welfare: Science and Society Working Together: The Welfare Quality Approach*, edited by Harry Blokhuis, Mara Miele, Isabelle Veissier, and Bryan Jones, 19–48. Wageningen, Netherlands: Wageningen Academic Publishers, 2013. https://doi.org/10.3920/978-90-8686-770-7_2.

Mikkelsen, Bent Egberg. "Images of Foodscapes: Introduction to Foodscape Studies and Their Application in the Study of Healthy Eating Out-of-Home Environments." *Perspectives in Public Health* 131, no. 5 (2011): 209–16. https://doi.org/10.1177/1757913911415150.

Miranda-de la Lama, Genaro C., Laura X. Estévez-Moreno, Wilmer S. Sepúlveda, M. C. Estrada-Chavero, Adolfo A. Rayas-Amor, Morris Villarroel, and G. A. María. "Mexican Consumers' Perceptions and Attitudes Towards Farm Animal Welfare and Willingness to Pay for Welfare Friendly Meat Products." *Meat Science* 125 (2017): 106–13. https://doi.org/10.1016/j.meatsci.2016.12.001.

Monteiro, Bronwyn Mariana Antonio, Tamara M. Pfeiler, Marcus D. Patterson, and Michael A. Milburn. "The Carnism Inventory: Measuring the Ideology of Eating Animals." *Appetite* 113 (2017): 51–62. https://doi.org/10.1016/j.appet.2017.02.011.

Morgan, Kevin. "Local and Green, Global and Fair: The Ethical Foodscape and the Politics of Care." *Environment and Planning* 42, no. 8 (2010): 1852–67. https://doi.org/10.1068/a42364.

Nagler, Rebekah H. "Adverse Outcomes Associated with Media Exposure to Contradictory Nutrition Messages." *Journal of Health Communication* 19, no. 1 (2014): 24–40. https://doi.org/10.1080/10810730.2013.798384.

Nash, Kate. "The 'Cultural Turn' in Social Theory: Towards a Theory of Cultural Politics." *Sociology* 35, no. 1 (2001): 77–92. https://doi.org/10.1017/S0038038501000050.

Nestle, Marion. *Food Politics: How the Food Industry Influences Nutrition and Health*. Berkeley: University of California Press, 2002.

"No Sign of Greenhouse Gases Increases Slowing in 2023." NOOA Research, April 5, 2024. https://research.noaa.gov/no-sign-of-greenhouse-gases-increases-slowing-in-2023/#.

Noonan, Chris, dir. *Babe*. Universal City, Calif.: Universal Pictures, 1995.

"Nutrition and Food." Gallup, accessed May 27, 2021. https://news.gallup.com/poll/6424/Nutrition-Food.aspx.

Ocejo, Richard. *Masters of Craft: Old Jobs in the New Urban Economy*. Princeton, N.J.: Princeton University Press, 2017.

O'Brien, Dave, and Lisa Ianni. "New Forms of Distinction: How Contemporary Cultural Elites Understand 'Good' Taste." *Sociological Review* 71, no. 1 (2023): 201–20.

O'Key, Victoria, and Siobhan Hugh-Jones. "'I Don't Need Anybody to Tell Me What I Should Be Doing': A Discursive Analysis of Material Accounts of (Mis)trust of Healthy Eating Information." *Appetite* 54, no. 3 (2010): 524–32. https://doi.org/10.1016/j.appet.2010.02.007.

Oldenburg, Brandon, and Limbert Fabian, dirs. *The Scarecrow*. Los Angeles: CAA Marketing, 2013. https://www.adforum.com/creative-work/ad/player/34489969/the-scarecrow/chipotle-mexican-grill.

Oleschuk, Merin. "'In Today's Market, Your Food Chooses You': News Media Constructions of Responsibility for Health through Home Cooking." *Social Problems* 67, no. 1 (2020): 1–19. https://doi.org/10.1093/socpro/spz006.

Oleschuk, Merin, Josée Johnston, and Shyon Baumann. "Maintaining Meat: Cultural Repertoires and the Meat Paradox in a Diverse Sociocultural Context." *Sociological Forum* 34, no. 2 (2019): 337–60. https://doi.org/10.1111/socf.12500.

O'Neill, Saffron, and Sophie Nicholson-Cole. "'Fear Won't Do It': Promoting Positive Engagement with Climate Change Through Visual and Iconic Representations." *Science Communication* 30, no. 3 (2009): 355–79. https://doi.org/10.1177/1075547008329201.

Orwell, George. *Animal Farm*. New York: Harcourt, Brace, & Company, 1946.

Ostrom, Thomas M. "The Relationship Between the Affective, Behavioral, and Cognitive Components of Attitude." *Journal of Experimental Social Psychology* 5, no. 1 (1969): 12–30. https://doi.org/10.1016/0022-1031(69)90003-1.

Otto, Natália, Josée Johnston, and Shyon Baumann. "Moral Entrepreneurialism for the Hamburger: Strategies for Marketing a Contested Fast Food." *Cultural Sociology* 16, no. 2 (2022): 190–211. https://doi.org/10.1177/17499755211039932.

Oussalah, Abderrahim, Julien Levy, Clémence Berthezène, David H. Alpers, and Jean-Louis Guéant. "Health Outcomes Associated with Vegetarian Diets: An Umbrella Review of Systematic Reviews and Meta-Analyses." *Clinical Nutrition* 39, no. 11 (2020): 3283–3307.

Perry, Janet, David Banker, and Robert Green. *Broiler Farms' Organization, Management, and Performance*. Washington, D.C.: Resource Economics Division, Economic Research Service, U.S. Department of Agriculture, 1999. https://www.ers.usda.gov/webdocs/publications/42203/13408_aib748_1_.pdf?v=8118.4.

Pfeiler, Tamara M., and Boris Egloff. "Examining the 'Veggie' Personality: Results from a Representative German Sample." *Appetite* 120 (2018): 246–55. https://doi.org/10.1016/j.appet.2017.09.005.

Philpot, Tom. "Joel Salatin's Unsustainable Myth." *Mother Jones*. November 19, 2020. https://www.motherjones.com/food/2020/11/joel-salatin-chris-newman-farming-rotational-grazing-agriculture/.

Piazza, Jared, Matthew B. Ruby, Steve Loughnan, Mischel Luong, Juliana Kulik, Hanne M. Watkins, and Mirra Seigerman. "Rationalizing Meat Consumption. The 4Ns." *Appetite* 91 (2015): 114–28. https://doi.org/10.1016/j.appet.2015.04.011.

Podberscek, Anthony L. "Good to Pet and Eat: The Keeping and Consuming of Dogs and Cats in South Korea." *Journal of Social Issues* 65, no. 3 (2009): 615–32. https://doi.org/10.1111/j.1540-4560.2009.01616.x.

Pollan, Michael. "An Animal's Place." *New York Times Magazine*, November 10, 2002. https://www.nytimes.com/2002/11/10/magazine/an-animal-s-place.html.

———. *The Omnivore's Dilemma: A Natural History of Four Meals.* New York: Penguin Books, 2006.

———. "Power Steer." *New York Times Magazine*, March 31, 2002. https://www.nytimes.com/2002/03/31/magazine/power-steer.html.

Polletta, Francesca. *It Was Like a Fever: Storytelling in Protest and Politics.* Chicago: University of Chicago Press, 2006.

Ponsford, Dominic. "Who Reads the Daily Mail? Why Biggest Print Title Still Has a Huge Influence." *Press Gazette*, March 10, 2023. https://pressgazette.co.uk/publishers/nationals/who-reads-the-daily-mail-circulation-and-readership/.

Poore, Joseph, and Thomas Nemecek. "Reducing Food's Environmental Impacts through Producers and Consumers." *Science* 360, no. 6392 (2018): 987–92. https://doi.org/10.1126/science.aaq0216.

Possidónio, Catarina, Jared Piazza, João Graça, and Marília Prada. "An Appetite for Meat? Disentangling the Influence of Animal Resemblance and Familiarity." *Appetite* 170 (2022): 105875. https://doi.org/10.1016/j.appet.2021.105875.

Presser, Lois. *Inside Story: How Narratives Drive Mass Harm.* Berkeley: University of California Press, 2018.

———. *Why We Harm.* New Brunswick, N.J.: Rutgers University Press, 2013.

Presser, Lois, and William V. Taylor. "An Autoethnography of Hunting: Animal Abuse and Criminology." *Crime, Law, and Social Change* 55, no. 5 (2011): 483–94. https://doi.org/10.1007/s10611-011-9299-0.

Pugh, Allison J. "What Good Are Interviews for Thinking about Culture? Demystifying Interpretive Analysis." *American Journal of Cultural Sociology* 1 (2013): 42–68. https://doi.org/10.1057/ajcs.2012.4.

Reed, Berlin. *The Ethical Butcher: How Thoughtful Eating Can Change Your World.* Berkeley: Soft Skull Press, 2013.

Rhee, Joshua J., Chelsea Schein, and Brock Bastian. "The What, How, and Why of Moralization: A Review of Current Definitions, Methods, and Evidence in Moralization Research." *Social and Personality Psychology Compass* 13, no. 12 (2019): e12511 https://doi.org/10.1111/spc3.12511.

Ricoeur, Paul. *Time and Narrative.* Chicago: University of Chicago Press, 1984.

Ritchie, Hannah, Pablo Rosado, and Max Roser. "Meat and Dairy Production." Our World in Data, last modified November 2019, accessed August 18, 2023. https://ourworldindata.org/meat-production#meat-production-by-type.

Rivis, Amanda, Paschal Sheeran, and Christopher J. Armitage. "Expanding the Affective and Normative Components of the Theory of Planned Behavior: A Meta-Analysis of Anticipated Affect and Moral Norms." *Journal of Applied Social Psychology* 39, no. 12 (2009): 2985–3019. https://doi.org/10.1111/j.1559-1816.2009.00558.x.

Rosenberg, Milton J., and Carl I. Hovland. "Cognitive, Affective, and Behavioral Components of Attitude." In *Attitude Organization and Change: An Analysis of Consistency Among Attitude Components*, edited by M. Rosenberg, C. Hovland, W. McGuire, R. Abelson, and J. Brehm, 1–14. New Haven: Yale University Press, 1960.

Rosenfeld, Daniel L. "The Psychology of Vegetarianism: Recent Advances and Future Directions." *Appetite* 131 (2018): 125–38. https://doi.org/10.1016/j.appet.2018.09.011.

Rosenfeld, Daniel L., and A. Janet Tomiyama. "Taste and Health Concerns Trump Anticipated Stigma as Barriers to Vegetarianism." *Appetite* 144 (2020): 104469. https://doi.org/10.1016/j.appet.2019.104469.

Rothblum, Esther, and Sondra Solovay, eds. *The Fat Studies Reader*. New York: NYU Press, 2009.

Rothgerber, Hank. "'But I Don't Eat That Much Meat': Situational Underreporting of Meat Consumption by Women." *Society and Animals* 27, no. 2 (2019): 150–73. https://doi.org/10.1163/15685306-12341468.

———. "Can You Have Your Meat and Eat It Too? Conscientious Omnivores, Vegetarians, and Adherence to Diet." *Appetite* 84 (2015): 196–203. http://dx.doi.org/10.1016/j.appet.2014.10.012.

———. "Meat-Related Cognitive Dissonance: A Conceptual Framework for Understanding How Meat Eaters Reduce Negative Arousal from Eating Animals." *Appetite* 146 (2020): 104511. https://doi.org/10.1016/j.appet.2019.104511.

———. "Real Men Don't Eat (Vegetable) Quiche: Masculinity and the Justification of Meat Consumption." *Psychology of Men and Masculinity* 14, no. 4 (2013): 363–75. https://doi.org/10.1037/a0030379.

Roser, Max. "How Many Animals Get Slaughtered Every Day?" *Our World in Data,* last modified September 26, 2023. https://ourworldindata.org/how-many-animals-get-slaughtered-every-day.

Rowntree, Jason E., Paige L. Stanley, Isabella C. F. Maciel, Mariko Thorbecke, Steven T. Rosenzweig, Dennis W. Hancock, Aidee Guzman, and Matt R. Raven. "Ecosystem Impacts and Productive Capacity of a Multi-Species Pastured Livestock System." *Frontiers in Sustainable Food Systems* 4 (2020): 544984. https://doi.org/10.3389/fsufs.2020.544984.

Rozin, Paul, Jonathan Haidt, and Clark McCauley. "Disgust." In *Handbook of Emotions*, edited by Lisa Feldman Barrett, Michael Lewis, and Jeannette M. Haviland-Jones, 815–34. New York: Guilford Press, 2016.

Rozin, Paul, Maureen Markwith, and Caryn Stoess. "Moralization and Becoming a Vegetarian: The Transformation of Preferences into Values and the Recruitment of Disgust." *Psychological Science* 8, no. 2 (1997): 67–73. https://doi.org/10.1111/j.1467-9280.1997.tb00685.x.

Ruby, Matthew B. "Vegetarianism: A Blossoming Field of Study." *Appetite* 58, no. 1 (2012): 141–50. http://dx.doi.org/10.1016/j.appet.2011.09.019.

Sahakian, Marlyne, Laurence Godin, and Irène Courtin. "Promoting 'Pro,' 'Low,' and 'No' Meat Consumption in Switzerland: The Role of Emotions in Practices." *Appetite* 150 (2020): 104637. https://doi.org/10.1016/j.appet.2020.104637.

Salatin, Joel. "Our Production Models—Polyface Farms." Polyface Farms, accessed August 1, 2021. http://www.polyfacefarms.com/production/.

Sanchez-Sabate, Ruben, and Joan Sabaté. "Consumer Attitudes Towards Environmental Concerns of Meat Consumption: A Systematic Review." *International Journal of Environmental Research and Public Health* 16, no. 7 (2019): 1220. https://doi.org/10.3390/ijerph16071220.

Savory, Alan, and Jody Butterfield, *Holistic Management: A Commonsense Revolution to Restore Our Environment*, 3rd ed. Washington, D.C.: Island Press, 2016.

Scarborough, Peter, Michael Clark, Linda Cobiac, Keren Papier, Anika Knuppel, John Lynch, Richard Harrington, Tim Key, and Marco Springmann. "Vegans, Vegetarians, Fish-Eaters, and Meat-Eaters in the U.K. Show Discrepant Environmental Impacts." *Nature Food* 4 (2023): 565–74. https://doi.org/10.1038/s43016-023-00795-w.

Schatzker, Mark. *Steak: One Man's Search for the World's Tastiest Piece of Beef.* New York: Viking, 2010.

Schechinger, Anne. "Animal Feeding Operations Harm Environment, Climate, and Public Health." Environmental Working Group, March 19, 2024, accessed July 6, 2024. https://www.ewg.org/research/animal-feeding-operations-harm-environment-climate-and-public-health.

Scheff, Thomas J. "Shame and the Social Bond: A Sociological Theory." *Sociological Theory* 18, no. 1 (2000): 84–99. https://doi.org/10.1111/0735-2751.00089.

Schoolman, Ethan D. "Completing the Circuit: Routine, Reflection, and Ethical Consumption." *Sociological Forum* 31, no. 3 (2016): 619–41. https://doi.org/10.1111/socf.12266.

Scott-Reid, Jessica. "'Ultraprocessed' Plant-Based Meat Isn't as Bad for You as the Meat Industry Wants You to Believe." *Toronto Star,* July 6, 2024, https://www.thestar.com/opinion/contributors/ultraprocessed-plant-based-meat-isnt-as-bad-for-you-as-the-meat-industry-wants-you/article_7cd5cb1e-3944-11ef-98a3-630c7eb74f1d.html.

Serpell, James. "Having Our Dogs and Eating Them Too: Why Animals Are a Social Issue." *Journal of Social Issues* 65, no. 3 (2009): 633–44. https://doi.org/10.1111/j.1540-4560.2009.01617.x.

Shahbandeh, Mahsa. "Chicken Meat Production Worldwide in 2022 and 2023, by Country (in 1,000 Metric Tons)." Statista, accessed August 18, 2023. https://www.statista.com/statistics/237597/leading-10-countries-worldwide-in-poultry-meat-production-in-2007/.

———. "Number of Pigs Worldwide in 2023, by Leading Country (in Million Head)." Statista, accessed August 21, 2023. https://www.statista.com/statistics/263964/number-of-pigs-in-selected-countries/#:~:text=Unsurprisingly%2C%20China%20is%20the%20leading,and%20importers%20of%20pork%20worldwide.

Siegrist, Michael, and Christina Hartmann. "Impact of Sustainability Perception on Consumption of Organic Meat and Meat Substitutes." *Appetite* 132 (2019): 196–202. https://doi.org/10.1016/j.appet.2018.09.016.

Simons, Johannes, Carl Vierboom, Jeanette Klink-Lehmann, Ingo Härlen, and Monika Hartmann. "Vegetarianism/Veganism: A Way to Feel Good." *Sustainability* 13, no. 7 (2021): 1–19. https://doi.org/10.3390/su13073618.

Singer, Peter. *Animal Liberation: The Definitive Classic of the Animal Movement.* New York: NYRB Classics, 2009.

Singh, Manvir. "Is an All-Meat Diet What Nature Intended?" *New Yorker,* October 22, 2023.

Slocum, Rachel. "Whiteness, Space, and Alternative Food Practice." *Geoforum* 38, no. 3 (2007): 520–33.

Sofos, John N., and Ifigenia Geornaras. "Overview of Current Meat Hygiene and Safety Risks and Summary of Recent Studies on Biofilms, and Control of *Escherichia Coli* O157:H7 in Nonintact, and *Listeria Monocytogenes* in Ready-to-Eat, Meat Products." *Meat Science* 86, no. 1 (2010): 2–14. https://doi.org/10.1016/j.meatsci.2010.04.015.

Springmann, Marco, et al. "Options for Keeping the Food System within Environmental Limits." *Nature* 562 (2018): 519–25. https://doi.org/10.1038/s41586-018-0594-0.

Spurlock, Morgan, dir. *Super Size Me 2: Holy Chicken!* Los Angeles: Samuel Goldwyn Films, 2019.

Standaert, Michael, and Francesco De Augustinis. "A 12-Storey Pig Farm: Has China Found the Way to Tackle Animal Disease?" *The Guardian.* September 18, 2020. https://www.theguardian.com/environment/2020/sep/18/a-12-storey-pig-farm-has-china-found-a-way-to-stop-future-pandemics-.

Stanley, Paige L., Jason E. Rowntree, David K. Beede, Marcia S. DeLonge, and Michael W. Hamm. "Impacts of Soil Carbon Sequestration on Life Cycle Greenhouse Gas Emissions in Midwestern USA Beef Finishing Systems." *Agricultural Systems* 162 (2018): 249–58. https://doi.org/10.1016/j.agsy.2018.02.003.

Stuart, Diana, Rebecca L. Schewe, and Ryan Gunderson. "Extending Social Theory to Farm Animals: Addressing Alienation in the Dairy Sector." *Sociologia Ruralis* 53, no. 2 (2013): 201–22. https://doi.org/10.1111/soru.12005.

Swidler, Ann. "Culture in Action: Symbols and Strategies." *American Sociological Review* 51, no. 2 (1986): 273–86. https://doi.org/10.2307/2095521.

———. *Talk of Love: How Culture Matters.* Chicago: University of Chicago Press, 2001.

Takacs, Christopher George. "Becoming Interesting: Narrative Capital Development at Elite Colleges." *Qualitative Sociology* 43, no. 2 (2020): 255–70. https://doi.org/10.1007/s11133-020-09447-y.

Tenbrunsel, Ann E., and David M. Messick. "Ethical Fading: The Role of Self-Deception in Unethical Behavior." *Social Justice Research* 17, no. 2 (2004): 223–36. https://doi.org/10.1023/B:SORE.0000027411.35832.53.

Thorslund, Cecilie A. H., and Jesper Lassen. "Context, Orders of Worth, and the Justification of Meat Consumption Practices." *Sociologia Ruralis* 57, no. S1 (2017): 836–58. https://doi.org/10.1111/soru.12143.

Todorov, Tzvetan. *The Conquest of America: The Question of the Other.* Norman: University of Oklahoma Press, 1999.

Valdes, Mirjana, Annalijn Conklin, Gerry Veenstra, and Jennifer L. Black. "Plant-Based Dietary Practices in Canada: Examining Definitions, Prevalence and Correlates of Animal Source Food Exclusions Using Nationally Representative Data from the 2015 Canadian Community Health Survey-Nutrition." *Public Health Nutrition* 24, no. 5 (2021): 777–86. https://doi.org/10.1017/S1368980020003444.

Van Dyke, Nina, and Eric J. Drinkwater. "Relationships between Intuitive Eating and Health Indicators: Literature Review." *Public Health Nutrition* 17, no. 8 (2014): 1757–66. https://doi.org/10.1017/s1368980013002139.

Vermeir, Iris, and Wim Verbeke. "Sustainable Food Consumption: Exploring the Consumer 'Attitude—Behavioral Intention' Gap." *Journal of Agriculture and Environmental Ethics* 19 (2006): 169–94. https://doi.org/10.1007/s10806-005-5485-3.

Vonthron, Simon, Coline Perrin, and Christophe-Toussaint Soulard. "Foodscape: A Scoping Review and a Research Agenda for Food Security-Related Studies." *PLoS One* 15, no. 5 (2020): e0233218. https://doi.org/10.1371/journal.pone.0233218.

Waldron, Jamie, and Angela England. *Home Butchering Handbook: Enjoy Finer, Fresher, Healthier Cuts of Meat from Your Own Kitchen.* New York: Alpha, 2013.

Wang, Xia, Xinying Lin, Ying Y. Ouyang, Jun Liu, Gang Zhao, An Pan, and Frank B. Hu. "Red and Processed Meat Consumption and Mortality: Dose-Response Meta-Analysis of Prospective Cohort Studies." *Public Health Nutrition* 19, no. 5 (2015): 893–905. https://doi.org/10.1017/S1368980015002062.

Warde, Alan. *The Practice of Eating.* Malden, Mass.: Polity Press, 2016.

Waters, James. "A Model of the Dynamics of Household Vegetarian and Vegan Rates in the U.K." *Appetite* 127 (2018): 364–72. https://doi.org/10.1016/j.appet.2018.05.017.

"We Need to Talk About Meat." United Nations Climate Change, May 19, 2021. https://unfccc.int/blog/we-need-to-talk-about-meat?gclid=CjoKCQjwkqSlBhDaARIsAFJANkhoGnnZH7qb1Iid2nwPAQZsbtQiREjpWLqrwb7-wS--7Qs_aodzAEUaAgKNEALw_wcB.

White, E. B. *Charlotte's Web.* New York: Harper & Brothers, 1952.

Wilkie, Rhoda. *Livestock/Deadstock: Working with Farm Animals from Birth to Slaughter.* Philadelphia: Temple University Press, 2010.

Woodyatt, Cory R., Catherine A. Finneran, and Rob Stephenson. "In-Person Versus Online Focus Group Discussions: A Comparative Analysis of Data Quality." *Qualitative Health Research* 26, no. 6 (2016): 741–49. https://doi.org/10.1177/1049732316631510.

Zickfeld, Janis H., Jonas R. Kunst, and Sigrid M. Hohle. "Too Sweet to Eat: Exploring the Effects of Cuteness on Meat Consumption." *Appetite* 120 (2018): 181–95. https://doi.org/10.1016/j.appet.2017.08.038.

Zur, Ifat, and Christian A. Klöckner. "Individual Motivations for Limiting Meat Consumption." *British Food Journal* 116, no. 4 (2014): 629–42. https://doi.org/10.1108/BFJ-08-2012-0193.

Index

Page numbers in *italics* indicate figures and tables.

CULTURE AND ECONOMIC LIFE

---

*For a complete listing of titles in this series, visit the
Stanford University Press website, www.sup.org.*

The authorized representative in the EU for product safety and compliance is:
Mare Nostrum Group
B.V Doelen 72
4831 GR Breda
The Netherlands

www.ingramcontent.com/pod-product-compliance
Lightning Source LLC
Chambersburg PA
CBHW020458270326
41926CB00008B/655